UNDERSTANDING EDUCATIONAL RESEARCH
AN INTRODUCTION

PSYCHOLOGY AND HUMAN DEVELOPMENT
IN EDUCATION

NICHOLAS HOBBS, *Consulting Editor*

Understanding
Educational Research
AN INTRODUCTION

DEOBOLD B. VAN DALEN

Professor of Education, University of Pittsburgh

WITH TWO CHAPTERS BY

WILLIAM J. MEYER

*Associate Professor of Psychology and Education,
University of Pittsburgh*

McGRAW-HILL BOOK COMPANY 1962

New York   San Francisco   Toronto   London

UNDERSTANDING EDUCATIONAL RESEARCH

v

66880

THE MAPLE PRESS COMPANY, YORK, PA.

Preface

The formidable "foreign language" of research fences off many teachers from the exciting frontiers of educational thought, and the resulting paucity of teacher-researcher intercommunication impedes professional progress. Hence, constructing basic bridges of information to help classroom teachers comprehend the terminology and tactics of the research world is of paramount importance to society. Pioneers have struggled to erect some spans of understanding from both sides of the academic river, but a free flow of intellectual traffic to and from the classroom and the laboratory has not been achieved.

Popularized works that present deceptively oversimplified accounts of scientific endeavors ignite sparks of interest that flicker brightly but soon fade away. Students who wish to travel further into the hinterlands of research are left stumbling in darkness because insufficient illumination has been given to guide them. More technical books—those that discuss the procedures and techniques employed in various types of studies and the results of scientific research projects—provide a firmer foundation for understanding the complexities of scientific investigations. But many novices who plunge enthusiastically into these works quickly become perplexed and panic because too many of the signposts are unintelligible to them.

This text extends a helping hand to these students. The exposition proceeds from the familiar and concrete to the abstract. The viewpoint of those who are approaching the systematic study of research for the first time is constantly kept in mind. To aid students who have a limited background in psychology, logic, and mathematics, the text links scientific terminology and tactics to their everyday experiences. Through illustrations of commonplace activities in classroom and life situations, it explores techniques that men have devised to solve problems. With a minimum of technical jargon and some carefully constructed steppingstones of understanding, the text introduces students to the psychological and logical foundations of scientific investigation. As the chapters unfold, they acquaint readers with the goals, basic assumptions, limitations, and language of scientists—with the way researchers talk and how their minds work in getting results. The text imparts what Conant calls for in *Science and Common Sense:* some knowledge of the "tactics and strategy" and of "what science can and cannot accomplish."

After inviting readers into the world of research and exploring the psychological and logical substrata of scientific investigations, the text gives them some insight into how scholars tackle investigations: how they locate problems; some of the methods, procedures, and indispensable tools that they employ; the general sequence of events that occurs during an investigation; the skills and knowledges required to undertake various types of studies; the library and research tools that are available; and the study habits and attitudes that are conducive to fruitful work. Readers are also reminded that many of these tools and procedures can also help them improve their term papers and professional reports.

The objective of this book is to imbue students with a respect for the scientific spirit of inquiry and to acquaint them with problem-solving techniques that will prove useful in their academic, personal, and professional lives. The discussion is designed to help readers understand and appreciate the complexity of social science phenomena, the difficulties investigators encounter, the importance of promoting sound research projects, and the need for applying the findings of significant studies in the classroom. The text strives to encourage and enable teachers to locate and read some research reports in their field, to be more discriminating evaluators of published research reports that are found in professional periodicals, and to cooperate more intelligently with experts in the field. Perhaps this volume will also give some students the confidence and impetus to undertake modest investigations, to broaden and deepen their knowledge in this field, and eventually to prepare themselves for professional research work.

Although this text is suitable for any novice interested in research, it is expressly written for education students—mature upperclassmen and graduates pursuing their master's degree. It may also provide an orientation to research for doctoral candidates who have had only a limited exposure to the scientific method. This text merely opens the doors to the halls of research and provides a guided tour of some main corridors; it leaves the task of exploring the specific academic areas necessary to train professional workers to more advanced and specialized books.

An experimental draft of these chapters has been presented to classes for several years. As a result of these practical experiences, the many questions raised by students, and pertinent suggestions offered by colleagues, the author gained insights that helped him improve the manuscript. To the students, professional associates, librarians, and others who offered criticism, advice, or assistance during the preparation of the text, the writer expresses his deepest appreciation. He also wishes to acknowledge his indebtedness to the individuals whose names appear in the chapter references and bib-

liographies and to the publishers who generously gave permission to quote
or use materials from their publications.   Special thanks go to Dr. William
J. Meyer, University of Pittsburgh, and Dr. Peter T. Hountras, Northwestern University, for participating in the preliminary discussion concerning the structure of the text and to the former for finding the time to contribute two chapters.   The author is especially grateful for the patient help
and constant encouragement received from his wife, Marcella Madison Van
Dalen.

Deobold B. Van Dalen

Contents

CHAPTER 1

Social Progress and Research

What is research? You hear this word used almost daily. The manufacturer proudly announces that after years of research his company has produced a new fabric. The stock analyst claims that his market forecasts are products of sound research. When in need of help, teachers, housewives, farmers, politicians, and military men turn to research laboratories for aid. Yes, research is a common word, a magic word. But what does it mean? What is the nature and value of scientific investigations?

Research is defined by scholars as a careful, critical search for solutions to the problems that plague and puzzle mankind. Research is born of curiosity and nourished by the intense yearning to learn the truth and to improve our ways of doing things. Research is a precious possession, for it provides citizens with a key to social progress.

Down through the decades, a succession of scientists have served as practical pathfinders to progress. By solving a multiplicity of problems facing individuals and nations, they have paved the road to social betterment. Their work has improved men's physical well-being, standard of living, and military security. Their efforts have provided people with better quality, quantity, and variety of food; more attractive and diverse clothing; and innumerable comforts and conveniences that ease men's burdens and enliven their lives. Ideas fostered in research laboratories have increased the speed and ease of transportation; replaced the muscle-straining pick, plow, and shovel with powerful machines; and created complicated automatic devices to assume many monotonous duties of men. On every front, scientists have attacked drudgery and disease. As a result of their efforts, people live longer, possess better health, enjoy more leisure, see more of the world, endure less suffering, and experience less arduous labor.

ATTITUDES TOWARD RESEARCH

Having observed a parade of astonishing advances and having become increasingly indebted to science, citizens should have the greatest respect for research work. But many of them, unfortunately, do not have an intelligent

1

understanding of the nature and value of research and its relationship to their lives. Consequently, they consciously or unconsciously have developed attitudes toward science that hamper its progress. While reading the following paragraphs, perhaps you will recognize points of view expressed by some of your classmates or teaching colleagues.

Repressing Research. Because of vested interests in the *status quo* or a fearful distrust of new ideas or developments, some individuals and groups do not want scientists to jar people out of their traditional patterns of thought and behavior. To them, change is unnecessary and undesirable; hence, they rudely reject or ruthlessly repress researchers who present ideas or inventions that depart too far from prevailing beliefs or practices. Historians have repeatedly related tales of the severe measures taken by authorities to prevent scientists from advancing knowledge. Copernicus was excommunicated for publishing *On The Revolutions of the Celestial Orbs*. Tycho Brahe, the astronomer, was burned at the stake. Galileo was persecuted by the Inquisition. Darwin was severely censured for his *Origin of Species*. The discovery of the basic principle of genetics by Mendel was ignored by society for thirty-five years after it was published. Dewey and his disciples, who sought to make education more scientific, were vigorously attacked. Not uncommonly, a crown of thorns rather than an olive wreath has been the reward of research workers.

Ridiculing Research. Because of inertia, ignorance, or the belief that it is impossible to make further advances in knowledge, some people ridicule the efforts of research workers. They dismiss scientists as peculiar fellows who patiently putter with rats, chemicals, or books rather than ambitiously attacking problems in the practical world of affairs. These critics contend that all the important discoveries have been made. They believe that scientists busy themselves with trivial problems and camouflage the insignificance of their work by studding research reports with technical jargon and mounds of statistics. They charge that instead of following the good old ways of the good old days, researchers attempt to foist upon society foolish, newfangled theories that never work.

Worshiping Research. Not only ridicule and repression but also indiscriminate admiration of scientists can hamper social progress. Some educators and other citizens place research on the highest pedestal and blindly worship it. They believe scientists are gifted geniuses—a different species of humanity—who engage in grueling hours of work utilizing complicated procedures that ordinary men cannot possibly comprehend. Standing in absolute awe of science, they accept all research reports as revolutionary, reliable solutions to problems. With great enthusiasm they adopt each new drug, gadget, and remedy on the market. Digging deep into their pockets, they generously donate to any project labeled research. They swallow, hook, line, and sinker, whatever a research worker tells them.

Desiring to identify themselves as alert and progressive, they eagerly grasp and apply new theories whether they have an intelligent understanding of them or not. Abandoning all critical caution, they conclude that whatever is proclaimed to be a product of research is good.

Assuming that We Possess Superior Aptitude. Having witnessed a succession of dramatic scientific transformations, some men complacently accept such progress as automatic. Many Americans smugly assume that we are world leaders because we instinctively possess the "know-how" to solve problems. Earlier in the century, a similar nationalistic pride caused German chemists to proclaim that their successes resulted from the possession of special "moral qualities." But it is naïve for any nation to believe that it has a monopoly on scientific aptitude. Americans were abruptly forced to face this fact when the Russians put the first satellite in orbit. This incident awakened us to the necessity of providing our scientists with better training, equipment, facilities, and financial support.

Accepting More Applied than Pure Research. Laymen tend to sanction some types of research more readily than others. Most of them see great value in applied research that produces plainly practical and immediately useful findings—a polio vaccine, television set, or hearing aid. But they are less enthusiastic about supporting basic or pure research that strives to solve the fundamental mysteries of nature. Many men, for example, would contribute generously to an applied research program for the development of an anticancer pill or an arithmetic-teaching machine. They might balk, however, at supplying funds for a basic study on cellular growth or the nature of learning that does not guarantee to produce a product of immediate social and economic value. Yet the study on cellular growth eventually may throw light not only on the prevention of cancer but on a host of diseases. Likewise, a study on the nature of learning may provide a major breakthrough that will lead to improvement in teaching not only arithmetic but also many other subjects. Although basic research may ultimately lead to more fruitful developments than applied research, it is often difficult to obtain public support for it. Citizens cannot easily see how pure research will better their lives. They are leery of projects that do not promise specific and quick returns on their investments.

Accepting More Natural than Social Science Research. Society has exerted considerable effort to promote research in the natural sciences, but it has assumed a more skeptical and antagonistic attitude toward supporting research in the social sciences. Many people are quite willing to accept changes in physics and technical fields, but they are rather reluctant to alter their social institutions. Citizens who quickly turn to scientists for aid in solving industrial problems rely on do-it-yourself and trial-and-error techniques for improving educational practices. Men who would not think of providing for national defense by returning to the military hardware of

World War I confidently claim they can solve all educational problems by returning to the practices of the McGuffey reader era. Manufacturers and politicians who continually increase research expenditures to produce more comfort gadgets and deadly weapons are not equally eager to earmark funds for educational research. Seeking better means of developing the potentialities of our children does not command as much attention as creating a new model car. Technologically, society's attitude toward research is in the Space Age; educationally, it is hardly beyond the Horse and Buggy Age.

Acquiring Better Understanding of Research. Many undesirable attitudes toward research have developed because the public is not well-informed about scientific procedures and objectives. Our country must take steps to fill this intellectual vacuum. If citizens remain ignorant of research, they may impede social development and endanger national survival. In a democracy, all men play a part in determining policies. If they do not appreciate the value of scientific investigations, they will not make intelligent decisions when asked to support research projects. Scientific understanding, therefore, cannot remain the exclusive privilege of an intellectual elite. If citizens acquire sufficient knowledge of research to see the relationship between it and their individual and national well-being, they will be more willing to assume the responsibilities necessary to promote scientific investigations.

Scientifically informed citizens will appreciate that social progress is not inevitable, but must be won by seriously searching for answers to problems. Hence, they will insist upon recruiting talented youths for research work, supplying the selected scholars with superior training, and granting scientists the prestige due them. Moreover, these voters will realize that it is essential to support educational as well as natural science research and to finance basic as well as applied research. On no occasion will they permit social, political, economic, or religious bodies to curb the scientists' freedom of inquiry and right to question existing funds of knowledge. Nor will they allow individuals and institutions to pervert research efforts so as to obtain findings favorable to selfish interests. Rather than gullibly accepting claims made for new theories and products, they will evaluate whether the assertions are based upon sound research. Rather than ignoring reliable research findings or forcing sound scientific theories to remain locked in laboratories, citizens will quickly apply each advance in knowledge to everyday life.

EDUCATION AND RESEARCH

Despite the rather apathetic attitude of the general public toward educational research, a few lay and school leaders have been successful in developing agencies and organizations to promote it. Their progress has been slow and laborious, for it takes considerable time to win public support.

But some day society may feel as deeply indebted to the men who have founded educational research as it now does to pioneer research workers in the natural sciences.

Establishing Agencies of Research. Lively sparks of interest in solving educational problems through research began to stimulate men's minds in the late nineteenth century. Some seeds of the research movement sprouted at Leipzig in 1879 when Wilhelm Wundt established the first psychological laboratory. In England, about that time, Francis Galton and Karl Pearson were developing statistical methods, terms, and principles that were later used in educational research. After the turn of the century, the French scholar Alfred Binet initiated his studies in mental testing. During these decades, the American students who streamed to Europe for advanced study caught the scientific fever and returned home burning with enthusiasm for research.

Developing Research Institutions. Having been deeply impressed with the leadership, laboratories, and libraries European universities provided to help students engage in research, outstanding American educators agitated for the founding of similar institutions in this country. Francis Wayland of Brown University, Henry P. Tappan and James B. Angell of Michigan were among the early leaders who recommended sweeping educational reforms. Charles W. Eliot of Harvard, Andrew Dickson White of Cornell, and Frederick A. P. Barnard of Columbia also participated in the movement. In 1869, a committee of the National Teachers' Association strongly urged the nation to establish a "real university" that would push back the frontiers of knowledge by means of research.

Harvard, Yale, Columbia, Michigan, and other schools made some effort to offer advanced instruction fairly early. Real graduate schools did not exist, however, until the establishment of Johns Hopkins University in 1876, Clark University in 1888, and the University of Chicago in 1890 with Daniel Coit Gilman, G. Stanley Hall, and William Rainey Harper as their respective presidents. In the pioneer universities, scholars such as Cattell, Judd, Hall, Thorndike, Pintner, Courtis, Terman, and others initiated research studies and inspired their students to carry on the work. For example, Ben Wood, who served as an assistant to Thorndike, later directed numerous studies and research projects and provided outstanding leadership for the movement.

As the research movement gained momentum, society created additional agencies to further scientific investigations. Colleges established psychological laboratories and research centers, such as the child study laboratories at Yale, Iowa, Columbia, and Minnesota. By 1924, twenty-two institutions had established research bureaus. Private and public experimental schools and teacher-training laboratory schools planned special programs to study children and to apply research findings. Public school authorities selected particular schools or classes in which to conduct investigations or to try out new procedures. Foundations such as the W. K. Kellogg Foundation, the Ford Foundation, and the Russell Sage Foundation gave substantial grants for research studies. City, state, and national educational authorities added directors of research to their staffs. In 1922, the National Education Association (NEA) established the Research Division which now collects considerable data and conducts many studies of concern to its members. In recent decades, agencies promoting educational research have multiplied, and most institutions have expanded their facilities and programs.

Developing Research Periodicals and Organizations. Distinguished leaders in the research movement also founded many organizations and publications to disseminate information and advance their work. In 1876 the first psychological journal, *Mind,* appeared in England. G. Stanley Hall started *The American Journal of Psychology* in 1887 and *Pedagogical Seminary* in 1891. Binet's work on intelligence appeared in *L'Année Psychologique* which he founded in 1894. After it was founded in 1900, the *Teachers College Record* presented many of Thorndike's studies. *The Journal of Educational Psychology,* established in 1910, became a valuable publication for workers in the field. Taking note of the importance of research, many universities established bureaus to publish research monographs and educational association added research sections to their organizations and publications.

In 1915, pioneer workers established the American Educational Research Association (AERA) which became a department of the NEA in 1930. The AERA exerted a wide influence on the research movement. It was connected with the founding of the *Educational Research Bulletin* in 1920 and the *Review of Educational Research* in 1931. The AERA also produced the *Encyclopedia of Educational Research* to aid scholars.

In addition to the AERA, a number of other organizations have contributed to modern research. The American Council on Education and the National Society for the Study of Education have served as stimulating agencies. Phi Delta Kappa, a graduate fraternity of students interested in education and research, has initiated over ninety-two thousand members. Dozens of other educational organizations have established research sections and have produced periodicals and yearbooks that are devoted wholly or partly to research. During the past two decades, an increasing number of research textbooks have been published.

Expanding Areas of Research. At the turn of the century, it was a relatively small group of men who became dissatisfied with the traditional trial-and-error and private intuition methods of trying to solve educational problems. Realizing that it was impossible to improve educational processes merely on the basis of guesswork, these inspired leaders tried to establish more objective methods of obtaining reliable knowledge about learning,

children, and the status of education. For a couple of decades, only a few
men joined the intellectually disciplined ranks of research workers. But,
by mid-century, an army of investigators were conducting scientific studies
to determine the educational effectiveness of the curriculum, school plant,
teaching methods, guidance programs, and administrative practices. Down
through the years, the research workers have greatly expanded the scope of
their activities and have gradually exerted an influence on the practices in
every area of education.

Developing Tests. Measurement formed the cornerstone of the research
movement. "For there cannot be a science without fairly precise quantification: not that science is measurement, but that traits which are devoid of
any reasonably definite quality simply do not have the required specificity
for entering into the careful thinking essential to science. When quantities
are disregarded almost any generalization is true" (19:253–254). Recognizing this fact, Thorndike designed his famous battle banner for research
workers: "Whatever exists at all exists in some amount" (21:16). Following his advice, scholars soon began to employ quantitative methods of
inquiry to obtain precise facts about various areas of education.

Devising tests to measure intelligence was a major concern of Binet,
Terman, Otis, Pintner, Paterson, Wechsler, and other able investigators.
Developing aptitude tests also received considerable attention. The Sea-
shore Test of Musical Talent appeared in 1915. Thereafter, investigators
developed many other tests to measure specific types of capacity. Edward
L. Thorndike and his students constructed most of the early tests and scales
for measuring academic achievements of children. The Stone Arithmetic
Test appeared in 1908 and the Thorndike Handwriting Scale in 1910.
About this time, Stuart A. Courtis, who was also active in developing
standardized tests, was invited to New York City where he conducted the
testing in the first formal school survey in which such tests were employed.
Within a few years, many other investigators published composition, spelling,
language, and arithmetic scales. Research workers also became interested
in devising tests to measure personality, attitudes, and interests of students.
The information provided by the tests developed during the past fifty years
has led to many improvements in educational and vocational guidance
programs, curriculum construction, and administration.

Investigating the Learning Process. Psychologists made an effort to push
back the frontiers of educational knowledge by conducting investigations to
answer the question: How do children learn? Prior to this century, teachers
had rather vague concepts of the learning process. Many of them believed
that they could guarantee that learning would take place by administering
sufficient drill and discipline. Upon becoming acquainted with the theoretical explanations of learning constructed on the basis of research studies,
educators began to appreciate that learning was a more complex process than

they had thought.   Realizing that they were not producing the most effective learning in their classrooms, some educators critically evaluated and revised their teaching methods.   Throughout the nation, instructors began to give greater attention to the various factors that research studies revealed played a part in learning.

Investigating the Nature of Children.   Research workers also aided teachers by engaging in studies to acquire extensive data about the nature of children. . G. Stanley Hall is considered the founder of the child study movement.   Since his time hundreds of investigators have conducted studies to obtain a more accurate understanding of the physical, emotional, intellectual, and social growth and development of boys and girls.   The findings reported by Gesell, Baldwin, Dearborn, Rothney, Ilg, Ogg, Olson, and other workers in child study laboratories have considerably influenced the practices that teachers, parents, and social workers follow in guiding the development of youths.

Developing the Curriculum.   Curriculum research during this century has challenged some existing school practices, confirmed the desirability of continuing others, and encouraged the adoption of new practices.   Rather than unquestioningly accepting the classical curriculum, research workers have asked some pertinent questions: What knowledges and skills are most useful in society?   What subject matter should be chosen as the basis of instruction? How should subject matter be integrated?   What types of learning experiences should be included in the curriculum?   How can the school provide for a longitudinal sequence of learning experiences?   What kind of daily and weekly schedule of activities should be adopted?   By proposing answers for some of these questions Bobbitt, Charters, Tyler, Caswell, Alberty, and many others made significant contributions to curriculum construction.   The Eight-year Study, Southern Association Study, and various state curriculum studies played a part in encouraging schools to depart from some of their traditional practices.   As a result of curriculum research, most schools have attempted to eliminate excessive fragmentation of instruction and to provide for broad, integrated areas of study that are directly related to the needs of pupils and modern society.   All schools have not adopted the same type of program, but most of them have either (1) reorganized instruction within a school subject, (2) correlated related subjects or fields, or (3) constructed a core curriculum.

Improving School Administration and Evaluation.   School administrators have encouraged investigators to conduct studies concerning taxation, budgeting, purchasing, class size, grouping pupils, school-community relations, selection of teachers, and other problems.   Administrators also have made an effort to translate research findings into practice.   Since 1910, many school authorities have had experts survey their school systems and suggest how to improve them.   Early surveyors based their judgments on personal opinion, but leaders of the research movement soon began to objectify the appraisals by applying the newly devised standardized tests, scales, and measuring devices.   To clarify and define their evaluative judgments in specific areas, surveyors developed new rating scales and score cards such as the Strayer-Engelhardt Score Card for Junior High School Buildings, the Mort-Cornell Guide for Self-appraisal of School Systems, and the Bruner Criteria for Evaluating Teaching and Learning Materials and Practices.   As the survey movement developed, administrators recognized the need for continuous self-evaluation.   Consequently, they established their own bureaus of research to administer testing programs, to interpret research findings to classroom teachers, and to apply the products of research in the schools.

Improving the Quality of Research.   Having been nourished by the enthusiasm and effort of forward-looking educators, the infant educational research movement has experienced considerable growth.   Dedicated men have accomplished miracles, but much work remains to be done.   The growing pains, problems, and weaknesses common to other sciences in the early days of their development have also plagued educational research. Platoons of well-trained investigators did not spring up overnight to present the world with flawless solutions to educational problems.   Each generation of research scholars has had to build upon the work of its predecessors—correcting errors when possible, filling in gaps, and gradually constructing a body of concepts that are more useful in solving educational problems than the guesswork of laymen.   Under the leadership of able men, the research movement has made slow but promising progress.

Developing a Higher-Caliber of Research Personnel.   The limited training and experience of educational investigators has hampered the development of the research movement.   Many research workers have lacked the necessary foundation in basic sciences, mathematics, psychology, languages, and logic.   Some of them have not been thoroughly familiar with the literature in their field and the various research techniques and procedures. To meet the demand for higher-caliber and better-prepared research workers, graduate schools have raised admittance standards and have developed extensive educational programs and instructional materials to prepare students for research.   Compact information and useful guides for workers in the field, which once were obtainable only through the most laborious individual effort, now appear in textbooks, periodicals, and other publications.

Rather than relegating research to one-shot doctoral dissertation projects or a spare-time hobby for professors carrying a full teaching load, more and more institutions are developing divisions of research so that scholars can become thoroughly grounded in an area of study and can devote all of their energies to scientific investigations. In addition, many colleges are now providing release time for other staff members who wish to pursue postdoctoral studies.

Developing Higher Standards for Research Work. The early decades in the scientific movement were devoted to developing research tools and procedures and arousing interest in initiating investigations. By 1935, a tremendous quantity of research had been done, but leaders in the field were beginning to question the quality of the studies. Much of the work was localized, repetitive, trivial, biased, fragmentary, and defective in design and methodology; it made little, if any, contribution to a body of organized scientific knowledge concerning education.

Since the 1930s, a more critical attitude has developed toward research studies and the use made of their findings. Educators have become more modest and cautious in making claims about the products of research. Moreover, they have begun to look for the shortcomings and technical errors in earlier studies. To overcome some of the difficulties confronting them, they have devised new and highly imaginative investigative techniques and have designed more reliable research tools. Leaders in the field have recognized that merely collecting data and describing phenomena does not advance knowledge appreciably. Hence, they have endeavored to explain phenomena, and in doing so, they have developed principles that are of great value to classroom teachers. But they have not been as successful as physicists in producing all-embracing theories that explain, unify, and order large bodies of unrelated facts.

The research movement has progressed to the point where workers are beginning to survey and analyze the weaknesses in the over-all production of studies. They find the development of research has been uneven. Much more work has been done in some areas than others. There are more studies concerning young children, for example, than those of high school age. The time has come to strive for a greater balance and comprehensiveness in investigative efforts. Action also should be taken to eliminate the confusion arising from the fact that findings from different studies on the same problem are sometimes conflicting in nature. To unify education as a science, workers in the field should critically evaluate the conflicting explanations given to account for phenomena and reject the weaker ones.

The soul-searching self-criticism that has occurred in the field of educational research denotes the emergence of greater maturity. The active, expanding research movement is passing from infancy to a more sophisticated stage of development. The successful work produced by educators and psychologists during the war years, the growing public recognition of the need for studious inquiry in all fields, and the current critical examination of our schools is winning recognition and financial support for more vigorous investigative programs. Since mid-century, many exciting new developments have triggered enthusiasm for tackling fundamental problems that require highly imaginative concepts capable of explaining a great range of specific events or conditions.   This work may someday provide educators with basic principles and laws that will enable mankind to make giant strides of progress.

TEACHERS AND RESEARCH

Educational research is as important to you as a classroom teacher as it is to leaders in the profession.   Acquiring some understanding of research work, therefore, should be regarded as an essential part of your education. The experience not only will broaden and deepen your general fund of knowledge and give you some appreciation of the powerful part research plays in fashioning our lives, but also will improve your methods of solving personal and instructional problems.   An introduction to research will open up an interesting new world for you.   It will acquaint you with a promising array of opportunities to experience continuous personal and professional growth.   It will challenge you to search for truths that men can apply to make the world a better place in which to live.

Offering Student Guidance.   As an educator, you are obligated to become sufficiently informed about research to offer students sound guidance. In the classroom, you are expected to help pupils gain an understanding of the role scientific investigations play in promoting social progress.   Since better instructional procedures today are organized around problem-solving activities rather than rote memorization, you must also help students acquire skill in scientific methods of solving problems.   In addition, society holds you responsible for interesting exceptionally able youths in the pursuit of research as a career and guiding them in the selection of academic experiences needed to realize their aspirations.   You cannot perform these services satisfactorily unless you become well acquainted with research work.

Improving Classroom Practices.   By reading research studies that keep you abreast of educational developments, you will acquire new interests, new motives, and new insights that will replenish your energies and enthusiasms and revitalize your instructional procedures.   Research will awaken your curiosity, shatter some pet entrenched ideas and attitudes, and make you question traditional practices.   As a result, you will never become a senile instructional automaton engaged solely in the spiritless drudgery of regurgitating college-acquired knowledges and concepts.   Rather, you will embark on an exciting quest for new viewpoints and better ways of planning and guiding children's learning experiences.   The rigorous demand of the adventure will spur the development of your potential capacities further than you ever thought it possible.   The thrill of working on the frontiers of knowledge, the satisfaction of experiencing continuous professional growth, and the glow of personal pride that arises from doing superior work are the rich rewards you will experience from studying research findings and applying them in the classroom.

Reducing Lag in Application of Research Findings. A twenty-five-year lag between research findings and their application is commonplace in our schools and some studies never receive proper consideration. This situation suggests that teachers are unaware of educational investigations made by competent scholars, or unwilling to apply the outcome of research in the schools, or unable to put the knowledge into effect owing to inadequate facilities or restrictive administrative policies. Some delay between the discovery of knowledge and the application of it is inevitable, but the present lag appears to be unjustifiably long.

If you and fellow teachers remain ignorant of research studies or resist applying the findings in the classroom, you can nullify the efforts of the most brilliant research workers. Of what value, for example, is it to develop reliable measures of child aggressiveness and submissiveness and methods of dealing with them, if teachers fail to utilize this information when working with children? Of what value is it to discover measures of reading readiness, if teachers continue to organize reading instruction groups on an age or grade level basis rather than on the pupil's readiness to read? Parents, doctors, social workers, and school administrators can apply some products of research, but, as a classroom teacher, you play a key role in translating educational research findings into practice.

Strengthening the Profession. Teachers retard the professionalization of education if they regard research as an expendable academic appendage. It is of paramount importance to an instructor to recognize that research workers are essential agents who build the structural foundation of education. As a practitioner in the classroom, you are helpless when deprived of the rudder fashioned by theoreticians in the laboratory. Carefully constructed theories precede successful practices. Doctors cannot make medical decisions without referring to well-confirmed theories. Nor can you make the best educational judgments on the basis of whim, expediency, or habit. Sound decisions are based on facts and theories, and research provides the means of obtaining them. Educators cannot expect the field to gain public recognition as a full-fledged profession without building a body of competent research.

Only by learning to discriminate between superficial research studies and well-grounded investigations can teachers win public respect for the profession. If you merely develop an effervescent enthusiasm for research and impulsively stuff instructional cabinets with every nostrum on the market, you will find that some of the wonder drugs not only fail to cure students' ills but also produce harmful effects. You cannot gain the confidence of the public by prescribing new educational practices without evaluating their worth.   But, by becoming familiar with standards for evaluating the research studies, you can put into practice only the most significant and reliable findings.   By taking such action, you will not only strengthen the educational system, but also encourage the public to hold teachers in higher esteem, to look to them for leadership, and to grant them greater financial reward.

Developing a sincere interest in research will also help you establish better relationships with colleagues, administrators, and parents.   Your enthusiasm for finding better ways of doing things will have a stimulating effect on others.   Your willingness to appeal to facts for answers to problems will create a hopeful, healthful working atmosphere.   Rather than becoming involved in endless emotionalized arguments with associates and the public concerning who is right, you will direct discussions into more productive channels by asking: What is right?   What do the facts reveal?

Participating in Research Projects.   Although most classroom teachers are appliers rather than producers of research, a few do play a role connected with creative investigation.   To assist scholars in conducting research studies, you may be requested to offer your classroom for observational purposes, supply information about students, administer tests, or obtain student volunteers for experimental programs.   You may also become interested in playing a part in the action research movement, which encourages classroom teachers to attack practical problems that they encounter.

In the future, more and more teachers will be called upon to play a role in research.   Certainly you will be a more interested and intelligent participant if you possess some knowledge of scientific investigative procedures. The following chapters, therefore, will present a simple explanation of the researcher's work—his objectives, methods, problems, limitations, and difficulties.   The discussion will illuminate your understanding of what a researcher does and what he cannot do.   This entree into the world of research will enable you to read reports or summaries of research more intelligently; it will provide a foundation for more advanced study; and it may interest you in preparing yourself as a specialist in this field where the profession desperately needs qualified men.

BIBLIOGRAPHY

1. Abelson, Harold H., "The Role of Educational Research in a Democracy," *The Journal of Educational Sociology,* 21 (April, 1948): 454.

2. Allen, Francis R., et al., *Technology and Social Change.*   New York: Appleton-Century-Crofts, Inc., 1957.

3. American Educational Research Association, "Twenty-five Years of Educational Research," *Review of Educational Research,* 26 (June, 1956): 202.

4. American Educational Research Association and Department of Classroom Teachers, *The Implications of Research for the Classroom Teacher.*   Washington: National Education Association, 1939.

5. Conant, James B., *Modern Science and Modern Man.* New York: Columbia University Press, 1952.

6. Conant, James B., *On Understanding Science.* New Haven: Yale University Press, 1947.

7. Cubberley, Ellwood P., *Public Education in the United States.* New York: Houghton Mifflin Company, 1934, chap. 21.

8. Good, Carter V., "Educational Research After Fifty Years," *Phi Delta Kappan,* 37 (January, 1956): 145.

9. Good, Carter V., and Douglas E. Scates, *Methods of Research.* New York: Appleton-Century-Crofts, Inc., 1954, chap. 1.

10. Hillway, Tyrus, *Introduction to Research.* Boston: Houghton Mifflin Company, 1956, chaps. 1–3.

11. Lieberman, Myron, *Education as a Profession.* Englewood Cliffs, N.J.: Prentice-Hall, Inc., 1956, chap. 7.

12. Meyer, Adolph E., *The Development of Education in the Twentieth Century.* Englewood Cliffs, N.J.: Prentice-Hall, Inc., 1949, chap. III A.

13. Monroe, Walter S., "Educational Measurement in 1920 and in 1945," *Journal of Educational Research,* 38 (January, 1945): 334.

14. Monroe, Walter S. (ed.), "Science of Education," *Encyclopedia of Educational Research.* New York: The Macmillan Company, 1950.

15. Monroe, Walter S., and Max D. Englehart, *The Scientific Study of Educational Problems.* New York: The Macmillan Company, 1936, chap. 4.

16. Ross, C. C., *Measurement in Today's Schools.* Englewood Cliffs, N.J.: Prentice-Hall, Inc., 1947, chaps. 1 and 2.

17. Rugg, Harold, *Foundations for American Education.* New York: Harcourt, Brace & World, Inc., 1947, chap. 23.

18. Ryan, W. Carson, *Studies in Early Graduate Education.* New York: Carnegie Foundation for the Advancement of Teaching, 1939.

19. Scates, Douglas E., "Fifty Years of Objective Measurement and Research in Education," *Journal of Educational Research,* 41 (December, 1947): 241.

20. State of Michigan, *"What Does Research Say?"* Lansing, Mich.: Department of Public Instruction, 1937.

21. Thorndike, Edward L., "The Nature, Purposes and General Methods of Measurements of Educational Products," *The Measurement of Educational Products.* Seventeenth Yearbook of the National Society for the Study of Education, 1918, part II.

22. Wilds, Elmer Harrison, *The Foundations of Modern Education.* New York: Holt, Rinehart and Winston, Inc., 1942, chap. 16.

CHAPTER 2

Methods of Acquiring Knowledge

Down through the ages, man has searched for knowledge that would answer his questions about the world, satisfy his desire to know the truth, and aid him in improving his ways of living. When faced with unceasing toil, primitive man managed to lighten his burdens by discovering the wheel, the sail, and the lever. By gazing into the heavens with wonder and seeking explanations for what he saw, the Babylonian scholar was able to predict eclipses as early as the sixth century B.C. The yearly flooding of the Nile and the repeated task of mapping out fields caused the Egyptians to create a calendar and acquire knowledge of geometry. From ancient times to the present day, man repeatedly has encountered puzzling phenomena and disturbing difficulties. When seeking a solution or explanation for his problems, he has turned to the various sources of knowledge discussed in this chapter: (1) authority, (2) personal experience, (3) deductive reasoning, (4) inductive reasoning, and (5) the scientific method.

OLDER METHODS OF ACQUIRING KNOWLEDGE

Early man acquired knowledge by chance or the trial-and-error method. When something occurred that he could not understand, such as lightning or leprosy, he often ascribed it to supernatural influences or blindly accepted the explanations handed down by his ancestors. These methods of accumulating knowledge were rather unproductive and frequently led to gross inaccuracies. They did not build up a substantial body of reliable information about the world that could contribute appreciably to social progress.

After stumbling upon logic, a method of reasoning about things, man increased his opportunities to acquire knowledge. A few gifted Greeks in ancient times developed the deductive method of reasoning into a highly refined art. Later, churchmen in the medieval era found that this type of formal logic was particularly suited to their purposes. Some of them narrowed the use of the deductive method, however, until they transformed it into more of a mental exercise than a search for truth. In the late sixteenth century, Francis Bacon revolted against this form of reasoning and sought to replace it with the inductive method. The following paragraphs briefly review these older methods of obtaining knowledge and how men have tried to improve upon them.

Authority. Even in the earliest civilizations, man appealed to some authority when searching for knowledge. The savage begged the medicine man to tell him how to relieve his pain, plied the tribal chieftain with questions about the elements, and turned to ancestral customs for guidance in modes of behavior. Rather than attempting to determine truth independently, modern man also frequently appeals to the opinion of authorities. A trial lawyer may ask a psychiatrist to testify concerning the sanity of the defendant; a ballistic expert to give opinions concerning weapons; and a handwriting specialist to compare signatures. A housewife may consult a child care book or a doctor concerning the spots on her son's chest. Obtaining knowledge by turning to customs or authorities is often economical of time and effort, but it sometimes leads to error. Therefore, when seeking advice from authorities, a scientist critically evaluates their reliability and reserves the right to investigate and test their pronouncements to see whether he reaches the same conclusions.

Tradition. In many situations modern man does not evaluate the truth or falsity of his beliefs any more than his forefathers did. He unconsciously or unquestioningly accepts many traditions of his culture, such as the customary modes of dress, speech, food, worship, and etiquette. In the world of practical affairs this is often necessary, for one cannot question *all* things. But it is a mistake to believe that everything that customarily has been done is right or that it is always possible to arrive at truth by appealing to the accumulated wisdom of the ages.

Historical records reveal that throughout the centuries society has collected not only wisdom but also much intellectual nonsense. Many long-revered educational, medical, and scientific theories have since proved false. For instance, it was once commonly believed that children differed from adults only in size and dignity, that asafetida bags warded off disease, and that planets revolved around the earth. Truth is not a guaranteed product of a popularity contest: a statement is not true merely because "everyone knows it," or "everybody has always believed it." Age, alone, is not sufficient to establish the truth or falsity of a belief.

Church, State, and Ancient Scholars. Primitive man turned to tribal leaders when seeking knowledge. In medieval times, man believed that ancient scholars and churchmen had discovered the truth for all times and their pronouncements could not be questioned. The Scholastics, for example, accepted Aristotle's conjecture that women have more teeth than men as absolutely true, even though simple observation and enumeration could have proved it to be false. A scholar refused to look through a telescope when invited by Galileo to view the newly discovered moons of

Jupiter. He was convinced that the moons could not possibly be seen because Aristotle had not mentioned them in his discussions on astronomy. This man and most of the other medieval scholars blindly clung to faulty Grecian theories and bitterly attacked any new idea that contradicted the accepted authorities.

With the rise of strong secular states after the Middle Ages, man increasingly turned to kings, legislatures, and courts as sources of information. Today, for example, many citizens expect government officials to solve problems for them concerning agricultural surpluses, international trade, labor-management difficulties, "fair-trade" practices, unemployment conditions, and even the validity of certain theories, such as those proclaiming the superiority of particular races, or Darwin's theory of natural selection. Some people appeal to the courts for interpretations on basic issues confronting them, such as the segregated school practices in this country. From the earliest times to the present, man has sought guidance and information from his oracles, leaders, and rulers.

Man justifies authoritarianism on the basis that in searching for truth himself he might make errors, and, therefore, it is better to rely on the judgment of outstanding authorities whose beliefs have withstood the test of time. If modern man, however, can make errors when searching for truth, his ancestors must have been subject to the same weaknesses. If tradition, the church, and the state are to be the source of all truth, what happens when these institutions render opinions that conflict with one another? The authorities in different churches and states do not always agree and traditions of cultures vary. Consequently, one may encounter perplexing problems when he turns to the multiplicity of existing authorities in a search for truth. Referring to the cultural cumulations of the centuries is worthwhile, for little progress will occur if each generation completely rejects the collective judgment of the ages and starts from scratch to accumulate knowledge. But refusing ever to question any accepted belief—total reliance on dogmatic authority—will result in social stagnation.

Expert Opinion. When searching for knowledge, man sometimes seeks the testimony of experts who because of their intellect, training, experience, or aptitudes are better informed than other people. But, is expert opinion a reliable source of knowledge? Society, certainly, would not advance if it were unwilling to accept the opinions of specialists. One must exercise discrimination, however, when selecting experts. It pays to investigate whether the experts are recognized by other authorities in the field and whether they are in a position to know the facts about the particular problem under consideration. Although it is often necessary to consult experts, it is dangerous to accept their opinions unconditionally and for all time.

Personal Experience. When confronted with a problem, one often tries to recall or seek a personal experience that will help him reach a solution.

Ancient nomads who had to search for food probably remembered that certain berries always made them ill, that fish were more plentiful in some streams than others, and that grains ripened at particular times of the year. Today, a science teacher who wants to find the quickest way to work may time himself on different routes to arrive at an answer. When deciding where to plant seeds, a gardener may try to remember in what part of the yard flowers grew best last year. When given a handful of coins to divide with his brother, a small boy may recall that selecting the biggest piece of candy on a plate is usually a wise choice. Because of his previous experience with candy, he may decide to keep the big nickels and give his brother the little dimes.

Appealing to personal experiences is a useful and common method of seeking knowledge. When it is not used critically, however, it can lead to incorrect conclusions as the boy who selected the nickels with his "candy measuring stick" discovered. A person may make errors when observing or when reporting what he has seen or done. He may, for instance, (1) omit evidence that does not agree with his opinion, (2) use measuring instruments that require many subjective estimates, (3) establish a belief on insufficient evidence, (4) fail to observe significant factors relating to a specific situation, or (5) draw improper conclusions or inferences owing to personal prejudices. Thus, when the modern research worker turns to experience in his search for reliable knowledge, he exercises precautions that will help him avoid disastrous pitfalls.

Deduction.   Man may employ deductive reasoning as a leverage to obtain information. In deduction, man reasons that whatever is true of all instances of a class must also be true of any single instance that comes within its limits. Therefore, he endeavors to demonstrate that a particular instance under consideration logically falls within the instances of the entire class. To accomplish this task, he utilizes a device known as a syllogism.

A syllogism provides a means of testing the validity of a particular conclusion or fact. It is an argument consisting of three propositions. The first two propositions are called premises, since they furnish the grounds for the conclusion, which is the proposition standing last. Aristotle defines the syllogism as "a discourse in which certain things being posited, something else than what is posited necessarily follows from them." The following *categorical syllogism* is an example of such a discourse:

All men are mortal.	(major premise)
The emperor is a man.	(minor premise)
Therefore, the emperor is mortal.	(conclusion)

In a categorical syllogism two supposedly true statements stand in such a relationship that they logically imply a particular conclusion. If a person accepts the two premises, he must agree to the conclusion that follows.

A syllogism does not have to be composed exclusively of categorical propositions. As the following examples reveal, arguments may involve *hypothetical, alternative,* and *disjunctive* propositions.

Hypothetical:
> If the school is on fire, the children are in danger.
> The school is on fire.
> Therefore, the children are in danger.

Alternative:
> Either I will get a passing mark on this test, or I will flunk the course.
> I will not get a passing mark on this test.
> Therefore, I will flunk the course.

Disjunctive:
> It is not the case that it is both a rainy day and a good day to present the school pageant outdoors.
> It is a rainy day.
> Therefore, it is not a good day to present the school pageant outdoors.

As you note in the examples, each syllogism is labeled according to the type of proposition occurring in the major premise. Each type of syllogism is used in different stages of assurance concerning knowledge.

Categorical propositions represent a certain settled stage of our knowledge, and conclusions validly drawn from categorical syllogisms are unconditional. Hypothetical or conditional propositions, however, represent an unsettled stage in thinking and knowing. Hypothetical thinking proceeds on various levels, from the solution of simple problems of daily life, and the detection of crime, to the technique of identification and classification in science, and the search after scientific laws by means of the statement and testing of hypotheses. Likewise alternative arguments represent an unsettled state of knowledge, but within limits; the alternative often being quite well within the possibility of progressive elimination or verification. The disjunctive syllogism is a combination of knowledge and ignorance, like the alternative, but is an advance upon the alternative in the direction of more definite knowledge, and reaches a conclusion by means of what is known and can be asserted in the minor premise (16:114–115).

Deductive reasoning was the most important method of securing knowledge for centuries. Today, it continues to render useful service. In personal and professional life, you use it when solving problems. The lawyer, doctor, soldier, and detective often resort to deductive argument. In investigating a murder case, a prosecuting attorney may search through piles of evidence —existing knowledge—discard the irrelevant bits of information, critically select previously unconnected facts, and combine them in such a way that they logically imply a hitherto unsuspected conclusion. Deductive reasoning enables him to organize premises into patterns that provide conclusive evidence for the validity of his particular conclusion.

The modern research worker also utilizes deductive reasoning to carry out certain phases of his work. Some men scoff at the role of reason in research and contend that an investigator is only concerned with *facts* he can obtain through observation and experiment. But it is not sufficient to collect facts. Without deduction "most of our preoccupation with facts would be fruitless, since we could not fit them into the increasingly deductive systems which we call sciences. The latter are man's most economical instruments" (15:113). The scientist frequently tries to pigeonhole a particular instance under an already established principle from which it can be deduced. Through the hypothetical use of deduction, he manipulates and explores possibilities that may open up new areas of inquiry. Moreover, deductive logic helps the investigator check careless and confused thinking. It also provides him with a reliable method of testing the validity of the reasoning procedures employed in an argument.

Deductive reasoning is a useful tool to employ in problem solving, but it does have limitations. Deduction relies on verbal symbols which can be quite ambiguous. The same words do not mean the same things to all people and at all times. "Progressive education," for example, is a term that has aroused much controversy because of the various interpretations given to it. In the early 1900s the commonplace word "health" usually meant freedom from disease, the presence of muscular strength, or organic vigor. Today it denotes not only physical fitness, but also mental, social, and emotional well-being. Because of the shifting meaning of words, it is often difficult to evaluate an argument.

The categorical syllogism has another weakness: it can only deduce the consequences of preexisting knowledge. It does not probe beyond that which is already known. It does not give man an opportunity to make new discoveries and advance knowledge. In other words, a categorical syllogism is a device for pursuing the consequences of generally accepted statements rather than an instrument with which to gain new knowledge. If an investigator confines himself to this tool of research, he will not discover new truths.

The primary weakness of deductive reasoning lies in the possibility that one of the premises is not materially true or that the premises are unrelated. Although the conclusion drawn from the premises may be valid, it is of little value if the premises are not in accordance with reality. For example, examine the following argument.

> All professors of education hold doctorate degrees.   (major premise)
> Miss Jane Smith is a professor of education.   (minor premise)
> Hence, Miss Jane Smith holds a doctorate degree.   (conclusion)

The conclusion that "Miss Jane Smith holds a doctorate degree" is valid for it necessarily follows from the premises given, but it is not true in fact, for Miss Smith holds only a master's degree. The conclusion reached by a deductive argument can be trustworthy only if it is derived from reliable premises that are properly related. Thus, although deductive logic is a useful instrument to employ in obtaining information, it has certain limitations and deficiencies. Deductive logic cannot be relied upon exclusively in searching for the truth; it is not a self-sufficient means of securing dependable knowledge.

Induction. If the conclusions reached by deductive reasoning are true only if derived from true premises, man must find some way of determining whether his basic premises are true. Consequently, he has devised inductive reasoning to complement deductive reasoning as a means of searching for knowledge. In inductive reasoning, an investigator collects evidence that will enable him to establish a generalization as being probably true. He initiates his inquiry by observing particular instances (concrete facts), and from his examination establishes a general conclusion about the whole class in which these particular instances belong. If a man can arrive at general conclusions through induction, he can use them as major premises for deductive inferences.

Perfect Induction. One form of induction is complete enumeration. In this form of induction, man simply counts all of the instances in a given class and announces his results in a general conclusion. For example, to determine the occupation of the members in a club, he questions each member and tabulates his results.

Mr. Brown is a teacher.

A_1 B_1

Miss Smith is a teacher.

A_2 B_2

.   .

.   .

.   .

.   .

.   .

.   .

A_{25} B_{25}

Conclusion: All twenty-five members of this club are teachers.

Perfect induction is a means of securing reliable information. But how often does one have an opportunity to examine all the instances to which a conclusion refers? This type of enumeration cannot be employed as a method of investigation in the solution of most problems.

Baconian Induction. Francis Bacon (1561–1626) severely criticized the medieval practice of deducing conclusions from self-evident or authoritative premises. He held that man should not enslave himself to other men's thoughts. Rather than accepting the premises (generalizations-theories) handed down by authorities as absolute truths, Bacon believed the investigator should study nature closely himself and establish general conclusions on the basis of direct observation.

The system Bacon recommended for arriving at generalizations was laborious. He advised the investigator to tabulate all the facts concerning nature and to study these facts for their "forms," that is, the underlying essence of the phenomena. To do this, the investigator was to compile three tables, (1) positive instances—instances where certain phenomena appeared, (2) negative instances—instances where certain phenomena did not appear, and (3) instances where certain phenomena appeared in varying degrees and where the form varied accordingly. These tables were to help determine what properties were invariably connected with certain forms. Bacon cautioned against formulating any possible solution to a problem until all the facts had been gathered. His demand that the investigator first search for the facts was justified, but the exhaustive collection of facts he required was beyond the realm of human capacity.

Imperfect Induction. Whereas perfect induction establishes a conclusion by an exhaustive enumeration of *all* instances that are subsumable under it, imperfect induction arrives at a generalization by observing only *some* instances that make up the class. The research worker utilizes imperfect induction more often than perfect induction, for in most investigations he cannot examine all of the instances to which a conclusion refers. From observing *some* instances, however, he can draw a general conclusion regarding *all* similar instances, some of which he has not observed.

Thus, when it is not practical to examine all the instances of a class under consideration, the investigator does the next best thing: he arrives at a generalization by observing an adequate and representative sample from the entire class. To check on the purity of the water in a swimming pool, for instance, a health officer may take a single sample of water, test it, and draw a conclusion about the purity of the water in the entire swimming pool. Perhaps on the same day his friend, a restaurant owner, purchases five hundred steaks. To ascertain whether they are of choice quality without examining each steak, he selects at random a few steaks and finds that they are choice grade. From his selective observations, he draws the conclusion that all the steaks are probably of choice quality.

Drawing an inference about a whole class of things after sampling a few of its members does not necessarily yield absolutely certain knowledge. The size and representativeness of the instances observed largely determine whether one arrives at a sound conclusion. If the material observed is homogeneous, one or a few samples may be adequate for arriving at a generalization. If the material is not homogeneous, the same number of samples probably will yield a less reliable generalization. For example, the conclusion drawn from one sample of water may be more satisfactory than one drawn from several samples of steak. Previous knowledge of the composition of water gives the health officer greater assurance that all the water in the pool is like the small sample, than his friend can expect from a larger number of instances taken from cattle of different breeds and environments. Through imperfect induction, an investigator merely arrives at conclusions of varying degrees of probability, for the possibility always exists that some unexamined instances of the class do not agree with his conclusion.

MODERN METHOD OF ACQUIRING KNOWLEDGE

About the seventeenth century, man developed a new method of acquiring knowledge and as a result gave birth to the modern scientific movement. Francis Bacon planted the seeds of the scientific method when he savagely attacked the deductive method of reaching conclusions on the basis of authoritative premises and recommended reaching general conclusions on the basis of observed facts. As was previously noted, Bacon's method of continually gathering random facts produced masses of unwieldy information. To construct a more practical method of attaining reliable knowledge, men such as Newton, Galileo, and their successors eventually combined the inductive and deductive thought processes. This synthesis of reason and observation produced the modern scientific method of research.

Steps in the Scientific Method. In the scientific method, purposeful fact gathering replaces unsystematic fact gathering, and premises are tested probabilities rather than assumed truths. When using the scientific method, man shuttles back and forth between deduction and induction; he engages in reflective thinking. In 1910, John Dewey in *How We Think* analyzed the stages of activity involved in the act of reflective thinking. The following discussion distinguishes five stages in the act of problem solving:

1. *A felt difficulty.* Man encounters some obstacle, experience, or problem that puzzles him.

a. He lacks the *means* to get to the *end* desired.

b. He has difficulty in identifying the character of an object.

c. He cannot explain an unexpected event.

2. *Location and definition of the difficulty.* Man makes observations—gathers facts—that enable him to define his difficulty more precisely.

3. *Suggested solutions of the problem—hypotheses.* From his preliminary study of the facts, man makes intelligent guesses about possible solutions of the problem. The solutions—generalizations he offers to explain the facts causing him the difficulty—are called hypotheses.

4. *Deductively reasoning out the consequences of the suggested solutions.* Man deductively reasons that if each hypothesis is true, certain consequences should follow.

5. *Testing the hypotheses by action.* Man tests each hypothesis by searching for observable evidence that will confirm whether or not the consequences that should follow actually occur. By this process, he finds out which hypothesis is in harmony with observable facts and thus offers the most reliable answer to his problem.

These steps in the act of reflective thinking reveal how induction and deduction serve as opposing blades of the scientific shears that cut out segments of truth. "Induction provides the groundwork for hypotheses, and deduction explores the logical consequences of the hypotheses, in order to eliminate those that are inconsistent with the facts, while induction again contributes to the verification of the remaining hypothesis" (16:4). The research worker continually shifts between collecting facts; making generalizations (hypotheses) to explain facts; deducing the consequences of his hypotheses; and seeking additional facts to test the hypotheses. By employing both induction and deduction, he is able to arrive at reliable knowledge.

The scientific method of thinking is presented in steps to give a better insight into the process. These steps, however, do not always take place in successive order; they are not necessarily separate phases in thinking. Considerable fumbling occurs; a scientist may go back and forth between the steps several times. Some steps may require little effort; others may seem to absorb a disproportionate amount of time.

Illustration of the Scientific Method. The five steps or processes in reflective thinking will be discussed in greater detail in later chapters. For the time being, however, the following homely illustration may give you a better insight into the scientific method of securing knowledge:

A man returns from his vacation and discovers his garden is destroyed (felt-difficulty—step 1). He examines the garden and finds a twisted fence, flattened flowers, and uprooted stakes (concrete facts that help him precisely locate and define the difficulty—step 2). While searching for an explanation of these facts, it occurs to him that the neighbors' children may have deliberately destroyed the garden (hypothesis or generalization explaining the facts—step 3). His hypothesis goes beyond existing knowledge. He did not see the children perform the act, but this hypothesis offers one possible explanation of the facts. It also occurs to him that a bad storm may have wrecked the garden. Thus, he has a second hypothesis which may explain the facts. Consequently, he suspends judgment until he can establish proof.

By deduction, man reasons out the consequences of his first hypothesis (step 4). If the children wrecked the garden, they had to be at home during the time he was on his vacation. To test his hypothesis, (step 5) he asks where the children were and finds that they were away at camp while he was on vacation. Thus, he must reject his first hypothesis, for it is not in harmony with observable facts. He, then, deductively, reasons out the consequences of his second hypothesis (step 4) : If a severe storm destroyed the garden, it probably wrecked other nearby gardens. He tests this hypothesis (step 5) by observing other gardens and finds they have also been destroyed. He checks in newspapers and finds an account of a storm which destroyed many gardens in his section of the city. A neighbor tells him he watched the hail and wind uproot the garden. The man concludes that his second hypothesis is a reasonable explanation of the facts.

Thus, in reflective thinking man moves from particular facts to general statements of explanation about these facts, and from his general statements of explanation to a search for facts that will support them. He continues to do this until he establishes a defensible or reliable explanation of the facts. Research workers follow procedures similar to those of the garden owner, but they carry them out in a more systematic manner.

Applicability of the Scientific Method. The scientific method of reflective thinking is a tool that investigators use to solve diverse types of problems. A pure research worker striving to ferret out new knowledge about the mysteries of the universe employs it. The applied research worker seeking to develop a new product that can immediately improve some existing condition employs it. As former President J. R. Angell of Yale University pointed out, "The objects of research in pure science and the motives inspiring the work may be appreciably different from those encountered in the field of applied science. But the technique of the procedure in the two cases may be all but indistinguishable" (1:27). The scientific method of reflective thinking provides a key to advances in both pure and applied research.

In recent years classroom teachers have become interested in solving the practical problems they encounter when working with children. As a result, they have developed the *action research movement*. Educators engaged in action research have objectives similar to those of applied research workers; they are interested in research as a means to improve existing practices. In the cooperative type of action research, teachers describe current difficulties they experience in their classrooms (step 1). They ask trained research consultants to help them analyze these problems and carry out their investigations. Together, teachers and research consultants strive to bring the problems into focus by precisely determining the pertinent causal factors (step 2). From their study of data, they construct hypotheses that seem to offer possible explanations for the causes of their difficulties (step 3). Subsequently, they reason out the consequences of their hypotheses (step 4) and test the most appropriate hypothesis by an acceptable technique (step 5). Step by step they follow the scientific method of finding answers to problems.

Generally speaking, classroom teachers do not engage in drawn-out, complex investigations that require the mastery of complicated research techniques; they do not establish as rigid controls as are necessary for scientific experiments; and they do not build up a body of systematized scientific knowledge. But classroom teachers do find that the scientific method that the pure research workers employ to unravel the riddles of the universe can also aid them in solving immediate, local school problems.

Progress Made in Acquiring Knowledge. Man has made considerable progress in developing better methods of seeking knowledge down through the ages and, in doing so, has learned to approach the unknown with greater humility. Man once believed that he possessed a body of absolutely reliable knowledge that enabled him to give completely authoritative answers to questions. The modern research worker is less dogmatic, for he knows that the revolutionary advances made by science within the past century have overthrown some long-standing theories. This knowledge makes him more willing to challenge accepted theories when he becomes suspicious about their validity. Moreover, after carrying out an investigation, he makes no claim that his conclusions are infallible, but, rather, invites others to confirm, modify, or refute them. If his hypothesis is found to be incompatible with reliable evidence produced in later experiments, he abandons or alters it.

The scientific method does not lead to absolute certainties, yet it is more reliable than some methods that claim they do. Cohen and Nagel contrast the scientific method of securing knowledge with some other methods as follows (7:195):

> The other methods discussed are all inflexible, that is, none of them can admit that it will lead us into error. Hence, none of them can make provision for correcting its own results. What is called *scientific method* differs radically from these by encouraging and developing the utmost possible doubt, so that what is left after such doubt is always supported by the best available evidence. As new evidence or new doubts arise, it is the essence of scientific method to incorporate them—to make them an integral part of the body of knowledge so far attained. Its method, then, makes science progressive because it is never too certain about its results.

The scientific method of searching for truth is a slow process, but its tentative solutions to problems can be accepted with greater confidence than guesses, arbitrary assumptions, and pontifical pronouncements that preclude any further investigation. Consequently, the scientific method is a powerful and practical torchlight for man to use in lighting the way to the discovery of new truths.

Despite the improvements man has made in searching for knowledge, he has not yet arrived at a perfect method for seeking the truth. Authority, experience, and inductive and deductive reasoning all have certain weaknesses or limitations as research tools. Reflective thinking, the scientific method employed by research workers, has proved to be an especially useful means of seeking knowledge in the natural sciences. It has also helped educators probe problems. But it has not been a suitable instrument for seeking answers to certain types of questions.   James B. Conant declares that "only an occasional brave man will be found nowadays to claim that the so-called scientific method is applicable to the solution of almost all the problems of daily life in the modern world" (8:10).   The many lively debates that appear in scholarly periodicals reveal that authorities have not reached a common agreement concerning the breadth of the applicability of the scientific method.

Some critics contend that the scientific method cannot be used except in the natural sciences.   Others question whether the scientific method follows a *single* method of investigation.   Most scholars today think it is impossible to establish a rigid set of logical rules for the physical scientists, archaeologists, mathematicians, psychologists, sociologists, educators, and historians to follow in their respective undertakings.   Sciences differ from one another and consequently there are a multiplicity of methods.   Nevertheless, there are numerous common features in scientific inquiries that suggest a unity of scientific method.   Therefore, when questioned about the existence of a general scientific method, some scholars (4:5) reply that

. . . on a highly conceptual level science may be considered a general method. When scientists study specific problems, however, this general method is modified in numerous ways, and many of these adaptations are of sufficient importance and sufficiently general in nature to be considered methods within themselves.   Science, then, is a very general method, modified in various ways into many less general methods that are utilized in the study of specific problems.

Although some controversy exists concerning the scientific method, it is one of the most promising tools that man possesses for pushing back the frontiers of knowledge and increasing the accumulation of tested and verified truth.   Thus, you will want to become better acquainted with this type of scholarly investigation.   The overview of the steps in the scientific method presented in this chapter has merely given you some pegs of memory upon which you can attach more detailed information.   Research is not as simple and orderly a process as the elementary analysis and illustration you have studied may suggest, rather it is an extremely complex and exacting process. To give you a deeper insight into the scientific method, the succeeding chapters will probe further into some of the problems and procedures involved in research.

BIBLIOGRAPHY

1. Angell, James R., "The Organization of Research," *Journal of Proceedings and Addresses of the Association of American Universities.* Chicago: University of Chicago Press, 1919.

2. Benjamin, A. Cornelius, "Is There a Scientific Method?" *Journal of Higher Education,* 27 (May, 1956): 233–238.

3. Black, Max, *Critical Thinking.* Englewood Cliffs, N.J.: Prentice-Hall, Inc., 1952.

4. Brown, Clarence W., and E. E. Ghiselli, *Scientific Method in Psychology.* New York: McGraw-Hill Book Company, Inc., 1955, chap. 1.

5. Churchman, C. West, and Russell I. Ackoff, *Methods of Inquiry.* St. Louis: Educational Publishers, Inc., 1950, chaps. 1–8.

6. Cohen, Morris R., *Reason and Nature.* Glencoe, Ill.: Free Press, 1953.

7. Cohen, Morris, R., and Ernest Nagel, *An Introduction to Logic and Scientific Method.* New York: Harcourt, Brace & World, Inc., 1934.

8. Conant, James B., *On Understanding Science.* New Haven: Yale University Press, 1947, chap. 1.

9. Copi, Irving M., *Introduction to Logic.* New York: The Macmillan Company, 1955.

10. Dewey, John, *How We Think.* Boston: D. C. Heath and Company, 1933.

11. Doughton, Isaac, *Modern Public Education: Its Philosophy and Background.* New York: Appleton-Century-Crofts, Inc., 1935, chap. 6.

12. Furfey, Paul Hanly, *The Scope and Method of Sociology.* New York: Harper & Brothers, 1953, chaps. 2, 3, and 11.

13. Good, Carter V., A. S. Barr, and Douglas E. Scates, *The Methodology of Educational Research.* New York: Appleton-Century-Crofts, Inc., 1941, chap. 1.

14. Hillway, Tyrus, *Introduction to Research.* Boston: Houghton Mifflin Company, 1956, chap. 1.

15. Larrabee, Harold A., *Reliable Knowledge.* New York: Houghton Mifflin Company, 1945, chaps. 1, 3, and 4.

16. Searles, Herbert L., *Logic and Scientific Methods.* New York: The Ronald Press Company, 1948.

17. Underwood, Benton J., *Psychological Research.* New York: Appleton-Century-Crofts, Inc., 1957, chap. 1.

18. Whitney, Frederick L., *The Elements of Research.* Englewood Cliffs, N.J.: Prentice-Hall, Inc., 1946, chap. 1.

CHAPTER 3

General Concepts
Concerning the Scientific Method

The scientific method has evolved out of the various attacks scientists have devised to solve problems down through the years. Since the beginning of this century, particularly, scholars have critically analyzed the scientific method and attempted to delineate its basic procedures. The steps listed in the last chapter summarize an analysis that eventually materialized. This simplified account provides a thumbnail sketch of the activities involved in scientific investigations. But to comprehend the conceptual framework upon which the scientific method is founded, an examination of its underlying assumptions, aims, complexities, and difficulties is necessary. This chapter briefly reviews these topics because they directly affect the research worker in the pursuance of his activities.

ASSUMPTIONS UNDERLYING THE SCIENTIFIC METHOD

The scientific method rests upon certain fundamental assumptions about nature and the psychological processes. These assumptions directly influence all of a researcher's activity: they form the basis for his procedures, influence his methods of executing them, and affect the interpretation of his findings. Probing the validity of these propositions falls within the domain of the philosophy of science. The researcher merely accepts them on a common sense basis because he cannot proceed in his quest for scientific knowledge without assuming that they are valid.

Assumption of the Uniformity of Nature. Most of the assumptions about natural phenomena can be classified under the heading "the uniformity of nature." The principle of the uniformity of nature means that "there are such things in nature as parallel cases; that what happens once, will, under sufficient degree of similarity of circumstances, happen again, and not only again, but always" (13:184). The scientist must accept the assumption that nature is so constituted that whatever is true with any one case is

29

probably true in all cases of a similar description, that what has been found to be true in many instances in the past will probably continue to hold true in the future.   In other words, nature is not a chaotic mass of isolated facts, but rather an ordered system.   It is not necessary to assume that nature is absolutely uniform in all respects; but science is only possible to the extent that nature is uniform.   If the scientist does not assume there is uniformity of nature, he cannot go to work and cannot prove anything.   The uniformity of nature is a major premise of all scientific reasoning.

By dividing the assumption of the uniformity of nature into individual postulates, it can be examined in greater detail.   Thus, the following paragraphs discuss the postulates of (1) natural kinds, (2) constancy, and (3) determinism.

Postulate of Natural Kinds.   When man observes natural phenomena, he notices that some objects and events possess a number of striking likenesses. Consequently, he examines phenomena to determine their essential properties, functions, or structures.   After finding several objects or events that have common characteristics, he places them in a group and gives them a class name, such as thermometers, metals, administrators, visual aids, or achievement tests.   The resemblances he notes may be of color, size, shape, function, texture, properties, structures, occurrences, for example, or varied combinations of associations between these resemblances.   Thus, an investigator may group people by the color of their hair; or he may observe structural resemblances, such as an association between blond hair and delicate skin, or functional resemblances, such as poor muscular coordination and poor typing or mechanical skills; or he may correlate structural and functional resemblances, such as a cleft palate and difficulty in pronunciation. Resemblances between phenomena intrigue the scientist: he continually looks for factors that objects or events have in common, groups like things, and then searches for and expects to find additional resemblances among these phenomena.

Pigeonholing like events, experiences, facts, and objects is one of the first steps an individual or a science takes to arrive at useful knowledge.   Man has always turned to grouping similar phenomena when searching for answers to problems.   In the interest of survival, for example, primitive man learned to classify berries as edible or poisonous, animals as dangerous or harmless, and his neighbors as friendly or unfriendly.   For generations children have appealed to classification when searching for answers in the ancient game "Animal, Vegetable, Mineral?"   Classification is characteristic of the early developmental stage of any science.   It is necessary for the research worker to have some knowledge of the resemblances and uniformities in nature before he can possibly discover and formulate scientific laws.

By classifying phenomena in accordance with their resemblances, scientists organize masses of information into a coherent and unified structure that is useful to man.   A classification system provides one with a tool that helps him identify, understand, and evaluate new phenomena that he encounters. Biologists, chemists, criminologists, for example, have benefited from the systems established for their use.   In the eighteenth century, Linnaeus, the Swedish botanist, devised a grouping system based on the number and arrangement of stamens.   This system had certain weaknesses, but it led to the development of better schemes for classifying plant life.   With a knowledge of the properties and structures of chemical elements, Mendeleev worked out a periodic table which proved invaluable to men doing research in the field.   The international system of fingerprinting proposed by J. E. Purkinje in 1823 enabled law enforcement agencies to classify millions of fingerprints under the heads of arches, loops, whorls, and composites.   When strange plants, chemical elements, or criminals' fingerprints were discovered, these classification systems simplified the location and identification of them.

Educators have also made some attempts to classify phenomena in their field.   A committee of college and university examiners, for example, has classified educational objectives within the cognitive domain (4).   The major classes in the taxonomy are knowledge, comprehension, application, analysis, synthesis, and evaluation.   Subclassifications are clearly defined for each of these classes; analysis, for example, is subdivided into analysis of elements, analysis of relationships, and analysis of organizational principles. This classification scheme was devised to ensure greater accuracy of communication about phenomena in the field; to aid research workers in formulating hypotheses about the learning process; and to provide a guide for the development of the curriculum, tests, and instructional techniques.

Good classification schemes serve useful purposes, but poor ones hinder progress.   By looking for resemblances between things and classifying them into groups, a researcher can increase his knowledge about them.   But if he attributes importance to resemblances that are of no significance, his classification scheme is of little value.   If all the girls who flunk chemistry in a given class wear the same shade of lipstick, this may be a noticeable resemblance, but it is not the key factor causing failure.   If an alcoholic notes that he always adds soda to his bourbon, gin, or scotch, he has recognized a resemblance between his drinks, but giving up soda will not cure his drunkenness.   Classification schemes can be unfruitful and lead to fallacies, but schemes that classify the relevant factors—which often are not the most obvious ones—can help the scientist arrive at valuable information. If the scientist cannot assume that objects have some common characteristics, if he has to consider every phenomenon as an isolated entity, he cannot cope with the resulting jungles of information.   Only by assuming that there is some uniformity in nature which makes it permissible to group and order data, can progress be made in advancing knowledge.

Postulate of Constancy.   The postulate of constancy assumes that natural phenomena maintain their essential characteristics under specified conditions over a definite period of time. This postulate states that there is relative permanency and orderliness in nature and rejects the possibility that nature is unstable, capricious, temporary, or moody. It holds that relatively constant conditions exist in nature; that is, there are phenomena that do not perceptibly change their basic characteristics over a given period of time. Most people accept this postulate; they assume that their parents, school, typewriters, or town will remain about the same from day to day; they expect some permanency of these phenomena.

The postulate of constancy does not demand absolute conditions of fixity, persistency, or permanency, nor does it deny that rates of change vary for different phenomena. Some phenomena remain substantially unchanged over the years; other phenomena exhibit relatively marked rates of change. The sun, planets, and diamonds display exceptionally enduring qualities down through the decades. The walls, stoves, and plumbing in a home economics laboratory may change slightly from year to year, but in general these things remain quite the same. But a dish of ice cream, a dozen eggs, or a fruit fly in the same environment will exhibit less permanency over an extended period of time. In other words, different types of phenomena have different rates of change.

Social phenomena generally are less stable in time than physical phenomena. On the whole, the physical world changes rather slowly. Although some social data remain relatively constant, other social phenomena undergo rather rapid and drastic changes. For instance, peripheral human personality traits may change considerably as the individual reacts to certain kinds of experiences. Yet each individual possesses a central core of traits that does not vary appreciably even when subjected to radical environmental changes. It is this core of traits that lends stability to the personality. Consequently, a classroom teacher expects to meet children who exhibit about the same characteristics from day to day, to witness about the same quality and quantity of performance from each one, and to observe the same type of behavioral responses from students when he confronts them with similar situations. Yet he knows that under certain conditions shy children may become more gregarious; sometimes students will exceed or fall short of their expected performance; occasionally they will react unpredictably to the "same" situation. Social phenomena, whether it is observed on the local school, national or international level, does not remain as changeless as chemical elements or planets. In some respects John and Mary may remain more or less the same throughout grade school; in other respects they may change rapidly. Society may enjoy relatively long eras of peace and tranquility and then suddenly experience devastating wars, financial crises, horrendous epidemics, or technological advances that cause revolutionary changes.

Although some phenomena change more rapidly than other phenomena, the difference in the rate of change does not necessarily impair the work of the scientist. All that he demands is that the rate of change in objects and events take place gradually. The phenomena must change slowly enough so that the scientist will have time to study the data thoroughly. Other workers must have an opportunity to observe the happenings so as to provide necessary confirmations. Moreover, society must have time to apply the findings of the study before subsequent events render the knowledge useless.

The postulate of constancy is a prerequisite for scientific advancement; without it, there can be no science as we know it. If phenomena do not maintain definable and definite characteristics with respect to time, science has no means of attacking problems to secure useful knowledge. If phenomena were not consistent for a given period of time, all inquiries into the innermost secrets of nature would be fleeting, fruitless, historical accounts. The knowledge gained in one study could never be applied when dealing with the same phenomena in the future if the characteristics of the phenomena could not be depended upon to remain relatively the same. Without some permanence of natural phenomena, science cannot carry out one of its primary functions—the ability to predict accurately the occurrence of an event. If science denies the postulate of constancy, its predictions possess little value, for they merely rest on blind speculations and chance occurrences.

Postulate of Determinism. This postulate denies that the occurrence of an event is a matter of chance, an accidental situation, or purely a spontaneous incident. Rather, the postulate affirms that all natural phenomena are determined. That is, an event has a cause or a set of causes: certain essential conditions invariably precede an event. If water is to boil, a definite set of contributing conditions must exist before the event will take place. If a doctor discovers his patient has diphtheria, he does not consider it a chance coincidence. He concludes that this condition has arisen because the patient has come into contact with a particular germ—Klebs-Löffler bacillus, *Corynebacterium diphtheriae.* If an explosion results, man is certain that sufficient and necessary circumstances existed to make this event happen and whenever these conditions occur he can be certain there will be an explosion. Thus, the postulate of determinism assumes that all natural phenomena are dependent upon and conditioned by their causes.

Man has probably been aware of orderliness in nature since earliest times. Even primitive man noticed regularities in nature: day followed night and seasons came in a regular order. To understand nature, he also searched for causes of events, but often ascribed them to supernatural forces or concluded that whatever immediately preceded an event was the cause of it. Hence, he reasoned that the floods were caused by the thunder of angered gods and a good day of hunting was the result of finding a rare flower at dawn. By attacking problems more systematically and going more deeply than mere time sequence to find causation, the modern research worker has been able to discover regularities in nature that are not detected through casual observation.

Determinism is a fundamental concept that underlies science. Yet rigidly interpreted determinism, belief in eternal natural stability and absolute certainty of uniformity, is questioned as a result of modern developments in physics. Determinism, at least some of its phases, has also been attacked by certain religious groups. Despite these criticisms, the essential meaning of this broad assumption continues to play an indispensable role in any research that goes beyond the purely classificatory level. If it is possible for any phenomena to fall outside the definition of this postulate, it is also outside the realm of science.

Science requires lawfulness in the events of nature. No pattern or scheme for setting up and controlling an experiment can be established and no predictions about what will happen in the future can be made if the assumption that what has happened in the past will happen again is false. If a scientist must consider each phenomenon as a capricious rather than a determined event, he is deprived of a means of attacking problems that enables him to formulate laws capable of explaining large bodies of phenomena. The best he can do in an indetermined situation is to describe the character of an isolate incident.

Assumptions Concerning the Psychological Process. Every research worker accepts the assumption that he can gain knowledge of the world through the psychological processes of perceiving, remembering, and reasoning. The scientific method cannot operate without utilizing these processes. Perceiving, remembering, and reasoning, however, are subject to error. If inaccurate processes are at work, they subsequently reflect their unreliability in the results of the investigation and invalidate it. Thus, the research worker must acquaint himself with the nature of these psychological processes and take the necessary steps to obtain the highest possible degree of accuracy when employing them.

Postulate of the Reliability of Perceiving. In the laboratory the investigator routinely records information he has experienced through his senses. Yet he knows that the human sense organs are limited in range and in fineness of discrimination. His dog can hear the high tones of a whistle that are inaudible to him. His colleagues may be able to hear a greater range of sounds than he can. His sense perceptions may differ not only from those of his friends, but also in successive observations he makes himself. Because his senses are subject to fatigue and adaptation, he may experience varied perceptions when repeatedly exposed to the same sound, taste, or odor.

Errors in visual perception are as commonplace as those in auditory perception.   When a child is given a puzzle picture of a village scene to study, he may not notice that a house has no door, the American policeman is wearing a swastika emblem, and an automobile has three wheels. Because he expects a house to have a door, a car to have four wheels, and a policeman to wear the traditional badge, he thinks he has seen them even though they are not there.   Adults as well as children can jump to inaccurate conclusions about what they see.   Recently, twenty subjects in a psychological experiment viewed a line drawing of a man's expressionless face on a screen. After seeing the word "happy" intermittently flashed beneath the picture, they thought the face gradually became happier even though it had not changed.

Through illusions, hoaxes, and shifts of attention a chic dress designer, deft magician, war camouflage expert, clever criminal, or football strategist can lead people to make false judgments and inferences.   Everyone experiences visual deceptions.   On her annual August vacation, an elementary teacher may encounter several perceptual puzzles.   At the railroad station, she may have the illusion that her train is pulling out, when it actually is standing still, but the train on the next track is beginning to move in the opposite direction.   At the beach, she may notice that her vertically striped swimming suit makes her appear thinner than the one with horizontal stripes and the straight stick that she places partially in the water appears crooked.   When she looks down the road, her eyes will tell her that it converges at a point in the distance.   On hikes, she may not see animals that are nearby because their protective coloration makes them blend into the surrounding background.

The scientist has no more natural immunity to faulty perception than the elementary teacher.   When working on a problem, he may make inaccurate observations because of momentary distractions, strong intellectual biases, personal prejudices, emotional sets, and inaccurate discriminations.   Sometimes he may see what he expects to see whether it is there or not, or he may fail to perceive relevant factors.   History is studded with stories of scientists who failed to track the trail to truth because they were guilty of making perceptual blunders.

Despite the untrustworthiness of the perceptual processes, the research worker accepts the assumption that one can obtain fundamentally reliable knowledge through his sense organs.   But since it is easy to make mistakes when observing phenomena, he checks his findings in various ways to make them more trustworthy.   Having familiarized himself with the common sources of errors, he takes the necessary precautions to prevent them from creeping into his work.   He repeats his observations and checks his findings with those of other experienced observers.   Rather than using vague terms to describe phenomena—guesses, estimates—he weighs, measures, times, tests, and accurately ascertains the amount or type of phenomena under investigation.   Rather than writing sweeping descriptions, he records well-defined, concrete, detailed accounts of what he observes.   Furthermore, the scientist strives to maintain an "open minded" attitude toward his work so as to guard against emotional and intellectual biases that might distort his perceptual experiences.

Postulate of the Reliability of Remembering.   Remembering, like the activity of perceiving, is subject to error.   Everyday experiences indicate the frailties of man's mental processes.   A teacher may be unable to recall the name of a former student, the title of the textbook he ordered last year, the items he is to bring to the school picnic, or where he parked his car.   After taking a month's trip through Europe, he may not be able to remember in which city certain museums were located.   An individual often recalls only those things he wants to recall.   A boy may vividly remember that his mother promised to take him to the circus on Saturday, but quickly forget that she asked him to mow the lawn.   A scientist may remember things that support his beliefs rather than those that do not.

Despite the weaknesses of the human memory, the research worker accepts the assumption that one can obtain fundamentally reliable knowledge from this source.   He must accept this assumption, for his work constantly requires him to recall specific and related facts.   Progress would terminate if one seriously questioned the accuracy of every single fact.   But, since it is easy to forget information or to recall it inaccurately, a scientist develops systematic methods of recording information; periodically reviews these data; and sometimes takes photographs, movies, recordings, or X rays of conditions or events for future reference.   By adopting such practices, he improves the range, accuracy, and completeness of his memory.

Postulate of the Reliability of Reasoning.   Reasoning, like perceiving and remembering, is subject to errors.   Reasoning, even by exceptionally intelligent individuals, is beset by many potential pitfalls.   Mistakes in reasoning occur because of the use of false premises, the violation of the rules of logic, the presence of intellectual biases, the failure to grasp the exact meanings of words, and faulty judgments made regarding the suitability and use of statistical and experimental techniques.

Despite the limitations of the reasoning process, the scientist recognizes its value as an implement of research.   He resorts to reasoning when selecting and defining his problem; when framing a solution; when deciding what observations to make; when devising techniques for obtaining data; and when determining whether to accept, modify, or reject his hypothesis.   Without mentally manipulating ideas, the scientist cannot make much progress in any investigation.   Therefore, he accepts reasoning as a generally reliable tool of research.

Because the careless or inappropriate use of this or any research instrument can lead to disaster, a scientist applies checks to detect errors in his thought processes. He examines the premises on which his reasoning is based to determine whether they are factually true, probably true, or only possibly true and subjects his arguments to the rules of logic that govern correct reasoning. Since confused reasoning can stem from the slovenly use of language, he endeavors to assign clear, correct, consistent, and specific meanings to words, phrases, and terms. Because personal prejudices and wishes may cause him to ignore facts and to reason illogically, he deliberately searches for and gives fair consideration to evidence that does not conform to his hypothesis.

GOALS OF SCIENCE

The goals of science are not unlike those of man down through the ages. A craving for knowledge of the world about him caused man to construct crude explanations for phenomena centuries ago. Longing to know what the future held in store for him, he beseechingly turned to wise men, fortune tellers, prophets, and astrologers for answers. His deepest desire was to acquire knowledge that would enable him to control floods, famines, diseases, and other forces impinging upon his life. With more refined methods, the modern scientist also seeks to understand the phenomena he observes. Discovering order in the universe, comprehending the laws of nature, and learning how to master the forces of nature are his objectives. The goal of the scientist is to improve his ability and success in explaining, predicting, and controlling conditions and events.

Explanation as a Goal of Science. The essential purpose of research is to go beyond mere description of phenomena and provide an explanation for them. A scientist is not completely satisfied with naming, classifying, or describing phenomena. Rather than terminating his investigation with simple observations, such as that apples fall down, balloons rise, tides ebb and flow, some children stutter, or certain diseases kill, he probes more deeply to find reasons for the occurrence of these events. Going behind casually observed factors to search for some underlying pattern that explains them is his objective. After discovering a possible cause for the occurrence of the particular event or condition, he frames a verifiable generalization that explains how the variables involved in the situation behave. Explanation—not mere description—is the product of his effort.

Science does not *want* to know only what phenomena are, but also *how* phenomena act as they do. A man may notice, for example, that on a hot summer day a steel cable expands as do streetcar tracks and metal beams. From his observation of these particular incidents, he may propose the generalization that heat expands metal. This low-level explanation is useful information for it describes *what* happens to heated metals, but it does not reveal *how* metals expand when heated.

When scientists tried to find some underlying principle to account for the fact that heat expands metal, they framed the following explanation: all heat is caused by the motion of molecules of matter; the greater the motion of the molecules, the greater is the heat of a body. The agitation of the molecules makes them jostle one another apart; hence, they take up more space. Thus, an increase in temperature results in expansion. This generalization gave man a better understanding of the phenomena observed, for it revealed the causes of the expansion of metal.

Once man understood and confirmed this scientific principle, he was able to apply it to other facts. Thereafter, upon encountering any phenomena involving expansion, he looked for heat as a possible cause; whenever heat was present, he considered expansion as a possible effect. Thus, the principle not only helped him to understand a particular phenomenon, but also enlarged his capacity to explain a large range of natural events. Basically, science seeks to explain natural phenomena by locating their place in a larger body of systematic coherent relations.

Formulating generalizations—conceptual schemes—that explain phenomena is a major goal of science. But generalizations can offer various levels of explanation. A generalization may present a conceptual scheme that explains a very limited body of phenomena. This generalization is useful, but the objective of science is to develop ever more far-reaching conceptual schemes. Hypotheses, theories, and laws are generalizations of gradually increasing generality. Since the generalization that offers the most comprehensive explanation is of the greatest value, a law is of greater importance than a theory or hypothesis. For example, a generalization that explains the movement of one planet is useful, but a law that explains the movement of all planets is of considerably greater value.

Science aims at the progressive unification of its generalizations. The ultimate goal of science is to seek laws of the highest generality—laws of the utmost comprehensiveness. Newton's theory of gravitation is an example of such comprehensive explanation. Before Newton was born, Galileo formulated his law of falling bodies which explained the motion of bodies on the surface of the earth. About the same time that Galileo proposed his explanation for terrestrial motion, Kepler formulated the laws of celestial motion. When Newton came upon the scene, he devised a more comprehensive generalization that applied to *all* massive bodies, whether terrestrial or celestial. His new theory performed the work of the two generalizations it replaced. Thus, Newton helped science take a giant stride in its continuous campaign to construct generalizations that explain a wider and wider range of phenomena. Since his time, a procession of creative geniuses have been endlessly "lifting science from problem to problem and adequate theory to more adequate theory with greater and greater generality"

(14:29). Their successively more comprehensive theoretical explanations have given mankind important keys to understanding the universe.

Prediction as a Goal of Science. An explanation that does not increase man's power over nature is useful, but it is not as valuable as one that enables him to predict events. Thus, the scientist is not satisfied merely with formulating generalizations that explain phenomena. He also wants to make predictions concerning the way a generalization will operate in new situations. His objective is to take known data and accepted generalizations and from them to predict some future event or hitherto unobserved phenomena. For example, by noting gaps in the periodic table that classified the known chemical elements, Mendeleev, in 1871, was able to predict the existence of a new element, germanium, fifteen years before it was discovered. By studying the data, theories, and laws available in their fields, modern research workers can also make rather accurate forecasts, such as the coming of an eclipse, future weather conditions, or the probable scholastic success individual members of the freshman class will attain in college.

The natural scientist has been able to make predictions in many fields, and some of them possess such a high degree of probability that it almost amounts to absolute certainty. The social scientist has found it much more difficult to make predictions, and those they have proposed are of an approximate character or confined to relatively simple problems. Because of the difficultness of the feat, whenever science does attain its goal of accurate prediction it is a satisfying and spectacular achievement.

Control as a Goal of Science. Science strives to attain such a thorough understanding of the laws of nature that it is able not only to predict but also to control an increasing range of events. Control refers to the process of manipulating certain of the essential conditions that cause an event so as to make the event happen or prevent it from occurring. For example, a doctor knows that if the pancreas fails to secrete insulin the body is unable to utilize properly the carbohydrates in the body. The doctor can predict what will happen to a patient when this condition—diabetes—exists. Moreover, he can control diabetes by giving the patient injections of insulin. Therefore, when a doctor predicts and controls a diabetic condition, he is actually demonstrating his understanding of the nature of the disease.

Scientists do not restrict the term "control" to conditions and events of a practical nature, such as the diabetic condition of the patient in the above example. The pure scientist, particularly, uses the term in an abstract and theoretical sense. He logically shows how a particular outcome can be obtained by controlling conceptual situations he devised according to the implications of his theory. Einstein, for example, in the development of the theory of relativity, utilized the concept of control in the abstract and theoretical sense rather than in a sense of controlling a practical situation.

Controlling natural forces is the deepest desire of the scientist. Assuming that a certain amount of constancy and consistency exists in nature that will enable him to predict that what has happened once will probably happen again, he digs deeply into the nature of phenomena to discover the specific factors and relationships that cause a particular condition or event. After acquiring a thorough and intimate knowledge of his subject matter, he gains an insight into the particular factors that he must manipulate to produce a desired event or to prevent an undesired condition. Such knowledge has enabled man to harness rampaging rivers and to convert their power into a rich resource for mankind. Diseases, such as tuberculosis, diphtheria, malaria, and poliomyelitis, which once took their terrible toll upon society, have come under effective control in many parts of the world as a result of the research work done in scientific laboratories.

Psychologists and educators have long been investigating the skills and aptitudes that lead to success in particular vocations. They hope that sufficient understanding of the conditions necessary to become a superior dentist, teacher, doctor, or electrician will make it possible to give aptitude tests that will predict the caliber of work an individual will do in a given field. If such knowledge can be obtained and predictions can be made with a sufficiently high degree of accuracy, good vocational guidance will prevent square pegs from trying to force themselves into round holes. By controlling the selection of students trained in each field through an aptitude testing program, the nation can be assured of a more effective utilization of the human potentialities in our society.

Science's ultimate goal is to control nature, but it is not easy to achieve this objective. There are many areas in which man can predict but cannot control natural events. Qualified individuals are able to predict the weather, the coming of a comet, or the course of cancer with varying degrees of success, but they are unable to control the conditions causing these phenomena. Scientists can neither predict nor control some events. They cannot predict, for example, when and where earthquakes will take place nor can they control them. In general, scientists have made greater progress in learning to control natural than social phenomena. One of the desperate demands of society today is to discover means of controlling phenomena, such as destructive wars, juvenile delinquency, human oppression, and group intertensions that weaken our social structure.

DIFFERENCES BETWEEN THE SOCIAL SCIENCES AND THE NATURAL SCIENCES

As we have noted, the natural sciences, such as physics, chemistry, geology, and astronomy, have made considerable progress in achieving some of the aims of science. The social sciences, such as history, economics, and education, have lagged far behind. A few leaders believe that the social sciences never can become scientific. Some men contend that the social sciences will gradually make some progress but will not reach the high level of the natural sciences. Other authorities admit that the social sciences are on an immature level, but they claim that research in these areas eventually will become as scientific as in the natural sciences. A number of obstacles, however, will prevent the ready realization of this objective. In their endeavor to obtain a better understanding of the fundamental factors underlying human behavior so that they can explain, predict, and control social phenomena, the social scientists encounter many difficulties. The following paragraphs discuss some of their problems.

Complexity of Subject Matter. The social and natural sciences deal with parts of the same subject matter. Certain factors, however, distinguish the social sciences from the natural sciences. The natural sciences are concerned with physical phenomena. Social facts have physical elements; but something other than the laws of physics or biology often are needed to explain social phenomena. If a teacher spanks a child, the laws of chemistry, physics, and physiology partially explain the event, but they fail to account for some significant aspects of the act: Why did the teacher punish the child? How did the child feel about the punishment? What was the reaction of the parents or the school board to this act?

The subject matter of the natural sciences is simpler than that of the social sciences, for it deals with phenomena on one level—the physical. On the gross physical level, a comparatively small number of variables (the set of conditions required for an event) are involved, and they can be measured quite precisely. Because the social sciences are concerned with man as an individual and as a member of a group, they present a much more complex situation. Social problems may involve such a large number of variables that they overwhelm the investigator with possibilities to consider.

When a natural scientist investigates a chemical explosion, a *relatively few physical factors* will account for the event. When a social scientist investigates a human crime, *innumerable factors*, some of which are not physical, may be involved: a switchblade knife, force and direction of the blow, blood vessels severed, intoxicated condition of the murderer, strength of the adversary, faulty biological heredity, gang social pressures, lack of police protection, hot and humid evening, rejection by parents, poverty, and strained race relations.

A number of physical explanations may be given for a crime or any other social phenomenon. Moreover, social phenomena may be observed not only on the physical level, but also from the sociological, psychological, and biological point of view or any combination of these. They can be explained —just to mention a few—in patterns of growth, time, type, place, institution, activities, motivation, or trends. This state of affairs creates many difficulties for the social scientist. He is always plagued with the problem of what points of view and what variables he must select to explain phenomena satisfactorily.

Observability of Subject Matter. Direct observation of phenomena is more difficult in some respects for the social scientist than it is for the physical scientist. A social scientist cannot see, hear, touch, smell, or taste phenomena that existed in the past, nor can he repeat these social events for the purpose of direct observation. An economist cannot acquire knowledge of the depressions of 1819 and 1873 by observing the conditions with his own eyes. An educator studying colonial schools cannot personally view the children, teachers, and instructional procedures of that early era in American history. A psychologist cannot put ingredients into a test tube and conjure up the exact events of an adult's childhood. A chemist or physicist can set up the same desired conditions again and again and directly observe what takes place, but a social scientist cannot repeat the American Revolution or the fight to establish public schools in the United States. The nature of past social phenomena precludes direct and repeated observation.

The social scientist can observe some present social phenomena directly but he cannot bring others into the open for scrutiny. In a child study laboratory, an investigator can observe when John Jurk slaps a companion, how many words he reads in a minute, and what range of sounds he can hear. But some social factors, such as Johnny's preferences, motives, and dreams are matters of inner consciousness and are not accessible to direct public examination. The investigator must either (1) interpret that "inner state" himself, which he can do only in light of his own life experience, which leaves room for error, or (2) accept his subject's description of his "inner state," which may be inaccurate.

Social facts are more variable than physical facts. For most purposes in chemistry, an observation of any cubic centimeter of sulfuric acid will be as good as another. But observations of 30 seventh-grade pupils in one city will not necessarily coincide with the observations of a like number and age of pupils in another city. The height, weight, size of vocabulary, play participation, and arithmetic achievement of one 10-year-old may vary widely from that of his age mates. In some situations a social scientist can treat all individuals alike, such as in the tabulation of births. But because of the wide range of differences in humans, he often finds it dangerous to attribute to a whole class what is true of selected samples.

Non-repeatability of Subject Matter. Social phenomena are less repeatable than natural phenomena. Many phenomena of the natural sciences are highly uniform and recurrent. Consequently they lend themselves to abstraction and the precise, quantitative formulation of generalizations and universal laws. Social problems usually deal with specific historical happenings. They are concerned with singularities, with events that occur but never reoccur in exactly the same way. Some generalizations can be made about social life and human behavior. Generalizations can be formulated, for example, about certain features that wars, raids, and revolutions or adults, adolescents, and infants have in common. Yet a social phenomenon has its unique and nonrepeatable character that needs to be comprehended in its entirety if it is to be understood. Thus, abstracting factors that are common to several social events so as to formulate a generalization cannot be carried too far without falsifying the material. Because social phenomena are less uniform and recurrent than natural phenomena, it is more difficult to establish and verify social laws.

Relationship of Scientists to Their Subject Matter. Physical phenomena such as chemical elements are impersonal. They have no emotions. The natural scientist does not have to consider either conscious or unconscious purposes or motives on the part of planets or oceans. His subject matter is not influenced by human whim or will. Since social science is concerned with man as a member of a group, its phenomena are more personal. Man is a purposeful creature who seeks certain desirable ends and who possesses the capacity to make choices which enables him to modify his conduct. Social science subject matter, therefore, is strongly influenced by human will and human decision. It is constantly changing as a result of the action taken by human beings.

The natural scientist inquires into nature's processes and tries to formulate general laws governing these processes. He does not expect to alter nature or to approve or disapprove of its processes. He merely hopes his knowledge of physical phenomena will enable him to make better use of nature's processes. When the natural scientist constructs a hypothesis to explain a physical phenomenon, he knows that his generalizations will not cause the phenomenon to modify its character. If an astronomer formulates a generalization to explain the orbits of planets, he does not expect them to react to it in any way. The celestial bodies will remain unchanged by his pronouncements. They will not call a celestial congress to campaign for the adoption of new patterns of movement.

Because the social sciences are integrally interwoven with the social fabric, they present a different situation. Generalizations made to explain social phenomena may affect social events and conditions. If men accept an explanation of social phenomena, they may decide to readjust social patterns in view of this knowledge and thereby create conditions which make the generalization invalid. Consequently, accurate prediction is more difficult in economics and education than in astronomy or physics. If a social scientist states that 360 people will die in automobile crashes over the Memorial Day holiday, his prediction may not come true. The public may become alarmed by his pronouncement and conduct nationwide safety campaigns that reduce the anticipated highway slaughter. The findings in natural science lose their strength only when they are replaced by better insight into the phenomena. But findings in the social sciences can lose their value because the knowledge they provide can cause humans to change the social conditions.

Research workers can more easily achieve a detached and objective attitude toward natural phenomena than toward social phenomena. The social scientist is not an impartial observer who stands outside of society to watch its processes. He is an integral part of the subject matter he observes. Man can impartially observe physical phenomena such as the structure of protoplasm, but his own interests, values, preferences, and purposes influence his judgment when he observes social phenomena. It is more difficult to be objective about human reactions in school segregation incidents than chemical reactions in test tubes, social stress in slum areas than physical stress in physics, the communistic system in society than the solar system in nature. Emotional attachments to particular systems of values tend to make the social scientist approve or disapprove of particular social processes. Thus, it is difficult to eliminate personal biases when observing social science phenomena.

The natural scientist is concerned with problems of fact; he confines his investigations to the conditions that exist in nature. The social scientist is also interested in problems of fact. To ascertain what conditions exist in society, he conscientiously studies and describes the characteristics and causes of unemployment, juvenile delinquency, reading failure, or similar problems. But the social scientist is interested not only in society as it is, but also in developing theories to designate what ought to be— what is socially desirable. Although some social scientists contend they are not concerned with social ends, they may unconsciously accept the prevailing order as the ideal. While some researchers may ignore social ends, the findings of their studies may cause others to seek the development of an ideal social order. Because social science subject matter is intimately related to man who is a purposeful, value-seeking creature, it presents types of problems that the natural sciences do not present.

Social scientists must overcome many obstacles if they hope to make significant advances in explaining, predicting, and controlling human conduct. Progress can be made only by persistent and patient probing. Because of the phenomenal advances the natural scientists have made in unleashing the secrets of the physical world in the past century, it is imperative that the social scientist attack human problems with renewed energy. The development of atomic energy, high-speed transportation, and automation processes has created a multiplicity of complex social problems that must be solved if society is to survive. In our modern world there is a most urgent need for psychological, educational, sociological, and economic research.   More and more people must be trained to meet this need of mankind.

BIBLIOGRAPHY

1. Beck, William S., *Modern Science and the Nature of Life*. New York: Harcourt, Brace & World, Inc., 1957, chap. 10.

2. Beveridge, W. I. B., *The Art of Scientific Investigation*. New York: W. W. Norton & Company, Inc., 1951, chap. 7.

3. Black, Max, *Critical Thinking*. Englewood Cliffs, N.J.: Prentice-Hall, Inc., 1952, chap. 11.

4. Bloom, Benjamin S. (ed.), *Taxonomy of Educational Objectives: The Classification of Educational Goals*. New York: Longmans, Green & Co., Inc., 1956.

5. Brown, Clarence W., and E. E. Ghiselli, *Scientific Method in Psychology*. New York: McGraw-Hill Book Company, Inc., 1955, chaps. 2 and 3.

6. Cohen, I. Bernard, "The Wonderful Century," *The Atlantic*, 200 (October, 1957): 84.

7. Cohen, Morris R., and Ernest Nagel, *An Introduction to Logic and Scientific Method*. New York: Harcourt, Brace & World, Inc., 1934, chap. 12.

8. Copi, Irving M., *Introduction to Logic*. New York: The Macmillan Company, 1955, chap. 13.

9. Doughton, Isaac, *Modern Public Education*. New York: Appleton-Century-Crofts, Inc., 1935, chaps. 6 and 7.

10. Feigl, Herbert, and May Brodbeck, *Readings in the Philosophy of Science*. New York: Appleton-Century-Crofts, Inc., 1953.

11. Furfey, Paul Hanly, *The Scope and Method of Sociology*. New York: Harper & Brothers, 1953, chap. 3.

12. Larrabee, Harold A., *Reliable Knowledge*. Boston: Houghton Mifflin Company, 1945, chap. 8.

13. Mill, John S., *A System of Logic*. New York: Harper & Brothers, 1846.

14. Northrop, F. S. C., *The Logic of the Sciences and the Humanities*. New York: The Macmillan Company, 1949.

15. Searles, Herbert L., *Logic and Scientific Methods*. New York: The Ronald Press Company, 1948, chap. 11.

16. Spahr, Walter E., and Rinehart J. Swenson, *Methods and Status of Scientific Research*. New York: Harper & Brothers, 1930.

17. Underwood, Benton, J., *Psychological Research*. New York: Appleton-Century-Crofts, Inc., 1957, chap. 1.

CHAPTER 4

Nature of Observation

Observation is fundamental in research, for it produces one of the basic elements of science—facts. Observing is an activity the research worker engages in throughout the several stages of his investigation. By utilizing his senses of hearing, seeing, smelling, feeling, and tasting, he gathers facts that help him locate and define a problem. Through alert and skillful observation he discovers clues that enable him to construct a theoretical solution for his problem. When conducting an experiment to determine whether there is evidence that will support his solution, he again makes careful and accurate observations. From the inception of an inquiry to the final confirmation or rejection of his proposed problem solution, a research worker relies on observation to keep him on the trail to truth.

Because observation, facts, and theories are closely related factors that play a significant role in scientific investigations, it is important to understand their nature, function, and relationship. The layman is quite familiar with these terms but his concept of their meaning is usually quite different from the definition a scientist would give. Therefore, this chapter will explore the following questions: What is the nature of scientific observation? What is the nature of a fact? What is the relationship between theory and fact in research?

CONDITIONS NECESSARY FOR OBSERVATION

Everyone uses his sensory capacities to become aware of phenomena in his environment. The act of "recognizing and noting some fact or occurrence" can be of a very simple nature or it can involve the most complex modern research techniques. The simplest kind of observation is an uncritical report by a casual observer of something he has experienced through the use of his senses. If you ask a friend whether it is snowing outside, he replies in the affirmative. How does he reach this conclusion? His answer is simple: "I know it is snowing because I have just *seen* snowflakes land on the window sill." Scientific observation is not ordinarily as direct and simple as this; it usually is an indirect and complex process that requires careful planning. Scientific observation involves the deliberate selection of some significant aspect of the phenomena in a certain situation and at a definite time; a close scrutiny of it which may require the use of precision procedures and instruments; and the presentation of the results in a form that is suitable for public verification. Thus, although observations can be made by anyone, accurate and fruitful ones are usually the product of considerable practice and training.

Since observation is essential in scientific inquiry, a neophyte should learn how to establish the conditions within himself and his working environment that will enable him to obtain reliable facts with maximum efficiency. The four psychological factors involved in observation that he must give due consideration are attention, sensation, perception, and conception.

Attention.   Attention is a necessary condition for successful observation. This condition is characterized by a mental set or a state of alertness which an individual assumes so as to sense or perceive selected events, conditions, or things. Being bombarded constantly by a multiplicity of stimuli, the nervous network of the human organism cannot simultaneously channel all of them to the cortex for interpretation. Hence, an observer sifts out the specific ones from which he wants to receive messages. This process of selection is attention. Adequate attention is imperative if one is to acquire clear, concise, and detailed information about phenomena. If thoughts about the weekend dance or the attractive girl across the aisle are flashing through your mind at the moment, you are probably receiving blurred messages from this printed page. Indeed, you may "read" the whole page without acquiring any knowledge of its contents, for your attention is elsewhere: you are not ready to receive the stimuli of the printed word.

The observational powers of man are limited. He often fails to perceive phenomena accurately when his attention is not intentionally concentrated upon them. Observing several things at once is beyond his capacity; he can give specific attention only to one thing at a time. If a researcher attempts to observe too much, he often overlooks significant events that occur because at the moment his attention is elsewhere. Consequently, a competent investigator directs his attention toward a portion of phenomena that is pertinent to his purpose, yet small enough to be encompassed.

Learning to "pay attention" is an important part of observational training. One must acquire the habit of placing himself in a state of readiness to sense and perceive the specific segment of phenomena that relates to his problem and to ignore other factors. By cultivating a deep interest in a particular point of view, it is easier to concentrate intensively upon the significant details relevant to a problem. Interest inspires one to watch things with an active, inquiring mind: it rivets his attention on the stimuli that can feed him the desired data. By exercising a high degree of self-control, one can keep strong and interesting extraneous stimuli from capturing his attention and can curb any natural restlessness that might permit his attention to wander. Gradually sustained and selective attention becomes so habitual a method of working, that an observer is not distracted easily by factors that are not absolutely essential to his investigation.

Although attention is necessary in observation, it can lead to certain errors that the scientist must guard against. By becoming too obsessed with his hypothesis—too set on looking for facts that support his proposed solution to a problem—one may observe only what he wants to find and ignore facts that do not agree with his theory. To eliminate such biases, an experienced investigator is extremely critical of his observation. When concentrating his attention on specific phenomena, he looks not only for facts that support his theory but also is on the alert to detect unsuspected facts that tend to disprove it. When making observations, he strives to notice all of the significant aspects of the situation—the unanticipated as well as the anticipated events and conditions. The ability to master this art is a distinguishing characteristic of a successful research worker.

The scientist controls not only personal factors that interfere with attention, but also characteristics of subject matter that prohibit effective observation. Man cannot successfully fix his attention upon objects or events that are exceptionally unstable or elusive. Thus, phenomena that are too big, too small, too fleeting, or too chaotic to be perceived with the senses and special instruments are not suitable subjects for an investigation. A researcher must study phenomena that are sufficiently stable, constant, and manageable that others can view them at the same time or check them at a later date.

Sensation. Man becomes aware of the world about him through his senses. When changes occur in his internal or external environment, they stimulate his sense organs which in turn excite his sensory nerves. When these sensory nerve impulses reach his brain, he experiences the event: a smell, a shape, or a sound. The accuracy of observation, therefore, depends on the acuity of the senses. A man with good sense organs can experience thousands of different visual and auditory qualities; he can feel pressure, pain, warmth, and cold; he can taste sweet, sour, salty, and bitter qualities; and he can distinguish different odors.

Yet, the sense organs have definite limitations. Man's senses are not reliable tools for making exact measurements of distance, speed, size, or intensity, and they are poor instruments for making comparisons. Because sense organs have a limited scope or sensitivity, they do not enable one to hear many tones, to see all the colors of the spectrum, or to feel the difference between distances that fall within a certain magnitude. Any defect of the senses, of course, reduces the possibility of observing phenomena accurately. Congenital imperfections, such as color blindness and tone deafness; temporary impairments due to fatigue, drugs, or emotional status; and gradual deterioration because of age or illness can distort observations. Fortunately, steps can be taken to avoid or compensate for some of these conditions. Moreover, rather than relying solely on the limited capacities of the senses, the researcher can employ specially devised instruments, such as the microscope, amplifying tube, and polygraph, to extend the range and clarity of his observations.

In addition to checking whether his senses are operating efficiently, a scientist also makes certain that he is getting clear, customary, and un-distorted signals from his phenomena. Strong competing stimuli or a confusion of extraneous ones may make it difficult for his senses to isolate the significant stimuli. A foreign or distracting medium that comes be-tween him and his subject matter can create many problems. A dirty test tube, for example, or undetected biases of subjects cooperating in an experiment can cause him to make startling but faulty observations. When investigating human phenomena, such as in a classroom or in a metropolitan slum, an investigator often finds that his mere presence on the scene makes subjects modify their behavior. Consequently, when studying the home life of Puerto Rican pupils, a social worker may assume some normal neighborhood role that will permit him to mingle with the people without arousing their suspicion and causing them to change their customary patterns of behavior. An educator studying cheating practices of pupils may take the precaution of observing them from a concealed position. By locating himself in the most favorable vantage point for observation, removing competing sensory stimuli, if possible and desirable, and checking to make certain he has an unobstructed, normal view of his subject matter, a scientist is able to make more accurate observations.

Perception. Observation is more than experiencing sensations. Ob-servation is sensation plus perception. Sensation is the immediate result of stimulating the sense organs: a sound, a smell, or a visual experience. This information is not useful until it is interpreted. One can hear a sound, but it remains a mere noise until he learns to identify it with the ringing of the telephone, rumbling of a streetcar, or mewing of the cat. Perception is the art of linking up what is sensed with some past experience to give the sensation meaning. When the Hontoon family is at the park, tiny baby Tim notices a moving object; his four-year-old brother Dale recognizes that it is a bird, for he has seen them in his storybooks; his mother explains that a recent magazine called these small yellow birds warblers; and his father, an ornithologist, identifies the bird as a Nashville warbler. Aside from the baby, each member of the family linked up what he had seen with his past experience; each engaged in perception.

Meanings are in men's minds rather than in the objects themselves.

Hence, when looking at the same object, everyone does not "see" the same thing. Moreover, one person may see the same object in different ways at different times. One may look at a line drawing of a cube, for example, and see that it is an open box at one moment, a solid cube of ice at another time, and a square wire frame at a later date. The drawing does not change, but the observer's organization of what he sees does.

Perceptions may be relatively simple or highly complex. They may involve a single sense organ, such as when one identifies the color of an object. On the other hand, several senses, a wide background of experience, and prolonged training may be required to give detailed interpretation of the sensations contributing to a given experience. When an orchestra leader listens to a recording, for example, he can identify the various instruments, visualize the score, and hear that the oboe is out of tune, while his teen-age nephews may only recognize the sounds as music that differs from jazz. The perceptions of a novice in any field—science, art, music—are apt to be vague, meager, and uncritical. Those of an expert are more definite, detailed, and discriminate.

Obstacles to Accurate Observation. The possibility of making errors in perception is much greater than in sensation. Man interprets his sensations in terms of his past experiences. All too frequently he quickly associates a sensory signal with some previously acquired knowledge and jumps to the conclusion that he has seen or heard something he really has not. When a small, dark object travels across a picnic table, he may immediately associate this occurrence with his storehouse of picnic information and conclude that the object is an ant, when it actually is a crumb that has rolled off the chocolate cake. Anticipation of an event can also cause him to make a faulty inference. Newspaper stories concerning flying saucers usually bring a rash of reports from readers who have seen a moving object and have concluded that it is a spaceship. The possibility of perceptual error is always present when the observer makes inferences on the basis of scanty sensory cues.

Strong personal interests tend to make the research worker see only those things he wants to see. After having reviewed many scientific studies made of animal learning, Bertrand Russell noted that (12:32–33)

. . . all the animals have behaved so as to confirm the philosophy in which the observer believed before his observations began. Nay, more, they have all displayed the national characteristics of the observer. Animals studied by Americans rush about frantically, with an incredible display of hustle and pep, and at last achieve the desired result by chance. Animals observed by Germans sit still and think, and at last evolve the solution out of their inner consciousness.

Because man can choose to interpret or ignore stimuli impinging upon him, his private passions and preconceptions can often serve as stumbling blocks to impartial observation.

Everyone is guilty of making faulty observations. In one evening, for example, each member of the Stetson family failed to achieve good perception of facts. At dusk, Professor Stetson saw someone walking rapidly in the distance and inferred from the graceful movements and familiar contours that it was Miss Richards, the dance instructor, whom he usually met at that time of day. As he came closer, he discovered the woman was a stranger who walked as gracefully as Miss Richards and was about the same size. While reading an exciting murder mystery, Jane Stetson heard a crackling noise outside the house and concluded that it was an intruder, when it actually was her mother returning unexpectedly. Mrs. Stetson came into the house exclaiming that she had observed a pathetic, shabby man on the street who obviously needed financial assistance. Jane peeked out the window and burst into laughter, for the man was Mr. Littlefield, a wealthy miser.

Obviously, perceptions are subject to distortions because of the observer's emotions, motivations, prejudices, mental sets, sense of values, physical condition, and errors of inference. Psychology professors often demonstrate the unreliability of human observation by staging a well-rehearsed mock shooting in the classroom and immediately asking students to write a description of what they have seen. The results are amazing! Not uncommonly students fail to agree on the size, age, dress, and number of participants in the incident, as well as the order of events and the type and number of weapons used. They not only miss seeing some important things, but also report details that are pure fabrications. When lawyers collect evidence for trials involving an accident, they commonly encounter similar situations. Moral: all human beings who are exposed to the same experiences do not necessarily perceive the same things.

A person tends to see what he knows. If a teacher, doctor, and architect inspect a school building, each will see the things that are of special interest to him and other matters will escape his attention. The teacher will notice the instructional situations, the doctor the health conditions, and the architect the structure and design of the building. If an individual knows little about a particular subject, he usually does not "see too much" when he observes it. If a Texan who knows nothing about ice hockey attends a game, he merely sees a number of padded players lining up in peculiar formations, skating swiftly with sticks in hand, pursuing a little black disk, bumping into one another, flaring into fist fights, and coming and leaving the field of play at frequent intervals. But the game does not make much sense to him because he does not know enough about the rules, the players' responsibilities, and the play formations to understand what is going on. He does not perceive as many details as the veteran hockey fan or a rival coach scouting the game, because he does not possess the knowledge needed to interpret the events transpiring before him.

Efforts to Objectify Observations. To increase the range, richness, and accuracy of his observations and to guard against errors in perception, a scientist takes a number of precautions. First, he acquires a broad background of knowledge in the field wherein his problem lies. This helps him to determine what facts to look for as well as where and when he may find them. It provides him with a greater fund of information to link with his sense experiences so as to give them meaning. Becoming thoroughly familiar with what to expect in a given situation places him in a better position to spot significant events that occur, as well as any conditions that are unusual or that do not conform to his beliefs or the accepted theories. Like the veteran hockey fan, he is able to perceive the relevancy of what takes place in a given situation because of his extensive knowledge about the subject.

To sharpen his perceptive powers, a scientist acquires abundant practice in the art of examining phenomena with an alert and questioning mind. He studies the special observational instruments and procedures designed to gather facts and constantly strives to become more proficient in employing them. Like the proofreader, piano tuner, teataster, or airplane spotter, he trains himself to discriminate between similar stimuli that workers encounter in his field. Since emotional and intellectual biases can prevent accuracy of observation, he takes positive action to counteract them. During an investigation, he makes a serious study of views that differ from his own, deliberately searches for facts that will explode his pet theories, compares his observations with those made by others, and invites colleagues to check his findings. Whenever possible, he repeats experiments to see whether the results will be the same on each occasion. Through the exercise of rigorous self-discipline, the establishment of systematic work methods, and the custom of striving to spot and eliminate reoccurring types of mistakes, a researcher gradually improves his receptivity to sensory stimuli and learns to detect more and more details about phenomena.

Because human frailties and biases can introduce errors into data gathering, a scientist often employs movie cameras, recordings, oscillographs, or similar instruments to make a permanent record of the occurrences in an investigation. These devices provide firsthand evidence that he and others can study immediately and can recheck as often as necessary in the future. Instruments do not eliminate the need for personal observation, however, for they cannot record certain factors. Even the most delicate and expensive ones do not have the varied observational powers of human beings. Moreover, instruments are of little value unless the investigator knows how to use them skillfully, understands their limitations, and checks their operational performance for precision and accuracy.

To avoid errors in perception that arise because of faulty recall, a researcher records his data as soon after making an observation as possible in an exact system of notation.   Waiting a day, a week, or a year to compile his notes, may cause him to forget relevant data, or to have blurred, distorted, or incorrect impressions of what happened.   When recording data, he includes every significant detail about the phenomena, equipment, procedures, and difficulties encountered.   To avoid overlooking important facts, he may construct a list of items to be noted during each observation. A novice observer usually errs in keeping too few and scanty notes.   Experience teaches the trained scientist to record comprehensive, complete notes, and to make detailed drawings of all pertinent incidents that transpire during an investigation, for these prove to be invaluable possessions when the time comes to analyze and interpret the data or to explain and defend his findings.

Scientific descriptions are written in precise, concrete terms.   One employs words and symbols that mean the same thing to other investigators as they mean to the writer.   Because vague generalizations and haphazard guesses are the products of sloppy thinking and provide useless information for problem solving, they are carefully culled from research reports. Rather than recording general impressions, one writes an exact account of each smell, sight, and sound.   Rather than stating that children in a class are disobedient, one lists the specific disobedient acts they perform, the number of children participating, and the frequency or duration of the acts.

A research worker soon learns that even words that seem to be specific can carry more than one meaning.   As one man suggests, "age" of the subject may refer to present age, age at last birthday, or age at next birthday.   Consequently, in scientific work one carefully defines his terms and checks each sentence to make certain that it describes exactly what he observes, and that no other interpretation can possibly be placed upon his words.   These systematic, precise, and thorough methods of work may seem pedantic, but they are essential if the collected data are to be of any value in solving problems.

Whenever possible, an investigator describes his data quantitatively: in terms of height, weight, distance, duration, speed, or number of units. Rather than describing pupils as large boys, he gives their anthropometric measurements.   Rather than recording that pupils look at television programs frequently, he records the number of minutes per day they view them.   Rather than describing his subjects as "a group of students," he states the exact number of pupils of each sex in the group and the range in their ages.   Numerical measures are more precise than word descriptions and may make possible further analysis of the problem by statistical procedures.   Consequently, if the scientist uses questionnaires, ratings, or lists to gather data he tries to put them in a form that requires quantitative answers.

As the preceding paragraphs indicate, scientific observation is not a casual procedure of viewing and making sweeping descriptions. Anyone can perceive phenomena, but achieving precision of perception is an art. Only through persistent practice can a research worker learn to make observations from which accurate and reliable knowledge can be derived.

Conception. Perception is extremely important, yet its deficiencies become apparent when an investigator relies upon it exclusively. There are occasions when one is confronted with a puzzling situation and is not able to perceive all of its relevant elements. To liberate oneself from such a dilemma and to understand the character of a problem, one is compelled to act on the basis of conception—to make various guesses about what probably is occurring in a given situation. One circumvents the limitations of perceptual experiences through the construction of imaginary concepts—hypotheses and theories—that visualize what one cannot directly perceive. These concepts provide one with new orientations for observing his problem. After constructing a conceptual scheme, one reobserves his puzzling situation to see whether he can find facts that fit into this framework. Concepts are mental constructs that suggest what one might profitably observe to solve his problem. To see how concepts function as part of the process of the scientific method, the reader must await a detailed discussion of it in the latter half of this chapter and in Chapter 8.

THE NATURE OF FACTS

The scientist makes observations to get at facts. But what are facts? Facts mean different things to different people. A layman frequently speaks of wanting the facts, but he usually has a rather narrow concept of their nature. He believes their meanings are self-evident and their nature is precise, permanent, final, unchanging. To the scientist, facts are not something that is self-evident, but rather data he discovers through purposeful probing. To him, facts are never permanent or final; they may undergo change as an investigation evolves; they are subject to reinterpretation or revision whenever man gains a better insight into phenomena. Rather than being dogmatic about the certainty of facts, he is constantly critical of them.

The scientist realizes that many facts are more elusive and less stable than the layman thinks they are. He does not expect all facts to be equally stable, precise, and accessible. His prolonged pursuit of facts has taught him that some can be expressed quantitatively, others can be expressed only in words, and some do not readily lend themselves to either mathematical or language descriptions. To the scientist, facts are any experience, change, occurrence, or event that is sufficiently stable and supported by enough evidence to be counted on in an investigation.

Accessibility of Facts.   All facts are not equally accessible to the observer. Personal or private facts, such as dreams, memories, fears, preferences, feelings, and revelations lie hidden deep within the individual.   They may be very real to him and pass his personal tests of reliability, but they are not accessible for examination by others.   Pink elephants are real to the alcoholic and horrible dreams are real to a child, but these specific facts cannot be verified empirically by someone else.   One cannot directly observe these inner, personal phenomena to see whether he draws the same conclusions about them as other observers or the individual having the experience.   If he relies on the individual's description of a personal experience, inaccurate information may be obtained.   Tommy may tell the doctor that his stomach hurts when the pain is actually located in his chest or when he feels good but has an intense longing to stay home from school.

A research worker may infer that an individual's private experience is like one he has had under similar circumstances, but this may not be true. In daily life people often make such errors.   Joe Adams assumes that his wife gets as much pleasure out of witnessing a boxing match as he does. An English teacher expects her nephew to experience the same enjoyment from reading *David Copperfield* as she always has.   Investigators studying people of a culture, social status, or era different from their own may fall into error if they conclude that their subjects experience the same reaction to given stimuli as they do. Raw fish eyes served at a puberty rite feast may be a nauseous form of nourishment to an American anthropologist, but a delightful delicacy to the natives.   Watching a child being flogged will not arouse the same response in a modern educator as it did in a teacher of ancient Sparta.   When seeking reliable information, it is always dangerous for a scientist to equate another man's inner experiences with his own.

Because of the hidden nature of personal facts, social scientists often ·have difficulty in interpreting a commonplace event.   For example, if a student takes the smallest piece of cake on the plate at a tea, what motivates this act?   Different observers will draw different conclusions. They may decide he is trying to be polite, doesn't like chocolate cake, or thinks the hostess is a poor cook.   The student may report that he took the smallest piece because his doctor has placed him on a diet.   Actually, he may be trying to conceal the fact that he has just eaten two candy bars and is not hungry.   Personal, inner facts are one man's knowledge.   Moreover, that man may not be willing or able to analyze his experience accurately.   Personal facts are socially unreliable knowledge because they cannot be verified by public tests of common perception.

Public facts—those which can be observed and tested by everyone—are relatively impersonal knowledge.   They do not depend on the peculiarities of a single individual for verification.   Because they are open to inspection by everyone and are agreed upon by a number of independent observers, public facts are much more reliable than inner, personal facts. If one man asserts that an object weighs ten pounds, for example, it is not necessary to take his word for it. Any normal person can test the validity of that statement by reference to evidence which is independent of the observers. If many men use their senses and special instruments to test the weight of the object and they all reach approximately the same conclusion, their findings can be accepted as being quite reliable. In time, public facts win common acceptance as the most trustworthy knowledge available to mankind.

The natural scientists deal primarily with public facts, but some of the most pressing problems demanding solution in the social sciences involve personal, inner facts or a mixture of public and personal facts. The natural scientists have devised a number of reliable instruments that enable men to weigh, measure, and time phenomena in their field. When social scientists attempt to create similar instruments, they are confounded by the concealed, elusive nature of private facts. Because of the nature of their subject matter, the social scientists encounter much more difficulty than the natural scientists when they observe phenomena.

Levels of Facts.   Facts are not all alike.   Some facts are derived directly from the impact of stimuli upon the senses, others are reached by conceptual manipulations. For purposes of illustration the following paragraphs discuss three levels of facts that range (1) from those that man becomes aware of through immediate sense experiences, (2) to those that man identifies by describing or interpreting his immediate experiences, (3) to those he identifies by engaging in a highly abstract reasoning process.

Facts of immediate experience are pure sensations without any names or labels. They represent raw experiences because no attempt is made to identify, interpret, or assign meaning to them. These facts are known by immediate apprehension alone. They are sometimes called "pure facts" or the most "factual of facts" because they have not been changed in any way by the individual's intellectual process. When facts of immediate experience undergo intellectualization, they no longer retain their pure character. It is doubtful that people, other than babies, can have such raw experiences, for human beings early in life begin to name or assign meaning to experiences.

The second level of facts, those describing or interpreting immediate experience, is not just raw experience. When man describes or interprets a sensation as a sound of a jet engine, he engages in perception or a low level of conceptualization. Through an intellectual process, he associates the raw sensation with his past experiences and identifies it with that class of things he calls sounds from jet aircraft. Facts describing immediate experiences are relatively close to sensory experiences. They are not highly conceptualized. Some, however, are more conceptual than others. Facts which are primarily sensory in nature, such as sound or smell, are less conceptual than those derived from thought or reasoning experiences, such as memories or ideas.

The third level of facts is highly abstract and conceptual in nature. These facts are remote from sensory experiences. They are derived primarily from human reasoning processes and cannot be directly observed by the senses. Although they are highly conceptual in nature, they are supported by enough empirical evidence to prove they exist and therefore are acceptable as facts. For example, through an involved reasoning process, man constructs the proposition: The world is "round."[1] Man cannot see that it is round with his naked eye, but he can provide sufficient evidence traceable to various forms of sensory experience to confirm this proposition. For example, a ship disappears over the horizon progressively—hull, cabins, and finally, smokestack. Another example of a fact derived from abstract reasoning is one that shows the relationship between two concepts. That reading ability is closely related to arithmetic ability is accepted as a fact. This relationship cannot be observed directly by an individual. It can only be experienced on the conceptual level. Ultimately, however, it can be traced to empirical referents; thus, it receives indirect substantiation as a fact. Most people do not realize how little of what they accept as facts is given by raw experience alone. Theorizing plays a major role in obtaining facts.

NATURE AND THE ROLE OF THEORIZING

The average man thinks the scientist deals with facts and the philosopher is concerned with theories. To him, a scientist is a disciplined, dedicated man who searches for the "true" facts rather than an unconventional, intellectual adventurer who creates imaginative structures. He thinks that facts are definite, real, concrete, and that their meaning is self-evident. Theories, in his opinion, are mere speculations—day dreams.

Many educators also scoff at theories and demand that researchers provide them with "practical facts" that will help them in the classroom. Yet, every act a teacher performs is based to some extent on a theory. An elementary teacher may select textbook *A* rather than *B* because the larger print is more suitable for younger students, or he may plan a field trip to a farm because varied sensory experiences aid the learning process. Without realizing it, perhaps, he has made these choices on the basis of theories. Indeed, an educator would flounder forever if no theories were available to guide him in making choices.

[1] Studies of the orbital flight of Vanguard I show the earth to be slightly pear-shaped rather than a bulging sphere.

Gathering masses of isolated facts can contribute little to the advancement of knowledge. Hence, the ultimate objective of the scientist is not to accumulate facts, but to develop theories that will explain a particular segment of phenomena. Consequently, rather than relying solely on induction—observing facts—he also engages in deduction—theorizing about facts. Because facts do not speak for themselves, he tries to see relationships between them, to structure imaginative concepts that supply missing links, and to keep manipulating ideas until he stumbles upon a key concept that enables him to order many facts into a meaningful pattern. Through arduous reasoning, he builds a theoretical structure that explains facts and the causal interrelationships among them. Thus, theories and facts are reciprocally interdependent. Theories are not mere speculations, for they are built partly upon facts; isolated facts are useless unless someone structures a theory that will make them fall into a meaningful pattern. Theories provide logical explanations for facts.

Progress in science would practically terminate if researchers were to reject reasoning and only accept facts that were immediately apprehended by the senses. Conceptual fertility—the capacity to structure bold and radical guesses about how facts are ordered—is the greatest gift a scientist can possess. Although science stresses objectivity, it is to a large degree concerned with the subjective act of theorizing. Science is "objective in that it is verifiable, within assignable limits of probability, but it is subjective in that the facts observed are immediately interpreted in terms of some pattern which enables man to make sense out of them" (13:33). Theorizing is not an ornamental instrument that men toy with in their "ivory towers"; it is a practical tool that enables them to explore the underlying mechanisms of their phenomena. Theorizing provides the road maps for research; without it new knowledge cannot be discovered. Hence, the following paragraphs will explore some of the ways that theory contributes to the advancement of knowledge.

Defining the Relevancy of Facts. To engage in research, men must determine what kind of phenomena they will study. Scientists cannot collect facts about everything. They must narrow the area of their interest to limited segments of phenomena and give them their undivided attention. Investigators, for example, may study the game of baseball in the sociological framework of play, in the physical framework of stress and velocity, in the economic framework of supply and demand, or in many other ways. But a multiplicity of facts are associated with any one of these problem areas. Not until researchers construct theoretical solutions for their problems do they know precisely what facts to observe. After theorizing that there is a relationship between A and B, they know which specific facts to locate; those that will provide the empirical evidence necessary to confirm or disconfirm their theory. It is the theory that determines the number and kind of facts that are relevant to their studies.   Facts do not identify themselves as relevant, only a theory can do that.

Classifying Phenomena and Structuring Concepts.   Every science develops a structural foundation to facilitate research.   Scientists cannot work efficiently and effectively with masses of assorted facts; they need some scheme for ordering the data in their fields.   Therefore, the first stage in any science consists in constructing theoretical frameworks for classifying their facts.   The older sciences have been quite successful in devising these systematic conceptual schemes.   Geologists have developed systems for classifying rocks and botanists have developed systems for classifying plants. The younger behavioral sciences have also striven to locate key characteristics of their subject matter that will enable them to construct the most useful classification systems.

Educators have devised some classification schemes for phenomena in their field.   The attempt to classify educational objectives in the cognitive domain has been mentioned previously.   A widely known administrative taxonomy POSDCORB attempts to place into a single table all the functions of administration.   The table includes planning, organizing, staffing, directing, coordinating, reporting, and budgeting.   Many of the classification systems that educators have constructed have been crude, but the practice of carefully examining phenomena; noting the similarities, differences, and relationships between them; and structuring a framework to categorize them will gradually enable workers to gain a deeper insight into them.   If they fail to develop theoretical structures to order and describe the complex and diverse facts relating to their subject matter, they will be severely handicapped in their work and unable to advance knowledge appreciably.

Through theorization educators have structured certain concepts concerning the nature of phenomena in their field.   Because the vocabulary of everyday discourse does not enable them to express these ideas, they have created distinctive symbols and terms to describe them.   Lewin introduced the concept of valence—the attraction or repulsion value of an object for a person—for example, and utilized a symbolic method for representing it. Educators employ such terms as IQ, conditioned reflex, sociometric measurement in the pursuance of their work and present formulas or draw figures to represent conceptual schemes.   These shorthand symbols are often unintelligible to the layman, but they convey considerable compact information to scientists, and thus make it easier for them to manipulate facts and communicate their findings.

Summarizing Facts.   Theorization is used to summarize knowledge within a given field.   These summaries are stated with varying degrees of comprehensiveness and precision.   They may range from relatively simple generalizations to exceedingly complex theoretical relationships.   A summarization may describe a limited range of events, such as when an educator makes a generalization about the practice of granting varsity letters to high school athletes. This low level of summarizing is not usually referred to as a theory. But the educator might construct a more complex generalization, one that describes the relationship between phenomena. After observing such phenomena as honor societies, varsity letters, certificates of achievement, for example, he may note a relationship between them and draw the generalization that public recognition rewards are a means of motivating pupils. Summarization on a high scientific level, of course, involves integrating the major empirical generalizations into a more comprehensive theoretical framework. In the natural sciences, Einstein strived for this in the unified field theory. Social scientists are constantly striving to summarize knowledge about human behavior with the hope that they may someday construct comprehensive generalizations that will explain the great motivating force of human nature. Thus, theorizing integrates pertinent facts into compact frameworks of knowledge that give man a better understanding of phenomena. A more comprehensive theory denotes a more mature science.

Predicting Facts. A generalization about data—a theory—enables one to predict the existence of unobserved instances conforming to it. For instance, investigators have made the following generalization: When children learn a baseball throwing skill, much improvement occurs during the initial learning stages. On the basis of this theory, one can anticipate that a class of elementary pupils learning this or any similar skill will experience an achievement spurt during the early practice periods. Correspondingly, one can expect that where children have acquired proficiency in these skills, the pattern of their improvement will have conformed to this theory. Similarly, if the generalization that a high rate of truancy is associated with slum areas has been confirmed, one can look for and expect to find this pattern in a slum area where no truancy statistics have been compiled. Theory enables one to predict where data are not presently available; it tells one what he should be able to observe. Theory serves as a powerful beacon that directs man in his search for facts.

Pointing Out the Need for Further Research. Since theories generalize about facts and predict facts, they also indicate areas where knowledge is deficient. Theories, particularly in the social sciences, may lack supporting evidence in one or more aspects. Such theories need further supporting evidence to provide the maturity and vitality essential for their proper functioning. Because theories suggest where evidence is lacking, they are an excellent source to turn to when in search of research problems.

Even a rather low level of theorization can point out the need for further research. For example, a research study may arrive at the following generalization: a rather high relationship exists between the physical endowments and proficiencies of students in a suburban junior high school and the frequency, duration, and nature of their play activities. This generalization suggests where to search for additional facts. It raises the following questions: Does the general relationship above hold true for elementary and high school children? Does this pattern hold true for rural groups or youths in other countries? Is there any difference in the general relationship between the sexes? Does grouping the junior high school children according to their intelligence reveal any difference in the magnitude of the correlations between the groups? Does grouping the children in accordance with their body builds (mesomorphy, ectomorphy, and endomorphy) influence the general relationship in any way? To what extent do children of low physical abilities prefer to indulge in other activities because they are barred from successful competition by their better physically endowed age-mates? Theorization on any level tends to open up new avenues of inquiry even as it did in this instance.

RELATIONSHIP OF FACTS TO THEORIES

In pushing back the frontiers of knowledge, scientists are very dependent upon the process of theorization, but they cannot construct or confirm any theory without the aid of facts. Throughout a scientific investigation, facts and theories interact constantly; no gulf exists between them; one depends upon the other; they are inextricably interwoven. Science cannot continue its steady march toward a deeper understanding and greater control of phenomena unless it engages in the discovery of new facts and the development of new theories by encouraging each process to stimulate and supplement the other.

Stimulating Theorization by Facts. The scientist does not theorize in a mystical vacuum. The history of science is replete with instances of simple observation of facts that have led to the formulation of important theories. When Archimedes observed water overflowing while he was taking a bath, for instance, he grasped the principle of displacement. When Newton saw an apple fall, he developed the principle of gravitation. When Watt watched steam escape from a teakettle, he visualized the principle of steam power. Facts are prods that stimulate the theorizing process.

Of course, everyone is not capable of leaping from a fact to a theory; many men made the same observations as Newton, Watt, and Archimedes without being intellectually stimulated. Several scientists noticed the inhibition of bacterial growth by molds before Fleming saw the significance in this fact that led to the discovery of penicillin. As Pasteur pointed out, when men make observations "chance favors the prepared mind." A scientist must have a broad background of knowledge if he is to recognize an unusual fact and utilize this sudden insight to structure an explanation for the nature of the phenomena. Facts can only initiate theorization when an alert, disciplined, and imaginative mind observes them and mentally constructs a possible explanation for them.

Testing Theories by Facts. Facts are essential for the establishment of a scientific theory: they determine whether a theory can be confirmed or should be rejected or reformulated. Facts may not be available immediately for the confirmation or rejection of a theory, but they are necessary for the eventual acceptance or abandonment of it. The discovery of pertinent facts that support a theory strengthen it. But, if facts are found that do not conform to the theory, one must reject it or reformulate it to fit the new evidence. Theories must be tailored to fit the facts and remodeled whenever new facts reveal the need for such action.

Theoretical formulations do not necessarily retain their original structures. New evidence being unearthed in research laboratories may lead to the revision of old theories or may spur the formulation of new explanations for phenomena. Theoretical explanations of learning, for example, have undergone revolutionary changes within the past several decades. The association and behavioral psychologists formulated some of the earlier theories of learning. When their work came to be accepted almost as definitive, dramatic developments occurred as a result of investigations made by the Gestalt and the topological psychologists. These field psychologists challenged both the basic assumptions and the research techniques of their predecessors. Facts revealed by their laboratory experiments and clinical studies caused them to formulate a new explanation of the learning process.

Clarifying Theories by Facts. Theories are refined and clarified as knowledge accumulates. New theories in the social sciences are apt to be elusive and ill-defined; they often give a rather crude, general explanation of phenomena. Further observation and experimentation, however, may reveal facts that not only agree with the theory, but also specify in detail and with precision what the theory states in a general way. For instance, modern psychologists have developed the so-called "field theories of learning" which contribute to our general understanding of the learning process. Yet, investigations conducted by Tolman, Lewin, Anderson, Murphy, and many others have added considerable substance and depth to these general theories of learning. Their work illustrates how additional facts can give greater specificity and breadth to a theory.

Interdependence of Facts and Theories. The marriage of facts and theories produces many advances in science. Man is forever searching for a more abundant life and better understanding of the world in which he lives. Finding answers to his questions entails a persistent search for facts that will aid him in building mental constructs capable of explaining phenomena. Facts supply the raw building materials: man's imagination and intellect supply the theoretical plan or framework that postulate underlying mechanisms that account for the phenomena under consideration.

Facts alone are a rather useless pile of bricks, and theories must rely on facts for their conception and confirmation. In science, man puts his trust, "not in facts as such, but rather in the interaction of many minds observing similar facts, projecting these facts against different conceptual backgrounds, testing the divergent interpretations by means of further observation, and seeking explanations of any final differences" (13:34). Science rests on facts and on ideas; it is both objective and subjective; it is a product of empirical knowledge and imaginative mental constructs; it advances under the power of inductive and deductive thought processes.

BIBLIOGRAPHY

1. American Educational Research Association, "Twenty-five Years of Educational Research," *Review of Educational Research,* 26 (June, 1956).

2. Beveridge, W. I. B., *The Art of Scientific Investigation.* New York: W. W. Norton & Company, Inc., 1951, chap. 8.

3. Brown, Clarence W., and E. E. Ghiselli, *Scientific Method in Psychology.* New York: McGraw-Hill Book Company, Inc., 1955, chap. 1.

4. Cohen, Morris R., and E. Nagel, *Introduction to Logic and Scientific Method.* New York: Harcourt, Brace & World, Inc., 1934, chap. 11.

5. Furfey, Paul H., *The Scope and Method of Sociology.* New York: Harper & Brothers, 1953, chap. 13.

6. Goode, William J., and Paul K. Hatt, *Methods in Social Research.* New York: McGraw-Hill Book Company, Inc., 1952, chap. 2.

7. Hanson, Norwood R., *Patterns of Discovery.* Cambridge: Cambridge University Press, 1958, chaps. 1, 2, and 4.

8. Kingsley, Howard L., and Ralph Garry, *The Nature and Conditions of Learning.* Englewood Cliffs, N.J.: Prentice-Hall, Inc., 1957, chap. 11.

9. Larrabee, Harold A., *Reliable Knowledge.* Boston: Houghton Mifflin Company, 1945, chap. 4.

10. Madge, John, *The Tools of Social Science.* London: Longmans, Green & Co., Ltd., 1953, chap. 3.

11. Northrop, F. S. C., *The Logic of the Sciences and the Humanities.* New York: The Macmillan Company, 1949, chap. 2.

12. Russell, Bertrand, *An Outline of Philosophy.* London: George Allen & Unwin, Ltd., 1927.

13. Scates, Douglas E., "The Conceptual Background of Research," *The Conceptual Structure of Educational Research.* Chicago: University of Chicago Press, 1942.

14. Searles, Herbert L., *Logic and Scientific Methods.* New York: The Ronald Press Company, 1948, chaps. 10 and 11.

15. Van Dalen, D. B., "A Study of Certain Factors in Their Relation to the Play of Children," *Research Quarterly,* 18 (December, 1947):279.

16. Werkmeister, W. H., *An Introduction to Critical Thinking.* Lincoln, Nebr.: Johnsen Publishing Company, 1948, chap. 17.

CHAPTER 5

Printed Resources for Problem Solving

A few centuries ago a scholar aspired to acquire an encyclopedic education that would acquaint him with all available knowledge. Since modern libraries bulge with a myriad of materials on almost every subject, this goal is no longer attainable. Printing presses annually spew thousands of new books and periodicals on the market. An educator cannot possibly keep abreast of all these publications. But the explosive expansion of knowledge does make it imperative for him to become proficient in locating, selecting, and utilizing references from an ever-increasing variety of printed resources.

Today, a mastery of library skills is a prerequisite for research. Hence, prowling through stacks and reference rooms and thumbing through books and indexes until one becomes thoroughly familiar with the varied library facilities and resources can save a researcher months of time in his future work. When locating materials becomes as easy and automatic a process for him as finding the light switches in his home, a researcher has acquired a professional tool that carries a lifetime guarantee of usefulness. To aid you in achieving such skill, this chapter provides a study guide for surveying (1) the types of available references, (2) the nature of information that each contains, and (3) how to use them.

REFERENCE BOOKS

Utilizing the reference room facilities is a satisfying and stimulating experience for an expert investigator who possesses the tools and techniques to mine the various sources for "pay dirt" information. But it is a frustrating experience for a neophyte who wanders in the endless tunnels of facts and does not know how to dig out the gems he wants. Since locating specific facts or compact overviews is frequently necessary, one should become well acquainted with reference books that can help him, such as encyclopedias, dictionaries, yearbooks, and directories.

To ease and speed the search for a reference book, one can consult the following carefully compiled volumes: *Guide to Reference Books* by Constance M. Winchell (10), which has supplements (11 and 12) between

64

editions, describes and evaluates over five thousand references. *Basic Reference Sources* by Louis Shores, 1954, covers fewer references but gives more detailed descriptions. Mary N. Barton's *Reference Books: A Brief Guide for Students and Other Users of the Library,* 1959, is a helpful but considerably shorter guide. *How and Where to Look It Up,* by Robert W. Murphey, 1958, is a comprehensive bibliography of basic reference works. It also offers guidance in the preparation and style of research papers. By adding one of the following books to his personal library, an educator may obtain an excellent introduction to the literature in the field: *How to Locate Educational Information and Data* by Carter Alexander and Arvid Burke (1) and the briefer *Library Resources in Educational Research* by Ruth E. Seeger (8).

If the reader wants to obtain more detailed bibliographic information about the sources listed in this chapter, he can find them in the preceding guides. Even after becoming thoroughly familiar with various reference books, it is advisable to check Winchell or the other guides occasionally to discover whether any useful new references are available or whether any changes have been made in the author, editor, title, publisher, or scope of material covered by the older references. If one fails to take such action, he may continue using a periodical index long after it has discontinued including the information that interests him; moreover, he may never discover that materials that were once published in one journal or index are now being presented in another source or under a new title.

Encyclopedias. Encyclopedias are good references to consult, in order to check a fact or to obtain a brief overview of a topic. These storehouses of information usually contain well-rounded discussions and selected bibliographies that are prepared by outstanding specialists. To make the most efficient use of encyclopedias, one should check dates of issue, consult the annual supplements that bring the materials up-to-date, and scan the indexes. To discover which general encyclopedia presents the best treatment of subjects in his field, one should examine some of the better known ones, such as *Encyclopedia Americana; Encyclopaedia Britannica; New International Encyclopaedia,* now out of print; and the useful one-volume *Columbia Encyclopedia.*

Every educator finds the comprehensive *Encyclopedia of Educational Research,* Chester W. Harris, editor, 1960, an invaluable reference. This book is arranged alphabetically by subject and for each field of research it (1) presents a critical evaluation and summary of the work that has been done, (2) suggests needed research, and (3) includes a selective bibliography. Other volumes that can be consulted are *Encyclopedia of Modern Education,* Harry N. Rivlin and Herbert Schueler, editors, 1943, and the old, scholarly five volumes of *Cyclopedia of Education,* Paul Monroe, editor, 1911–1913. In addition, there are many special field encyclopedias available, such as

The New Encyclopedia of Sports, Frank G. Menke, editor; *Encyclopedia of Child Guidance,* Ralph B. Winn, editor; and *Encyclopedia of Vocational Guidance,* Oscar J. Kaplan, editor.

The following list gives samples of other types of encyclopedias that educators might use: *Encyclopaedia of the Social Sciences,* 1930–1935, 15 vols.; *Van Nostrand's Scientific Encyclopedia; Catholic Encyclopedia; Jewish Encyclopedia; International Cyclopedia of Music and Musicians,* Oscar Thompson; *Encyclopaedia of World History,* William L. Langer, 1948; *Encyclopaedia of Religion and Ethics,* James Hastings and John A. Selbie.

Dictionaries. Good dictionaries that provide information concerning the spelling, pronunciation, derivation, syllabication, and correct usage and meaning of words are the constant companions of a researcher. Generally speaking, dictionaries that are unabridged, of recent date and compilation, responsibly edited, and specialized are better for investigative purposes than older, less comprehensive, and more general works. Among the better-known general dictionaries are: *Oxford English Dictionary,* 12 vols.; *Dictionary of American English on Historical Principles,* 4 vols.; *Funk and Wagnalls New Standard Dictionary;* and *Webster's New International Dictionary of the English Language.*

Because it is frequently necessary to define educational terms with precision, a researcher in this field usually owns a copy of the *Dictionary of Education,* Carter V. Good, editor, 1959. He also has a good abridged dictionary on his desk as well as Henry Fowler's *Dictionary of Modern English Usage* or Margaret Nicholson's *Dictionary of American-English Usage* and Peter Roget's *Thesaurus of English Words and Phrases.* Some of the special field dictionaries he may use are: *Dictionary of Sociology,* Henry P. Fairchild, editor; *Dictionary of Social Sciences,* John T. Zadrozny, editor; *Comprehensive Dictionary of Psychological and Psychoanalytical Terms,* H. B. English and Ava C. A. English; and *Dictionary of Statistical Terms,* Maurice G. Kendall and William R. A. Buckland.

Almanacs and Yearbooks. A wealth of current information can be found in almanacs and yearbooks. Up-to-date statistics and data concerning events, progress, and conditions in a wide variety of social, educational, industrial, political, financial, and religious fields appear in the *World Almanac,* 1868—,[1] and *Information Please Almanac,* 1947—. Statistics on population, standard of living, prices, labor, and business are presented in the *Economic Almanac,* 1940—.

Educational Yearbooks and Handbooks. Recent statistics and discussions on educational problems, thought, and practices are found in several outstanding yearbooks. Some yearbooks cover a new topic of current interest each year, others give more general reviews of events. One of the most

---

[1] Interpret reference of this nature as follows: published from 1868 to the present.

valuable yearbooks has been put out since 1902 by the National Society for the Study of Education. Each yearbook in this series is now issued in several parts; thus, a reference to this source must indicate the part as well as the year.

About fifteen departments of the NEA publish yearbooks or annual reports. Some of them, such as those compiled by the American Association of School Administrators, have made major contributions to education. The *NEA Handbook for Local, State, and National Associations,* 1945—, lists its publications, gives accounts of its work, and includes facts about education in general. A report of the programs, meetings, and activities of the NEA and its departments, commissions, and committees has appeared in the annual volume of *Addresses and Proceedings* since 1857.

Many worthwhile yearbooks are also published in special fields. Educators may consult the *Mental Measurements Yearbook* (title and years of publication vary—1938, 1941, 1949, 1953, 1959) which is compiled by Oscar K. Buros. It lists all commercially available educational, psychological, and vocational tests published during the period covered by the volume and gives price, publisher, grade level, and evaluations. *The Yearbook of School Law,* edited by M. M. Chambers, 1932 to 1942, and by Leo O. Garber, 1950—, presents abstracts of important court cases dealing with education as well as a few feature articles.

Statistical Information. Statistics concerning public and private schools on all levels appear in the indispensable *Biennial Survey of Education in the United States* for the years 1916 to 1918—. This work contains data on such things as personnel, enrollment, receipts, expenditures, salaries, attendance, buildings, and per-capita costs. The U.S. Department of Health, Education, and Welfare, Office of Education,[2] publishes some of these statistics in advance in *School Life* and *Higher Education.* The NEA publication, *Research Bulletin,* which is issued four times a year, is an excellent source for recent statistics and discussions on topics such as salaries, working conditions, educational practices, and teacher supply and demand.

The United States Census Bureau's ten-year reports and its *Census Abstract* are reliable and detailed. The annual *Statistical Abstract of the United States,* 1878—, gives more recent statistical information about the political, social, industrial, and economic organization of the nation. Since 1947, UNESCO has published international economic statistics in the *Statistical Yearbook* and population and social statistics in the *Demographic Yearbook.*

International Information. International surveys and descriptions of educational systems in many countries are found in the *Year Book of Education,* 1932 to 1940, 1948—. The early volumes, which reviewed educational

[2] Hereafter, the shorter term, Office of Education, will be used to designate this agency.

developments in the major European and English-speaking nations, were edited by G. B. Jeffery, University of London Institute of Education. In 1953, the sponsors of this yearbook joined Teachers College, Columbia University, to prepare an annual work under the same title. Each year they examine some particular aspect of education at length, for example, the theme of the 1960 edition was "Communications Media and the School." The *International Yearbook of Education*, which is issued jointly by UNESCO and International Bureau of Education, 1948—, reviews the educational developments of approximately 45 countries, including the United States and Canada. Prior to 1948, this yearbook was published in French. The *World Handbook of Educational Organization and Statistics*, 1951, and the new and enlarged *World Survey of Education*, 1958, are issued by UNESCO. Similar volumes of up-to-date statistics concerning many educational systems in the world will be published periodically by UNESCO.

Special Fields. Many topics that are closely related to teaching problems can be found in yearbooks from other fields, such as the *Social Work Year Book*, 1929—. Since an educator frequently has to locate specific information or statistics about government organizations, services, problems, trends, officials, and addresses, he may also use the following references which give information about all phases of government, including education: *The Statesman's Year Book*, 1864—, presents current facts about governments of the world. The *United States Government Organization Manual*, 1935—, is an invaluable guide to the work of the Federal government. *The Book of the States*, 1935—, and *the Municipal Year Book*, 1934—, are useful references for their respective fields.

Directories. Directories are as valuable in professional life as a personal address book is in private life. An educator uses them to locate the names and addresses of persons, periodicals, publishers, organizations, or firms when he wants to obtain information, interviews, a grant from a foundation, or research materials and equipment. By consulting directories, he can find people or organizations who have similar professional interests or who are qualified to answer his questionnaires or problems.

The *Education Directory*, published by the Office of Education, is a widely used reference. It has five parts and includes the following data: (1) state and territorial school officials; (2) county and city school officials, including some parochial superintendents; (3) higher educational institutions—enrollment, curricula, officers, accrediting agency, and statistical tables; (4) officers of educational associations, religious and international organizations, and educational foundations; (5) Federal educational officials. Similar information appears in *Patterson's American Education*. The *NEA Handbook* lists the NEA departments and affiliated associations and their officers. Many educational associations include membership lists in their yearbooks.

Information about educational institutions is presented in *Patterson's American Education* and the government's *Educational Directory*, Part 3, which were cited above. The following guides published by the American Council on Education are also useful: *American Universities and Colleges*, *American Junior Colleges*, and *Universities of the World Outside U.S.A.* Other references in this field include *The College Blue Book*, C. E. Burckel; *A Guide to Graduate Study*, Frederic W. Ness, editor, Association of American Colleges; *Handbook of Private Schools*, Porter Sargent. *Index Generalis* lists institutions of higher learning, academies, libraries, gardens, museums, and observatories throughout the world.

Business firms can be located in the *Guide to American Business Directories*, Marjorie V. Davis. *Patterson's Schools Classified* has a section on educational business firms and more comprehensive guides are provided by *American School and University*; *A Yearbook Devoted to the Design, Construction, Equipment, Utilization, and Maintenance of Educational Buildings and Grounds*; and *Sweet's Catalog File (Architectural)*. A directory of periodicals and publishers is included in the *Education Index* and the major publishers are listed in the *Publishers' Trade List Annual*.

An educator might also have occasion to consult specialized directories, such as *A Directory of Educational Research Agencies and Studies*, compiled by Raymond J. Young, 1957, which lists agencies doing research, types of work done, and a bibliography of studies completed, and *University Research Bureaus and Institutes*, 1960, published by Gale Research Company. The following directories also contain information that is frequently sought by educators: *Youth-serving Organizations*, American Council on Education; *American Foundations and Their Fields* and the *Encyclopedia of American Associations*, Gale Research Company.

Biographical Sources. When carrying out a research study, one may have to obtain a specific fact about a person, such as his birthdate, degrees, publications, present position or professional affiliations. It may also be necessary to locate general information concerning the background, competency, prestige, or biases of a person. This type of information can be found in encyclopedias, large dictionaries, or the following specialized sources.

The *Biography Index*, 1947—, provides a comprehensive guide to biographical materials appearing in current books, periodicals, and the *New York Times*. This quarterly, which has annual and three-year cumulations, indexes items by profession and occupation as well as by names. It includes persons both living and dead, lists obituaries, and indicates which articles include portraits (see Figure 1). Winchell (10) describes some useful earlier guides to biographical materials by Marian Dorgan, Edward H. O'Neill, and the co-compilers, Helen Hefling and Jessie Dyde.

Reference books that contain biographies of notable personalities both living and dead are *Webster's Biographical Dictionary,* which gives brief sketches, and the comprehensive *National Cyclopaedia of American Biography,* 35 vols. Deceased notables are found in the reliable and scholarly *Dictionary of American Biography,* 22 vols., and *Who Was Who in America,* 2 vols. Notable contemporaries are listed in sources, such as *World Biography; Who's Who in America,* a biennial with monthly supplements; and similarly named publications in other countries. *Current Biography,* a monthly with a cumulative index, gives lively sketches of recent newsworthy names throughout the world. Some educators are included in the *Directory of American Scholars* and the *American Men of Science* and many are listed in *Leaders in Education* and *Who's Who in American Education.* Similar references have been compiled to cover art, music, government, industry, and many other fields.

DEWEY, John, 1859-1952, philosopher
Nathanson, J. John Dewey. (In Mason, Gabriel Richard, ed. Great American liberals. Starr King press '56 p 143-53)
Pillsbury, W. B. John Dewey, 1859-1952. (In National academy of sciences. Biographical memoirs. Columbia univ. press '57 p 105-24) bibliog por autograph

DE WINT, Peter, 1784-1849, English painter
New York (city). Museum of modern art. Masters of British painting, 1800-1950. The museum '56 p52-3 bibliog il

DEWITT, Anna (Drury) 1884?-1957, political leader
Obituary
N Y Times p29 Ja 17 '57

DIONNE, Cecile, 1934- one of the Dionne quintuplets
First of the quints to say mais oui. il pors Life 42:57 Ap 8 '57

DIOR, Christian, 1905- French costume designer
Dictator by demand. il pors Time 69:30-4+ Mr 4 '57
Dior stages a dress rehearsal. il pors Look 21:88-9 Ap 2 '57
Pictorial works
Dior celebrates a decade at the very top. Life 42:129-32+ Mr 4 '57

DIRKS, Rudolph, 1877?- cartoonist
Dirks's bad boys. il por Time 69:48 Mr 4 '57

Fig. 1. Typical entries in the *Biography Index.* (*The H. W. Wilson Company.*)

Bibliographical Sources. Compiling a bibliography is one of the first and last things a researcher does in conducting a study. This essential task is less arduous and time-consuming if he is well acquainted with the various "laborsaving" devices at his disposal. By spending a few minutes consulting guide books in the library reference room, he usually can locate relevant bibliographies that have already been compiled. Of course, the bibliographies will vary in type and quality; some will be exhaustive and others selective or brief; some will be annotated and others will not be. If the bibliographies are compiled by experts in the field and give clues as to the content, general value, scholarship, and significant features of the publications, they may save the researcher weeks of searching time.

Since 1937, the excellent *Bibliographic Index* has provided a guide to bibliographies in all fields (see Figure 2). It includes bibliographies that are published as separate books or pamphlets as well as those appearing in books, pamphlets, and periodicals, both in English and foreign languages. This semiannual subject index has annual and larger cumulations. For materials published earlier than 1937, an educator can consult Winchell (10) under the heading Bibliographies.

To locate educational bibliographies published since 1928, the best source is the *Education Index*. In this guide, bibliographies are listed as a subhead under a mainhead subject (i.e., mainhead Social Sciences, subhead Bibliography). Earlier bibliographies can be found in *Bibliographies and Summaries in Education to July 1, 1935* by Walter S. Monroe and Louis Shores.

Excellent educational bibliographies also can be found in the *Encyclopedia of Educational Research* and issues of the *Review of Educational Research*. Books or articles in special fields, such as William W. Brickman's *Guide to Research in Educational History* often includes a list of bibliographies. An

---

EDUCATION—*Continued*

South

Harlan, Louis R. Separate and unequal; public school campaigns and racism in the southern seaboard states, 1901-1915. Univ. of N.C. press '58 p270-81 annot
Southern education reporting service. With all deliberate speed; segregation-desegregation in southern schools; ed. by Don Shoemaker. Harper '57 p218-24

United States

Mathewson, Robert Hendry. Strategy for American education; an inquiry into the feasibility of education for individual and social development. (Education for living ser) Harper '57 incl bibliog
EDUCATION, Audio-visual. See Audio-visual education
EDUCATION, Compulsory
See also
School attendance
EDUCATION, Consumer. See Consumer education
EDUCATION, Elementary
Archer, Clifford Paul. Elementary education in rural areas. Ronald '58 incl bibliog. annot

EDUCATIONAL guidance
Guide to guidance; a sel. bibliog. of 1957 pubs. of interest to deans, counselors, advisers, teachers, and administrators. (V20) Syracuse univ. press '58 58p annot
See also
Personnel service in education
EDUCATIONAL group work. See Group Work
EDUCATIONAL laws and legislation
Yearbook of school law, 1958. Garber '58 p 175-80 annot
Young, R. J. Suggested basis for examining legal and regulatory requirements affecting curriculum. Educ Adm & Sup 43:415-17 N '57
EDUCATIONAL measurements
Baron, Denis, and Bernard. Harold W. Evaluation techniques for classroom teachers. (McGraw-Hill ser. in education) McGraw '58 incl bibliog annot
Furst, Edward J. Constructing evaluation instruments. Longmans '58 incl bibliog
Noll, Victor Herbert. Introduction to educational measurement. Houghton '57 incl bibliog annot
Ability—Testing
Intelligence tests
Tests and scales

Fig. 2. Typical entries in the *Bibliographic Index.* (*The H. W. Wilson Company.*)

educator sometimes finds that the *Art Index, Agriculture Index,* or similar publications are the best source to consult for his purposes. Textbooks, some professional magazines, and various organizations also provide bibliographies. The U.S. Department of Health, Education, and Welfare publishes a number of bibliographies, for example, *Administration of Higher Education: An Annotated Bibliography*, Bulletin 1960, contains 2,708 studies and *Research Relating to Mentally Retarded Children*, 1960, includes 458 studies.

BOOKS AND MONOGRAPHS

Books and monographs are major research resources. Unless a student can quickly ascertain what publications the local library has on his subject and knows how to find the title and location of those that are available elsewhere, he cannot make much progress with an investigation. Examining everything that has been written on a subject either will be impossible or will consume an exorbitant amount of time; consequently, one must master the art of selecting books discriminatingly. To judge which books are most useful for his purpose, one must learn how to locate and interpret the information provided by the card catalog, book lists, and reviews.

Card Catalog. The card catalog is the key to the local library's collection of books and some other items. The "dictionary type" catalog contains (1) author, (2) title, and (3) subject cards arranged alphabetically. An author card is filed last name first. A title card is filed under the first principal word in the title of the book (initial articles—a, the, an—are disregarded). A subject card has a heading, usually typed in red, which indicates what a book is about. If a book falls under several subjects, it is filed under each pertinent subject heading. Subject headings that have several entries are subdivided and the division headings are listed alphabetically; for example, the subject heading Education, may be followed by the division headings Aims, Bibliographies, History, and Philosophy. Cross-reference cards which carry the notation "see" or "see also" are inserted in the catalog when the information sought can be located under other subject headings or when the author uses a pseudonym.

A library may use its own typed cards in the catalog or those published by the Library of Congress or the H. W. Wilson Company. Some libraries are now dividing their card catalog into two sections—one for authors and title cards and the other for subject cards. They also may have separate catalogs for dissertations, reserved books, and other special collections.

The wealth of information that appears on the cards in the catalog can be exceedingly helpful if the researcher knows how to interpret it. Merely by checking the author card, which carries the most detailed data about a book, he can find a number of valuable clues that will indicate whether the book will meet his needs. Notice, for example, the amount of information given on the author card in Figure 3.

Other items sometimes noted on cards are bibliographies; maps; portraits; illustrations; tables or tabulations if given; series if any in which a book appears; a brief description or quoted evaluation of the book; whether the book is a translation and who did the work; whether the author uses a pseudonym; and the number of pages in the preface, body of the text, and index (xii, 320, xv p.).

Books Not Located in the Local Library. What does an educator do if he needs information about a book that is not available in the local library? How can he determine whether a book has been published on a given subject? How can he get data to correct or complete a reference listed in his bibliography? How can he obtain information about a book that was published by an author in 1940? How can he find out which libraries have a copy of the book he wants? By becoming familiar with some of the following guides, one usually can answer such questions.

Books from Other Libraries. If a book is not in the local library, it may be available in another institution. Regional and national union catalogs which contain entries of works cataloged by many libraries give such information. By consulting them, the local reference librarian can discover what institution has a particular book and may be able to obtain it for a

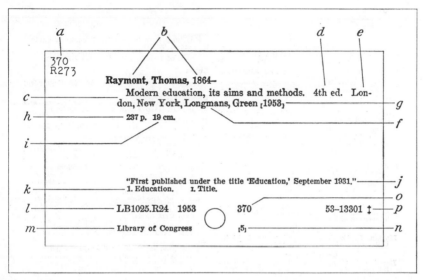

Fig. 3. Illustration of an author card. (*a*) call number; (*b*) author and year of birth; (*c*) complete title; (*d*) edition; (*e*) place published; (*f*) publisher; (*g*) publication date; (*h*) number of pages; (*i*) size (height); (*j*) former title; (*k*) other headings to look under; (*l*) Library of Congress call number; (*m*) card publisher; (*n*) date of card code number; (*o*) Dewey system call number; (*p*) order code number of this card. *Library of Congress.*

patron on an interlibrary loan. By checking the *Union List of Microfilms,* the librarian can ascertain whether any institution has a microfilmed copy of a nonlendable book. For a small fee, the larger libraries will prepare a typed copy or photostat of a few pages in a book. Before requesting any of these services, of course, one must obtain complete bibliographic information about the book and must make certain that it is not available locally.

General Lists of Books. A number of sources can be consulted to find the title, author, or publisher of books. The most recent books published in the United States are listed in *The Publishers' Weekly.* Books published in past months or years can be found in recent issues of the *Cumulative Book Index,*

1928—, or one of its larger cumulations. This world list of books in the English language includes most publications, but omits pamphlets, government documents, and maps. Entries in the *Cumulative Book Index* are cataloged by author, title, and subject in one alphabetical list; the author entries give the complete bibliographical information (see Figure 4). Older books can be found in the *United States Catalog* which lists books in print 1899 to 1928 and the *American Catalogue of Books* which covers the 1876 to 1910 period.

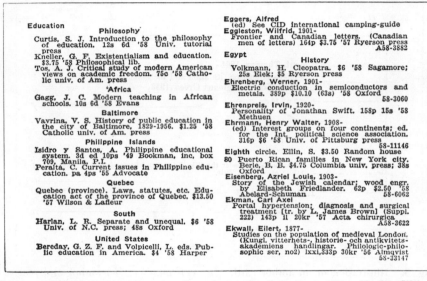

Fig. 4. Typical entries in the *Cumulative Book Index*. (*The H. W. Wilson Company.*)

Books in Print. Sometimes it is necessary to know whether a book is in print. If the author or title of the book is known, it may be found in *Books in Print;* otherwise, it may be found in *Subject Guide to Books in Print.* Both of these works are edited by Sarah Prakken. Out-of-print books can sometimes be found through the columns of the weekly *Antiquarian Bookman.*

Educational Publications. Books in the field of education, with the exception of elementary and high school texts, are listed in the body of the *Education Index* which also presents a helpful "check list" of current publications in the front of each monthly issue. Current pedagogical textbooks can be found in an annual publication, *Textbooks in Print.* Most educational organizations compile lists or catalogues of the publications that they produce or that can be obtained from other sources. The NEA, for example, annually puts out *Publications,* a list of over a thousand books, pamphlets, periodicals, research reports, and audio-visual materials. Many lists such as this one can be obtained upon request from publishers and the national headquarters of educational organizations.

Government Publications. Books, pamphlets, and other publications from various governmental agencies are a rich source of information, for they include statistical data, research studies, official reports, laws, and other materials that are not always available elsewhere. Locating government documents can be difficult, especially if one does not know that librarians index government publications under the name of the official body responsible for them rather than the author's name. If one reads the brief overview concerning government publications written by Louis Shores (9) and the chapter of detailed suggestions presented by Alexander and Burke (1:267–283), he will find it easier to locate government materials.

The publications of the Office of Education are listed in the *Education Index* under the main heading, United States. A list of items that are for sale, which is entitled *Education,* Price List 31, can be obtained by writing to the Superintendent of Documents, Government Printing Office, Washington, D.C. *The 1937–1959 Publications,* Office of Education, presents a more comprehensive single list. Alexander and Burke (1:247–266) present a detailed guide on how to locate Office of Education publications. To find publications of other government agencies, an educator can refer to the two general source books: the *Monthly Catalog of United States Government Publications,* which lists entries by departments and has a subject index, and the *Monthly Checklist of State Publications* issued by the Library of Congress.

Book Lists and Reviews. How can an educator decide which books are the most useful and reliable sources? From experience he learns that some authors and publishers maintain higher standards than others and the information given in the card catalog provides him with some clues. In addition to these guides, he can consult book lists, book reviews, and editorial comments to obtain an estimate of a book's value.

Book Lists. Since carelessly prepared book lists are worthless, it pays to become acquainted with reputable ones, such as those compiled by the competent staff members of the Research Division of the NEA, the American Library Association, and the Enoch Pratt Free Library. The staff of the Pratt Library compiles a comprehensive list on a single topic which appears in the spring issues of *Educational Horizons* and a list of outstanding educational books of the year which appears in the May issue of the *NEA Journal.* Current educational book lists are found in the *Education Index* under the main headings Reading Lists, Book Lists, Books and Reading with the subhead Best Books, and Education with the subhead Bibliography. Many lists can also be found in the *Bibliographic Index* under the following headings: Reading Lists, Book Lists, Books and Reading, Bibliography, and Education.

Book Reviews.   More detailed information about books can be obtained from book reviews.   But, if they are used to evaluate books, due consideration must be given to the special interests, biases, and competencies of the reviewers as well as the standards of the periodicals printing them.   Book reviews can be located in several sources.   The *Education Index* has a

BROWN, SLATER. Gray bonnets; il by Fritz Kredel. (American heritage series) 192p $1.75 Aladdin

54-6317

Historical novel of Boston in the days of Roger Williams. Written for young readers in grades 6-9.

Chicago Sunday Tribune p28 N 14 '54 20w

Reviewed by M. J. Taylor
Christian Science Monitor p12 N 11 '54 20w

"Simple but clear definitions of Quaker and Puritan beliefs and the more flagrant outrages of the controversy. Good."
+ Kirkus 22:438 Jl 15 '54 80w

"An absorbing story for modern American youth." H. S. McEntee
+ Library J 79:2499 D 15 '54 80w

" 'Gray Bonnets' is a perfect example of what can happen when an author gives a character an impossible task. . . As it stands, the plot is incredible; the motivation simply is not strong enough to justify Dan's actions. What Dan does is admirable, but it is hard for the reader to believe in it." Eithna Sheehan
N Y Times pt2 p26 N 14 '54 70w

Fig. 5.   Illustration of entries in the *Book Review Digest*.   (*The H. W. Wilson Company.*)

heading, Book Reviews, under which it lists items alphabetically by author. Reviews of elementary and high school texts are not included in the *Education Index*.   Every month the *Book Review Digest* gives condensed reports of book reviews appearing in a wide variety of sources.   This publication lists entries alphabetically by the author of the book reviewed.   An entry describes the purpose and scope of the book, notes where reviews are located, indicates whether they are favorable or unfavorable by the use of a plus or minus sign, and may include excerpts from some reviews (see Figure 5).   The *Technical Book Review Index* is a useful guide to reviews in technical, scientific, and trade journals.

PERIODICALS AND OTHER SERIALS

New ideas and developments frequently appear in periodicals long before books incorporate them.   Periodicals also publish articles of temporary, local, or limited interest that never appear in book form.   Consequently, periodicals constitute one of the best sources for reports on recent research studies and the older volumes provide a priceless record of past proposals, accomplishments, conflicts, attitudes, propaganda, ideas, and events.   Since all periodicals are not of the same caliber, an intelligent reader forms the habit of checking their reliability by asking some of the following questions: Do the publishers have a good reputation?   Are the editors and contributors competent?   Are the periodicals listed in recognized indexes?   Are the footnotes and bibliographies adequate?

Periodical Indexes.   What a hopeless task a researcher would face if he had to leaf through all the magazines in the library to find the articles he needed!   Fortunately, expertly compiled periodical indexes are available that serve as guides to the contents of magazines just as card catalogs serve as guides to books.   These periodical guides usually list the selected magazines they index on the inside covers or near the front of each issue.   This list changes occasionally when new periodicals are indexed or old ones are dropped.   Consequently, before using a periodical guide, an experienced researcher always checks to make sure it indexes the magazines that are likely to answer his problems.   Before writing out a call slip for a periodical, he also checks whether the local library subscribes to it.   In the reference or periodical room he usually can find a list or file of current magazines and volumes of back issues that are kept by the library.

Educational Indexes.   One of the greatest work-saving devices ever created for educators is the *Education Index*.   Since 1929, it has provided the most extensive and detailed guide to professional literature in the field.   It lists all. articles in outstanding educational journals and many educational articles in nonprofessional periodicals.   In addition, it lists many educational books, pamphlets, monographs, government documents, important yearbooks, college education textbooks, workbooks, courses of study, tests and scales, book reviews and lists, bibliographies, biographies, and reports.   Almost all of the publications of the NEA and the Office of Education are in the *Education Index*.   This valuable guide is published monthly, except for June and August, and is cumulated frequently.

All main entries in the *Education Index* are alphabetically listed with appropriate subheadings.   The plan of indexing is by author and subject and the author entries give full bibliographic data.   By utilizing the "Key to Abbreviations," and the "List of Periodicals Indexed," which are located at the front of each issue or cumulation, it is easy to interpret an entry.   For example, the entry under author Lindberg in Figure 6 conveys that Lindberg's

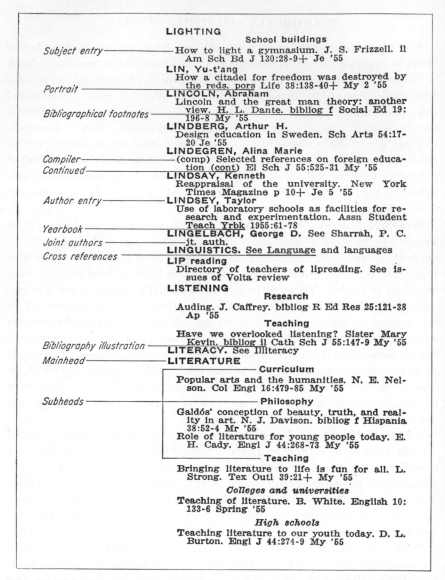

LIGHTING

School buildings

Subject entry ——————— How to light a gymnasium. J. S. Frizzell. il
Am Sch Bd J 130:28-9+ Je '55

LIN, Yu-t'ang
How a citadel for freedom was destroyed by
Portrait ——————— the reds. pors Life 38:138-40+ My 2 '55

LINCOLN, Abraham
Lincoln and the great man theory: another
Bibliographical footnotes ——— view. H. L. Dante. bibliog f Social Ed 19:
196-8 My '55

LINDBERG, Arthur H.
Design education in Sweden. Sch Arts 54:17-
20 Je '55

LINDEGREN, Alina Marie
Compiler ——————— (comp) Selected references on foreign educa-
Continued ——————— tion (cont) El Sch J 55:525-31 My '55

LINDSAY, Kenneth
Reappraisal of the university. New York
Times Magazine p 10+ Je 5 '55

Author entry ——————— **LINDSEY, Taylor**
Use of laboratory schools as facilities for re-
search and experimentation. Assn Student
Yearbook ——————— Teach Yrbk 1955:61-78

LINGELBACH, George D. See Sharrah, P. C.
Joint authors ——————— jt. auth.

Cross references ——————— **LINGUISTICS. See Language and languages**

LIP reading
Directory of teachers of lipreading. See issues of Volta review

LISTENING

Research

Auding. J. Caffrey. bibliog R Ed Res 25:121-38
Ap '55

Teaching

Have we overlooked listening? Sister Mary
Bibliography illustration ——— Kevin. bibliog il Cath Sch J 55:147-9 My '55

Mainhead ——————— **LITERACY. See Illiteracy**

LITERATURE

Curriculum

Popular arts and the humanities. N. E. Nel-
son. Col Engl 16:479-85 My '55

Subheads ——————— Philosophy

Galdós' conception of beauty, truth, and reality in art. N. J. Davison. bibliog f Hispania
38:52-4 Mr '55
Role of literature for young people today. E.
H. Cady. Engl J 44:268-73 My '55

Teaching

Bringing literature to life is fun for all. L.
Strong. Tex Outl 39:21+ My '55

Colleges and universities

Teaching of literature. B. White. English 10:
133-6 Spring '55

High schools

Teaching literature to our youth today. D. L.
Burton. Engl J 44:274-9 My '55

Fig. 6. Typical entries in the *Education Index.*   (*The H. W. Wilson Company.*)

article "Design Education in Sweden" can be found in *School Arts,* volume 54, on pages 17 to 20 of the June, 1955, issue.

If a novice researcher wants further information on how to use the *Education Index,* he will find that Alexander and Burke provide an excellent guide (1:106–122).   To locate periodical articles that were published before the *Education Index* was established in 1929, he can examine a number of other guides: The *Record of Current Educational Publications* compiled by the Office of Education covers the period from January, 1912, to March, 1932; indexes have also been compiled for the early NEA publications (1:231 and 10), and the *Ohio State University Periodical Index* "Ohio File" includes articles published between 1919 and 1929 and thereafter specializes in local and state journals.

Readers' Guide.   Since 1900, the *Readers' Guide to Periodical Literature* has served as a faithful servant to library patrons.   This semimonthly (monthly in July and August) subject and author index lists general interest articles in more than one hundred magazines, but rarely duplicates those that appear in the *Education Index.*   Prior to 1929, it is one of the best indexes to educational literature.

International and Early Indexes.   For technical and specialized articles concerning education prior to 1929, the *International Index to Periodicals* is the most helpful source.   This excellent guide to scholarly articles covers many more periodicals than the *Readers' Guide.*   It indexes articles concerning the social sciences, humanities, and subjects of general interest and until 1955 it covered some foreign and scientific periodicals.   It is published quarterly and cumulated periodically.   This index was called the *Readers' Guide Supplement* until 1920.   The first volume of the series, 1907–1915, carried the index back to supplement the last volume of the pioneer guide— *Poole's Index to Periodical Literature,* 1802–1881, which is the traditional source to consult for the nineteenth century.   Another guide to periodicals in the last century is the *Nineteenth Century Readers' Guide to Periodical Literature* which covers the 1890 to 1899 period.

Special Field Indexes.   Educators find that specialized indexes prepared for other fields are superior guides for locating articles on some subjects. They may, for example, have occasion to refer to such sources as: the *Agricultural Index, Applied Science and Technology Index, Art Index, Business Education Index, Catholic Periodical Index, Index to Religious Periodical Literature, Occupational Index,* or *Quarterly Cumulative Index Medicus.*   Most of these indexes are similar to the *Education Index* in format and publication.

Pamphlets.   Many beginning researchers experience difficulty in locating pamphlets because they are not aware of the services offered by the *Vertical File Index* (formerly, *Vertical File Service Catalog*).   Since 1932, this monthly, except August, publication has listed the more important pamphlets, bulletins, maps, and posters in all fields, alphabetically by subject, and has included a title index in each issue.   It gives descriptive notes, prices, and the addresses of publishers.   The *Education Index* also lists many pamphlets.   When searching for pamphlets, it is important to remember that they usually are available only a short time after publication and some are produced for advertising or propaganda purposes.

Periodicals not Available Locally. Since the local library cannot subscribe to all periodicals that are printed each year, an educator sometimes must locate a publication elsewhere. By turning to the guide books that reveal which libraries have what volumes of a given publication, he usually can solve his problem. The old *Union List of Serials in Libraries of the United States and Canada* and its two supplements, 1941–1943 and 1944–1949, list alphabetically by title the publications held in over six hundred libraries. The publication of this work was terminated in 1949.

As a continuing supplement to the *Union List of Serials,* the Library of Congress publishes a guide which is now known as *New Serials Titles* (see Figure 7). This work lists the new serials received by the Library of

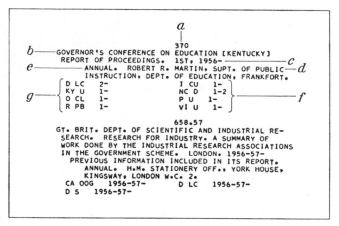

Fig. 7. Typical entries in the *New Serial Titles.* (*a*) Dewey decimal classification; (*b*) serial title; (*c*) initial publication date; (*d*) issuing body and place of publication; (*e*) frequency of publication; (*f*) library's holdings (volumes); (*g*) participating libraries, coded, i.e., D LC is the Library of Congress. A key on the inside cover of the work interprets the symbols used. (*Library of Congress.*)

Congress and many participating libraries. It is published monthly and is cumulated periodically. In this guide, titles are listed alphabetically, but a related monthly, noncumulative publication, *New Serial Titles—Classed Subject Arrangement,* contains the same entries arranged by the Dewey Decimal Classification numbers which reflect the subject contents of the serials. A key to the code used in the entries makes it possible to interpret what libraries have a magazine and whether they loan serials or furnish photocopies and microfilms.

Educators may find the *Union List of Technical Periodicals* helpful. It lists publications in two hundred libraries that are concerned with science and its application in various fields. The fourth edition is now being compiled. If a researcher wants to purchase back issues of a magazine for his private library, he can try the publisher, the Periodical Clearing House of the H. W. Wilson Company, or dealers who specialize in such service.

Newspapers. Current newspapers provide up-to-date information on speeches, reports, conferences, new developments, personalities, and a host of other topics. Old newspapers, which preserve a record of past events and the evolution of movements and ideas, are particularly useful in historical inquiries. The larger metropolitan Sunday editions, such as the *New York Times* and *New York Herald Tribune,* have special sections devoted to weekly news reviews and to educational affairs. Current events and educational news are also reported in periodicals, such as *Time, Newsweek, Life, Current History, Living Age,* and *Foreign Affairs.* The loose-leaf encyclopedia of current events, *Facts on File,* which is usually found in the reference room of a library, gives a weekly digest of world news in a few pages. Some general periodicals and many educational journals also have special sections devoted to news digest of educational events.

To locate articles in a newspaper, a reader can refer to the *New York Times Index,* a monthly publication with annual cumulations (see Figure 8). Since 1913, it has classified all important items in the paper alphabetically by subjects, personalities, and organizations. Since most news events of wide public interest are published immediately, the *New York Times Index* gives a reader clues concerning the dates when a particular item may have appeared in other newspapers.

Lists of early American newspapers and the location of existing files are found in Clarence S. Brigham's *History and Bibliography of American Newspapers, 1690-1820,* and Winifred Gregory's *American Newspapers, 1821-1936.* The *New York Daily Tribune Index,* 1875-1906, is useful for the dates it covers. Some libraries, state historical associations, and universities prepare lists of the newspapers and existing files in their local areas. Two English indexes that cover a span of many years are the *London Times Official Index,* 1906—, and *Palmer's Index to the Times Newspaper* (London), 1790—. Ayer's *Directory of Newspapers and Periodicals* has listed sectional or local American newspapers since 1880.

Directories to Periodicals and Newspapers. Sometimes a researcher has to find what publications are available in a particular field or geographical area. To proceed with some phases of his work, he may need the name, address, price, circulation figures, or date of origin of a periodical. To evaluate a magazine or newspaper, he may want to know the name of the publisher or editor, the political bias of a publication, or where it is indexed. By consulting one or more of the following directories, he can usually find answers to such questions.

America's Education Press: A Classified List of Educational Periodicals Issued in the United States of America is published on odd numbered years in the yearbook of the Educational Press Association of America. This list classifies periodicals under a number of educational subject headings and in-

Fig. 8. Typical entries in *The New York Times Index.* (*a*) Heading: Education; subhead Colleges, subhead United States, paragraph on finances, September, 28; (*c*) cross references; see Council for Financial Aid to Education under main heading Colleges, subhead United States, paragraph on finances, September, 28; (*b*) cross references: suggests other headings under which to look for information; (*d*) entry: (summary of story) i.e., "Population rise poses . . ."; (*e*) date, page, column: Sept. 21, page 27, column 1. (*The New York Times.*)

dexes them alphabetically by title.   The twenty-sixth yearbook differs from earlier works in that it was published jointly with UNESCO and carries international as well as domestic educational periodicals.   Later editions may or may not include the international list.   *Ulrich's Periodicals Directory* covers a list of about sixteen thousand foreign and domestic periodicals in all fields.   N. W. Ayer's annual *Directory of Newspapers and Periodicals, 1880—,* gives an extensive coverage for newspapers and periodicals of all kinds.   It contains several lists, such as agricultural; college; Negro; religious; and trade, technical, and class publications.   The main catalog list of over one thousand pages is arranged geographically, first by state, and then by city or town of publication.

Microfilms and Audio-Visual Aids.   Through the magic of microfilm the modern researcher can examine copies of the Bay Psalm Book[3] of 1640, a colonial or modern newspaper, an 1898 educational periodical, rare books in foreign libraries, or a 1961 doctoral dissertation.   The local library may own some microfilms and may help patrons obtain copies from other institutions or agencies.

A few guides have been published to help locate microfilms.   *Newspapers on Microfilm,* Library of Congress, is a source for many foreign and domestic newspapers.   Since 1942, the *Union List of Microfilms* and its later editions and supplements has listed thousands of periodicals and other titles reported by many institutions in the United States and Canada.   Since 1953, it has limited coverage to serials other than newspapers.   This publication is provided by the Philadelphia Bibliographical Center and Union Library Catalogue.   Any student engaged in research will have occasion to refer to *Dissertation Abstracts* (formerly *Microfilm Abstracts,* 1938–1952), which is put out by the University Microfilms, Ann Arbor, Michigan.

Articles concerning audio-visual aids have multiplied rapidly in recent decades.   The *Education Index* lists many articles.   In addition, some special reference tools provide information in this field.   The H. W. Wilson Company's *Filmstrip Guide* lists about six thousand recent filmstrips and its *Educational Film Guide* lists more than eleven thousand current 16 mm. films with complete bibliographical notes and brief descriptions of them.   Educators Progress Service, Randolph, Wisconsin, puts out *Educators Guide to Free Films; Educators Guide to Free Tapes, Scripts, and Transcriptions;* and *Educators Guide to Free Slide Films.*   The National Union Catalog, Library of Congress, now has two parts in special subject areas available: *Motion Pictures and Filmstrips* and *Music and Phonorecords.*   An annual *Blue Book of Audio-Visual Materials,* presents a list of films, filmstrips, and recordings.   It was previously issued separately, but since 1955 it has been a special issue of *Educational Screen.*

[3] The correct title is *The Whole Book of Psalms Faithfully Translated into English Metre.*

EDUCATIONAL RESEARCH

An educator cannot successfully engage in research unless he becomes adept at locating theses, dissertations, and the reports of studies that embody the bulk of the work done in his field. One can begin searching for this literature in the previously discussed *Education Index, Encyclopedia of Educational Research,* and *Bibliographies and Summaries in Education to July, 1935.* As soon as possible, one should form the habit of examining the following sources regularly.

Review and Abstracting Journals. An educator is usually well acquainted with the general periodicals in his field, but he may need to become

---

92.   CATTELL, RAYMOND B., & COAN, RICHARD W. (Univer. of Illinois, Urbana, Ill.) **Personality factors in middle childhood as revealed in parents' ratings.** Child Develpm., 1957, **28**, 439-458.   A sample of 68 girls and 77 boys, ranging from 6 years, 3 months, to 7 years, 4 months, was rated, each child on 55 forms of behavior, chosen to cover the personality sphere and to permit comparisons with personality structure found in ratings for adults, older children, and younger children in coordinated researches. The ratings were made by the children's parents, and comparisons are to be made with studies on the same children using teachers' ratings. A simple structure factor analysis yielded 16 dimensions, most of which could be confidently identified with patterns already known in adults or older children, though modification of expression with age could also be traced. The 16 source trait patterns were: A, Cyclothymia-vs.-schizothymia; B, General intelligence; C, Ego strength; E, Dominance; F, Surgency; G, Superego strength; H, Parmia; I, Premsia; K, Comention; O, Guilt proneness; M, Autia; Q_4, Ergic tension; and four factors connected with situation: insecurity from physical handicap, oldest child, female child, and only child patterns. It is suggested that research now be concentrated on change of form of these basic personality factors with age, and that measures of these factors be set up as a basis for quantitative studies of child development. —Authors' Abstract.

Fig. 9.   Typical entries in *Child Development Abstracts and Bibliography.*

---

more familiar with review and abstracting journals.   These journals give brief summaries of research studies reported in a wide variety of periodicals; hence, they are great timesavers.   They enable one to keep abreast of the work being done in his own field and also in related fields.

Review journals vary in content.   Some give brief summaries of individual studies and others go into greater detail (see Figure 9).   Some summarize all the work being done in an area rather than individual studies; in addition, they may trace trends, discuss new techniques, point out gaps in research, and present bibliographies.   Abstracts of research reports naturally lag considerably behind the original publication of the studies.

The *Review of Educational Research* gives an educator an excellent overview of the work that has been done in the field and helps him keep up with recent developments. In this publication, which has been issued five times a year since 1931, one can find reviews of the following eleven subdivisions of education: Administration; Curriculum; Educational Measurement; Educational Psychology; Educational Sociology; Guidance and Counseling; Mental and Physical Development; Language Arts, Fine Arts, Natural Sciences, and Mathematics; Research Methods; Special Programs; and Teacher Personnel.

Each of these eleven subdivisions is reviewed about every three years. Curriculum, for example, was reviewed in I:1 (January, 1931); IV:2 (April, 1934); VII:2 (April, 1937); XII:3 (June, 1942); XV:3 (June, 1945); XVIII:3 (June, 1948); XXI:3 (June, 1951); XXIV:3 (June, 1954); XXVI:2 (April, 1956); XXVII:3 (June, 1957); and XXX:3 (June, 1960). The back page of the *Review of Educational Research* presents a similar list of the issues that have reviewed each of the other subdivisions in the series. This list provides a researcher with an index to the summaries of research that has been done in his special field of interest since 1931. The extensive bibliographies in each issue give him additional leads to literature in the field.

Perhaps there is no better way to become acquainted with research techniques and progress than by reading several periodicals devoted primarily to abstracts and reviews. In addition to the *Review of Educational Research,* a student may examine some of the following: *Annual Review of Psychology,* 1950——; *Child Development Abstracts and Bibliography,* 1927——; *Dissertation Abstracts,* 1952——; *Education Abstracts* (UNESCO publication, title varies), 1949——; *Psychological Abstracts,* 1927——; *Psychological Bulletin,* 1904——; *Sociological Abstracts,* 1952——; *Biological Abstracts,* 1926——; *Chemical Abstracts,* 1907——; *Historical Abstracts,* 1775–1945, 1955——; *Mathematical Reviews,* 1940——; and *Nutrition Abstracts and Reviews,* 1931——.

Many other professional periodicals and yearbooks include some reviews of research progress, abstracts of studies, lists of dissertations, statistical information, and scholarly discussions of educational problems in one or all of their issues. Some of the sources that an educator may profitably consult are:

Educational Research

Journal of Educational Research, NEA Research Bulletin, Educational Research Bulletin, Educational and Psychological Measurement, Journal of Experimental Education, Mental Measurements Yearbook, Research Quarterly, Journal of Research in Music Education, and *Speech Monographs.*

Psychology

Journal of Educational Psychology, Journal of Psychology, Journal of Social Psychology, and *Journal of Applied Psychology.*

Sociology

Journal of Educational Sociology, American Journal of Sociology, American Sociological Review, and Social Forces.

General and Specific Fields

Harvard Educational Review, Educational Record, School Review, Educational Leadership, Phi Delta Kappan, Teachers College Record, Religious Education, Catholic Education Review, Journal of Negro Education, Journal of Home Economics, Nation's Schools, National Business Education Quarterly, Elementary School Journal, Vocational Guidance Quarterly, School and Society, and Journal of Teacher Education.

Yearbooks and Publications of Educational Associations

Some of the more important ones are sponsored by the American Council on Education, National Society for the Study of Education, Fund for the Advancement of Education, UNESCO, The NEA Educational Policies Commission, and various NEA organizations, such as the American Association of School Administrators and Association for Supervision and Curriculum Development.

Dissertations and Theses.   Theses and dissertations, which embody the bulk of present-day educational research, are usually housed by the institutions that award the authors their advanced degrees. Sometimes these studies are published in whole or in part in educational journals. Postgraduate studies are often released through research journals, bulletins, or monographs. It is possible to get some dissertations or microfilm copies of them from the Office of Education and through interlibrary loans. To locate theses and dissertations, a researcher can consult the sources discussed in the preceding paragraphs and the following specialized guides:

General Guides.   Doctoral dissertations in all fields, including education, can be found in sources compiled by various agencies. For the period of 1912 through 1938, the Library of Congress provided the annual *List of American Doctoral Dissertations* for published studies. From 1933–1934 through 1954–1955, the Association of Research Libraries sponsored the annual *Doctoral Dissertions Accepted by American Universities.* This service was continued by the *Index to American Doctoral Dissertations,* 1956—, which is published as an additional issue of *Dissertation Abstracts.*

The *Index to American Doctoral Dissertations* gives a comprehensive list of the dissertations from a number of universities. Many of these studies are summarized in the monthly, *Dissertation Abstracts.* By reading these abstracts, a researcher can often glean enough information to satisfy his needs. Moreover, in this one source, he can quickly scan not only education theses but also those from related fields, such as sociology, psychology, anthropology, economics, and political science. If he wants to read a complete study, he can order a microfilm copy for a small fee by using the code symbol given in the abstract. In addition to these sources, a researcher can consult various graduate schools' lists and abstracts of their students' dissertations. A source for such lists is the *Guide to Bibliographies of Theses—United States and Canada,* 1940, by T. R. Palfrey and H. E. Coleman.

Educational Guides. Lists of studies that are devoted exclusively to educational research are found in *Ten Years of Educational Research, 1918–1927* by Walter S. Monroe. Similar lists were compiled annually by the Office of Education from 1926 to 1940 under the title, *Bibliography of Research Studies in Education.* Since 1941, this work has been continued by Phi Delta Kappa under the title, *Research Studies in Education.* This series classifies studies by subject fields and now includes dissertations under way as well as those that have been completed. Prior to 1953, educational dissertations under way were published in the January *Journal of Educational Research,* 1931–1946, and in the spring issues of *Phi Delta Kappan,* 1947–1952. Master's theses for many institutions are listed in the annual *Master's Theses in Education,* 1951—, now edited by H. M. Silvey.

Special Field Guides. Most of the departments of the NEA and many educational societies annually or occasionally publish lists of research studies in progress or completed. Dr. T. K. Cureton, for example, compiled the "Doctorate Theses Reported by Graduate Departments of Health, Physical Education, and Recreation, 1930–46," for the Research Quarterly, March, 1949, and later he prepared a list for master's theses. Walter C. Eells prepared *American Dissertations on Foreign Education* (1884–1958) for the NEA Committee on International Relations. *Research in Industrial Education, 1930–1955,* is available in Bulletin 264, Vocational Division, U.S. Department of Health, Education, and Welfare. The National Art Education Association compiled *Research in Art Education,* 1956. Educators can also locate pertinent special field studies in the *Journal of Research in Music Education, Speech Monographs, Religious Education, Journal of Home Economics,* and many other professional journals.

Values of Searching the Literature. Mastering the multiplicity of guides to the literature that are presented in this chapter may seem a time-consuming task. But, if an educator remains ignorant of these professional tools and aimlessly attempts to attack the ever-expanding volume of literature, he will face insurmountable obstacles. Superficially skimming a few sources and dismissing the work as an unimportant research routine will also lead to failure. Reviewing the literature with a high level of professional skill is demanding work, but it is a rewarding experience. It provides one not only with the inspiration for undertaking a study, but also with the help needed to lay a sound foundation for his entire investigation.

Exploring the literature enriches and excites the intellect of the educator. From the hours spent in the library, one learns what others have already discovered in his field, notices gaps in knowledge and contradictory findings, and identifies needed research. Studying the work of other investigators acquaints one with methods of attack, facts, concepts, theories, and bibliographies that may prove useful in his own investigations. Examining the strengths and weaknesses of many research reports prevents him from plunging into some of the procedural pitfalls that have plagued his predecessors. He learns, for example, to avoid duplicating needlessly the work done by others and to refrain from utilizing techniques that have proved unsatisfactory. Because a thorough and critical review of the literature can help one increase the productivity and quality of his work, a researcher should make every effort to become skilled in the art.

BIBLIOGRAPHY

1. Alexander, Carter, and Arvid J. Burke, *How to Locate Educational Information and Data,* 4th ed.   New York: Bureau of Publications, Teachers College, Columbia University, 1958.

2. Barton, Mary N., *Reference Books: A Brief Guide for Students and Other Users of the Library,* 4th ed.   Baltimore: Enoch Pratt Free Library, 1959.

3. Barzun, Jacques, and Henry F. Graff, *The Modern Researcher.*   New York: Harcourt, Brace & World, Inc., 1957, chap. 4.

4. Cordasco, Franesco, and Elliott S. M. Gatner, *Research and Report Writing.* New York: Barnes & Noble, Inc., 1955.

5. Good, Carter V., and Douglas E. Scates, *Methods of Research.*   New York: Appleton-Century-Crofts, Inc., 1954, chap. 3.

6. Goode, William J., and Paul K. Hatt, *Methods in Social Research.*   New York: McGraw-Hill Book Company, Inc., 1952, chap. 9.

7. Larson, Leonard A., Morey R. Fields, and Milton A. Gabrielsen, *Problems in Health, Physical and Recreation Education.*   Englewood Cliffs, N.J.: Prentice-Hall, Inc., 1953, chap. 7.

8. Seeger, Ruth E., *Using Library Resources in Educational Research.*   Columbus: Bureau of Educational Research, Ohio State University, 1957.

9. Shores, Louis, *Basic Reference Sources: An Introduction to Material and Methods.*   Chicago: American Library Association, 1954.

10. Winchell, Constance M., *Guide to Reference Books,* 7th ed.   Chicago: American Library Association, 1951.

11. Winchell, Constance M., and O. A. Johnson, *Guide to Reference Books,* 7th ed. Supplement, 1950–1952.   Second Supplement, 1953–1955.   Chicago: American Library Association, 1954–1956.

12. Winchell, Constance M., John N. Waddell, and Eleanor Buist, *Guide to Reference Books,* 7th ed.   Third Supplement, 1956–1958.   Chicago: American Library Association, 1958.

CHAPTER 6

Library Skills for Problem Solving

The number of reading hours and the amount of notes logged by a researcher do not provide a reliable measuring stick of his problem-solving productivity. Time and motion studies of his work may reveal an enormous waste of effort. Moreover, laboring forever at this low level of efficiency may be his fate if he fails to master the library searching, reading, and note-taking techniques needed for carrying out an investigation.

IMPROVING LIBRARY SEARCHING

To conduct any study, you must be able to locate the best available sources pertaining to a problem and be able to extract the essential information from them. The previous chapter pointed out that this ability cannot be acquired until you are thoroughly familiar with the various library resources and services and the most efficient procedures for using them. Skill is not developed, of course, merely by becoming informed about sources; mastery comes from practicing techniques until they become automatic. The following discussion suggests some worthwhile searching habits for you to form.

Knowing the Library and Its Regulations. Before using a new library, familiarize yourself with its layout, facilities, services, and regulations. First, inquire whether there is printed material available to guide you on an orientation tour, and then proceed as follows:

1. Locate the card catalog, check how it is organized, and find out whether the library classifies books according to the Dewey or Library of Congress system.

2. Having noted the call number symbols under which most books in your field fall, locate them in the stacks. Browse through the shelves, and familiarize yourself with the nature and number of books available for various areas in your field.

3. As you proceed on the tour, examine the type and placement of materials in the reference, periodical, reserve book, rare book, and special collec-

tion rooms, and discover where most of the government and educational publications are kept.

4. Locate the microtext readers, picture files, recording library, coin typewriters, and other services.

5. To avoid future difficulties and disappointments, get a copy of the hours and regulations observed in various sections of the library, and, thereafter, plan your work to conform with them.

6. To obtain references as quickly as possible, become thoroughly acquainted with the procedures for withdrawing books for overnight or extended use; how to reserve a book that is now in circulation; and how to obtain back issues of periodicals, interlibrary loans, microfilms, records, or pictures.

Constructing a Guide to the Literature. The acquisition of a personal library and the construction of tailor-made guides to educational source materials can ease your investigative labors. If you discriminatingly select items and organize them, in orderly fashion, in private files and on book shelves, you will have a reliable corps of research assistants at your command. By turning to them, many questions that might cause frustrating delays and repeated trips to the library can be quickly answered. To increase the efficiency of your work in the years to come, immediately begin to obtain and construct some of the following guides:

1. Compile a personal who's who—include the names of leaders in your field and note their positions, publications, professional training, special interests, biases, and standing in the professional world.

2. Gradually collect information on research agencies and the chief collectors of statistics; note the nature and quality of their staffs, work, and facilities; the frequency of their publications and the issuing agencies; and the headings under which indexes and the card catalog list their publications.

3. Down through the years compile a list of libraries, museums, and individuals that have special collections in your field.

4. Obtain copies of the best bibliographies for your files; list the titles, nature, and location of others; and note which periodicals regularly, or occasionally, print such lists and the dates of the issues in which they appear.

5. In a card file or notebook keep a list of the best reference books, indexes, handbooks, historical studies, and legal references in your area of specialization.

6. In a similar manner, list the publishers and manufacturers who specialize in books and equipment you may need.

7. After carefully evaluating the reference books, textbooks, periodicals, and pamphlets in the field, purchase the more important ones for your personal library. If you intend to make research a life work, collect the pertinent back issues of outstanding professional periodicals that relate to your work.

8. To have finger-tip information about leading periodicals, organizations, and government agencies serving the field, keep a record of their names and special services.   In addition, list the titles, addresses, and procedures to use when requesting information from them.   Note also which periodical indexes cover their publications and under what headings.

9. Since the official names of periodicals, organizations, and government agencies frequently change, keep a record of the previous names and dates for each.   This information is often vitally important.   When writing an article for publication, for example, you do not want to use the present name of an organization when referring to the work it did under another name. Nor do you want to waste time futilely searching for a 1920 publication under its current name, if that title did not come into existence until 1960. When reading, you do not want to become confused because the same organization has had three different names during various stages of its development.

Developing Skill in Heading Searching.   Searching for references in a card catalog or index can be an extremely discouraging experience or an exciting adventure.   Is it arduous labor for you to perform the mental gymnastics required to recall various topical headings under which materials may be located?   If you cannot find a reference listed under the heading Grading, for example, do you give up in disgust or begin to look under topics, such as evaluation, testing, marking systems, student achievement, or report cards?   Does associational poverty completely paralyze your progress? If so, you can overcome this handicap by taking some of the following steps:

1. To familiarize yourself with typical headings used in the field, study the indexes of textbooks, card catalogs, *Education Index, Encyclopedia of Educational Research, Review of Educational Research,* and some abstracting journals.

2. When searching for references on a particular topic, write or mentally list synonymous titles or larger area classifications under which the items may appear, e.g., an Office of Education publication may be indexed under the United States or Department of Health, Education, and Welfare; aptitude tests under mental measurements; and a speech educational association under NEA, teachers, or education.

3. By keeping notes concerning commonly experienced classification difficulties, you can eliminate some reoccurring problems.   You may note, for example, that government publications are usually indexed under the name of the issuing agency and not the name of the author; older indexes are more apt to use the term, "teacher training," and the more recent ones "teacher education."   The *Education Index* does not cover certain periodicals in which you are particularly interested; book reviews and poems are listed only under those headings in the above index.

4. Guide books can help you find likely headings.   Near the card catalog,

some libraries keep a copy of *Subject Headings Used in the Dictionary Catalogs of the Library of Congress,* Marguerite V. Quattlebaum, editor. The larger cumulations of the *Education Index* give promising headings for the various topics covered. For example, in one two-year cumulative issue under the topic "Tests and Scales" appears the caption "See also" which is followed by approximately 150 cross references. Extensive lists of headings for education are presented by L. Belle Voegelein in *List of Educational Subject Headings,* 1928 and Clyde Pettus in *Subject Headings in Education: A Systematic List for Use in a Dictionary Catalog,* 1938. A number of professional leaders have also written guides for the literature in their special fields. The Bookwalters, for example, have compiled a suggestive list of headings for materials in the areas of health, physical education, and recreation (2:32–34).

5. Developing a good "date sense" also helps a researcher locate materials. By recalling the years in which a subject was of national interest, you usually can locate more references than by merely looking in current sources or searching blindly in older ones. Articles on teacher shortages, for example, usually appear during inflationary periods, academic freedom was an issue during the era of intensive communistic investigations, and science education articles peppered periodicals after the Russians launched the Sputnik.

6. Because vocabulary style changes occur in educational terminology, it is important for a researcher to know the older as well as the modern terms used in headings. Topics that are now classified under "school health services" probably would have appeared under "health inspection" earlier in the century; "school desegregation" under "civil rights" or "negro"; and "exceptional children" topics under "handicapped," "blind," "deaf," "hard of hearing," "crippled," "mentally retarded," "speech defective," or "gifted children."

Planning Library Work Procedures. Frittering away precious time on random reading and searching in the library should be avoided. This can be done if you outline work and plan how to accomplish each task most efficiently before going to the library.

1. After constructing a library worklist, keep revising it until the statements pinpoint the precise information to be located. If your note reads "get some information on teachers' salaries," probe further, asking: What do I want to find out about salaries? How are salary schedules constructed? Do I want up-to-date, last year, or last century data? Am I interested in local, state, national, or international salary information? Determining the specific type and amount of data required for your purpose will narrow the search for references, and, hence, will hasten the location of pertinent materials.

2. After stating each question to be answered as concretely as possible, jot

down the best sources to consult and some alternative references to consider if the first choices are unavailable or do not produce answers. Also mull over appropriate headings to look under for each topic.

3. To facilitate work at the library, group your questions in accordance with (1) areas in the library where answers will be found, and (2) accessibility of the references, i.e., reserve books in great demand, overnight books, and two-week loan books. After glancing at the groups, schedule the most logical order to follow in pursuing the work.

4. Check the schedule of library hours, note the peak patronage periods, and then plan to study when there is the least noise and competition for resources and services.

Acquiring Library Work Skills. What woes an inexperienced scholar can encounter in the library! When entering the building, you may be fired with enthusiasm about a topic. But after floundering from one section of the library to the other you may soon become mired in unpleasant bogs that dampen your spirits. The books you need are not available! The reserve book room is closed! A call slip is returned because some "insignificant item of information" is lacking! When the books eventually arrive, there is not enough time left to read them! Tensions mount and fatigue sets in as obstacles keep arising to impede progress. But many of these irritating delays may be avoided if you observe the following practices:

1. Whenever possible arrange to spend a block of time in the library that is sufficient to accomplish a specific task. When little time is available clear up questions that can be answered quickly in references that are readily accessible. The value of budgeting time and work units carefully cannot be overemphasized. The practice not only increases work productivity, but also gives one a pleasant feeling of satisfactory accomplishment at each library session which heightens one's interest and stimulates further intellectual effort.

2. Do your work in reserved books first or when they are in least demand and then move on to more accessible materials.

3. By reading all the required references in one part of the library before searching elsewhere, you can avoid retracing your steps and wearily waiting for materials.

4. After locating the title of a promising reference, copy down *all* information necessary to obtain it. Before closing the periodical index or card catalog, carefully *recheck* and *rectify* any errors or omissions. Such precautions pay dividends! Nothing is more annoying than a prolonged wait at the circulation desk that is rewarded by the return of the call slip rather than the desired publication. If you fail to copy down the volume number of a periodical, the title of a yearbook, the name of the government issuing agency, or spell the author's name **Roberts** instead of Robbins, you will experience many such **disappointments**.

5. Anticipate delays and the possibility that some source materials will not be available by making out call slips for all or most of the books needed in one session.   While waiting to receive the books, have a list of other work to do—perhaps checking items in the card catalog, index, encyclopedia, and dictionary or reviewing notes and references.

6. Before sending for an interlibrary loan or arranging to reserve a micro-text reader, ascertain whether you will have sufficient free time to use them profitably when they are available.

IMPROVING READING

Reading efficiency and a mastery of the evaluative techniques necessary for screening source materials are prime requisites for research work.   When locating and analyzing research problems, when reviewing the literature relating to a problem, when selecting investigative procedures, you have to devote many hours to reading.   Merely to keep abreast of the activities in education, you must scan the titles of hundreds of books and articles that appear each year, decide which ones can be ignored, which should be skimmed, and which should be read critically.   Since a great proportion of your time will be spent examining printed pages, it is only prudent to become proficient in the art of reading.   By observing the following practices, you can avoid committing some serious reading sins.

Screening Reading Materials.   Even before you see a reference, begin to evaluate its worth.   Prior to writing out a call slip for a book or periodical, squeeze every useful item of information about it that you can from the card catalog, or a periodical index, bibliography, or book review.   Check whether the reference includes maps, tables, illustrations, or a bibliography that will prove helpful.   If the date of the reference indicates that it is too old or too recent for your purpose; the number of pages reveals that the discussion is too comprehensive or too limited to serve your needs; the title or subtitle suggests that the reference covers the social aspects of the subject rather than the political information you want, do not write out a call slip for it.   If the periodical, publisher, or author does not have a reputation for maintaining high scholarly standards, you may also refrain from giving the reference further consideration.

After selecting the most promising materials relating to a problem, do not immediately engage in a cover-to-cover, word-at-a-time perusal of the references.   If you customarily do this, jar yourself out of this unprofitable habit!   It is a luxury no researcher can afford.   Before you read a book or an article always leaf through the pages to obtain a critical bird's-eye view of its contents.   Note the scope, purpose, bias, and distinctive features of the reference as you skim through the preface, foreword, and introduction and examine the table of contents, bibliography, figures, and appendix.   If the reference appears to present the type of information you are seeking, reexamine the table of contents and the index to locate the particular sections that will be useful to you. Carefully read the topical headlines, lead sentences, and summary paragraphs on these pages. As you read, jot down the number of the pages or lines that have sufficient significant passages to warrant a more detailed analysis at a later date.

Some novice researchers have a guilt complex about surveying and skimming source materials. To them, it is a careless work habit, if not a form of cheating. They are convinced that a complete, conscientious reading of all references is essential in research. Careful reading and analysis is required, but purposelessly plodding through every page in a book is a wasteful practice. A researcher must confine his attention to pertinent materials. A quick survey of a reference will enable you to locate the most important information and to eliminate much useless reading. Moreover, it will provide you with a key for interpreting the discussion. Page-by-page reading may leave you in a confused maze of details. If you can relate isolated passages to the structural design of the whole book, it is easier to grasp their meanings.

Mastering Reference Utilization Guides. Before using a reference, investigate whether the author or publisher has included any mechanical aids or information that will facilitate reading. Seek answers to several questions: Is the reference organized alphabetically, chronologically, or topically? Are summary paragraphs provided at the end of the chapter? Is there a table of contents and a subject or author index to aid in the speedy location of information? Are there any keys, codes, statements of explanation, pages of directions, or other conventions that will help you interpret abbreviations, symbols, and other data in the reference? Are these guides located on the inside covers, in the introductory pages, at the end of chapters, in the appendixes, or immediately after the items mentioned in the work? Learning to locate and utilize these guides is necessary if you want to benefit from the full potential of the printed resource.

Investigating the Scope of the References. How discouraging it is to spend minutes or hours examining a reference before you discover that the desired information is purposely excluded from the work! To avoid such unfortunate errors, carefully check each reference. Ask pertinent questions to ascertain the extent of the service and information it provides. Do the authors or editors definitely state the delimitations of the reference in the subtitle, preface, introduction, or elsewhere? (For example, a book or periodical may state that it lists printed but not unpublished dissertations, doctoral but not master's studies, American but not foreign research reports.) Does the publisher indicate whether the periodical is indexed in each issue, in an annual issue, or in a well-known periodical index? Does a periodical cover certain features monthly, in particular annual issues, or at any other stated interval? Does a particular cumulation of the periodical index cover the years in which the desired data will appear? Is the publication issued monthly, annually, biennially, or decennially? Are there any supplements that bring a reference up to date? Knowing the scope of the services and information that various resources offer saves precious time and energy when you are trying to locate answers to questions.

Reading Selectively. Learning to read only those materials that are pertinent to one's purposes and in proportion to one's needs is an art the novice must master. Reading an entire chapter or book to find a fact that can be located quickly in an encyclopedia, almanac, or dictionary cannot be justified. You do not have to obtain or read an entire biography on Horace Mann to find out where he was born. Conversely, when making a definitive study of a problem, you cannot confine the investigation to elementary textbooks and secondary source materials. Whenever possible, it pays to consult primary sources, for reading about a publication is never as satisfactory as reading the work itself. A translation or a summary of a book may satisfy one's needs in some instances, but the possibility of errors and misinterpretations in secondary sources always exists. Moreover, the literary taste and tang of the original is rarely retained in the rehashed version.

You may find it helpful to read simple explanations of topics before tackling more comprehensive discussions. To explore a new or difficult topic, procure an encyclopedia or elementary textbook that gives a brief overview of it. If possible, read several textbooks, for each one will explain some things more thoroughly or clearly than the others. After acquiring some background knowledges in the field, you can select more advanced references; elementary textbooks usually will direct you to the better sources.

When you have a problem to investigate, do not immediately collect and exhaustively examine every publication the library has on the subject. Rather check recent bibliographies and from them select four or five key references that give a well-rounded overview of the subject. Skim through these books to get some idea of the large natural divisions of the problem. Utilize this information to construct a crude outline for your investigation and then compile a working bibliography that will give a well-balanced coverage for each topic. If you fail to get a picture of the whole problem before studying special aspects of it, you may get bogged down in masses of detail. You may read volumes on some phases of a subject and completely ignore other equally important ones. Close scrutiny of detail after detail while reading is of little value if the facts are not mentally fitted into the mosaic of the total problem picture.

Learning to Concentrate. Before beginning to study, select a place and time to read that invites the fewest interruptions and distractions. Approach your work with eager anticipation and give concentrated attention to the specific problem at hand. If getting a brief overview of a book is the objective, devote yourself exclusively to skimming its contents—strictly refrain from reading paragraphs and chapters. When you read a chapter through for the first time, concentrate on grasping the author's ideas—do not stop to take detailed notes or get sidetracked in any way. A researcher cannot fragmentize his attention and read intelligently. If you attempt to read, take notes, check questionable points, and look up every reference the author mentions during the one hour available for work in the library, you will become irritated with the slowness of your progress and get a confused concept of the author's ideas. You cannot do everything at once, concentrate on one task at a time.

Checking Comprehension. An intelligent reader makes certain that he is getting the exact meaning that the author is trying to convey. Since unfamiliar terminology can make it impossible to follow or understand an author's discussion, you may find it helpful to have a set of vocabulary cards or notes at hand when reading new and difficult materials. As soon as you become confused, begin to construct these cards or lists. On them, place not only the definitions of the key terms in the reference, but also the particular sense in which the author uses certain common terms.

A good reader like a good driver judges his speed in accordance with the situations he meets. You can skim some materials, but must analyze other passages with great care. Whenever you fail to grasp the meaning of a paragraph, immediately try to locate the difficulty: Is it vocabulary? Did you fail to spot a key transitional sentence or word, the topic sentence, or the author's signal that something was to follow? Did you fail to relate the material to the topic headline or the over-all chapter organization? Did the author subsequently modify a definition or statement that he made earlier in the work? Accurately assimilating the author's ideas is vital in investigative work.

Reading Critically. Mechanically accepting the words on a printed page is a dangerous practice. Reference materials vary in reliability; consequently, you must test them. As you read, critically evaluate the merit of each fact, sentence, and argument. Keep asking questions: What does this information contribute to my problem needs?   Is this statement true? Does this author agree with other authorities? Did he borrow this idea from someone else? Does this statement contradict what he wrote earlier? Does he use this term in the same sense that Dewey did? From what source did he obtain these statistics? How were they derived? Has he arrived at this conclusion by a sound reasoning process? Do the statements that he presents as supporting evidence justify his conclusions? The more probing and pointed these questions are, the more productive your reading sessions will be. Critical analysis rather than passive absorption is required when reading for research purposes.

Developing Sound Study and Health Habits. Chronic fatigue, frequent colds, and other health problems cut down tremendously on your working efficiency. Reading without needed glasses, in insufficient light, and when extremely tired is unproductive. Excessive, unselective reading and note taking, making more professional and social commitments than you can reasonably meet, and loafing until it becomes necessary to plunge into exhaustive work orgies drain physical reserves and impede an investigation. To achieve success in research, you must schedule sensible working hours; establish timesaving routines; get adequate food, rest, relaxation, and medical attention; and change activities to refresh and relax your mind and body. These practices will keep you in tiptop physical condition for intensive intellectual effort.

IMPROVING NOTE TAKING

Note taking like reading is not an end in itself, but a means of furthering the whole investigative process. Note taking is a servant, not a master; a stimulus to thought, not mere copy work. When done properly, it keeps you mentally alert and makes you actively engaged in making comparisons, noting discrepancies, seeing relationships, analyzing arguments, and evaluating data. Good notes enable you to review and reconsider ideas encountered months previously in light of those read recently.

Critical note taking is an exciting, challenging experience; passive note taking is a monotonous, unproductive drudgery. A nonselective, unsystematic method of recording notes usually piles up tangled masses of data that are a greater obstacle than an aid to the solution of a problem. A good note-taking system preserves the most significant ideas in a form that permits you to shift, compare, group, and order items. Pertinent, precise, and flexible notes are easier to organize and synthesize into original thought patterns than continuous pages of rambling, jumbled information. Any note-taking system that successfully serves your needs is acceptable, but the following well-tested bibliographical and subject note procedures are worthy of consideration.

Bibliographical Notes. Bibliographical notes are made for several purposes: (1) to have a correct copy of the complete bibliographical information available for each book, magazine article, newspaper item, or other reference that may contribute to an investigation; (2) to be able to relocate a reference quickly in the local library; (3) to preserve a brief record of the general nature and value of a reference; and (4) to have the information necessary for constructing a formal bibliography.

Information on Bibliographical Notes. A bibliographical note carries all of the data necessary for the writer, reader, or librarian to relocate the reference. The following information is the minimum needed for a book bibliographical card: (1) full name of the author (two initials if the first name is not given, or issuing agent if author is not given); (2) full title of the work, underlined; (3) place, publisher, and date of the book's publication; (4) edition if given, and possibly (5) the total and/or particular pages used. In some instances a reference cannot be located unless the bibliographical card also gives (6) the volume and part number. A bibliographical card for a periodical or newspaper article is somewhat different. It includes (1) the full name of the author; (2) the full title of the article in

---

O.K.

Brodbeck, May, "The Philosophy of Science and
    Educational Research,"

Review of Educational Research
27 (December, 1957), 427.

                            U. of Pitt.
                            Educ. Lib.
                            Section D

Fig. 10.   Front of a bibliography card for a periodical.

quotation marks; (3) the name of the publication, underlined; (4) the volume number; (5) date of issue; and (6) the number of the initial page of the article or the range of the pages it covers.

Because you may refer to a reference several times during an investigation, it is advisable to make notations that will help relocate it speedily. To accomplish this, place on the front or back of the bibliographical card, but always in the same place and set conspicuously apart from the other information, (1) the library call number; (2) the name of the library if you patronize more than one; and (3) the room, department, division, or section that houses the work (see Figure 10).

After using several references, an investigator can become confused about what information was in the various volumes. By writing brief notes on the back of the bibliographical card concerning the nature, scope, special features, or chief strengths and weaknesses of the book and the page numbers of the most pertinent topics (see Figure 11), you can later recall what the reference can contribute to your study. Moreover, when compiling an annotated bibliography for a research report, you can refer to these notes to obtain useful information.

How to Take Notes. Economize on time and effort when taking bibliographical notes, by establishing good note-taking habits. To avoid accumulating many duplicate and useless bibliographical cards, always screen references before copying a single item. Refrain from hastily scribbling

```
Excellent review of literature (1948-1957) on:

    Operationalism         427
    Nomological Network     429
    Causation              433
    Theories               435
    Models                 439

Gives appropriate examples and implications
    for education.
Cites pertinent bibliography.
Points out criticisms of operationalism.
Draws attention to the form of operational
    definition—conditional or if-then sentence.
```

Fig. 11.   Back of the same bibliography card.

partial bibliographical information on notebook covers, backs of letters, class notes, or any available scrap of paper. Widely scattered, crudely written fragmentary notes on assorted sizes of paper are easy to lose, difficult to relocate and file, and hard to interpret.

Whenever possible copy each reference in full, once and for all, on a *separate* standardized size card or sheet of paper. If a few blank cards are kept on hand at all times, it will not be necessary to recopy references. Cards can easily be carried in a purse or pocket and they are more durable and easier to handle, sort, and file than lists of sources on sheets of paper. A 3- by 5-inch card is convenient to carry, but some researchers prefer a larger size because one can write more on them.

But before doing this, investigate the form and content of the entries that you will be required to use in the final report. Different professors, institutions, periodicals, and publishers establish style standards that vary slightly.

If they do not have their own style manual, they require scholars to conform to a recognized style, such as the one published by the University of Chicago Press (7 and 8).

If you form the habit of recording bibliographical notes in conformity with the recommended style manual, you can type the final bibliography directly from these cards without reorganizing the data. This practice eliminates the tedious task of shifting items on cards and avoids the errors that can creep into a bibliography during the recopying process. Always carry sample style cards for a book, periodical, and newspaper with you. By referring to them, you can immediately and properly write up the permanent bibliographical notes for the bulk of references. You may prefer to purchase printed bibliographical cards or to mimeograph cards that provide blanks for the required items.

Since some references require special information in their entries, it is also advisable to have a style manual accessible while working. By turning to it, you can quickly check the correct form to solve problems that arise, such as how to write up the entry when an organization is the author; a pseudonym is used; a translator or editor is noted; or the article comes from an encyclopedia, chapter of a yearbook, unpublished thesis, or newspaper editorial. When it is not convenient to consult a style manual, copy all the information and reorganize the contents on these particular cards before you include them in the formal report.

Before you take a single note from a reference, make out a bibliographical card neatly and legibly in ink. Procure the information for books from the title page rather than the cover of the book. After completing the task, carefully check whether you have omitted any necessary data—an item, word, letter, punctuation mark, or number—and also check the correctness of the spelling, punctuation marks, and call number. When you are finished, make an "o.k." notation on the card so that no doubts concerning its accuracy will arise later. The extra minutes expended in getting accurate bibliographical information is time well invested, for careless errors may later cause you to spend endless hours searching for missing items, recopying cards, and retyping entire bibliographies. Merely omitting the pages covered by an article on an entry may force you to make a special trip to the library, and, if the volume is out, a return trip and more wearisome waiting at the circulation desk will be necessary.

Filing Notes. After collecting a number of bibliographical notes, one must organize them into some meaningful order. An alphabetical arrangement by authors' surnames—or the first important word of the title if there is no author given—proves satisfactory in most studies. Some workers file their bibliographical cards under subject headings and then alphabetize them by authors' surnames. They make out duplicate or cross-reference cards for a work that is used in more than one section of the report, annotating its usefulness for each. In some studies, researchers classify cards under primary and secondary sources; under types of references, such as books, periodicals, and pamphlets; or under a chronological arrangement. Elaborate filing systems become too cumbersome; a simple system that readily locates references pertaining to the various aspects of the problem is best.

Subject Notes. Subject and bibliographical notes serve different purposes. Each type possesses its individual characteristics. From a practical standpoint, mongrel notes (part bibliographical and part subject) are useless. Copying full bibliographical data on each subject note would be excessively time consuming; failing to put full data on mongrel notes would cause difficulties; therefore, it is wise to keep the two types of notes separate.

The information that you record on subject notes depends upon the nature of your problem and your experiential background. During an investigation, you may (1) copy many specific facts from references, such as dates, places, names, statistics, formulas, and definitions; (2) summarize or copy arguments, questions, explanations, opinions, illustrations, or descriptions presented by authors; (3) write comments about your reactions to reference materials; (4) state relationships, conclusions, or interpretations that come to mind during the reading and contemplative phases of your work; and (5) jot down items that require further checking.

Subject notes usually comprise the bulk of the notes taken in any study; they form a reservoir of facts. When writing a report you may draw upon them to (1) support a particular position; (2) illustrate a point of view; (3) make comparisons; (4) weave a web of logical evidence; or (5) buttress arguments with vivid, pertinent passages by recognized authorities. Subject notes are the building blocks that help solve problems; good ones enable you to construct sound reasoning structures; poor ones can cause your investigation to collapse.

Taking Notes after Evaluating Items. Indiscriminately copying copious notes about every item that remotely relates to your problem is a bad practice. You not only waste time writing worthless pages of material, but also must later spend hours filing, reexamining, and eventually culling them. Before taking any notes you should quickly skim through a few of the best references and then as you critically reread the pertinent pages record the location of the important facts or passages. If you own the book underline these items; if not, list the location of them on a card in an abbreviated form, such as 198:2, 4–6 (page 198, paragraph 2, lines 4 through 6). Later you can reevaluate the underlined or listed passages and copy or paraphrase the most pertinent ones.

Taking Flexible, Durable Notes. A system of note taking that produces permanent, easy-to-handle notes saves a researcher much time and lessens the labor involved in assembling data for the final report. Writing notes in bound books or consecutively on pages of paper is an unwise practice, for the items will later have to be relocated, reclassified, and either recopied or elaborately indexed. A note is of the greatest value, if it is a complete unit that can be found quickly in a sheaf of notes, traced readily to the original source, and transferred easily from one position in your outline to another.

When each note is on a separate card or page, you can run through items taken from many sources and at different times, slip out those that pertain to the same subject, and quickly reorganize them in a logical sequence for your report. When several items of information are on one card, they may fall logically into different sections of the report. Hence, the process of shuffling and ordering cards so as to place facts in the proper report sequence becomes an extremely complicated and arduous task. Moreover, it is easy to overlook important items of information that are buried among other data and to make the mistake of combining unrelated facts in a report merely because they were on the same card.

Writing Intelligible Notes. When writing a report, smeared penciled notes or illegible pen scratchings that are crammed with complicated forms of abbreviations can thwart your progress. To avoid such stumbling blocks, habitually type notes or write only in ink, carefully form each letter and figure, and consistently use a simple, intelligible abbreviation system. After taking a note, check to make certain that you or a secretary can decipher each word accurately now and in the future.

Using Uniform-size Note Sheets. Because assorted shapes of note sheets are clumsy to organize and important items can easily get lost, it is best to write all subject notes on paper or cards of the same size. Some workers prefer to use note paper because it is not as bulky as cards, provides more space for writing, and is more convenient to use when typing; others prefer cards because they are more durable and easier to sort and arrange. The nature of the study and idiosyncrasies of the writer determine what size card or paper is most serviceable. Subject notes generally require a larger size card than bibliographical notes.

Using One Side of Paper. Writing notes on both sides of a paper is a mistake. If you must constantly flip papers when organizing notes into a logical order, it is difficult to see them as a whole and easy to overlook items. Many a researcher has searched days for a note, only to find it tucked away on the back of a page he assumed was blank. If an entire note cannot be placed on one side of a page, it is best to complete it on a second card— writing "to be continued" on the first card and "continued from card one" on the second. Stapling these cards together is another precaution to take.

Using Topic Headings That Conform with the Report Outline. When taking notes, indicate what they are about by placing suitable topic headings consistently at the top-left or -right hand side of the subject cards. If these headlines are the same as the topics and subtopics in your tentative report outline, they will facilitate not only locating, sorting, and classifying cards, but also writing the report.   If you encounter materials in a reference that suggest a new or more effective topic heading, use it and revise your outline accordingly.   If it is difficult to decide where to file a note, you probably have not carefully studied its relationship to the subject or your outline contains overlapping, vague, or insufficient subject headings.   Initial attempts to construct an outline and assign headings to notes will not be perfect.   But, during the course of an investigation, you will spot weaknesses and discover ways to correct them.

```
Brodbeck, Philos. of sc., 427-428.  Opera-
                          tionalism, nature of
        Concept formation in science is opera-
    tional.  That is, the meanings of terms are
    not defined by listing the observable attri-
    butes of objects--shape of chair--but by
    reference to more abstract properties--IQ--
    obtainable by dividing M.A. by C.A.  There-
    fore, operationalism holds that concepts
    derive their meanings from the techniques
    employed in observation or investigation--
    their operations.

      *Check P. W. Bridgman's, Logic of Modern
       Physics for his explanation.
     **Sometimes called operationism, why?
    ***Does this definition have application to
       historical research?
```

Fig. 12.   A summary subject note with comments.

Noting Location in Reference.   On each subject card place the source from which the information was obtained, either on the bottom of the card or opposite the topic heading at the top of the card.   Since bibliographical cards carry the complete data for references, the subject card may merely identify the source by author or by author and an abbreviated title, but it must indicate the exact page or pages from which the note is derived (see Figure 12).   Remember, your final report will have to be documented and each footnote will have to state the complete bibliographical information for the reference and the exact page on which the quotation can be found. Consequently, forgetting to record the source and page of a note can cause discouraging delays when you are ready to write up the study.   Days can be spent in obtaining a reference again and rereading it to locate a quotation —and the search will not always culminate in success!

Quoting Reference Properly. After locating pertinent material in a reference, you may decide to copy it verbatim, paraphrase it, or summarize it. Your decision will determine the type and form of the note you make. Never copy a statement word-for-word unless it is especially significant and striking and vitally important to your study. Immediately enclose a copied statement in quotation marks so that you will not later assume these are your own words and innocently commit an act of plagarism. Copy quoted passages exactly as they appear in the original. Permit errors to stand, but call attention to them by adding the notation [sic] immediately after their occurrence in a passage. If you insert a word or phrase to clarify a quotation, enclose the addition in brackets. For example, "A former department head [James Damber] wrote the report." If you omit words, insert ellipses marks—three periods with alternating spaces—to convey this information. For example, "Professor Thomas Wood . . . first outlined the program in 1910." If you omit something from the end of a sentence or delete more than one sentence, add an additional period—making four periods in all. Errors can easily be made when copying quotations; therefore, always exercise great care: recheck each word, punctuation mark, and capital letter to make certain that you have not made a mistake or omitted anything.

Learning to Paraphrase. Paraphrasing or summarizing an author's ideas rather than mechanically copying pages of direct quotations forces you to (1) analyze, evaluate, and get the full meaning out of the material and (2) compose notes that may then be woven into the first draft of your report with little or no recasting. Stringing quotations together to form a research report is an indication of sloppy, superficial thinking; such compilations make dull reading and no significant contribution to the advancement of knowledge. A good report is a product of the investigator's critical thinking: it represents his own ideas and is written in his own words. By disciplining yourself to paraphrase the material taken from references, you immediately become involved in critical thinking. Absent-mindedly copying notes verbatim merely postpones the time when you must analyze and synthesize the source materials.

Paraphrasing and summarizing are skills that require more practice than perfecting a golf swing. Copying phrases, words, or partial sentences usually produce unsatisfactory notes, for after a lapse of time these isolated items may not convey significant meanings and the partial quotes may be mistaken for one's own words or may be easily distorted. You cannot assimilate an author's ideas if you merely copy fragments of his sentences or change a word or two. Assimilation requires effort: you must concentrate on passages until you eliminate unessential details, single out the significant ones, and recast these ideas into sharply coined, original sentences that faithfully reproduce the intent of the author. A few carefully drafted notes are extremely valuable; a profusion of inaccurate, ambiguously stated ones are worse than none at all.

Recording Reactions to References. Disturbing doubts and challenging questions may seep into your mind as you read a reference. You may ask: Did the author use primary sources? Is this definition of "hypothesis" different from that given by Professor Jones? Isn't Galileo spelled differently in the *Encyclopaedia Britannica?* Are the author's conclusions based on facts? Did he observe these conditions himself? Critical reading will produce many questions such as these. Keeping a record of them and seeking answers to them will prod your investigation toward a successful solution. Personal reactions to reference materials may be written on separate notes or below a summary or quotation note. If you register a personal reaction to a source material directly on a subject note, distinguish your words from those of the author by enclosing them in brackets or by placing asterisks or some similar symbol beside them (see Figure 12).

Recording Flashes of Insight. Early in an investigation you begin to examine your collected notes. During this process you search for meaningful relationships, patterns of order, and possible inconsistencies in data. Flashes of insight that help marshal facts into logical chains of evidence may come to you at any time—when deliberately trying to put tangled thoughts into some meaningful order, or, at unexpected moments, while engaged in other activities. These mercurial ideas may produce the crucial clues that solve problems; immediately record them, for they can easily escape your memory forever. Since weeks or months may elapse between the time when the thoughts first occur to you and the actual writing of the report, it is only wise to write clear, detailed statements of what prompted each idea and what implications each has for your study.

Recording Temporary Notes. Brief notes may be made of items that vie for your attention when you are trying to concentrate on something else. While reading, note taking, or engaging in some other pursuit, you may encounter a worthwhile reference, suddenly see a desirable method of classifying some facts, question a point, or become concerned about a personal problem. To avoid becoming sidetracked and to prevent any worthwhile ideas from escaping you, jot these thoughts down quickly in abbreviated form to preserve them for later consideration. Once recorded, they are less likely to keep intruding on your train of thought, and interrupting your progress with the work at hand.

Notes of a temporary nature can be listed in a notebook and those of a more permanent nature on cards. Divide these notes into research and personal items. For example, Research: "Good bibliography on Russian education, Staley, p. 322. Check average salary of Russian high school teachers last year. How long did Mr. Sach observe Russian schools? Did he speak the language?" Personal: Obtain a copy of *New York Times*. Ask Professor Jacks for a conference on Thursday. Get stamps." Each day check some of these items during spare moments and periodically set aside definite blocks of time to clear up any unfinished business. When you check an item cross it off your list.

Filing Notes. To prevent materials from getting lost during the collection of data, regularly file your notes in a convenient depository. Use vertical files, letter files, accordian files, work organizers, or large manila folders and a cardboard box of the right size. To speed the filing of notes and to order them in a manner that will facilitate writing the final report, label the file guide cards with the main- and sub-topics in your report outline. Keep your filing system up to date. If a category that was once important is no longer useful, destroy the notes or place them under other topics. Add new topics when it is necessary and fit them properly into the organizational scheme of the report.

BIBLIOGRAPHY

1. Alexander, Carter, and Arvid J. Burke, *How to Locate Educational Information and Data,* 4th ed. New York: Bureau of Publications, Teachers College, Columbia University, 1958, chaps. 2, 3, and 11.

2. American Association for Health, Physical Education and Recreation, *Research Methods in Health, Physical Education, and Recreation.* Washington, 1959.

3. Barzun, Jacques, and Henry F. Graff, *The Modern Researcher.* New York: Harcourt, Brace & World, Inc., 1957, chaps. 2 and 15.

4. Cordasco, Franesco, and Elliott S. M. Gatner, *Research and Report Writing.* New York: Barnes & Noble, Inc., 1955.

5. Dow, Earle W., *Principles of A Note-system for Historical Studies.* New York: Appleton-Century-Crofts, Inc., 1924.

6. Good, Carter V., and Douglas E. Scates, *Methods of Research.* New York: Appleton-Century-Crofts, Inc., 1954, chap. 10.

7. *A Manual of Style.* Chicago: University of Chicago Press, 1949.

8. Turabian, Kate L., *A Manual for Writers of Term Papers, Theses, and Dissertations.* Chicago: University of Chicago Press, 1960.

CHAPTER 7

Analysis of the Problem

Chapter 2 briefly reviewed the steps in the scientific method of solving a problem. The next two chapters will present a more detailed consideration of the processes involved in (1) discovering and defining a problem, and (2) constructing and testing hypotheses. Again, it is important to emphasize that the various steps in problem solving are not necessarily well delineated one from another nor taken in successive order; the research worker moves back and forth from one step to another—changing, searching, altering, and clarifying. He tackles a problem like an artist who works constantly on his whole composition rather than first perfecting an eye, then a nose, and then a mouth. No two scientific investigators proceed in exactly the same manner, but they do become involved in the closely related and overlapping steps during the course of their investigations. Their work is creative and individualistic rather than mechanical, but it is not a completely haphazard undertaking. Like any art, it entails necessary disciplines and procedures. By abstracting some of them for analysis the following chapter may give you a deeper insight into research work.

DEVELOPMENT OF A PROBLEM

Finding and analyzing a problem is a prerequisite for conducting a research study, but an inexperienced investigator often overlooks this fact. Quite commonly, he has an unrealistic, glamorized conception of his work. The excitement of executing an investigation completely commands his attention and causes him to engage in frenzied activity on the superstructure of the study before he has constructed a firm foundation upon which it can rest. The laborious task of analyzing a problem does not intrigue him; he dreams of playing the starring role in a dramatic experiment that culminates in an earth-shaking discovery. In this imaginative drama, he visualizes himself masterfully manipulating intriguing technical procedures, complicated questionnaires, electric computers, batteries of tests, or intricate statistics while the public observes with awe and admiration.

A novice investigator is usually as anxious as a child to leap to the answer stage of problem solving.   Impatiently he listens to advisers who ask, "Have you defined your problem clearly?   Do you know what variables are involved?   Do you possess the basic skills to solve it?   Have you constructed a sound theoretical framework for this problem?"   Without giving these questions serious consideration, he plunges headlong into gathering copious notes and setting up an elaborate experiment.   Since he is employing sophisticated terminology, statistics, and research procedures, he smugly assumes that the solution to his problem will automatically materialize.   But the elation he experiences while conducting this pseudo-scientific experiment is quickly extinguished when critics attack his problem design.

Competent research does not consist of play acting with scientific paraphernalia and techniques to produce a senseless stack of statistics, a grab bag gathering of facts, and a casual collection of glossy generalizations unsubstantiated by acceptable evidence.   Solutions to problems are not produced by toying with laboratory tools.   Research tools are means to an end; they must be employed purposefully to be of value; and they cannot be used intelligently unless an investigator knows what problem he is trying to solve.   It is the planning that counts in research, carrying out the plans is largely a mechanical process which requires more persistence than profundity.

Identification of a Problem.   Problems cannot be solved unless a research worker possesses the intellect to isolate and comprehend the specific factors giving rise to the difficulty.   Locating and analyzing a problem is a crucial step in research, yet many novices grasp at any straw and label it a problem.   They spend months or years laboriously gathering data relating to their large, vague topics without ever defining a specific problem.   The end result of their furious figuring and fact finding is a formless, frustrating fund of data.   Having never decided precisely what to solve, they roam rudderless in a sea of facts with their mapless voyage obviously committed to failure.

Since identifying the exact nature and dimensions of a problem is of major importance in research, it is essential that an investigator learn how to recognize and define one.   How does one locate problems?   What conditions give rise to them?   John Dewey answered these questions by suggesting that a problem arises out of some felt-difficulty.   Something puzzles or disturbs an individual; a gnawing dissatisfaction nibbles at his peace of mind until he can locate precisely what is bothering him and find some means of solving it.

Suppose that late at night the sound of rushing water awakens and alarms you.   Having been plunged into a problematic situation, you immediately strain to pinpoint the difficulty.   Is the water rushing from the eaves?   Is the creek flooding?   Has a water pipe burst?   What precisely is your problem?   Not only household but also scientific problems spring from puzzling experiences. A problem materializes when a scholar senses that something is not right or needs further explanation. Perhaps he fails to produce the customary results when carrying out a familiar experiment, finds some facts that do not agree with accepted theories or beliefs, detects inconsistencies between his observations and those made by other investigators, or observes something he cannot explain. When a scientist has an inkling that something is wrong or needs to be explained and is anxious to obtain a clearer concept of the factors causing this puzzling or commonplace occurrence, he has established some of the conditions necessary for identifying a problem.

A vague feeling that something is wrong or that some theory is not adequate does not constitute a problem, however; it merely indicates an area in which a problem may exist. If a doctor examines a patient with a fever and a rash, he knows that a problem exists. But, before he can cure the patient, he must diagnose the exact nature of the difficulty. If a teacher becomes disturbed about the amount of time correcting test papers consumes, he is aware of a problematic situation but has not identified the specific difficulty. To bring the causes of his problem into clearer focus, he can ask several probing questions. Do I correct tests when I am too tired or experience too many interruptions? Is the form of the test difficult to correct? Would a shorter test serve the purpose equally well? Until the teacher and the doctor locate the key to their difficulties, they cannot solve their problems. Recognizing a general problematic situation provides a starting point for an investigation; but, before proceeding too far, one must isolate, sharpen, and clarify the pertinent points giving rise to the problem.

If a researcher narrows a problem before his imagination has had an ample opportunity to view it from varied vistas, he may overlook the most promising approach to it. Eventually, however, he must trim his investigation to a manageable size and this may be a difficult task. Having experienced a felt-difficulty about the "world situation," classroom discipline, children's attitudes, or religious education, one may think that he has located a problem. But years can be devoted to collecting data on these broad subjects without unearthing all of the relevant materials. If a scholar wishes to investigate religious education, for example, he can accumulate unmanageable mounds of data about the training of infants, adolescents, and adults among Jews, Christians, Mohammedans, ancient Romans, and modern suburbanites. Where does he stop? This grandiose religious problem and its multiplicity of variables will keep him busily engaged in an interminable investigation that never will arrive at a solution. If he delimits his study, however, to an investigation of the religious education programs provided for teen-age youths by Ohio Methodist churches since 1900, he has a measuring stick for determining what facts to include and exclude and can reasonably expect to collect the required data. Imaginatively exploring a selected segment of phenomena until he locates a specific problem and then thoroughly investigating it may enable a researcher to advance knowledge in his field.

Analysis of a Problem. The process of identifying and analyzing a problem may be better understood by tracing the step-by-step development of a simple educational research inquiry (10). Thus, the following discussion reveals how Miss White, a conscientious and enthusiastic teacher, encounters a difficulty in her classroom that many educators have experienced. By asking pertinent, analytical questions and procuring considerable data, she gradually determines the dimensions of her problem. Although her investigation lacks the preciseness and controls of sophisticated research procedures, it gives some insight into the inductive and deductive thought processes involved in clarifying the specific factors giving rise to a problem.

Felt-difficulty Stimulates Inquiry. Miss White's investigation originates from a felt-difficulty—as all problems do. In a teachers' meeting she expresses a dissatisfaction with the reading progress of her pupils and a desire *to solve the reading retardation problem.* This classroom difficulty is sufficient to stimulate an inquiry, but the initial problem statement is too vague to serve as a guide to a fruitful solution. Unless Miss White delimits the inquiry to a more specific situation and probes deeply into it, she may fish facts forever out of the vast reservoirs of reading data. In desperation, she may blindly accept a superficial generalization or a personally favored explanation for reading retardation without analyzing whether these facts and explanations are biased or directly related to the pupils' difficulties. Miss White cannot profitably search for a solution until she precisely identifies the problem.

Collecting Information That May Relate to the Problem. By analyzing a general problematic situation—the elements, conditions, characteristics, and situations that seem to be related to it—one may locate the specific factors giving rise to the difficulty. Thus, to bring the constituent elements of the reading problem into clearer focus, Miss White compiles a list of (1) known and suspected factual items of information and (2) possible explanations that may have a bearing on it.

Number of retarded readers	Amount of vocabulary drill
Sex of retarded readers	Phonics background
Speed of reading	Enunciation of teacher
Comprehension	Classroom noise
Hour of day that class is taught	Dietary problems
Intelligence of students	Hearing impairment
Time devoted to reading	Visual impairment
Size of textbook print	Lack of sleep

Foreign language spoken exclusively at home

Class too large for effective instruction

Broken or unhappy home conditions

Class too heterogeneous for effective instruction

Children's experiential background

Attitude of parents toward reading development of their children

Textbook materials not sufficiently varied to meet different interests

The more known and suspected facts and possible explanations that Miss White can think of, the better are the chances that she will locate the causes of the children's reading difficulty. Undue haste in analyzing any problem can result in disaster. Crude guesswork may be a speedy method of obtaining answers, but it seldom leads to successful solutions. Probing into the simplest educational problem usually reveals that the phenomena are enormously complex. Obtaining a picture of all the factors involved and their interrelationships will consume considerable time—but unless this is done the problem cannot be solved.

Deriving Meanings from the Information. To squeeze as much meaning as she can out of these possible constituents of the problem, Miss White looks for relationships between facts and facts, explanations and explanations, and facts and explanations. She may inquire, for example, whether a relationship exists between hearing impairment, classroom noise, and the teacher's poor enunciation that reveals a key to the difficulty. Facts and explanations that first come to mind may yield more precise knowledge of the difficulty if she probes them for more detailed information. Upon becoming suspicious that a dietary problem exists, for example, she should ask more penetrating questions: Is the real cause a lack of a balanced diet, conditions under which meals are eaten, or improper preparation of the food? Is there empirical evidence available to confirm that a relationship exists between the nature of the breakfast consumed by children and their work capacity?

By digging more deeply into the problem, Miss White may discover that conditions which first appeared to be important causes of the difficulty are not the specific factors responsible. If the class is taught late in the morning, should she assume the hour is the relevant factor responsible for the reading retardation or are other conditions connected with the time of day more significant? Are the children restless and uninterested because they do not get enough sleep and adequate breakfasts? Would a rest and milk period prior to reading class be wise? Is the late morning hour of instruction causing the difficulty or the fact that the school band practices outside the classroom at that period? Factors that may seem most important when the analysis first gets under way may merely be clues that lead to the real causes of the difficulty.

Examining Assumptions Underlying the Suggested Constituents. When analyzing her problem, Miss White also examines the assumptions underlying the possible constituent elements. Are they true? Preconceived notions, hidden beliefs, and false basic assumptions may render Miss White blind to the real source of the problem or may lead her down dead-end alleys for solutions. Will vocabulary drill improve reading progress? What kind of drill? How often? How much? Can it have adverse effects? Does homogeneous grouping of pupils guarantee greater reading progress than heterogeneous grouping? Is reading retardation associated with sex, race, or socioeconomic status of pupils? What evidence is there to support these contentions? Is there any evidence to disprove them?

Men have often fallen into error by failing to question the assumptions underlying their reasoning. In the past, brilliant scholars assumed the earth was flat, no living organism existed in a drop of water, and blood-letting cured illnesses. Only a few years ago doctors assumed that post-operative patients would recuperate best if they had a period of complete bed rest; today, they get many patients up within twenty-four hours after an operation. Keys to many of our most difficult problems have been blasted to the surface by daring investigators who challenged facts traditionally assumed to be true. When asked how he discovered relativity, Einstein simply stated that he challenged an axiom. The assumptions underlying Miss White's suggested constituent elements of the problem may be sound, but it is only prudent for her to examine them carefully and to assemble as much evidence as possible to support them before proceeding too far with the investigation.

Searching for Facts to Clarify the Problem. After listing the items she thinks might be relevant to the problem, trying to see relationships among them, and examining the assumptions on which they are based, Miss White searches for facts to determine whether these items are relevant to her problem; whether there are flaws in her reasoning regarding the nature of the problem; and whether there are additional facts, explanations, or relationships that play a determinate role in the reading retardation of her pupils.

To obtain the required facts she closely observes her pupils while they are reading, studying, and playing. She also explores the literature related to reading problems and reviews other investigations concerning retarded reading. To locate some facts, she checks health records, intelligence tests, reading tests, and the information volunteered by pupils, parents, other teachers, and the school nurse.

As a result of her investigation, Miss White discovers that ten boys and two girls are not making satisfactory progress. They miss basic sight words, stumble over easy words, call "wrong" words, attack unfamiliar words unconfidently, and read word by word; they ignore thought sequences, pictures and context clues, and punctuation. They exhibit an indifference toward reading, daydream, or engage in disruptive activities during reading periods. When someone reads to them their comprehension is much better than when they read to themselves. Most of the children come from modest homes in which English is spoken; only two of them have divorced parents. Pupils have little reading material in their homes and they have not had varied or extensive home, community, travel, and educational experiences. Although some of the students are shy, none of them gives evidence of being deeply emotionally disturbed. In mental ability they range from an IQ of 82 to 129. In academic subjects they do fairly well except in spelling.

This detailed analysis gives Miss White a clearer picture of the problematic situation. When she discovers that only twelve of the thirty pupils are retarded readers, she can limit further study to them. When facts reveal that some of her "guessed at" explanations for unsatisfactory reading progress are not the causes of the difficulty—mental, emotional, and visual conditions—she can eliminate these irrelevant items from the investigation. While searching for facts, Miss White may uncover some new clues to the reading difficulty which she adds to her list. Moreover, she may find evidence that indicates certain clues on her original list are worthy of further consideration. By collecting reliable information that justifies eliminating or retaining listed items and continuing to trace the relationships between the remaining items, Miss White gradually penetrates to the core of the difficulty and brings the problem into sharp focus.

Statement of the Problem. While analyzing her problem, Miss White keeps reformulating her original vaguely expressed explanation of the reading retardation difficulty. After singling out all of the pertinent facts and explanations causing the difficulty and tracing their interrelationships, she organizes them into a formal descriptive statement that gives a unified picture of the problem in all of its dimensions. To pinpoint the precise factors that require investigation, she raises the following questions: Are these twelve children retarded readers because they (1) lack varied sensory and oral experiences that enable them to associate printed symbols with words and ideas, and (2) have not developed the habit of utilizing picture, context, and punctuation clues to help them derive meaning from printed materials?

Writing a description of a problem requires infinite care. Miss White's experience gives a simplified picture of the process; it does not reveal all the complexities involved in more sophisticated research. Regardless of the scope of an investigation, however, the objective is to present the exact dimensions of the study in a concrete word picture. In the formal statement of a problem one describes the background of the study, the theories on which it is based, and the assumptions underlying the analysis. One also stipulates specifically what persons, materials, situations, factors, and causes will and will not be considered; consequently, there will be no question about what the research worker is to do. An adequate statement of the problem encompasses the sum total of all the relevant facts and explanatory concepts that the analysis indicated have a bearing on it. These factors are not merely listed in an encyclopedic fashion; they are placed in relationship to one another. Through a skillful grouping and subgrouping of the factors one formulates the specific question or questions that the investigator must answer to solve the problem.

The investigator is confused by a vaguely or ambiguously stated problem rather than guided to sources of information necessary for its solution. Because word symbols are exceedingly elusive and complex, misunderstandings may arise over the meaning of the simplest statement. In any language many words have different meanings in different contexts and a number of words can convey substantially the same idea. It is also possible to observe a situation or event and find no word that conveys the exact shade of meaning to describe it. In such instances, a researcher must coin a word and stipulate the sense in which he proposes to use it. Many investigators believe that operational definitions are necessary in scientific inquiry. Rather than giving detailed descriptions of the properties of a concept, they specify the measuring operations that one uses to identify phenomena. In a child development study, for example, they would define chest girth by specifying the precise acts that one performs to ascertain chest girth. Forging problem statements that carry precise meaning is difficult, but it is a skill that one must master.

When constructing a problem statement, a research worker evaluates each word and symbol to ascertain whether it will call up the same core of meaning to all competent workers in the field. If a word fails to meet this requirement, he substitutes a more specific term—one that relates directly to an observable event—or retains the word and adds a definition that will convey the same idea to everyone. An investigator soon discovers that commonplace words can cause as much confusion as coined, figurative, or unusual ones. Educational terms such as extracurricular and school day are not foreign to educators, for example, but what do they mean? Does the school day begin when the building is unlocked, when the first child or teacher arrives, or when the first class starts? Are extracurricular activities part of the school day or do they lie outside the school day? The simpler a term is, the more meanings it may have acquired; consequently, the greater may be the need for defining it. Rarely can a researcher conclude a study without preparing a list of definitions that describe the exact meaning that is to be attached to words, expressions, and symbols.

The first draft of a problem statement usually requires successive refinements. Skilled scientists report that they formulate and reformulate problem statements dozens of times during their investigations. They

weave back and forth in their inquiries, analyzing the problem and reformulating the statement of it. When they gain a deeper insight into
the problem, they become dissatisfied with their original description of it.
While searching in libraries, experimenting in laboratories, conducting

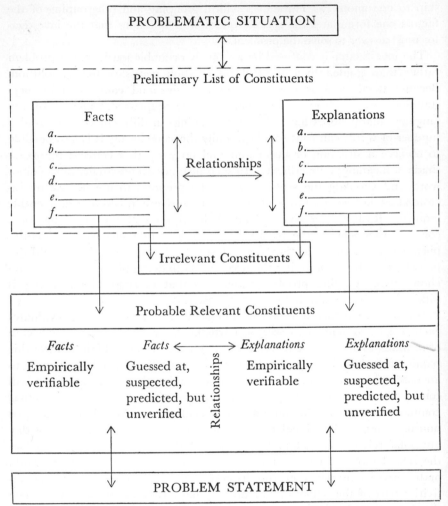

Fig. 13. Schematic analysis of a problem.

pilot studies, constructing scaled models, or utilizing diagrams or mathematical symbols to refine their thinking, they often discover evidence that
makes it imperative to reformulate the problem statement. Rarely does
a scientist find that the description of the problem that he places in his
final report is the same one he originally formulated.

The preceding discussion reveals that one engages in many activities when analyzing a problematic situation. The following list summarizes these tasks:

1. Accumulating the facts that might be related to the problem
2. Settling whether they are relevant through observation
3. Tracing any relationships between facts that might reveal the key to the difficulty
4. Proposing various explanations (hypotheses) for the cause of the difficulty
5. Ascertaining through observation and analysis whether they are relevant to the problem
6. Tracing relationships between explanations that may give an insight into the problem solution
7. Tracing relationships between facts and explanations
8. Questioning assumptions underlying the analysis of the problem (see Figure 13)

Through this painstaking probe, one gradually eliminates irrelevant ideas and forces into view the pertinent facts and explanations involved in the difficulty.

EXAMPLES OF PROBLEM ANALYSIS

The procedures employed in problem analysis are determined by the type of problem under investigation. An analysis may seek to understand the structural or functional relationship in a situation, try to determine the causal connections between certain variables, or strive to ascertain the authorship of a disputed document. Investigators, therefore, do not utilize exactly the same procedures to analyze all problems, but they do follow the general course of action outlined earlier in this chapter. A review of two problems that were undertaken by experienced investigators will give you a clearer comprehension of the problem identification and analysis aspects of research work.

Definition of Force. Several centuries ago, Galileo observed a phenomenon that did not seem to conform to the accepted theories of his time. When shooting off a projectile, he noticed its movement did not conform to Aristotle's explanation of motion. By mentally mulling over this projectile phenomenon, Galileo sought to put his finger on the source of the difficulty. He examined the traditional assumptions about what causes motion and finally decided that the difficulty was not located in the flight of the projectile, but rather in Aristotle's definition of force. Having somewhat identified the nature of the problem, he dropped further fact-collecting about the projectile and concentrated his attention on the definition of force.

According to Aristotle, force is that which produces movement. It follows then, that when force ceases to act on a body, the body will stop moving. Aristotle's definition gives a reasonable explanation of force that holds true in most instances. If you push a box, it moves; when you stop pushing a box, it stops moving. In case of the projectile, however, the force stops acting the moment the explosion takes place, but the projectile continues to move for some time and distance after the explosion. As Galileo discovered, the projectile phenomenon contradicts Aristotle's definition.

Having identified the difficulty that puzzled him as a need for an all-embracing definition of force, Galileo began to search for the facts required to construct a new definition. To analyze the problem, he selected the most elementary example of a force acting on a moving object he could —a ball falling freely under the force of gravitation. While closely observing the ball fall to the floor, he tried to determine what factors might be involved in the relationship between force and motion. Some scientists had previously concluded that temperature, smell, color, and shape of bodies were irrelevant to the problem. The ancient scientists had also assumed that distance and duration of the fall were irrelevant. But Galileo's mathematical, physical, and philosophical background, and his familiarity with the works of certain contemporaries and predecessors, caused him to reject the latter assumption.

After making observations, collecting facts, recalling previous experiences, reviewing scholarly studies, and searching for the relationships that might be involved in the difficulty, Galileo concluded that there were three factors upon which the fall might depend: (1) the weight of the object, (2) the distance it traveled, and (3) the time required for the fall. Thus, by thoroughly analyzing the problem, he was able to locate and describe the precise factors that had to be investigated before an acceptable definition of force could be formulated. The next chapter will reveal how Galileo tested each of these factors so as to arrive at an adequate explanation of force.

Assessment of Teacher Effectiveness. Skipping a few centuries, let us turn our attention to a recent analysis of an educational problem (6). The investigators were disturbed about a longstanding educational problem: how to determine the effectiveness of teachers and to predict the degree of success a potential teacher will achieve in a classroom. After analyzing this problematic situation, they decided there were four major factors involved in teacher effectiveness. To bring these four types of variables and their interrelationships into clear focus, they constructed a simple diagram (see Figure 14). Study this diagram as you read the following explanation of it.

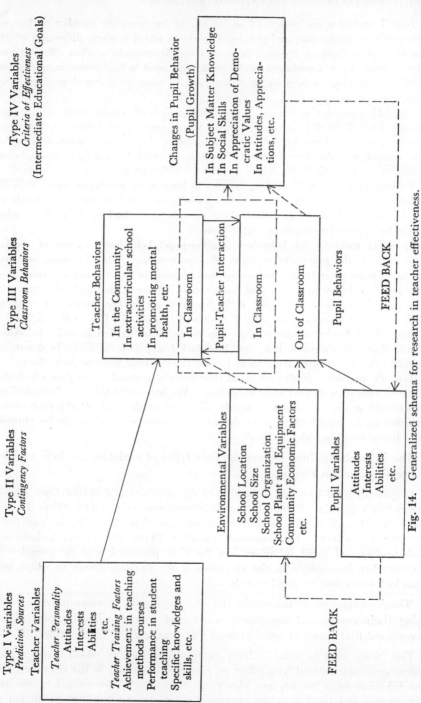

Type I Variables
Prediction Sources

Teacher Variables

Teacher Personality
Attitudes
Interests
Abilities
etc.

Teacher Training Factors
Achievement in teaching
methods courses
Performance in student
teaching
Specific knowledges and
skills, etc.

Type II Variables
Contingency Factors

Environmental Variables

School Location
School Size
School Organization
School Plant and Equipment
Community Economic Factors
etc.

Pupil Variables

Attitudes
Interests
Abilities
etc.

Type III Variables
Classroom Behaviors

Teacher Behaviors

In the Community
In extracurricular school
activities
In promoting mental
health, etc.

In Classroom

Pupil-Teacher Interaction

In Classroom

Out of Classroom

Pupil Behaviors

FEED BACK

FEED BACK

Type IV Variables
Criteria of Effectiveness
(Intermediate Educational Goals)

Changes in Pupil Behavior
(Pupil Growth)

In Subject Matter Knowledge
In Social Skills
In Appreciation of Demo-
cratic Values
In Attitudes, Apprecia-
tions, etc.

Fig. 14. Generalized schema for research in teacher effectiveness.

Type I variables are composed of an almost inexhaustible number of human characteristics [personality and training factors] on which teachers differ and which can be hypothesized to account, in part, for differences in teacher effectiveness. Ideally some Type I variables ought to be estimated before young people begin training as teachers, others by their very nature must be deferred until training is underway or completed.

Type II variables are contingency factors [school environment and pupil variables] which modify and influence the whole complex of behaviors that enter into the educational process. If Type II variables play a commanding role in the achievement of educational objectives, then we will be required to replicate studies of teacher effectiveness in a great many different situations, and predictions of teacher success from Type I variables will have to be contingent upon Type II variables. Some Type II environmental variables are undoubtedly inaccessible to measurement and to manipulation; these must be controlled or their effects minimized by appropriate experimental designs.

Type III variables, or behaviors [teacher-pupil behavior] . . . are of crucial significance in the process of assessing effective teaching. The classroom provides the focal point wherein the personality and training of the teacher are translated into actions. Likewise school and background influences on pupils determine in part pupils' classroom behavior. It is primarily out of the interaction of these elements that we expect educational goals to be attained. Or, as Ryans has indicated, the behavior of the teacher that ought to be studied is social behavior. Considering that classroom behaviors bear such heavy responsibilities in determining educational outcomes, remarkably little is known about them or their effects.

Type IV variables [pupil growth] are the criteria or standards against which the whole of educational effort must be judged. We have subtitled them intermediate educational goals, meaning measurable outcomes at the end of a period of instruction to distinguish them from the ultimate criterion which might be phrased as "a better world in which to live."

The interrelationships among the four types of variables are indicated by connecting lines on Figure 14.

In general, solid lines are indicative of direct effects and dotted lines suggest indirect or tangential effects. In such a scheme teacher variables (Type I) and pupil variables (Type II) are direct determinants of teacher behavior and pupil behavior respectively. Environmental variables (Type II) indirectly influence both teacher and pupil behaviors. In the view presented here the complex of pupil-teacher interactions in the classroom is the primary source to which one must look to account for pupil growth.

The investigators in this study (6) also explored the assumptions underlying their conceptual assessment scheme of teacher effectiveness. They recognized that it rested upon at least two fundamental assumptions.

First, there must be some stability in human personality which exerts a consistent governing or modifying effect on a teacher's behavior in the classroom. If the behaviors of a teacher are wholly, or even largely, determined by the environmental and pupil variables operating at any given time, then prediction of behavior seems foredoomed to failure. The second assumption is that the teacher (or more precisely, the teacher's behavior) as contrasted with the home, the school equipment, the principal, or other factors, is the primary causative factor in accounting for pupil growth toward the goals of the school. It is on this premise that the whole structure of professional education of teachers is based. Intuitively, we tend to feel that teachers are important, even though we do not yet possess the evidence to show what it is about their behavior that is crucial to children's learning.

The general conceptual framework presented in Figure 14, delineating the factors involved in teaching effectiveness, evolved out of a thorough analysis of the problem. By searching for facts and explanations relating to teacher effectiveness, and tracing their relationships, the investigators gradually brought the relevant factors into focus. By constructing the diagram, they placed this information into meaningful relationships that presented a unified picture of the problem in all of its dimensions. The diagram provided a useful backdrop against which many investigations could be projected.

Observe, for example, how the diagram guided investigators in conducting a longitudinal study (6) beginning with the 1953–1954 class of student teachers in the municipal colleges in New York City. They explained their project as follows:

Of these approximately 1,800 young persons, biographical and test data were initially obtained from about 1,600 of them. In order to study their persistence in teaching we have maintained correspondence with more than 90% of these teacher education graduates. To be able to assess their effectiveness as teachers from the basic group, we chose a sample of 75 who had accepted their first-year positions in the New York City public schools, teaching grades three through six. . . .

During October and November the pupils in 56 teachers' classes were tested with a reading test, an arithmetic test, a group-solving test, and a test of mental ability for a control variable. During the early spring months of the school year six observers working in teams each made two half-hour visits in the classrooms of these beginning teachers. Thus a total of 588 half-hour classroom visitations were made to observe the teacher and pupil behaviors occurring in the class rooms. . . . A carefully designed objective observation schedule . . . was employed by the observers to record classroom behaviors. This schedule was constructed after a review of the papers by Cornell on measurement of individualities of schools and classrooms, with Withall on social-emotional climate and by Harold Anderson on dominative and integrative behavior of kindergarten teachers. . . .

During the months of April and May of 1955, 904 pupils were retested with equivalent forms of the achievement instruments used in the previous fall. With these procedures we laid the basis for the development of pupil growth criteria in reading ability, in arithmetic skills, and in group problem-solving ability. Two less crucial criterion variables, a measure of teacher-pupil rapport and a measure of classroom disorder, were obtained from a 47-item pupil reaction inventory given to the youngsters and entitled *My Class*. Gross controls on mental ability levels and school effects were provided in the design. Furthermore, we obtained detailed classroom behavior records for 49 teachers which are being analyzed and combined into meaningful descriptive dimensions.

This briefly sketched description of an investigation gives you some insight into the value of thoroughly exploring the factors involved in a problematic situation before trying to define and delimit a particular problem for investigation. It reveals how a general problem analysis aids in locating potential problems and in determining what information to search for when conducting the study.

AIDS IN LOCATING AND ANALYZING PROBLEMS

Some graduate students become extremely dissatisfied and discouraged when they cannot quickly locate a problem. As the text noted earlier, their disgruntlement springs from the misconception that the researcher's real responsibility is to conduct a crucial experiment. They think that finding and analyzing a problem is a simple, uncomplicated, non-time-consuming task that one quickly performs before he engages in the exciting experimental work. Consequently, when difficulties arise, they resent expending considerable effort on an analysis and seek an "easier way out." Not uncommonly they select a general topic for investigation and without thoroughly analyzing it, begin to swing their mental machetes through a jungle of facts, piling them up like cord wood, never dreaming that their efforts will culminate in failure. Competent research workers, on the other hand, often devote more time and thought to the analysis of their problem than to any other single aspect of it.

The initiation of a scientific inquiry is not an easy task nor an unimportant consideration. Isolating points giving rise to the difficulty requires painstaking care and thought, for so much depends upon this all-important incident. The statement of the problem influences all subsequent phases of the investigation. It gives direction to the selection of the facts necessary for a solution, determines what investigative methods and procedures are most appropriate, aids in the control of biases, and establishes the philosophical environment for the study. A thorough knowledge of the problem is a prerequisite for finding a satisfactory solution; if a hasty and superficial analysis is made, there is nothing but disillusionment waiting at the conclusion of the study. An uncritical preliminary examination of the problem may result in missing the solution to it even though the scientist employs the most sophisticated methods in executing the subsequent phases of the investigation. Any small error made in this initial step of research may spell the difference between the success or failure of the undertaking.

The importance of clarifying the precise dimensions of a problem is a lesson that many young scholars learn only through bitter experience. You will find no magic elixir on the market that can guarantee to deaden the pain or quicken the process of locating and solving problems. But before actively engaging in research, you can become acquainted with some practices that appear to enliven the critical and creative capacities of research workers.

Steeping Yourself in the Literature. Problems spring from felt-difficulties, but one cannot expect to remain idle and aloof waiting for a formal introduction to a difficulty. An impoverished intellect has little opportunity to meet or recognize difficulties. Problem ideas do not germinate in barren brains but rather in minds enriched by varied experiences and fertile layers of knowledge. By reading extensively in educational and scientific publications, you can prepare an intellectual soil in which ideas will readily sprout.

When searching for a problem, explore the literature in a particular area of interest and construct an overview of the theories that have been developed by others. While critically studying this theoretical framework, you may spot weaknesses, inconsistencies, or gaps in knowledge that point to problem possibilities. Or you may be able to make deductions from the theories that are worthy of investigation or to develop a more comprehensive theory.

Promising problem seeds lie dormant in professional periodicals awaiting your discovery. These publications directly or indirectly point to unsolved problems in their (1) reports of current research; (2) articles that discuss or question assumptions, procedures, techniques, and generalizations commonly accepted in the field; and (3) surveys that summarize the frequency of investigations in various areas, thereby indicating where gaps exist and where further research is needed. By examining doctoral dissertations and technical papers published by workers in education and allied fields—particularly the concluding paragraphs—you may also encounter concrete suggestions for follow-up studies.[1] These publications may inspire you to undertake similar studies or to challenge, verify, or extend the coverage of the findings reported. A familiarity with the annual bibliographies,

---

[1] E. Ginzberg and D. W. Bray, for example, in their book *The Uneducated*, 1953, present a searching analysis of men who were rejected for military service in World War II on the ground of mental deficiency and a study of men who were accepted but who were illiterate or semi-illiterate. Their book provides valuable data and raises several important problems that exist in the area of mental retardation. For another example of problem suggestions see Ellfeldt and Metheny's concluding paragraphs in Appendix E.

interpretative summaries, and critical reviews of research will also help you locate problems in the field. Worthwhile scientific studies are not discovered by chance, but rather by prepared minds; consequently, steeping yourself in the literature is essential in research work.

Exposing Yourself to Professional Stimulation. By placing yourself in a dynamic research environment, you increase your opportunities for finding and solving problems. Spirited intellectual intercourse in which ideas are presented, explained, analyzed, and challenged is a rich source of inspiration. Graduate courses, seminars, professional meetings—particularly those in which papers are read and criticized—conferences with stimulating professors, lectures by eminent men in education, "gabfests" with fellow research workers, visits to laboratories, and part-time jobs in research centers often give birth to ideas worthy of investigation or provide clues needed for the solution of problems. Nothing promotes the growth of "problem ideas" more readily than actively engaging in research; one investigation usually points up other problems that need to be solved.

Examining Everyday Experiences. Since all problems spring from life situations, a practitioner in the field of education is in a favorable position to locate problems. Every day you encounter difficulties with students, equipment, tests, textbooks, guidance, discipline, parents, curriculum, supervision, or administration. You experience dissatisfaction with certain conditions—wonder how or why they developed—and notice things or relationships for which you know of no satisfactory explanation. Seize upon these felt-difficulties and thoroughly explore them to discover whether they have been or can be solved. An alert mind, sensitively studying classroom situations, serves as an excellent detector of research problems.

Keeping Notes. Ideas are born in fleeting moments and may vanish from your mind forever unless you immediately jot them down. Fruitful ideas appear at the oddest times. They will not always pop up when you are working on the particular problem concerned. A flash of insight may occur when you are busy with other tasks, engaged in conversation, listening to a lecture, teaching a class, reading a book, or relaxing at home. Even though this idea may seem perfectly clear at the moment and too important to forget, there is always a chance that it later may escape you. Therefore, whenever a kernel of thought sprouts in your mind, immediately preserve it in writing for future consideration. Keeping systematic notes throughout an experiment stimulates critical thinking and leads to the discovery of new ideas.

Adopting a Critical Outlook. Problems are neither discovered nor solved by complacent educators who are habitually subservient to traditional authority, smugly satisfied with the *status quo,* or perpetually parroting popular pedagogical jargon. Knowledge is advanced by creative minds filled with curiosity. A research worker cannot afford the comforts of conformity. You must experience the difficulties and delights of challenging existing theories and practices. Therefore, while reading, conversing, teaching, observing, attending classes, seminars, and professional meetings, adopt a critical attitude toward the information, generalizations, assumptions, and procedures you encounter. Question them; challenge their validity; look for deficiencies and contradictions; maintain a healthy skepticism. Keep asking questions: Is it true? Did the investigator interpret the results of the experiment accurately? Is there a better explanation for this phenomenon worthy of investigation? Follow Francis Bacon's advice: "Read not to contradict and confute, nor to believe and take for granted . . . but to weigh and consider."

EVALUATION OF A PROBLEM

Before expending a tremendous amount of time on a problem, it is only prudent to evaluate its worth. Putting off the evaluation until the conclusion of the investigation is not a recommended practice. In research, evaluation is a continuous process: the investigator begins to evaluate when he first becomes aware of a problematic situation and during the entire analysis of the problem, he keeps questioning whether this is a feasible and worthwhile topic to investigate. Upon encountering evidence that indicates it would be imprudent to proceed, he either drops the problem or refashions it into a more acceptable form. Delaying his evaluation too long or terminating it too soon can cause a researcher to waste months of valuable time conducting a useless investigation or one that he never can complete.

A thorough evaluation of a major research study requires a familiarity with many complex methodological techniques that you can only acquire through considerable study. But an elementary discussion of the considerations involved in evaluation may give you some insight into the process. Because problems in education are multiform and multipurpose, the advisability of undertaking a particular study depends upon two factors: (1) who is doing the investigating, and (2) what is being considered for solution. The type of problem that is worthy of investigation will vary somewhat for classroom teachers, curriculum committees, research staffs of public and private agencies, and graduate students. No matter what type of problem a research worker evaluates, however, he takes both personal and social factors into consideration.

Personal Considerations. Boldly blustering into an investigation is foolhardy if one lacks the necessary qualifications, support, or facilities to complete it. To avoid making such an error, an intelligent investigator explores the following types of questions:

1. Am I genuinely interested in this problem but free from strong biases?

2. Do I possess or can I acquire the necessary skills, abilities, and background knowledge to study this problem?

3. Do I have access to the tools, equipment, laboratories, and subjects necessary to conduct the investigation?

4. Do I have the time and money to complete it?

5. Can I obtain accurate and adequate data?

6. Does the problem meet the scope, significance, and topical requirements of the individual, institution, or periodical for which it is to be prepared?

7. Can I obtain administrative support, guidance, and cooperation for the conduct of the study?

Since interest is a tremendous stimulus to work in any form of endeavor, an investigator should select a problem that he has a consuming desire to solve. The prodigious effort required in research cannot easily be maintained if one feels that his topic is meaningless and boring. An insatiable curiosity about a subject gives the investigator the extra enthusiasm and drive necessary to withstand the prolonged period of exacting work. Strong biases in favor of a particular viewpoint, however, can make it extremely difficult to maintain an objective attitude. Because of this, some workers in the field believe it is best to avoid problems that spring from beliefs to which the individual is deeply attached emotionally.

Interest alone will not lead to the solution of a problem. Success cannot be attained if social forces and raw realities prohibit it. Common sense demands that one work within the framework of the social milieu and his personal potentialities. Hence, when a researcher is extremely eager to undertake a particular study, he should proceed with caution. Insurmountable difficulties may later arise and doom his endeavors if he does not carefully check several factors: Is the college, foundation, company, school administrator, or professor sponsoring his work opposed to it? Are his advisers capable of offering competent guidance in this area? Are the necessary equipment, subjects, or facilities available? No matter how enthusiastic he is about a study, these and other stubborn actualities can prevent him from making any progress. A problem may require, for example, that he read Russian scientific journals, travel to various private libraries for data, obtain access to classified government documents, procure the correspondence of a deceased man from his uncooperative family, possess a knowledge of physiology, and use specialized equipment that is only available at a distant university. If one is unable to do these things, he must face reality and reject the problem—at least for the present.

Social Considerations. Social as well as personal factors must be carefully evaluated when selecting a problem, for a researcher works not only to achieve personal satisfactions, but also to advance knowledge for the good of mankind.   Thus, there are a number of other questions one asks when evaluating a problem—questions such as the following:

1. Will the solution of this problem advance knowledge appreciably in the field?

2. Will the findings be of practical value to educators, parents, social workers, or others?

3. What will be the breadth of the application of the findings in terms of range of individuals, years of applicability, and areas of coverage?

4. Will the investigation duplicate the work that has been or is being done adequately by someone else?

5. If this topic has been covered, does it need reworking or extending beyond its present limits?

6. Is the topic sufficiently delimited to permit an exhaustive treatment yet sufficiently significant to warrant investigating it?

7. Will the conclusions of the study be of doubtful value because the tools and techniques available to conduct the inquiry are not adequately refined and sufficiently reliable?

8. Will the study lead to the development of other investigations?

When a research worker becomes interested in a topic, he locates and evaluates all studies relating to it that have been completed or are under way.   If this survey reveals that his proposed problem has already been thoroughly explored, he usually abandons it.   He may persist in pursuing the problem, however, if he doubts the validity of the conclusions reached by others, believes new evidence or better techniques have been discovered that require a new investigation, or thinks that there are gaps to fill or extensions to be made in the organized body of educational knowledge.

A more detailed discussion of the remaining social questions a research worker evaluates before undertaking an investigation is presented in succeeding chapters.   But, perhaps some mention should be made here of another evaluative technique that is sometimes employed.   After having made a rather extensive analysis of his problem, a research worker may set up a pilot study.   This trial study, which precedes the main investigation, may reveal more closely how the variables in the situation operate. It may spot technical difficulties that will develop in establishing experimental controls and in measuring factors singled out for measurement. The pilot study will help the research worker evaluate whether it is advisable to launch into a full-scale investigation.

Serving society is the ultimate objective of scientists.   Thus, competent workers not only give practical considerations to their personal limitations when selecting problems, but also earnestly endeavor to overcome their deficiencies so that they can undertake the most challenging problems. Because some graduate students are driven by a strong desire to obtain an advanced degree as quickly as possible, they utilize expediency rather than excellency as their problem selection measuring stick. They craftily circumvent any investigation that requires them to become proficient in utilizing a difficult statistical procedure, to interview people in distant cities, to master a new field of knowledge, or to do considerable detective work in locating primary source materials. Rather than searching for ways to make the most significant contribution to research, they myopically hunt for a problem that will demand the least possible effort on their part. The insignificant inquiries undertaken by these easy-degree seekers are neither challenging nor interesting; consequently, completing them is the dullest drudgery. Society also suffers, for mankind profits little from surface-skimming investigations. When a profession has a multitude of pressing problems to solve, it is tragic that any of its members should waste precious time and talent on trivial studies. Neither the educational profession nor its practitioners will experience satisfactory growth and a sense of significance by side-stepping difficult problems.

BIBLIOGRAPHY

1. Beveridge, W. I. B., *The Art of Scientific Investigation.* New York: W. W. Norton & Company, Inc., 1951, chap. 1.

2. Brown, Clarence W., and E. E. Ghiselli, *Scientific Method in Psychology.* New York: McGraw-Hill Book Company, Inc., 1955, chap. 7.

3. Good, Carter V., and Douglas E. Scates, *Methods of Research.* New York: Appleton-Century-Crofts, Inc., 1954, chap. 2.

4. Hillway, Tyrus, *Introduction to Research.* Boston: Houghton Mifflin Company, 1956, chap. 7.

5. Hodnett, Edward, *The Art of Problem Solving.* New York: Harper & Brothers, 1955, chaps. 2–4.

6. Mitzel, Harold E., "A Behavioral Approach to the Assessment of Teacher Effectiveness." Mimeograph, 1957.

7. Northrop, F. S. C., *The Logic of the Sciences and the Humanities.* New York: The Macmillan Company, 1949, chap. 2.

8. Rummel, J. Francis, *An Introduction to Research Procedures in Education.* New York: Harper & Brothers, 1958, chap. 2.

9. Spahr, Walter E., and Rinehart J. Swenson, *Methods and Status of Scientific Research.* New York: Harper & Brothers, 1930, chap. 7.

10. Taba, Hilda, and Elizabeth Noel, *Action Research.* Washington, D.C.: Association for Supervision and Curriculum Development, 1957.

11. Whitney, Frederick L., *The Elements of Research.* Englewood Cliffs, N.J.: Prentice-Hall, Inc., 1946, chap. 3.

CHAPTER 8

The Solution of the Problem

Problems are solved by a complex, creative process that involves unique forms of conceptualization similar to those employed in producing great works of art and music. Creative thought is not a step-by-step process that one can master by following directions in a "how-to-do-it" manual. Original ideas are not produced by idle and vacuous minds; they do not materialize without the expenditure of considerable effort. A successful scientist may appear to pluck problems magically out of the academic atmosphere, but months or years of patient plodding usually precede the exciting moment when he can pinpoint a particular event or condition that requires explaining. And no blinding flash of intuition immediately illuminates his mind with a brilliant solution; usually, a long period of arduous intellectual activity ensues before he evolves an adequate explanation.

CONSTRUCTING HYPOTHESES

When attacking a problem, an educator, chemist, or detective systematically observes phenomena and meticulously gathers facts. But an investigator is not interested in "facts and nothing but the facts," for problems are never solved by facts alone. One may collect facts for years without reaching a solution, for undirected observation may never reveal the significant facts or their relevant connections. Strangely enough, the most efficient way to attack a problem involves considerable speculation about it.

Bold, imaginative guesswork solves problems. Consequently, after locating a puzzling phenomenon, a researcher engages in dexterous mental gymnastics. Through disciplined daydreaming he structures *hypotheses— various possible explanations for the condition or event* (Dewey's step 3). These hypotheses are his most useful tools for mining knowledge; they play as important a part in solving his problems as hard, stubborn facts. If he does not construct them he has nothing to direct him in selecting and patterning facts to solve his problem, for "facts never speak for themselves

129

but only *to* someone who has an hypothesis which he wishes to test" (17:123–124).

Nature of Hypotheses. When and how does the scientist construct a hypothesis? While analyzing a problematic situation—perhaps the cause of an airplane crash or some form of pupil behavior—an investigator may notice that some data are vague or incomplete, some elements do not appear to be related to other known elements or to fit into any particular order, or there are no adequate interpretations for some phenomena. He is disturbed and keeps asking: How can I complete the data, systematize the information, or give some interpretation that will explain the unknown factors? Now the investigator is standing on the threshold of research! If he can imagine some unknown facts that when combined with observed facts and an existing body of theory will form a reasonable explanation or solution for the problem, the researcher will take a giant step forward. By leaping beyond the known facts and constructing hypotheses—intelligent guesses that offer possible solutions to the problem—he may eventually push back the frontiers of knowledge.

Man uses hypotheses to solve his simplest as well as his most complex problems. If the lamp on your desk does not light, for example, you will try to obtain an explanation for this phenomenon by proposing possible solutions: (1) the bulb is burned out, (2) the cord is not plugged in the outlet, or (3) the cord is severed. By combining the "known fact" that the light is out with certain "unknown facts" that you imagine, suspect, or predict may be related to the difficulty, you form possible solutions to the problem. Thus, hypotheses guide you in locating and patterning the facts needed to solve the problem. After listing several hypotheses, you begin to test them. If you test the bulb in another lamp and it lights, you know that hypothesis (1) is not the solution to your problem. If you continue to test the hypotheses one by one, you may find that number (3) fits all the evidence and satisfactorily explains why the desk light is out. Hypotheses, as Hodnett has aptly described them, "are your eyes as you try to approach problems in a scientific manner. Through them you look into the disorder that is a problem and see the possibilities of order" (13:120).

To summarize, hypotheses are suggested problem solutions which are expressed as generalizations or propositions. They are statements consisting of elements expressed in an orderly system of relationships which seek to explain conditions or events that have not yet been confirmed by facts. Some elements or relationships in hypotheses are *known facts* and others are *conceptual*. The conceptual elements are products of the research worker's imagination. Thus, hypotheses include facts and transcend the known facts to give plausible explanations for unknown conditions. They may provide the conceptual elements that complete the known data, conceptual relationships that systematize unordered elements, or conceptual meanings and interpretations that explain the unknown phenomena. By logically relating known facts to intelligent guesses about unknown conditions, hypotheses are able to extend and enlarge our knowledge.

Conditions Conducive to Creativity. As a teacher you may never actively engage in a formal research project, but you will repeatedly construct hypotheses to solve personal and professional problems. No precise rules can be given you for formulating them, for that is the creative aspect of the scientific enterprise. Hypotheses differ in their subtlety, in the obscurity of their origins, and in the details of their evolution. Their creators cannot always explain from whence they spring. Probably no two scientists arrive at the solution of problems in exactly the same way. But scholars are convinced that some conditions are more conducive to hypothesis construction than others.

Hypotheses are calculated guesses, but these guesses are not merely "happy accidents" as some scientists modestly suggest. Fruitful hypotheses are the products of gifted and informed minds. The quality and quantity of hypotheses a person can construct depend largely upon two factors: (1) the range and richness of previously assimilated knowledge that he can bring to bear on the present problem, and (2) the flexibility, versatility, and discrimination that he exhibits in selecting, organizing, and rearranging concepts into unique explanatory patterns.

Background Knowledges. The priceless ideas preserved in the literature are treasured possessions, for each generation of scholars builds upon the foundations constructed by its predecessors. A scientist cannot be an isolated rebel who relies on personal observation, alone, to create fruitful hypotheses. His work will be hopelessly hampered if he is not thoroughly familiar with established facts, existing theories, and previous research relating to his problem. Organizing relevant raw materials drawn from these sources in various patterns will help locate the key associations or missing data needed to explain puzzling phenomena. Supplying the imaginative concepts—missing pieces—needed to solve a problem is his ultimate objective, but to produce these concepts he must be familiar with all the known facts and must be able to order them imaginatively.

Familiarity with the literature relating to a problem ordinarily gives the trained person a tremendous advantage over the neophyte or outsider in arriving at a successful solution, but complete slavery to traditional source materials and excessive specialization in a field can crush creativity. Knowledge of masses of educational data mentally suffocates some scholars. When attacking a problem, they cannot see the forest for the trees. They cannot abstract the data necessary to formulate a solution. Intensive preoccupation with the literature may also fix traditional thought patterns firmly in their minds and render them incapable of seeing problems from fresh viewpoints. Because this occurs, some successful scientists avoid perusing the literature during the initial stages of an inquiry. To keep their minds from becoming shackled to the thought patterns of predecessors, they give their imagination free reign when first searching for solutions. For this reason, some industrial concerns place an intellectually able man who is unfamiliar with the particular field of inquiry on each research team to help the group see the problem through "virgin eyes." Any hypotheses, however, that are produced by such "free reign" explorations are later evaluated in light of the existing body of theory.

Provincial minds tend to see problems from limited and prejudiced viewpoints; liberally educated minds are more likely to look at them from the multiple angles suggested by their myriad of experiences. Scientists find that diverse knowledges from related or even distant fields sometimes provide them with the keys to problem solutions that extensive knowledge of their own field fails to produce. Perhaps one of the most productive means of creating hypotheses is to examine conceptual schemes developed by other disciplines and to decide whether they provide insights that would help explain educational phenomena. Kurt Lewin, for example, drew on the concept of force in physics to help him explain human behavior. Ellfeldt and Metheny (see Appendix E) borrowed the philosophy of symbolic transformation developed by Cassirer and Langer for their theory of movement and meaning.

Significant hypotheses may spring into the consciousness of cultivated minds that are not trained in the particular branch of knowledge, but they are rarely if ever brought into focus by feeble intellects. The scientists who make outstanding discoveries in fields other than their own always bring a varied background of knowledges and skills from their own fields to bear on these problems. Approaching a problem from a fresh and fertile foreign viewpoint can lead to the solution of problems, but ignorance is never a useful tool for attacking problems; an extensive and intensive educational background is absolutely essential in research work.

Imagination. Since the possession of a versatile intellect is of paramount importance if one wants to create hypotheses, a scientist conscientiously cultivates work habits and attitudes that will keep him mentally alert. He not only obtains a broad experiential background in his own and other fields, but also strives to increase the range, richness, and accuracy of his observations. By employing safeguards to minimize his emotional and intellectual biases, he strips himself of stereotyped blinders that might prevent him from originating useful hypotheses. However, this wealth of information and these observational skills are of little value unless he also develops one other ability: his imagination. He must learn to free himself from traditional thought patterns, to entertain radical ideas, and to fit facts into new and meaningful interpretive structures.

Imagination, the magic catalyst in research, is the product of an adventuresome attitude and an agile intellect. A competent researcher approaches problem solving with an enthusiastic and challenging attitude. He assumes that the explanation for the phenomena may be different from what obviously seems to be true or always has been assumed to be true. Stubborn skepticism stimulates him to search for flaws in old theories and to examine phenomena from new positions and different viewpoints. Resisting the temptation to coast along blindly accepting current theories, he deliberately breaks free from established thought processes and purposefully entertains new and varied combinations of ideas. Rather than dismissing strange ideas that pop to the surface momentarily and sticking strictly to traditional thought patterns, he takes advantage of any "happy accident" that gives him a new insight into a situation. Associational fluency enables him to select, shift, and combine seemingly unlike and previously unconnected known and imaginary facts until he constructs a simple, coherent explanation for some aspect of nature that troubles mankind.

In the hypothesis constructing stage of research, caution is temporarily abandoned. Wild experimental associations are made; risks are taken— they must be taken for discoveries are not made by jogging along in the ruts of past experience. Being unconventional in thinking does not guarantee solutions to problems, but it holds greater promise of advancing knowledge than credulously clinging to old ideas. But jarring oneself loose from the emotional and intellectual ties of traditional thought requires a stronger will power and richer imagination than the average person possesses. Following hundreds of hunches that lead up blind alleys before finding one that leads in the right direction requires more patience and persistence than most men ever develop.

Order and Analogy. Most scientists agree that perspiration rather than inspiration plays the greater role in research. Concentrated attention and enormous effort are required to produce original ideas. A research worker completely saturates himself with the problem: he observes phenomena, collects facts and theories that are relevant to it, and attempts to detect relationships between them. To facilitate the process of prying loose the key information that will solve a problem, he may resort to two ancient techniques: seek patterns of order, or structure useful analogies.

Ordering data so as to discover fundamental laws of nature is the purpose of research. In each investigation the researcher is faced with a puzzle—a disordered, disturbing situation—and a crude trial-and-error method is unlikely to provide a solution. But by looking for some order in the phenomena, by trying to perceive a pattern or a deviation from a known pattern, he may discover an explanation for it. When he wants to know the cause of teacher ineffectiveness, why Johnny can't read, or how to interpret aggressive behavior manifested by the student, he begins by looking for factors that seem to be associated with the phenomenon, their relationships, the frequency of their occurrence, and the order in which they occur. During this careful, prolonged examination of phenomena, he continually strives to structure disordered items of information into a pattern that will explain the condition or situation.

Analogy is another universal problem-solving device. Man has traversed this well-worn bridge from the known to the unknown down through the ages. When faced with a problem the modern researcher also trods this pathway: he searches for a successful previous ordering of nature that might illuminate his present difficulty. Upon spotting some similarity between a new situation and an old one that he knows a lot about, he examines his past experience to determine whether it will provide clues that will solve his present problem. He reasons that if these two situations have some resemblances in common, they may be analogous in other as yet unknown respects.

1. If A (new situation) resembles B (old situation) in regard to X factor
2. and he knows from previous experience that B is related to Y and Z as well as X
3. then, perhaps A is also related to Y and Z.

Thus, the analogy leads the investigator to clues he might not otherwise stumble upon and hints at hypotheses that he might find it worthwhile to test.

Analogies are useful but not foolproof tools for finding solutions to problems. They can easily lead to error, for the assumed similarities may not actually exist. If any essential dissimilarity prevails, the analogy is false as Miss Wilson, an elementary school principal, discovered to her dismay. When the poor attendance at the afternoon PTA meeting disturbed her, she recalled that young matrons had doubled the weekly attendance in her Sunday School class by organizing a nursery to care for members' children during their meetings. Miss Wilson reasoned that since the PTA and Sunday School class both had many young mothers as members and similar attendance difficulties, the same solution might work in both cases. Miss Wilson failed, however, to detect an important difference in the two situations: the school children's mothers were career women and could not leave their jobs to attend afternoon meetings even if a nursery were provided. Miss Wilson's experience indicates that problem solvers must be not only exceptionally adept at noting similarities between things, but also meticulously careful about detecting any differences between them that might make the analogies false. Despite the danger of mistaking an analogy for evidence, scientists favor using it with caution. They recognize that its reliability is restricted, but with all of its hazards it is one of the more helpful means of discovering hypotheses.

Other Practices. Research workers find they are more apt to devise hypotheses if they allot sufficient blocks of time—uninterrupted by distractions—to mull over, organize, and reorganize their collected data. After periods of intensive work, they sometimes temporarily abstain from conscious intellectual effort on the project and direct their attention to other work or just relax. In moments of relaxation their subconscious minds may continue to consider the problem and pop up with a useful hypothesis when they least expect it. Dropping a problem periodically permits them to escape from unprofitable ruts of thought they stubbornly have been following and to renew their labors later with fresh and more objectives viewpoints. Conversations with colleagues and authorities from different fields may aid them in checking their reasoning errors and may stimulate them to venture up new avenues of thought. Lecturing or writing about the puzzling phenomena may clarify their thinking and force the "key clue" to the surface. Drawing diagrams, constructing models, or forming mental images of the factors involved in the problem may also help them "break through" to a plausible explanation for the phenomena.

Examples of Hypothesis Construction. Formulating hypotheses is a commonplace activity that individuals engage in whenever they try to solve problems or explain facts. Hypotheses, therefore, can range from relatively simple to highly sophisticated statements. The average schoolboy devises elementary explanations for ordinary life or classroom occurrences while the genius creates elaborate theories concerning complex physical, social, or psychological phenomena. You engage in hypothesis construction everyday when searching for solutions to problems such as: Where did I leave my glasses? Why won't my car start? Why did so many students fail the last English test? Perhaps the following illustration will help you recall the mental processes involved in making a constructive attack on a problem.

Personal Problem. If you periodically experience symptoms similar to a cold—dripping nose, watering eyes, annoying sneezes—and yet never develop a cold, the situation is unpleasant and puzzling. You have a problem and want to obtain some explanation for the repeated occurrence. To initiate the inquiry, you collect empirically verifiable facts about the phenomena such as when, where, and how frequently they occur. At the same time you begin to think of explanations for the phenomena. From your previous experiences—reading, conversations with friends, observations of people with similar problems—you cull some of the following possible solutions: Does dust cause it? Do I eat, wear, or become exposed to something that is irritating? Am I allergic to wool or feathers? Do the chemicals I use at work cause it? Do some flowers or plants cause it? Do I have hay fever? These hypotheses are mere hunches at this stage. They have to be further analyzed and developed. Empirically verifiable facts have then to be found to support them.

By examining and reexamining the facts and explanations and tracing relationships between them, you try to determine which hypothesis is in agreement with all the facts in the case and gives a better explanation of the phenomena than any of the others. If dust causes the phenomena, you should suffer the most during the spring and fall housecleaning seasons. Since you actually experience the greatest difficulty in August and December, the dust hypothesis does not stand up under analysis. If chemicals used at work cause it, you should sneeze more at work than at home. But this is not true, for the greatest discomfort occurs during the August and December vacation weeks. Could it be hay fever? The December facts negate this possibility. Could it be a wool allergy? The August facts negate this possibility. Just what is the relationship between August and December? You probe this possibility further, searching for additional facts and eventually you recall that the phenomena occur most frequently outdoors in August and indoors in December.

In one magic moment at an August beach party, a reasonable solution springs into your mind. Because the miserable cold symptoms have reoccurred, you are particularly irritated by daughter Janie's whining questions. But one of those unwelcome questions suddenly supplies the missing clue that solves your problem. Janie complains, "There are too many old cedar trees around the porch. Why don't we cut them down for our Christmas decorations instead of always taking one from the clump down by the lake?" Sitting up—suddenly tingling with excitement—you pounce upon her words and mentally examine them as the possible missing link to your puzzle. Cedar trees grow around the cottage where you stay in August; during the Christmas holidays you use them for decorations in your city apartment. Is cedar the cause of your difficulty? This is a more concise and testable hypothesis than the original vague explanation that some plant, dust, chemical, wool, or flower caused your suffering. The hypothesis still has to be tested to determine whether cedar is actually the cause of the difficulty. You have an informed guess to work on, however, that has a reasonable chance of being the correct answer to the problem.

Educational Problem. If you will recall, Miss White, whom you met in Chapter 7, went through many of the same steps in hypothesis construction. She was disturbed by a problematic situation: her pupils were not making satisfactory progress in reading. With this glimmering of a problem as a prod to action, she began to make observations and gather facts to clarify it: Which children were having difficulty? How many? What sex were they? What difficulties did they have? At the same time she began to recall from her previous experiences—working with children, reading professional literature, conversations with colleagues, doctors, nurses, parents—some theories or explanations for reading difficulties.

Miss White mulled over various explanations and asked, "Are these particular children having difficulty because of their low intelligence level, impaired hearing or vision, inadequate sensory experiences, or emotional instability?" Through further observation and analysis she endeavored to trace the relationship between her accumulated facts and explanations. When doing this, she found it necessary to search for additional data. By adding, subtracting, and reorganizing materials in this manner, she gradually obtained a clearer and clearer picture of the facts and explanations that were relevant to the problem. Facts produced by intelligence tests caused her to dismiss low intelligence as an explanation for the difficulty. After obtaining verifiable evidence relating to the other hypotheses, she was able to reject some and retain others for further consideration.

Through this thorough analysis and development of the problem and a careful definition of terms, Miss White gradually removed many ambiguities and uncertainties. Eventually she crystallized a hypothesis that seemed to agree with all the facts in the case and to offer the most logical explanation of the problem. She framed the first draft of her hypothesis as follows: Twelve third-grade pupils are retarded from one year, seven months to two years, six months in reading because they lack varied sensory experiences that can help them associate printed symbols with words and ideas.

TESTING HYPOTHESES

A hypothesis is a provisional or possible explanation which accounts for the factors, events, or conditions that the research worker is trying to understand. But even after a hypothesis is critically analyzed for logical consistency and completeness, it is not acceptable as an explanatory device. A hypothesis remains a mere guess—and possesses little explanatory value—until empirically verifiable evidence is produced to support it. Thus, after formulating a hypothesis, it is necessary to (1) deduce its consequences (Dewey's step 4), (2) select or develop tests that will determine through experiments or sense observations whether these consequences actually occur, and (3) carry out these tests (Dewey's step 5), thereby collecting facts that will either confirm or disconfirm the hypothesis.

Deducing the Consequences. Some hypotheses can be tested quite quickly and directly; others, particularly scientific explanations, can be tested only indirectly. If a man guesses that a noise is caused by rain beating on the roof, he can look outdoors and confirm or disconfirm his hypothesis by direct observation. If he guesses that Mr. Jones shot Sally Lake, the world is "round" rather than flat, or the professor applying for a job is an impostor, he cannot directly observe these facts or conditions, but he can indirectly test the truth of the hypotheses. By studying them to see what they logically imply, he can deduce the consequences that must occur if these hypotheses are true. He reasons: if these hypotheses are true, then certain consequences are observable and can be tested directly.

Perhaps a fictitious example will clarify this process. Suppose Dean Henry is suspicious of the college training and degree records that Professor Silnatch has included in his application for a job. Since the Dean cannot tell whether the man is an impostor merely by looking at him or his application, he proposes the following hypothesis and deduces the consequences that it logically implies.

> If job applicant, Professor Stanley Silnatch, received a doctorate from Jones University in 1938,
> then (1) Jones University will have a record of awarding him the degree;
> then (2) his doctoral project will be listed in *Doctoral Dissertations Accepted by American Universities;*
> then (3) he will recall the names of the members on his doctoral dissertation committee;
> then (4) his signature will be similar to the one on college records;
> then (5) college health records and photographs of student Stanley Silnatch will reveal a number of facts that are characteristic of the job applicant (general height, bone structure, color of eyes, and physical handicaps).

These five consequences can be tested directly. If Dean Henry can find empirically verifiable evidence that agrees or disagrees with these consequences, he indirectly confirms or disconfirms the hypothesis. Thus, it is the consequence rather than the hypothesis itself that is tested in scientific investigations.

Deducing consequences from hypotheses that can be empirically verified cannot be a hurried or casual procedure. In major research projects the indirect method of attacking problems may lead through extremely intricate and remote channels of reasoning. In any investigation one must check his reasoning to make certain that the consequences actually do issue from the hypothesis, for there is no point in testing them if they are not logically related to the hypothesis. Furthermore, they must be expressed in clear, precise terms, for testing ambiguously stated ones is a difficult if not an impossible task.

Imaginative and disciplined intellectual effort is required in the deductive elaboration of hypotheses. When a significant hypothesis is proposed, the process may go on for years with a number of scientists deducing and testing various consequences. Thus, in many investigations the researcher does not originate his hypothesis, but rather tests consequences deduced from other men's explanations of phenomena.[1] Through this process he obtains additional evidence that either strengthens the confirmation of the hypothesis or disconfirms it (also see Appendixes D and G).

Selecting Test Procedures. Having determined what consequences are logically implied by the hypothesis, the researcher next devises a factual situation that will test them. A study by Durkheim (7) may quickly give you an insight into this three-step procedure. (1) He proposed the hypothesis that although the progressive division of labor increases material wealth, it decreases group cohesiveness and, hence, personal happiness. (2) If this hypothesis was correct, he deduced that the following consequences should be observable: (a) suicide rates would be higher in nations with greater material wealth, (b) higher in city than in farming areas, (c) higher in some occupations than others, and (d) higher among religious groups requiring little cohesiveness than in others requiring more. (3) To test whether these deduced consequences were observable, he examined international records on suicides.

Selecting and perfecting suitable testing procedures requires the most careful consideration. Weak, unreliable, or inappropriate tests will produce results of questionable value. A foolish error made when structuring a questionnaire, selecting subjects, controlling experimental conditions, or checking the authenticity of a document, may prove to be a fatal flaw in an investigation. If tests do not measure precisely what one wishes to measure, they are of no value. A one-hundred-yard dash, for example, cannot measure the maximum running speed of six-year-old children, for it tests endurance rather than speed of that age youngsters. Nor does an English version of an intelligence test ascertain the IQ of children with little or no command of the language. The appropriateness of the empirical test depends upon the nature of the deduced consequences; to be acceptable, a test must factually fulfill the specific requirements of the consequence. Hence, one must always make certain that there is logical consistency between all tests and the deduced consequences they are supposed to check.

In his stiff appraisal of testing procedures, a competent researcher asks:

[1] When reading research literature, you may become confused because some workers refer to the proposed solutions to problems as theories and to the deduced consequences of a theory as hypotheses. Even the present author sometimes resorts to the shorthand method of stating that "one tests the hypothesis" rather than the longer but more accurate statement, "one tests the deduced consequences of the hypothesis." Whatever language may be used to explain the process, the important thing to keep in mind is that the researcher presents an explanation for phenomena that he or someone else has originated, deduces the consequences that must occur if that explanation is accurate, and then tests to determine whether these conditions or events do occur.

Do these tests correctly and adequately represent the particular factors, conditions, or relationships of the consequences? Are they valid, reliable, and objective? Will they enable me to collect the necessary evidence with a minimum of effort? Since improper administration of a test or interpretation of the data will cause critics to reject his findings, he also exercises every precaution during these stages of his investigation.

Keeping accurate records of testing procedures is also essential in research. Writing a complete description of what he intends to do before initiating the full investigation makes it possible for the researcher to spot and correct obvious weaknesses. Keeping a diary of all procedures employed during the testing process places him in a better position to compile an account of them at the conclusion of the investigation. When the researcher presents his study to other scholars for consideration, he is obligated, of course, to include a detailed and accurate description of the subjects selected; statistical techniques employed; apparatus used; controls established; or any factor, condition, or event that played a part in the testing situation. If any procedure is based on some assumption, he states that also. Similar care and precision are exercised when presenting the test results, for omission of data or an ambiguous account will create a mystery rather than solve a problem.

Because tests are needed to meet a variety of demands, hundreds of them have been developed. A more detailed discussion of the selection, administration, evaluation, and interpretation of them is presented in later chapters. This text, however, merely provides an introduction to the subject. Anyone who wishes to pursue research work as a career must study and attain proficiency in employing a wide variety of test procedures. Acquiring a limited familiarity with investigative techniques will limit the range of work one can do and may cause one to make unfortunate technical errors. Mastery of a certain procedure, for example, will enable a researcher to conduct some studies successfully, but it may tempt him to apply his "pet method" to other situations where it is less adequate or not applicable.

Confirming the Hypothesis. A hypothesis is not confirmed unless the results of the tests conducted by the research worker present evidence that agrees with the consequences. When Dean Henry endeavored to confirm whether the job applicant, Prof. Stanley Silnatch, had been awarded a doctorate degree by Jones University in 1938, he found considerable evidence to support some of his consequences. The published list of doctoral dissertations indicated that Stanley Silnatch had produced a study in 1938. The Jones University records revealed that in 1938 a doctorate had been awarded to Stanley Silnatch. Dean Henry was almost convinced that his suspicions were unjustified, when he noticed that the student's signature on college records was quite different from the job applicant's signature. This puzzled him. When checking Stanley Silnatch's college health records and photographs, he discovered the key evidence that solved his problem. According to the 1938 records, Mr. Silnatch was over 6 feet tall, had blue eyes, and had lost three fingers on his left hand. Obviously the job applicant was an impostor for he was 5½ feet tall, had brown eyes, and possessed all his fingers. Dean Henry had discovered evidence that contradicted a deduced consequence; hence, he had definitely disconfirmed his hypothesis. The job applicant was merely masquerading as a student he had known well when he attended Jones University.

Requirements for Confirmation. To confirm a hypothesis, the researcher must provide factual evidence that agrees with every consequence logically implied by it. If Dean Henry had claimed that the hypothesis was confirmed merely because a number of facts fitted the theory perfectly, he would have been in error. Whenever *any evidence* produced by a test flatly contradicts one or more consequences and no errors have been made in test procedures, the researcher must abandon or modify his original hypothesis. No matter how much evidence is obtained to support a hypothesis, a single item of contradictory evidence can disprove it.

A hypothesis, then, is not confirmed unless it meets all of the following requirements: (1) all the factual evidence collected in the empirical tests corresponds with the consequences; (2) the test situation adequately represents the essential factors expressed in the consequences; and (3) the consequences are logically implied by the hypothesis. The substantiation of the hypothesis requires that each of these steps and relationships be fully realized (see Figure 15).

Strength of Confirmation. A scientist confirms rather than proves or verifies a hypothesis. The term "prove" carries the connotation of finality and absolute certainty. The term "verification" often appears in research literature, but the word literally means "to prove true" which is not an exact description of what the testing process produces. Hypotheses are never *proved* by producing factual evidence that is in harmony with the consequences; they are established only as *possessing a degree of probability.*

Finding factual evidence that supports one consequence of a hypothesis involves the "fallacy of affirming the consequence." Formal logic rules that if a minor premise affirms the consequent, as it does in the following example, the hypothetical argument is not valid.

Major premise:	If a child is bitten by a rabid dog, then he will die.
	(antecedent) (consequent)
Minor premise:	The child died. (factual evidence)
	(affirms the consequent)
Conclusion:	Therefore, he was bitten by a rabid dog. (inferred fact)

Since many causes other than a rabid dog bite could bring about death, this argument is invalid logically. To present evidence that affirms the consequent—death occurred—does not permit an inference as to which of many causes of death was responsible in this particular case.

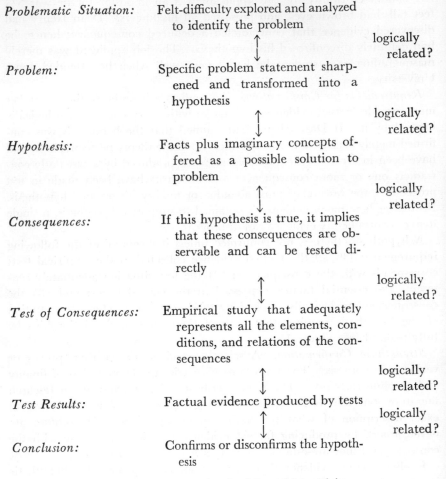

Problematic Situation: Felt-difficulty explored and analyzed to identify the problem

logically related?

Problem: Specific problem statement sharpened and transformed into a hypothesis

logically related?

Hypothesis: Facts plus imaginary concepts offered as a possible solution to problem

logically related?

Consequences: If this hypothesis is true, it implies that these consequences are observable and can be tested directly

logically related?

Test of Consequences: Empirical study that adequately represents all the elements, conditions, and relations of the consequences

logically related?

Test Results: Factual evidence produced by tests

logically related?

Conclusion: Confirms or disconfirms the hypothesis

Fig. 15.   Processes involved in problem solving.

In education or any field, an investigator can make the mistake of assuming that he has found the real cause of some phenomena merely because he has obtained empirical evidence that supports a consequence of his hypothesis. The following example reveals the flaw in this type of argument:

If low intelligence is the cause of juvenile delinquency, then low intelligence is observed in a disproportionate number of children with criminal records.

Low intelligence is observed in a disproportionate number of children with
criminal records (empirical evidence).

Therefore, low intelligence is the cause of juvenile delinquency.

It is possible that low intelligence is associated with juvenile delinquency,
but many other factors may also be associated with it.   Perhaps low intelligence is merely associated with heredity, early environment, or some
other factor or combination of factors which may be the true cause of
juvenile delinquency.   Perhaps low intelligence is as frequent among law-
abiding youths as among juvenile delinquents who come from the same environment.   The most satisfactory hypothesis is the one that explains all the
facts relating to the problem.   The investigator, therefore, tries to show
that no alternative hypothesis can account for the facts relating to the
problem as adequately as his hypothesis.   To accomplish this, he obtains
empirical evidence to support consequences in a number of widely scattered
areas.   Not until he clearly eliminates all other possible explanations, can
he claim that his hypothesis is the only one that adequately explains the
phenomena.

The affirmation of one consequence cannot prove that a hypothesis is
true.   The affirmation of several consequences cannot prove it is true
either, but building up a web of evidence makes the hypothesis "more
probably true."   Scientists recognize that they cannot achieve "absolute
certainty," but they try to come as close to this goal as possible by finding
as much evidence as they can to support their hypotheses.   If only a little
evidence is produced to substantiate consequences of a hypothesis, it is
poorly or weakly confirmed.   If considerable factual evidence is produced
to support several deduced consequences, the degree of probability that the
hypothesis offers a satisfactory explanation approaches greater certainty.
But, remember, even a well-confirmed hypothesis is held only tentatively
and provisionally; it is subject to modification or abandonment whenever
new factual evidence demands it.   Empirical support merely confirms,
strengthens, or substantiates hypotheses; it does not *prove* something is
absolutely true for all time.

Reformulation or Abandonment of a Hypothesis.   An inexperienced research worker often feels that he must prove something and wants to prove
it on the first try.   After hastily constructing a hypothesis, he rushes headlong into testing its deduced consequences.   His intense desire to confirm
his hypothesis may cause him to avoid evidence that will disconfirm it.
After formulating the hypothesis that "all geniuses exhibit antisocial behavior," for example, he may eagerly search for data concerning drunkenness, dope addiction, riotous living, and immorality among great painters,
writers, scientists, and musicians, but fails to investigate the lives of Einstein,
Pasteur, and other "well-behaved geniuses."   Incandescent infatuation with

his hypothesis may blind him to its faults and cause him to ignore evidence that can explode it.

Parting with a pet hypothesis is a particularly painful experience if intellectual poverty makes it difficult for an investigator to construct alternative solutions. Because a successful scientist possesses a rich intellect and vivid imagination that enables him to originate many hypotheses, he is not reluctant to abandon an untenable one. As W. Stanley Jevons pointed out, "It would be an error to suppose that the great discoverer seizes at once upon the truth, or has any unerring method of divining it. In all probability the errors of the great mind exceed in number those of the less vigorous one. Fertility of imagination and abundance of guesses at truth are among the first requisites of discovery" (14:577). Before stumbling upon a fruitful hypothesis, one may explore and abandon dozens of hopeless hunches.

By clinging tenaciously to a disconfirmed hypothesis, an investigator commits professional suicide. Advances in knowledge are never made by nursing dead ideas. Successful scientists agree that hypotheses are not sacred slogans to be preserved at all costs. Darwin once declared that he could not remember ever formulating a hypothesis that he did not later greatly modify or abandon. Einstein observed that probably ninety-nine out of a hundred of his conclusions were false. Hypotheses are mere guesses, and the vast majority of them prove to be wrong. Most hypotheses quickly go to their graves, some experience a short life, and only a select few are handed down from generation to generation.

Although a scientist may find it difficult to do so, he should drop or revise a hypothesis when he obtains evidence that it is inconsistent with observable facts. But there is a difference between abandoning a disconfirmed and an unconfirmed hypothesis. If no evidence disconfirms a hypothesis, one does not abandon it merely because finding the supporting evidence is difficult. Some scientists have conducted hundreds of tests and endured years of frustration before they were able to produce evidence confirming their hypotheses. A research worker must be capable of judging when he has no choice but to reject a hypothesis and when he should persevere with one. An investigation may have to be set aside, temporarily, of course, if the tools or techniques needed to obtain confirming evidence have not yet been devised. It also may have to be put off until the required testing conditions arise. One of the consequences of the theory of relativity could not be tested, for example, until a total eclipse of the sun occurred.

Types of Confirmation. The social sciences encompass many specific subject fields with a wide variety of problems in each area. Each social science problem is distinctive, but most of them fall into two broad categories: (1) problems of fact and (2) problems of value. Each type of problem raises a different kind of question. Many scholars believe that the scientific method simply cannot deal with problems of value; others (16,19) argue that it can. Some of the difficulties involved can best be understood by reviewing the nature of problems of fact and value.

1. *Problems of fact.* Problems of fact propose questions that ask: What is the actual state of affairs in a given society? These problems raise questions which require the determination of facts. An educator, for example, might propose that the ratio of left-handed to right-handed children who stutter is three to one. To confirm this hypothesis, the educator must find factual evidence in the existing culture that corresponds exactly with it. For the solution of his factual problem, he resorts to the scientific method of inquiry.

2. *Problems of value.* Problems of value raise questions that ask: What kind of society should man aim to achieve? Normative social theories answer these problems by defining the ideal society. Different people have different concepts of the social norms at which they aim. The Russians and Americans, for example, do not envisage the same form of ideal social organization. Problems of value sharply differ from problems of fact for they question what the ideal society ought to be like, not what the facts of the situation are in any given culture. The democratic or Christian ideal, for example, is not realized completely in practice, but this does not mean that it is invalid. Yet, this is exactly what an investigator would have to conclude if he confirmed *normative* social theories and *factual* social theories by the same method.

To be valid, a factual theory must be absolutely in accord with the facts in a given society. The objective of the normative social theory is to change the actual status of society rather than to coincide completely with the facts in a particular culture. Hence, an investigator cannot solve problems of value by exactly the same method as problems of fact. Different types of problems require somewhat different methods for solution.

Some scholars argue that some value as well as fact problems can be attacked by the scientific method, but the method of confirmation in the two types of problems differs. To verify factual theories, an investigator checks his theory against the *conditions in society,* and if they agree completely, his theory is confirmed. According to Northrup, an investigator can verify a normative social theory, not by checking it against the *facts in society,* now or in the future, but by checking it with the *facts of nature.* For example, American educators believe that a good educational system is one that provides for individual differences. If this theory is checked against the facts in society, it will not be verified empirically for many schools do not provide for individual differences. But, if this theory is checked against the *facts of nature,* it will be confirmed for it is possible to verify empirically that children differ in capacities. If the normative social theory agrees with the facts of nature, it is sound; if it does not, it should be rejected. Thus, in the opinion of some scholars, the social scientists have a scientific method of determining which is the most adequate social theory of those created by men.

Examples of Testing Hypotheses. The preceding chapter discussed two examples of problem analysis, one undertaken by Galileo centuries ago and the other by Miss White, a modern classroom teacher. Perhaps the following review of how they deduced consequences from their hypotheses and tested them will give you a clearer insight into the procedures involved in confirming or disconfirming hypotheses.

Galileo's Experiment. On the basis of his problem analysis, Galileo constructed three hypotheses that might offer satisfactory explanations for the phenomenon, motion, that he was trying to understand. These hypotheses were merely proposed solutions; they lacked confirmation. To determine whether any one of them could be confirmed, he had to deduce the consequences of each hypothesis and test them.

Galileo as well as others before him gave consideration to the relationship of weight and the motion or velocity of falling bodies. Thus, he first examined this ancient hypothesis: The velocity with which bodies fall is proportional to the weight of the body. From this hypothesis he could deduce the following consequence: If this hypothesis is true, then when bodies of different weights are dropped simultaneously from the same height, they will reach the earth at different times. Common sense would seem to indicate that the heavier objects would hit the ground before the lighter ones. But Galileo was not willing to accept this explanation merely because it was logical; he insisted upon putting it to an empirical test. In the Tower of Pisa experiment (or if this is mythical, some similar test), he discovered that except for differences caused by the resistance of air, objects of different weights fall at the same speed (and in a vacuum they would hit the ground at the same time). Hence, Galileo had disconfirmed the hypothesis that the velocity with which a body falls depends on the weight.

Galileo next examined his second hypothesis: Velocity is proportional to the distance through which the body travels. But he rejected this hypothesis because he thought he had demonstrated mathematically that one of its consequences presented an impossibility. Thus, he turned to consider his third hypothesis: Velocity is proportional to the length of time during which the body falls. In other words he proposed that the acceleration or change in velocity during any unit interval of time is constant.

Galileo's third hypothesis could not be tested directly. But Galileo deduced that if this hypothesis were true, the distance covered by free falling bodies was proportional to the square of the time of their fall. Thus, if a body fell one unit of time and covered one unit of distance, in two units of time it would travel four units of distance, and in three units of time it would cover nine units of distance. If such evidence could be found, it would strengthen his hypothesis that the acceleration of falling bodies is constant.

To obtain empirical evidence that would confirm or disconfirm his hypothesis, Galileo set up an experiment. He placed a metal ball on an inclined plane which allowed the ball to move down freely, but relatively slowly, and observed how many units of time the ball consumed in covering different units of distance. As a result of this experiment, he was able to present empirical evidence that the relation between distance and time was in accord with his consequence. Therefore, Galileo's third hypothesis possessed empirical support and provided the basis for a new understanding of motion.

Having acquired a better understanding of motion, Galileo was able to construct a more satisfactory definition of force. According to Galileo's definition, force was not that which produces motion or velocity as Aristotle had described it, but that which produces a change of velocity —acceleration of movement. Thus, an object, such as a projectile, experiences continuous acceleration as long as it is being acted upon by force. According to Aristotle's definition of force, the projectile would have to stop moving as soon as the force of the explosion ceased to act. According to Galileo's definition, it does not stop moving when the explosion ends, it merely ceases to change velocity. It would continue to move with a constant velocity, if the force of gravitation did not draw it toward the earth. By solving the problem that had puzzled him, Galileo was able to present the world with a new, all-embracing definition of force that applied to any motion whatever.

Miss White's Experiment. Unlike Galileo's problem in which a limited number of variables operating on a purely physical level were involved, Miss White's classroom problem involved twelve children and a number of variables operating on at least four levels—physical, social, mental, and emotional. Consequently, she could not isolate and control the factors involved in her problem as easily and with the same precision as Galileo had. Despite the lack of a sophisticated research environment, Miss White arrived at a solution to her problem more efficiently by establishing a hypothesis, deducing its consequences, and testing the latter, than she could have by employing trial and error procedures.

You will recall that she proposed a number of hypotheses or explanations for the reading retardation. She quickly tested some of these: Is low intelligence a satisfactory explanation? Intelligence tests revealed that it was not. Were broken homes a cause? Home records revealed only two broken homes. After rejecting several hypotheses, Miss White decided that the following seemed to offer the most promising explanation:

These ten boys and two third-grade girls are below their reading expectancy level because they lack the sensory experiences that can help them associate printed symbols with words and ideas. Therefore, if they are to meet their reading expectancy level it will be necessary to devote a total of 200 minutes per school week for 20 consecutive weeks to sensory experiences directly related to their specific disabilities and progressively developed to strengthen and enlarge their language tools.

Having constructed a hypothesis, she deduced its consequences: If these children are below their reading expectancy level because they lack sensory experiences to help them associate printed symbols with words and ideas,

then (1) they will improve their reading ability by devoting 40 minutes per school week for 20 consecutive weeks to concrete sound, sight, touch, taste, or smell experiences that provide experiential background for words that appear in the reading text;

then (2) they will improve their reading ability by spending 100 minutes per school week for 20 consecutive weeks on concrete experiences accompanied by discussion to elicit responses that aid them in utilizing context clues in their reading selections;

then (3) they will improve their reading ability by devoting 60 minutes per school week for 20 consecutive weeks to word analysis and phonics.

To test her hypothesis, Miss White engaged in a number of activities. Before initiating the experiment, she gave the pupils reading achievement tests. To provide sensory experiences relating to the reading materials she selected a booklet, a related film, and a film strip with various captions used in the film. She also checked the booklet with the Flesch formula to determine whether it was suitable for third-grade pupils. Before introducing the unit, she made cards for the one hundred sixty words in the booklet, tested the pupils' comprehension of them, and found that there were forty-eight words that no pupil recognized.

After designing a systematic procedure for presenting the film, film strip, and text, Miss White gave the children many oral experiences with words they would later read. By skillfully eliciting questions and responses in class discussion, she encouraged pupils to utilize pictures, context clues, and sensory experiences when interpreting printed materials. As the need developed, she introduced phonics training to meet particular problems. The experiment also included games, field trips, displays, and creative media that enabled the children to observe, interpret, or play with sounds, experiences, and objects that appeared as words and ideas in their booklet.

Throughout the experiment, Miss White kept a detailed anecdotal record of each child's reactions to his experiences. At the conclusion of the experiment, Miss White checked to see how many of the forty-eight unfamiliar words had been learned and discovered the pupils knew two-thirds more than they had at the start. When she gave them an alternative reading achievement test, their gains ranged from one month to one year and three months. The entire discussion of Miss White's study (20) has been simplified and adapted to suit our needs. The study lacks the sophistication, preciseness, and controls that characterize real research, but it does reveal the general nature of the procedures involved in testing a hypothesis.

EVALUATING HYPOTHESES

Some hypotheses are more satisfactory than others. But how can a scientist determine whether there are weaknesses in a hypothesis? How can he judge whether it is advisable to give serious consideration to his suggested problem solution? When two hypotheses seem to explain the same facts, is there any way of determining which is the more desirable? What characterizes the most significant hypotheses? Certain criteria for evaluating hypotheses have been mentioned in this and previous chapters and the following paragraphs will expand, extend, and summarize this discussion.

Plausibility of Explanation. One of the first questions that a researcher asks is: Does this hypothesis present a relevant and logical possibility? An explanation that does not pertain to the problem under consideration or that contains contradictory terms is not acceptable. Nor does an explanation that suggests a physical impossibility provide a satisfactory solution to a problem. It is of little value, for example, to suggest that the government can cut expenditures for military uniforms by controlling the growth of young men so that they all require the same size garments. This hypothesis presents a physical impossibility; hence, it is worthless. To suggest that the fall of the French government caused twenty pupils in a particular Muskegon, Michigan, school to fail an algebra test is an unacceptable explanation. The failure of the students is not logically implied by the hypothesis. The explanation has nothing to do with the problem; it is irrelevant. To repeat, a properly structured hypothesis is logically consistent, pertinent to the question under consideration, and does not contradict the laws of nature (See Appendix F).

Testability of Explanation. Another question that a researcher asks when evaluating the worth of a hypothesis is: Can its consequences be tested empirically at the present time or in the foreseeable future? Unless a hypothesis implies consequences that can be checked by observational tests, it can never pass from the status of a "guess" to that of a confirmed fact. Unfortunately, some of the problems that are of the greatest interest to educators cannot be attacked because the techniques for testing the proposed solutions are not yet available.

If grandiose hypotheses require such prolonged and complicated testing procedures that the process can never be completed, they are of little value. Obviously, it is also useless to propose a hypothesis such as—evil spirits cause children of the Xandu tribe to steal chickens, but some educational hypotheses that men cherish contain variables that cannot be measured or observed any more easily than evil spirits. An untestable hypothesis or one that requires interminable testing may be highly treasured by its originator, but it is not a practical tool for prying loose reliable knowledge. A hypothesis that can be neither confirmed nor disconfirmed cannot advance science; it remains a mere guess; and genuine knowledge rests upon more than guesses.

The testability of a hypothesis is determined in part by the clarity and preciseness of the terms used to express it and its consequences. To test something you must know exactly what to consider in your experiment. What evidence would you have to produce, for example, to check this hypothesis: Modern pupils' failure to read is due to insufficient practice in the use of phonics. Exactly who, what, and how much does this hypothesis suggest that you check? What constitutes "modern pupils," "failure," and "insufficient"? It is impossible to determine what these vague concepts imply. They fail to indicate exactly what evidence must be located or measured to confirm the hypothesis. If a hypothesis is to be tested, each term in it must denote a specific measurable phenomenon that any observer can check by empirical tests.

Embedding value terms such as "good," "poor," "bad," "ought," and "should" in hypotheses also causes problems. Consider the following hypothesis, for example: Poor students view television programs more than good students. What constitutes "good," "poor," "more"? A hypothesis cannot consist of ambiguous, obscure, and emotionally spiced prose passages. Clear and precise terms are required—if possible, terms that enable the investigator to count, weigh, measure, time, or in some way quantify the factors to be checked by direct observation. If "poor students" becomes students in Cedar Falls High School who failed two or more stipulated subjects in the past semester, any investigator can count them and arrive at the same answer. A good hypothesis always states a specific condition that can be empirically examined. Consider, for example, the hypothesis that water temperature does not affect the performance of or the physiological stress (heart beat and body temperature) on University of Pittsburgh varsity swimmers. This hypothesis is satisfactory as a basis for research because the variables (water temperature, performance, heart beat, body temperature) are definitely stated, the relationship between water temperature and the other variables is clearly cited, and the variables are measurable.

Adequacy of Scope. A good hypothesis explains all the facts that are relevant to a problem and contradicts none of them. Many hypotheses are able to explain some phenomena relating to a problem, but lack the power to explain others. One reason for the unsatisfactory situation in educational psychology today is the limited scope of the several hypotheses explaining the nature of learning. Each hypothesis accounts for some phenomena of learning but ignores factors that other hypotheses explain. In the field of medicine, two schools of thought have created different explanations for schizophrenia. One suggests that the cause and cure are psychic and the other that it is physiological in origin. When more research has been done, perhaps some scientists will be able to construct an all-inclusive explanation.

In the early stages of development in any field, the hypotheses are apt to be limited in scope. This is a natural situation, for men cannot leap to the pinnacle of thought in one jump. Innumerable limited explorations are usually made before some genius creates a hypothesis that represents a major "breakthrough" in knowledge. Modest hypotheses make necessary and valuable contributions to science, but investigators work continuously toward the formulation of more adequate and more comprehensive ones.

The more facts a hypothesis brings into a system or order through its explanation, the greater is its worth. If H-I (hypothesis one) explains A and B, and H-II explains A, B, and C, and H-III explains A, B, C, and D, the last is preferable. A hypothesis is of greater value if it establishes a generalization that can be applied in many fields. If a geographer develops a hypothesis that enables zoologists, historians, and geologists to explain phenomena that have been puzzling them, it is of greater worth than a hypothesis that accounts only for phenomena in one discipline. Theories formulated about gravitation, atoms, and evolution are examples of hypotheses that possess extensive explanatory powers. As science advances, investigators continually strive to devise more comprehensive concepts to account for phenomena that were previously explained by different, rival, or unrelated theories. In the unified field theory, for example, Einstein attempted to bring gravitation, light, and electricity—all of them manifestations of energy—into one grand formula. The highest goal of any science is to develop a few comprehensive explanations that will account for all the facts that come within its scope.

The most satisfactory hypotheses not only explain all the known facts that gave rise to the original problems, but also enable scientists to make predictions about things that previously were not known or even suspected. If H-III can explain A, B, C, and D, and also successfully can predict E, F, and G—previously undiscovered phenomena—it will be greatly strengthened. The heliocentric theory acquired added weight, for example, because it enabled scientists to predict the existence of Neptune long before they sighted the planet through a telescope. Whenever predictions projected from a hypothesis are confirmed, the hypothesis gains tremendously in stature.

Usefulness of False Hypotheses. Hypotheses need not be the correct answers to problems to be useful. In almost every inquiry a scholar constructs several hypotheses and hopes that one will provide a satisfactory solution to the problem. By eliminating the false hypotheses one by one, he keeps narrowing the field in which the answer must lie. If a doctor, for example, tries to determine why students became ill after a school picnic, he may theorize that the potato salad, cream pie, chicken, or drinking water made them ill. If his tests indicate that the first three items were not responsible, he is on his way to finding that the water was the causative agent. A researcher makes a contribution to science even though none of his hypotheses solve a problem. Pointing out lines of inquiry that are unprofitable to pursue lightens the task of his successors. Testing false hypotheses is also of value if it directs the attention of the investigator or other scientists to unsuspected facts or relations that eventually help solve the problem. History is sprinkled with stories of investigators who have stumbled upon clues leading to a successful hypothesis while testing a false one.

Roots in Existing Theories. Science develops by building cumulatively on the existing body of facts and theories. A useful educational hypothesis, therefore, adds something to previously established knowledge by supporting, qualifying, refuting, or enlarging upon existing theories. A hypothesis that is compatible with well-attested theories is in a favorable position to advance science. It does not have to agree with all the established facts, but should be consistent with a substantial body of them. Science cannot build sound, well-knit theoretical structures with isolated and conflicting hypotheses. If progress is to be made new hypotheses must fit into the framework of existing theories and transform them into more perfect explanatory schemes.

Hypotheses that are incompatible with established theories are regarded with suspicion, but such radical suggestions sometimes spark spectacular advances in science. Newton, Darwin, and Einstein, for example, proposed hypotheses that temporarily upset accepted bodies of theory and led to the reorganization of knowledge in their fields. Concepts introduced by Dewey, Thorndike, Kohler, and Lewin revolutionized educational thought. But scientists do not readily relinquish well-established theories. Rather than completely rejecting all older knowledge they usually try to correct errors, extend coverage, or reconcile conflicting theories. If a new hypothesis explains phenomena previously explained by two or more hypotheses, it receives careful consideration. Hypotheses that overthrow existing theories win support if they successfully eliminate contradictions in the existing ones. Einstein accomplished this fact when he constructed the theory of relativity which eliminated conflicts in the basic laws of classical mechanics and electrodynamics. In his unified field theory he attempted to reconcile conflicts in the relativity and quantum theories. Thus, even the more revolutionary theories are not completely disassociated from the existing body of knowledge.

Suitability for Intended Purpose. Several hypotheses may explain the same phenomenon, and each may be acceptable. If fifty children lose their lives in a school fire, an architect, pathologist, psychologist, and fire chief may offer different explanations of the event. Each hypothesis will reflect the past experience, special branch of knowledge, and particular frame of reference of its creator. Obviously, an explanation for the loss of life that satisfies the fire chief will not be the same as that which satisfies the pathologist. But, each hypothesis that offers a satisfactory explanation of what it intends to explain is useful for that purpose. The various explanations cannot contradict each other, of course, and each is not useful for any purpose. All hypotheses do not have to be cast in a single mold, but each must be adequate for the purpose it claims to serve.

Simplicity of Explanation. If two hypotheses are capable of explaining the same facts, the simpler one is the better. Simplicity in this instance does not imply ease of comprehension nor a low level of significance. Rather, it means that the hypothesis explains the phenomena with the least complex theoretical structure. The theory of relativity, for example, is not easy to comprehend, but it is admired and accepted, in part, because of its logical compactness. The classic example of simplicity is in the field of astronomy. Both the heliocentric theory and the geocentric theory explain the movements of the sun, moon, and planets. Both theories introduce epicycles to account for the positions of heavenly bodies, but the heliocentric theory introduces fewer epicycles. Because the heliocentric theory offers a less elaborate and complex explanation, it is more satisfactory. The hypothesis that accounts for all the facts with the fewest independent or special assumptions and complexities is always preferable.

Place in Hierarchy of Knowledge. Perhaps the value of hypotheses can best be comprehended by tracing their relationship to facts, theories, and laws. Through inductive and deductive methods of searching for truth, scientists gradually build a hierarchy of knowledge: (1) hypotheses, (2) theories, and (3) laws. Since everyone does not employ the same language when referring to these levels of knowledge, students often become confused. In the research literature, for example, the terms law and theory, and theory and hypothesis are sometimes used interchangeably and theorizing may refer to the formulation of hypotheses, theories, or laws. The following discusssion will distinguish between these levels of knowledge by using the more commonly accepted terminology.

Hypotheses and Facts. A hypothesis is the first step beyond random suggestions in the direction of scientific truth. In the hierarchy of scientific knowledge, it is the lowest on the scale. This temporary working principle requires testing to determine its worth. If empirical evidence can be found to support the hypothesis, it can gain the status of a fact. It retains this status thereafter unless evidence is discovered later to discredit it. Whether or not a hypothesis possesses the status of a fact depends upon the supporting evidence it can secure and hold.

Hypotheses and Theories. Hypotheses and theories are alike in that they are both conceptual in nature and both seek to explain phenomena. A theory usually offers a more general explanation than a simple hypothesis. Because it presents a more comprehensive conceptual scheme than a hypothesis, it deals with more facts. A theory actually may contain several logically interrelated hypotheses in its framework. A greater amount of empirical evidence is needed to support a theory than to support a hypothesis. This mass of evidence makes the probability of its certainty greater than that of a weakly confirmed hypothesis, but does not establish it as an absolute truth.

Hypotheses and Laws. Some hypotheses receive sufficient confirmation to become or to lead to the formulation of theories; some become laws. A law represents the highest level of scientific certainty. It offers the most comprehensive explanation of phenomena and is, therefore, applicable to a wide variety of situations.   Laws are developed by a long and painstaking process, during which they receive extensive empirical confirmation. Hence, they are accepted with little question. A law, nevertheless, retains its lofty position only by continuing to explain every instance which it claims to explain. If new evidence arises that does not conform to its tenets, the law no longer retains its preeminent status. It is either reconstructed to conform to the new evidence or abandoned, depending on the nature of the data that are discovered.

IMPORTANCE OF HYPOTHESES

Upon first becoming acquainted with research, students sometimes question the value of hypotheses construction. To them, it appears to be a "make work" project that is unrelated to the practical tasks involved in problem solving. They think that science is concerned with gathering facts objectively rather than guessing about answers to problems. They do not appreciate that a good guess provides the quickest and most efficient route to the solution of a problem.

No scientific undertaking can proceed effectively without well-conceived hypotheses; any attempt to do so is like working in the dark. For, as John Dewey pointed out, hypotheses regulate "the selection and weighing of observed factors and their conceptual ordering" (6:71). Hypotheses are indispensable tools, for they enable the researcher to map and expedite the exploration of the phenomena under consideration. Hypotheses serve as a "crutch" to thought. They help the investigator determine what facts to locate, what procedures to employ when conducting the study, and how to organize and present the findings. To reemphasize the importance of constructing sound hypotheses, the following discussion will review the more significant services they perform in a scientific investigation.

Pinpointing of Problems by Hypotheses. Without a hypothesis to guide him, a research worker often wastes time conducting a directionless investigation. If he produces meaningful results, it is largely due to chance. Chiseling out a specific promising hypothesis makes the research worker abandon a superficial or generalized attack on the problem. It compels him to make a thorough analysis of all the factual and conceptual elements that are pertinent to the problem and to determine their relationship to one another. By isolating and combining all relevant information into a systematic conceptual context and expressing it in an all-encompassing statement, the research worker constructs a solid foundation for a successful investigation. He is no longer fumbling with nebulous notions, but rather has clarified the issues at stake and crystallized the problem for investigation.

Using Hypotheses to Determine the Relevancy of Facts. Selecting facts necessary to conduct research is a matter of crucial concern. Aimlessly collecting a mass of data on a given subject is futile, for the infinity of possibilities prohibits any rational manipulation of them. The strategic facts needed to solve a problem do not automatically label themselves as relevant to it; they must be carefully selected. The hypothesis serves as the organizing principle that makes it possible to accomplish this task. It provides the structural framework around which pertinent data can be organized. The hypothesis guides the investigator in ascertaining what facts to collect and enables him to decide how many facts he needs to test its consequences adequately. Without a hypothesis the research worker drifts into an unfocused, trial and error inquiry in which he may become hopelessly confused by a welter of irrelevant facts and never stumble upon a successful problem solution. A hypothesis is required to direct action into productive channels.

Research Design Indicated by Hypotheses. A hypothesis helps the investigator determine what research procedures and methods are appropriate and adequate for testing the suggested solution to the problem. The different types of questions raised by hypotheses require different testing methods. Owing to the manner in which a hypothesis points up the pertinent issues at stake, it immediately rules out many testing methods as irrelevant. A well-constructed hypothesis often indicates the particular modes of attack that will meet its specific demands. It may suggest, for instance, what subjects or data are sufficient; what instruments or operations are adequate; what statistical methods are appropriate; or what events, facts, or circumstances are required to evaluate its consequences satisfactorily. Thus, the hypothesis may not only indicate what to look for in an investigation but also how to proceed with the inquiry.

Explanations Presented by Hypotheses. Providing explanations is the primary function of hypotheses. Science strives to supply the reasons for the occurrence of events or conditions. Scientific inquiry goes beyond the amassing of facts or mere describing and classifying of them in accordance with their superficial properties. Rather than merely tabulating symptoms of diseases, characteristics of aggressive behavior, or facts about juvenile crime, a serious research worker seeks to determine the underlying patterns that explain the structural interrelations of the phenomena under observation. As the text has previously pointed out, to do this he engages in a high order of conceptualization. He imaginatively creates elements or relationships and mentally combines them with known facts to account for the factors that require explanation. Thus, fact and fancy are artfully welded into hypotheses that provide man with a most useful instrument for exploring and explaining the unknown.

The Framework for Conclusions Provided by Hypotheses. A hypothesis helps the research worker organize and present significant conclusions in his study. A hypothesis is a tentative principle or generalization that accounts for some given phenomena; it retains the character of a guess until pertinent facts are found to support it. Through appropriate testing situations, the necessary facts are collected and, in the conclusions of the research report these findings are organized in terms of the purposes that initiated the investigation. If the factual evidence agrees with the original proposal, it confirms the hypothesis; if it disagrees with the original proposal, it discredits the hypothesis. Merely collecting facts on a subject and citing them *per se* or classifying them according to one's whims in the conclusions of the study does not advance knowledge appreciably; a hypothesis is required to provide a framework for stating the conclusions in a meaningful manner.

Further Research Stimulated by Hypotheses. An explanatory hypothesis enables man to extend and unify his knowledge. A well-conceived hypothesis offers a general principle that renders more understandable the phenomena under consideration. But rather than merely being an end in itself, a good hypothesis is a means to further understanding. It serves as an intellectual lever by which investigators can pry loose more facts to be fitted into other or more inclusive explanations.

The most useful hypotheses create a base from which new lines of investigation branch out in various directions. One report on teacher characteristics (18:399), for example, lists seventeen of the many suggestions that could be forwarded where further research is needed in this area. The Salk poliomyelitis vaccine, which stemmed from hypotheses relating to tissue culture and viruses that had been established by many earlier investigators, in turn, opened up some of the following questions: Can safer strains be produced? How long can immunity be achieved? Is it possible to develop a perfect immunity? Is it possible to reduce the number of injections? Can effective vaccines be developed for measles, encephalitis, common colds, etc.? Thus, one well-structured explanation can stimulate the formulation of a number of other hypotheses. These, in turn, can lead to new investigations and thus to the discovery of additional knowledge. A hypothesis is not advanced as a final statement; as Max Weber said, "it asks to be outdated and surpassed." It is our passkey to the unknown, leading us from one problem to another, from modest explanations to more adequate conceptual schemes that successively open up exciting new areas on the frontiers of knowledge.

BIBLIOGRAPHY

1. Beveridge, W. I. B., *The Art of Scientific Investigation.* New York: W. W. Norton & Company, Inc., 1951, chap. 5.

2. Black, Max, *Critical Thinking.* Englewood Cliffs, N.J.: Prentice-Hall, Inc., 1952, chap. 16.

3. Brown, Clarence W., and E. E. Ghiselli, *Scientific Method in Psychology.* New York: McGraw-Hill Book Company, Inc., 1955, chap. 8.

4. Cohen, Morris R., and Ernest Nagel, *An Introduction to Logic and Scientific Method.* New York: Harcourt, Brace & World, Inc., 1934, chap. 11.

5. Copi, Irving M., *Introduction to Logic.* New York: The Macmillan Company, 1955, chap. 13.

6. Dewey, John, *Logic: The Theory of Inquiry.* New York: Holt, Rinehart and Winston, Inc., 1938.

7. Durkheim, Emile, *Suicide,* translated by John A. Spaulding and George Simpson. London: Routledge & Kegan Paul, Ltd., 1952.

8. Furfey, Paul H., *The Scope and Method of Sociology.* New York: Harper & Brothers, 1953, chap. 11.

9. Galilei, Galileo, *Dialogues Concerning Two New Sciences.* Evanston, Ill.: Northwestern University, 1946.

10. Goode, William J., and Paul K. Hatt, *Methods in Social Research.* New York: McGraw-Hill Book Company, Inc., 1952, chap. 6.

11. Hall, A. R., *The Scientific Revolution.* London: Longmans, Green & Company, Ltd., 1954, chaps. 3 and 4.

12. Hillway, Tyrus, *Introduction to Research.* Boston: Houghton Mifflin Company, 1956, chap. 8.

13. Hodnett, Edward, *The Art of Problem Solving,* New York: Harper & Brothers, 1955, chaps. 15 and 18.

14. Jevons, W. Stanley, *The Principles of Science.* London: Macmillan & Co., Ltd., 1924.

15. Larrabee, Harold A., *Reliable Knowledge.* Boston: Houghton Mifflin Company, 1945, chap. 5.

16. Northrop, F. S. C., *The Logic of the Sciences and the Humanities*. New York: The Macmillan Company, 1949.

17. Report of the Committee on Historiography, *Theory and Practice in Historical Study*. New York: Social Science Research Council, 1946.

18. Ryans, David G., *Characteristics of Teachers*. Washington, D.C.: American Council on Education, 1960.

19. Stanley, William O., and B. Othanel Smith, "The Historical, Philosophical, and Social Framework of Education," *Review of Educational Research*, 26 (June, 1956): 308.

20. Taba, Hilda, and Elizabeth Noel, *Action Research*. Washington, D.C.: Association for Supervision and Curriculum Development, 1957.

21. Travers, Robert M. W., *An Introduction to Educational Research*. New York: The Macmillan Company, 1958, chap. 4.

22. Van Dalen, D. B., "The Role of Hypotheses in Educational Research," *Educational Administration and Supervision*, 14 (March, 1957): 21.

23. Werkmeister, W. H., *An Introduction to Critical Thinking*. Lincoln, Nebr.: Johnsen Publishing Company, 1948, chap. 21.

CHAPTER 9

Patterns of Historical Research

Because educational research embraces segments of many related disciplines and utilizes a great variety of procedures, it is somewhat difficult to obtain an overview of the work. Educators undertake studies in all subject matter fields; they investigate phenomena in the areas of curriculum, administration, guidance, methods, and teacher preparation; and they probe fundamental problems concerning the nature of learning and of child development. Several volumes would have to be written to explore the work being done in each of these fields. Moreover, the discussion would become repetitive because investigators in the various fields employ somewhat similar techniques and procedures. Hence, the remainder of this text discusses (1) the three general methods that educators utilize to solve problems—the historical, descriptive, and experimental methods; (2) the tools that researchers employ; and (3) how they write and evaluate research reports.

This chapter will examine the historical method of research. This method is employed by researchers who are curious about conditions and occurrences that have taken place in the past. Obtaining knowledge about the past has always intrigued men. Ancient wandering tribesmen handed down colorful accounts of their forefathers' lives in song and story. Later, a procession of scribes, churchmen, and learned scholars laboriously recorded the history of their cultures. In both primitive and highly civilized cultures, men have carefully preserved accounts of the past for posterity.

The roots of historical narrative are buried deep in the cultural soil of antiquity, but the purpose and scope of historical writing have changed down through the ages. Most of the early works in this field sought to achieve literary rather than scientific objectives. Writers preserved beloved folk tales or created stirring epics to entertain or inspire the reader. A few ancient Greek scholars, however, directed their efforts toward different goals. they envisioned history somewhat as a science—a search for truth. Thucydides, who wrote his famous historical accounts in the fifth century B.C., aspired to be more than an imaginative storyteller. His objective was to present an accurate account of the past in order to aid "in the interpretation of the future." To achieve this goal, Thucydides based his writings on his own observations or the reports of eyewitnesses that he subjected to detailed tests of reliability. For centuries most historians ignored the exacting methods and lofty aims of Thucydides; many of them wrote history to glorify the state or church rather than to arrive at objective truth. Some historians were disciplined by rigorous critical standards of research, however, and this practice became more commonplace particularly after the vigorous academic discussions of the historical method that took place shortly after the turn of this century.

Today, historians strive to recreate the past experiences of mankind in a manner that does no violence to the actual events and conditions of the time. They collect, examine, select, verify, and classify facts in accordance with specific standards, and endeavor to interpret and present those facts in an exposition that will stand the test of critical examination. They apply the same scholarly standards whether the problem is concerned with the history of a nation, the evolution of American universities, the life of an outstanding educator, or the history of a state educational association. Modern historical research is critical; it is a search for truth.

The historical method of investigation is of particular interest to scholars because of the universality of its application. One can apply it not only to subject matter that is commonly referred to as history, but also to ascertain the meaning and reliability of past facts in the natural sciences, law, medicine, religion, or any other discipline. Even if a researcher is not engaged in a historical study, he may employ historical research techniques. The critical standards established by historians can help him evaluate previous studies relating to his problem, the tools and procedures utilized by his predecessors, and the circumstances that conditioned the results of the previous studies. Hence, every researcher should be familiar with this method of investigation.

When undertaking a historical study, a scholar engages in some activities that are common to all investigations, but the nature of his subject matter presents him with some peculiar problems and requires him to apply some special standards and techniques. In general, a historian becomes involved in the following procedures: (1) selecting the problem, (2) collecting source materials, (3) criticizing source materials, (4) formulating hypotheses to explain events or conditions, and (5) interpreting and reporting the findings. These are not necessarily separate or successive processes, but for the sake of convenience and clarity, they will be considered separately in the following discussion. After reviewing these steps, the chapter will conclude with an evaluation of the historical method.

SELECTING THE PROBLEM

Earlier chapters in this text discussed the selection and delimitation of problems in detail as well as the general bibliographical tools and other library resources that one can use to locate them. Repeating this information is unnecessary, because the general considerations for choosing a problem remain the same regardless of the type of investigation one undertakes. It is sufficient, then, to acquaint you with representative historical studies and the need for research in the field.

A compilation of all the historical studies that have been completed in education would make an impressive list. Some describe education in different periods, geographical areas, or fields of specialization. Others investigate the development of institutions, organizations, teaching methods, curricula, legislation, or school buildings. Some give accounts of old textbooks; methods of school support, control, or administration; or the contributions of leaders to education. The studies cited in the bibliography (1,8,15,18,23,24,28) are examples of specific problems that have been investigated. Reviewing the literature in the field and examining historical doctoral dissertations, will give you an overview of other work that has been done and may help you spot some problems that are worth investigating. The bibliographies and discussions of historical research in educational history presented by Brickman (3) and Good and Scates (11:170–254) will also prove helpful not only when you are exploring problem possibilities, but also when you are searching for source materials and conducting an investigation.

Abundant opportunities for investigating historical problems exist. Woody once called physical educators' attention to the need for more research, and what he had to say to them also applies to other fields of specialization. Woody pointed out that, "if really little has been done by digging in the local quarries of intellectual history, less has been attempted in regard to physical education. . . . Institutions, movements, men and women, associated with the development of play and physical education, are waiting for an historic interview" (31:186). Many other aspects of education also are awaiting investigation. Unless the profession devotes more attention to historical research, much important source material will be permanently lost to mankind. Each year valuable letters, documents, and other materials are discarded from the files of retiring professors; embryonic educational organizations fail to preserve records of their activities; old textbooks, school and community records, and equipment are cleared from attics and storerooms and destroyed. Young scholars can make an important contribution to the profession by rescuing some of these primary source materials from oblivion. With a little probing, they can find a multiplicity of urgent and worthwhile historical problems to investigate.

COLLECTING SOURCE MATERIALS

Obtaining the best data available to solve a problem is an initial and important task of a historian. Thus, early in any study, he sifts through the vast and varied traces of human activity that testify about past events and selects evidence that is relevant to his problem. Although he may begin his search by examining secondary sources, his ultimate objective is to locate primary sources. Hence, he must be able to distinguish between the two types of source materials and must become adept at locating them.

Primary and Secondary Sources. Since a historian cannot observe past events for himself, he endeavors to obtain the "best evidence" available from *primary sources:* (1) the testimony of able eye and ear witnesses to past events, and (2) actual objects used in the past that can be examined directly. The importance of these sources cannot be overemphasized: through these surviving traces of men's thoughts and activities a historian can gain some understanding of the past; without them he is helpless— "Without them history would be only an empty tale, signifying nothing" (31:185). Primary sources are the basic materials of historical research.

Because a historian knows the worth of "firsthand" evidence, he makes every effort to locate it. But, sometimes, he finds it necessary to consult *secondary sources:* summaries of information written by a person who did not directly observe the event, object, or condition. These summaries appear in encyclopedias, textbooks, almanacs, newspapers, periodicals, and other references. Some secondary source materials are actually based on third-, fourth-, and fifth-hand information. Naturally the more interpretations that come between the past event and the reader, the less trustworthy is the evidence.

A rigid classification of source materials is not always possible, for both first- and secondhand information may appear in the same report. A principal's report of a school fire, for example, may describe incidents that he personally observed as well as those that other people described to him. In some instances, an item may be classified as either a primary or secondary source, depending upon how it is used. A general history of education textbook, for example, is many times removed from the original events, and is, therefore, a secondary source. If a scholar is studying how authors organized history of education textbooks and the emphasis they placed on various topics, however, it is a primary source.

A historian tries to obtain evidence from the closest witness to the past events or conditions. A newspaper account of what transpired at an NEA executive meeting would not satisfy him if he could possibly obtain a copy of the official minutes of the meeting. A translation of an educational document would not satisfy him if he could obtain and read the original document. Whenever possible, he would prefer to visit an old school building or playground rather than merely to study pictures of it. Primary sources are highly prized by a historian, but he sometimes finds that secondary sources also serve useful purposes. They may acquaint him with work that has been done in an area that he is exploring, may suggest problem possibilities and working hypotheses, and may introduce him to important primary sources. Secondary sources may provide him with background information for an investigation. He may use them to obtain an overview of a problem area and to develop the general setting for his problem. Later, of course, he will have to alter his problem outline, whenever firsthand information indicates it is imperative to do so.

Records and Remains. For the most part the historian's source materials are *records that have been preserved with the conscious intent of transmitting information.* Diverse types of records of past ideas, conditions, and events are available in written, pictorial, and mechanical forms, for example:

1. *Official Records:* Legislative, judicial, or executive documents prepared by Federal, state, or local governments, such as constitutions, laws, charters, court proceedings and decisions, tax lists, and vital statistics; the data preserved by churches, such as baptismal, marriage, financial, and board meeting records; the information compiled by Federal and state education departments, special commissions, professional organizations, school boards, or administrative authorities, such as the minutes of meetings, reports of committees, administrative orders or directives, catalogs, school surveys, annual reports, budgets, courses of study, class schedules, salary lists, honors and awards, attendance records, health records, safety and accident reports, and athletic records

2. *Personal Records:* Diaries, autobiographies, letters, wills, deeds, contracts, lecture notes, and original drafts of speeches, articles, and books

3. *Oral Traditions:* Myths, folk tales, family stories, dances, games, superstitions, ceremonies, reminiscences of eyewitnesses to events, and recordings

4. *Pictorial Records:* Photographs, movies, microfilms, drawings, paintings, and sculpture

5. *Published Materials:* Newspaper, pamphlet, and periodical articles; literary and philosophical works that convey information about education

6. *Mechanical Records:* Tape recordings of interviews and meetings, phonograph records of pupils' speech or reading efforts

In some instances, the historian does not have to rely on the records, reports, or words of others, but actually can handle objects of the past that have been preserved. *These remains or relics which are handed down from the past without the specific intent of imparting facts or information constitute an unconscious testimony of incidents in the lives of people.* The toys, weapons, implements, and skeletal remains found on a burial site, for example, may convey considerable information about the past. Remains sometimes reveal the actual practices and conditions better than official documents. A law may be found, for example, stating it was compulsory for children to remain in school until they were sixteen years of age. But payroll records, pictures taken in factories and fields, and other unpremeditated evidence may reveal that many pupils left school before that age.

Various types of remains a historian might find are:

1. *Physical Remains:* Buildings, facilities, grounds, furniture, equipment, costumes, implements, awards, and skeletal remains
2. *Printed Materials:* Textbooks, blank diplomas, record blanks, contracts, certificates, attendance forms, report cards, and newspaper advertisements
3. *Handwritten Materials:* Pupil manuscripts, drawings, and exercises

Since relics and remains are tangible evidence that the researcher can examine personally, they are more trustworthy as sources than records. The historian can measure, weigh, and describe an ancient instrument that was once used to punish children. To interpret how, when, or why it was used, however, he usually must search for clues in reports made by men in the past.

Source materials do not necessarily fall into exclusive categories. An item may be either a record or relic depending upon the purpose for which it is used and the intention of the producer of the document or relic. A blank form for recording academic studies and achievements, for example, is a remain. But, if someone writes the courses, the grades, credits earned, and the name of the student on it, the form conveys information intentionally; thus, it is a document. Similarly, a recording may be made of a pupil's speech merely to test the equipment and with no intention of conveying information; or it may be made to have a record of the pupil's speech patterns for future analysis.

Location of Source Materials. In his preliminary search for historical data, a researcher will find that the card catalog, periodical indexes, bibliographies, historical reviews, dissertations, and research journals provide helpful leads. Although he may locate useful materials in his local library, his search probably will extend to other institutions and to specialized depositories that have business, government, legal, or private papers relating to his problem.

Some individuals and agencies have exerted considerable effort to collect educational records and remains and have established a number of historical depositories to preserve them. The types of resources and completeness of the accumulations in the various depositories vary greatly: some contain extensive collections of a particular kind of materials and others have fragmentary collections of items from different fields. Owing to the wide expanse of time and the broad scope of educational endeavors, no one depository, however excellent, can possibly house all the available materials.

The Library of Congress, the New York Public Library, and some universities and specialized libraries have valuable collections in particular educational areas. The Museum of the City of New York and similar institutions in other communities possess local educational remains. Some state and local historical societies have museums that contain important remains, newspaper files, and documents. Educational organizations have preserved documents and relics pertinent to their interests, for example, the American Association for Health, Physical Education, and Recreation has established a depository at Queens College. A few universities have kept libraries, equipment, and effects of outstanding educators who have served on their staffs. Private citizens and prominent educators have also accumulated exceptional collections, such as the thousands of old school textbooks that Dr. John Nietz acquired and presented to the University of Pittsburgh.

Not all source materials, of course, are conveniently collected for a researcher. Private probing expeditions can often turn up valuable evidence. Important data may be discovered by talking with "oldtimers" in the profession; exploring secondhand stores, book shops, and attics; visiting sites of schools and playgrounds; getting permission to examine the correspondence, lecture notes, manuscripts, and files of retired teachers and professors; or studying court, town, church, professional, school, and institutional reports and records.

CRITICIZING SOURCE MATERIALS

A historian does not assume that a remain is genuine or that a record presents an authentic account of past happenings. He meticulously examines each one and attempts to determine how trustworthy it is. Detecting whether a document contains unintentional errors or is a deliberate deception is an essential part of his work. Any investigator who fails to take this precaution is foolhardy, for research based on unreliable sources is labor lost. "In historical studies doubt is the beginning of wisdom" (17:50). To give mankind a credible account of past events, a historian must subject his source materials to rigorous external and internal criticism.

External Criticism. Through external criticism the historian checks the genuineness of the document or relic—whether it is what it appears or claims to be—to determine whether it is admissible as evidence. To discover the origins of source materials, he asks many questions: When or why was the document produced? Who was the author or creator? Did the credited author write the material? Is this the original or an accurate copy of the author's work? If not, can the original text of the document be restored? Questions, questions, questions—the researcher keeps asking them until he can ascertain when, where, why, and by whom a document or relic was produced.

Establishing authorship is a common test performed by a historian, for some documents do not carry the name of the writer, conceal his identity with a pseudonym, or present a man as the author who wrote little or none of the work. Educational committees and school administrators, for example, frequently issue reports that do not clearly identify the writer. Although three committee members may sign a report, only one of them may have written it—or a subordinate of one member may have compiled it. To ascertain the authorship of a superintendent's annual report, a historian may have to investigate several things: Did the superintendent write it, one of his assistants, or was it a compilation of reports made by various school administrative heads? If the superintendent used other people's materials, did he correct, alter, omit, suppress, or expand parts of their reports?

Enterprising and exacting detective work is often required to establish authorship, trace anonymous and undated documents, ferret out forgeries, discover plagiarism, spot incorrectly identified items, or restore a document to its original form. When sleuthing for clues, the historian attentively examines items and asks pertinent questions, such as: (1) Are the language, style, spelling, handwriting, and printing of the document typical of the author's other work and the period in which it was written? (2) Did the author exhibit ignorance of things a man of his training and time should have known? (3) Did he write about events, things, or places that a man of that period could not have known? (4) Did anyone intentionally or unintentionally alter the manuscript by copying it incorrectly, adding to it, or deleting passages? (5) Is this an original draft of the author's work or a copy? If it is a copy, is it reproduced in the exact words of the original? (6) If the manuscript is undated or the author unknown, are there any internal clues in the document that reveal its origins?

When cross-examining his silent witnesses to determine the genuineness of a document or relic, a researcher experiences greater success if he possesses a rich fund of historical and general knowledge. He also needs a good "chronological sense," a versatile intellect, good common sense, an intelligent understanding of human behavior, and plenty of patience and persistence. To solve some problems he must be familiar with philology, chemistry, anthropology, archaeology, cartography, numismatics, art, literature, paleography, or various modern and ancient languages. A historian cannot have a knowledge of everything, of course, but he usually acquires special training in auxiliary fields that are most closely related to his educational problem. If he is not qualified to undertake certain aspects of textual criticism, he seeks the help of competent experts in the field.

Internal Criticism. After completing the external criticism of a source material, the historian engages in internal criticism. External criticism is concerned with establishing the time, place, and authorship of the document and restoring the original form and language employed by the author. Internal criticism is concerned with ascertaining the meaning and trustworthiness of the *data within the document.* To do this, the historian probes for answers to the following questions: (1) What did the author mean by each word and statement? (2) Are the statements that the author made credible? The intent of internal criticism is to determine the conditions under which a document was produced, the validity of the intellectual premises upon which the writer proceeded, and the correct interpretation to be placed upon data.

Determining the meaning of a statement, technical term, or archaic word can be a complicated task requiring considerable knowledge of history, laws, customs, and languages. Many words in older documents do not mean the same thing today that they did in earlier times. Interpreting words and statements in recent publications is a less arduous task, but some words do not convey the same meaning to all people. When English and American writers use the word "football" or "public school," for example, they are not referring to the same thing. Nor do all authors have identical meanings in mind when they use the term "progressive education" or "juvenile delinquent."

Reading a document "through the author's eyes" is easier if one is familiar with the geographical, social, political, religious, economic, and domestic environment that the writer experienced. If one knows why an author wrote a particular report, he may also be able to interpret its meanings more accurately. The possession of such background information helps an investigator detect whether the author is writing seriously, humorously, ironically, or symbolically. It helps him determine whether the author is voicing his real sentiments or pious, polite, or conventional phrases for public consumption. Whenever a researcher uses a translation of a historical document or does the work himself, he makes certain that the translated materials convey exactly the same meaning as the original. Accurate analysis and interpretation of the author's meaning is of paramount importance if a scholar is to recreate a reliable account of past events.

A historian remains skeptical of statements made in source materials until he critically tests them. To evaluate the credibility of passages in a document, he intensively investigates whether the author was willing and able to tell the truth in each instance. When conducting this probe, he asks some of the following questions: (1) Is the author accepted as a competent observer and reliable reporter by other authorities in this special field? (2) Were his facilities, technical training, and location favorable for observing the conditions he reported? (3) Did emotional stress, age, health conditions, or lack of intelligence cause him to make faulty observations or an inaccurate report?   (4) Did he report on direct observations, hearsay, or borrowed source materials?   (5) Did he write the document at the time of observation or weeks or years later?   (6) Did he write from carefully prepared notes of observations or from memory?   (7) Did he have biases concerning any nation, region, race, religion, person, political party, social or economic group, professional body, period of history, old or new teaching methods, educational philosophy, or activity that influenced his writing? (8) Did anyone financially assist his research work with the hope of securing a report favorable to a specific cause?   (9) Did the author write under any economic, political, religious, or social condition that might have caused him to ignore, misinterpret, or misrepresent certain facts?   (10) Was he motivated to write by malice, vanity, or a desire to justify his acts?   (11) Was his objective to win the approval of succeeding generations or to please or antagonize some group?   (12) Did the author distort or embellish the truth to achieve colorful literary effects?   (13) Did the author contradict himself?   (14) Are there accounts by other independent, competent observers of different backgrounds that agree with the report of the author?

Examples of Criticism. Many questions arise when one engages in historical criticism. To give you some insight into typical problems that a researcher encounters, the following discussion presents a case of (1) determining authorship, (2) identifying an unknown manuscript, (3) assessing authenticity, (4) restoring a document, (5) ascertaining meaning, (6) finding the correct spelling, and (7) checking origin.

Determining Authorship. Sometimes a man will be credited as an author of a work for years and in many reputable references before anyone questions the fact. A book on gymnastics that was used in some early American schools, for example, has the name of Salzmann on the title page. Scholars who traced the origins of this text, found that Johann C. F. Guts Muths, a teacher in Salzmann's school, was actually the author of the original book, *Gymnastik für die Jugend,* which was published in 1793. In 1800, an English publisher translated Guts Muths's book and placed Salzmann's name on the title page. A footnote explained that there was no doubt that Salzmann wrote it, for his name was subjoined to the advertisement in which it was announced (22:80). This error of authorship was repeated in the American work of 1802. Moreover, a comparison of the original Guts Muths edition with the translated versions, reveals that the latter editions were also altered and condensed.

Identifying an Unknown Manuscript. An interesting story of tracking down the author, time, place, and purpose of a document has been told by Thomas Woody (31:188–189). In the University of Pennsylvania Archives, an old manuscript was found with other original manuscripts relating to the University. It was in relatively good condition, apparently free from alteration or mutilation, but devoid of any external indication of its origin.

After carefully examining the manuscript for clues, Woody was able to formulate the following hypotheses: (1) the document was all or part of an original document or a translated account of the rules and operation of *Pädagogium Regii,* a school established by Francke at Halle, Germany; (2) the appearance of certain awkward expressions suggested that the writer or translator was unfamiliar with the English language; (3) the reference to money in terms of Pennsylvania currency suggested that the author expected the information to be used in that locale; and (4) a reference made to 1726 indicated that the manuscript was probably produced sometime after that date.

To test his hypotheses, Woody turned to the most promising source—"The Trustees' Minutes"—for supporting evidence. In the minutes, he found that the Trustees in 1750–1751 appointed a committee to draw up regulations for the new institution that had been established and placed under their care. The committee, wishing to be better informed about institutional regulations, requested "the Trustees to get a Translation made of a Pamphlet written in the German Language, recommended by the Revd. Mr. Whitefield, containing the Rules and Orders observed by the celebrated . . . School at Hall [Halle]" (31:189). The minutes stated that the Trustees unanimously agreed to the committee's proposal.

Woody suggested that, "from the foregoing, it seems reasonably certain, but the proof is not complete, that the English manuscript *may be the translation* of a document which, presumably, Mr. Whitefield had in his possession" (31:189). This conclusion was also supported by the fact that many of Mr. Whitefield's letters express admiration for the institutions established by Francke. Woody concluded "Further search would probably lead to discovery of the original pamphlet, or a copy of the same, from which this MS. translation was made, and many other matters" (31:189). But his discussion is sufficient to reveal some of the steps and techniques involved in tracing an unknown manuscript.

Assessing Authenticity. Historians are curious about whether a document actually is what it claims to be. Hoaxes and intentional falsifications are not common in educational literature, but doubts sometimes arise concerning the real nature of a document. This happened in the case of *A Young Girl's Diary* (16), an anonymous work that was claimed to be a genuine and unedited diary of an early adolescent. This book, which Freud described as a "gem" in a brief introductory letter, gained wide recognition in psychological circles as a revelation of the beginning of sexual consciousness, its development, and its incorporation into maturer thought patterns.

When a few readers (4) began to suspect that the diary was not the work of an early adolescent, they suggested that it might be a reproduction of childhood experiences by an adult. To support their position, they pointed out that the style of writing and sustained logical thinking was too mature for an eleven- to fourteen-year-old girl. Moreover, the length of the entries —sometimes two thousand words a day—was too taxing for a child. The critics held that the continuity, coherence, and clarity of the diary was extraordinary, particularly because it had to be kept secret from an anxious mother and inquisitive sister. Unexplained allusions and unconnected incidents did not impede the reader's understanding of the passages as would be expected. One did not need editorial notes to explain who characters were and each incident reported contributed to building the main dramatic theme. Inconsistencies were noted when checking the girl's references to the weather on certain days, visits to places that were nonexistent at the time, and other items (20). Consequently, some men concluded that the diary probably was not written by a young girl during the years the events took place.

Restoring a Document. An author's words are not necessarily preserved in print exactly as he wrote them. *The Autobiography of St. Thérèse of Lisieux* (19), for example, was published after her death and became a best seller. When she was canonized, the original script of her autobiography was located and analyzed. In comparing it with the printed work, scholars noted many differences. During the process of restoring the autobiography, they discovered that seven thousand changes had been made in the manuscript!

Ascertaining Meaning. When men want to settle questions, they may turn to traditional sources of authority for guidance. In recent years, for example, some citizens have urged that sectarian religious instruction be fostered in public schools and that public funds be made available to private and parochial schools. Their opponents claim that such action would violate the principle of the separation of church and state expressed in the First Amendment, which reads: "Congress shall make no law respecting an establishment of religion, or prohibiting the free exercise thereof. . . ." The question raised is: "Does the ban on 'establishment of religion' prohibit 'co-operation' between church and state in education or is greater 'co-operation' than we now have both permissible and desirable? Does 'co-operation' amount to an alliance or fusion of church and state?" (5:xiii). To reach any decision, it is necessary to determine what the principle of separation of church and state means.

Professor Butts tried to discover the authentic meaning of "establishment of religion" by sifting through the available historical evidence. To trace what the term has meant in America from colonial days to the mid-twentieth century, he examined the deliberations and constitutions of colonial, state, and national bodies; the writings of outstanding leaders; and the school laws, legislative acts, and judicial decisions that had a bearing on the problem. Butts's analysis extended over two hundred pages, and his conclusions concerning the meaning of the term "separation of church and state" for education were summarized in ten statements (5:209–210). His study reveals the tremendous amount of labor that is sometimes involved in determining what a statement means.

Finding the Correct Spelling. Standard works of reference generally possess their quota of mistakes. For instance, the *Encyclopaedia Britannica* refers to the wife of the fourth President of the United States as Dorothy; the *Encyclopedia Americana* states that she is Dolly; the *Reader's Encyclopedia* says she is Dorothea. Recently, a group of scholars examined a number of documents including letters from Mrs. Madison to friends, a note to a minister, her will, and her mother's letters. The evidence in these sources indicates that Mrs. Madison's first name was Dolley—not Dolly.

Checking Origin. Our national pastime of baseball has also been the subject of historical criticism. Modern literature quite commonly credits Abner Doubleday as the inventor of the game. How he won this reputation and the historical criticism of the claim is an intriguing story that reveals how easily and innocently a picture of the past can be distorted.

When baseball became an extremely popular sport in this country at the turn of the century, enthusiastic fans began to claim that the game was of American origin. A British-born sportsman, Henry Chadwick, challenged this theory, for he believed the sport was a direct descendant of the English game of "rounders." A. G. Spalding, a popular baseball figure who supported the American theory, sought to settle the issue in "some comprehensive and authoritative way, *for all time*" (13:173) by establishing a commission of six public-spirited men to investigate.

The public was invited to send pertinent information to the commission. Two years later the members accepted the testimony submitted in a letter by Abner Graves who wrote that his boyhood friend, Abner Doubleday, originated the game. Without any additional supporting evidence, they announced that Doubleday invented and named the game "Base Ball" in 1839 when he marked off a diamond-shaped field and diagramed the location of players at Cooperstown, New York. This report remained unchallenged by most people for years and was copied in a number of textbooks, newspapers, and sports' books.

When Henderson critically examined the evidence, he presented some interesting conclusions (13:170–196). The report was primarily the work of the chairman of the commission, A. G. Mills, who was a military friend of Doubleday. Mills apparently based his findings solely on a letter written by Abner Graves, for no documents by any other person and no contemporary records were presented to support the Graves story. Henderson points out that when Doubleday originated the game in Cooperstown, he actually was in West Point and did not return to Cooperstown on leave. After retiring from the army, Doubleday wrote many articles for publication but none about baseball. Moreover, when he died in 1893 his obituary notice did not mention that he invented the game.

A critical examination of the commission's report revealed many other weaknesses. The name "Base Ball" and some of the rules that Doubleday supposedly invented in 1839 had appeared in print before that time. Although it was claimed that Graves was present when Doubleday traced the first baseball diamond in the dirt, the original Graves letter did not state this. A later letter that appears to have been written by Graves disclosed that he did not know "where the first game was played according to Doubleday's plan." Moreover, a few books printed before 1839 discussed or illustrated a baseball diamond. Comparisons of the two Graves letters revealed some inconsistencies, which was not surprising, for the man wrote from memory almost seven decades after the event.

Henderson believes that certain personal factors may have caused members of the commission to accept the report. Because of the pressure of other duties, they probably did not check the facts thoroughly. Perhaps patriotic prejudices also influenced their decision. Some of the men were anxious to prove that baseball was of American rather than British origin. The possibility that General Doubleday, a famous Civil War soldier, invented the great American game must have appealed to them.

General Principles of Criticism. The examples given of historical criticism reveal that researchers make many judgments when evaluating records and relics. Not all the principles of criticism can be fully discussed in this text, but the following suggestions made by Woody (31:190) will serve as a general guide.

(1) Do not read into earlier documents the conceptions of later times; (2) do not judge an author ignorant of certain events, necessarily, because he fails to mention them (the argument *ex silentio*), or that they did not occur, for the same reason; (3) underestimating a source is no less an error than overestimating it in the same degree, and there is no more virtue in placing an event too late than in dating it too early by the same number of years or centuries; (4) a single true source may establish the existence of an idea, but other direct, competent, independent witnesses are required to prove the reality of events or objective facts; (5) identical errors prove the dependence of sources on each other, or a common source; (6) if witnesses contradict each other on a certain point, one or the other may be true, but both may be in error; (7) direct, competent, independent witnesses who report the same central fact and also many peripheral matters in a casual way may be accepted for the points of their agreement; (8) official testimony, oral or written, must be compared with unofficial testimony whenever possible, for neither one nor the other is alone sufficient; (9) a document may provide competent and dependable evidence on certain points, yet carry no weight in respect to others it mentions.

For a more detailed discussion of the problems and principles involved in external and internal criticism, the reader can consult the excellent discussions and·interesting examples presented by outstanding authorities in the field (2,3,9,10,12,14,17). One must keep in mind that criticism of documents yields only isolated information and fails to meet the legitimate goals of the scientific method.

HERE

FORMULATING HYPOTHESES

Historians do not aimlessly collect records and relics, subject them to intensive criticism, and then present the mass of facts—names, events, places, and dates—to the public like "beads on a string." Unrelated bits of information do not advance knowledge appreciably. Even if scholars group their facts and arrange their groups in a logical order, they produce a narrative that is little more than a series of disconnected and unexplained events. Isolated facts lack meaning; consequently, research workers go beyond the amassing of data or merely describing and classifying them in accordance with their superficial properties. To produce works of value, they formulate tentative hypotheses that explain the occurrence of events and conditions. They seek the hidden connections, underlying patterns, or general principles that explain or describe the structural interrelations of the phenomena under study. After constructing hypotheses, they search for evidence that will confirm or disconfirm them.

When Woody traced the origin of a manuscript, you recall, he first hypothesized that it might be a copy of the regulations observed in a German school and then searched for evidence to test this guess. Other historians follow a similar procedure. After examining raw materials in some area of interest they (1) formulate and precisely state a hypothesis about the nature of a past event and (2) note any assumptions that underlie the structuring of their problem. Thus, a reader is informed of their objective and the political, philosophical, economic, social, or other views they hold that may influence the selection of data. Since a previous chapter discussed the structuring and testing of hypotheses in detail, perhaps the best way of gaining a deeper understanding of the process is to examine some concrete examples.

Principle of Separation of Church and State. When Butts undertook the task of determining the meaning of the principle of "establishment of religion," he observed the standards of sound scholarship. In the introduction of the study, he expressed his objective simply: (5:5-6)

This book is an effort to state as clearly, as briefly, and as objectively as possible what the weight of historical evidence means concerning the American principle and practice of separation of church and state. . . . In the pages that follow, a portion of the available historical evidence is presented in order to help the American people decide whether or not the principle of separation of church and state is an authentic and valid tradition in America.

Because his selection of evidence is necessarily conditioned by his beliefs, Butts frankly states that his work is written (5:xiii–xiv)

. . . in a framework of values which includes the following assumptions: that religious freedom is a foundation stone of American liberty, that the preservation of the equal rights of religious conscience is a necessity for genuine religious free-dom, that the guarantee of religious freedom is an essential function of our con-stitutional form of government, that public education is a bulwark of our common democratic values, that private education has a legitimate and desirable function to serve in American society, and that 'an establishment of religion' (as defined in Chapters 2, 3, and 4) is a threat to religious freedom and to the American tradition of democracy. This all means, by and large, that the historic principle of separation of church and state as defined in 175 years of American history is a desirable tradition to maintain in American education (as outlined in Chapters 5 and 6). These are the working hypotheses upon which the investigation in this book has been undertaken. Whether or not the conclusions reached are justifi-able depends in the last analysis upon public judgment.

Early Roman Education. A study of early Roman education caused Chiappetta to formulate a hypothesis concerning the period, "namely, that the Romans did not accept formal education or use it as a reliable or effective behavior changing device" (6:155). He noted that aside from the writing of Quintilian there were practically no reliable reports on educational practices during this period and there was also a "curious lack of archaeological remains which would indicate the existence of schools in any great number" (6:155). To test his hypothesis, Chiappetta ex-amined "some of the events which occurred, or more importantly, did *not* occur" and reported the following conclusions (6:155–156):

The scanty evidences indicate that only a small segment of the population at-tended schools. In general, the sons of the senatorial class became the next sen-ators or patricians, and at no time did the schools become a vehicle for social mobility. . . . Further, while the Romans . . . built not only an empire, but all the appurtenances that go with a complicated society—a language, a priesthood, commercial systems, an architecture, roads, bridges, sanitation systems, armies, navies, *ad infinitum*—at no time do we hear of schools which prepared the Ro-mans to do these outstanding deeds. Apparently there was no institutional edu-cational attempt to prepare people for the vast range of employments required in the constantly enlarged Roman-dominated area. The attempts at secondary and higher education seemed to concentrate on the production of the orator, and . . . the tyranny of the Roman emperors was in the process of becoming so absolute that Rome no longer needed statesmen, educated or not. . . . Finally, the late entry of the state into the support of education seems to indicate that the Ro-mans thought lightly of such matters.

Early New York Schools. Errors may appear in educational literature and be repeated for years before someone challenges them. About the turn of the century, for example, Andrew S. Draper stated that "all the English schools in the province [New York] from 1700 down to the time of the Declaration of Independence, were maintained by a great religious society . . . called the society for the propagation of the gospel in foreign parts [SPGFP]" (7:29–30). Other educational historians accepted and incorporated this hypothesis in their writings.

Years later, Professor Seybolt (27), apparently after reading a doctoral dissertation by Kemp (18) on the work of the religious society, began to doubt Draper's generalization. Kemp stated that the SPGFP continuously supported from five to ten elementary schools from 1710–1776 in New York. Seybolt got the notion that there were probably many "English Schools" in New York during those years that were not maintained by the religious society. To test his hypothesis, he critically examined eighteenth-century records and found evidence that there were at least two hundred schools not maintained by the SPGFP. Thus, Seybolt had produced facts to refute Draper's generalization and to support his own. In brief, he spotted a conflict in the literature, proposed a working hypothesis, collected data that supported his position, and thus confirmed his hypothesis.

Early American Textbooks. Sister Marie Léonore Fell utilized a hypothesis in her study of *The Foundations of Nativism in American Textbooks, 1783–1860.* Previous studies had indicated that considerable opposition to minority groups existed in the United States at this time, but the "contribution of biased text-books to political nativism" remained unknown. She examined more than a thousand reading, history, and geography texts to test the hypothesis that during the formative years of our country the compilers of textbooks "laid the foundations of the anti-Catholic and anti-foreign attitudes, which had their political conclusions in the Nativist movements of the 1830's and 1840's and in the Know-Nothing party of the 1850's" (8:vi). In reporting her findings, she stated that the study "reveals not so much an anti-foreign slant as an anti-Catholic attitude on the part of the compilers of the texts" (8:224). Thus, Sister Fell had established a hypothesis, examined primary source materials to test it, and announced her conclusions that the evidence revealed "intentional" anti-Catholic indoctrination in textbooks.

Origin of Sport. The recreations of people in the past reveal much about the character and conditions of the period in which they lived. Consequently, some men are interested in tracing the development of sports. After studying various ball games and wondering about their origins, Henderson formulated the hypothesis that "all modern games played with bat and ball descend from one common source: an ancient fertility rite observed by Priest-Kings in the Egypt of the Pyramids" (13:4). To test his hypothesis, he examined the religious ceremonies and folk customs of ancient man and traced the evolution of games played with a ball. Henderson reported finding evidence in rituals, customs, and tombs to support his thesis that the modern bat and ball games are vestigial remains of ancient religious rites.

REPORTING THE FINDINGS

After completing their investigations, historians write well-organized reports of their work. Chapter 15 gives a detailed discussion of the processes involved in reporting research. It is sufficient to state here that investigators' expositions include a statement of the problem, a review of the literature, the basic assumptions underlying the hypothesis, the statement of hypothesis, the methods employed in testing the hypothesis, the findings and conclusions reached, a bibliography, and possibly an appendix.

The hypothesis provides a framework for stating the conclusions of the study in a meaningful manner. It enables the historian to determine what is relevant to a study and to screen out irrelevant materials. Within the framework of the hypothesis, of course, the historian will pattern his material in some systematic order, such as chronological, geographical, topical, or a combination of these. He will also make judgments concerning the amount of emphasis or space to give to various evidence. Considerable information may be collected on relatively minor points in a study and little evidence on more significant events. Obviously, reporting everything would produce a distorted picture of the past. Determining which data are packed with the greatest significance and how many of them to include requires a continuous reevaluation of the hypothesis and the study as a whole.

Weaving raw data into a cohesive, well-proportioned, colorful exposition requires painstaking labor. To achieve the twin objectives of maintaining accuracy and interest, a historian refrains from embellishing narratives with dramatic flourishes that distort the truth, but strives for literary excellence. Stretching or supplementing the existing evidence to create a more spirited narrative is not permissible. Artfully fitting the pieces of established evidence into a simple, vivid mosaic that dramatically delineates past events is the difficult but desired ideal to attain. History is life—and it deserves better than a drab description. The historian cannot sacrifice accuracy for eloquence; but by developing his creative and critical skills he can learn to write lucid, lively, logical accounts without violating the rigorous rules of historical scholarship.

EVALUATING HISTORICAL RESEARCH

Historical research is an exciting and satisfying pursuit, but it is important to have a proper perspective of its achievements and limitations.

Some people credit historians with accomplishing more than is possible; others believe they cannot possibly produce scientifically reliable data. The truth probably lies somewhere between these two extreme positions. By reviewing some of their arguments, perhaps you can get a better insight into the problem and draw your own conclusions.

Nature of Historical Knowledge. Adulators of historical writing some-times assume that the researchers present them with the totality of past actuality. No historian can possibly do this, he can give only a fragmentary picture of the past. Historical knowledge is never complete; it is derived from the surviving records of a limited number of events that took place in the past. As Gottschalk points out (12:45),

. . . only a part of what was observed in the past was remembered by those who observed it; only a part of what was remembered was recorded; only a part of what was recorded has survived; only a part of what has survived has come to the historians' attention; only a part of what has come to their attention is credible; only a part of what is credible has been grasped; and only a part of what has been grasped can be expounded or narrated by the historian.

Hence, historical knowledge is partial, not total, knowledge of past actuality.

Application of the Scientific Method. Some men believe that historical researchers can adhere to the same principles and purposes that the physical scientists do. Other scholars contend that this is not possible: they argue that history embraces a different kind of subject matter than science, there-fore, it requires a different method and interpretation. Men from both schools of thought usually agree that the historical method is scientific in some respects, but they sharply disagree whether it is in other respects.

Hockett has described the scientific method as "consisting of three processes: observation, hypothesis and experiment" (14:58). He and others argue that modern historians are scientific in that they (1) critically and objectively examine their source materials, and (2) formulate hypotheses. But they recognize that historians encounter greater difficulty than physical scientists in applying the scientific method of research. Some of the prob-lems that arise are concerned with (1) critical examination of sources, (2) construction of hypotheses, (3) observation and experimentation, (4) tech-nical terminology, and (5) generalization and prediction.

Critical Examination of the Sources. Myriads of historical facts are established as scientifically as are facts of the physical sciences. If a re-searcher has critically examined a number of documents and checked and verified the testimony of his sources against one another, he can report the time and place of a particular event with almost the same certainty that a physical scientist can report that mixing two chemicals in certain proportions under given conditions will produce a certain precipitate. But, all facts that interest a historian are not concrete, single historical incidents that have been reported by reliable eyewitnesses.

Scientifically ascertaining the facts becomes difficult or impossible for the researcher if he cannot locate adequate reports of firsthand observations, or if he is interested in causes, motivations, influences, generalizations, or value judgments. After examining available records, for example, a researcher can determine whether or not Superintendent Hayes made a particular speech at a certain time or place, but he cannot ascertain with the same assurance that the speech caused eighty per cent of the voters to support the school bond issue. Within limits, historical research is scientific—its results can be verified by others—but in some cases, it is difficult, if not impossible, to isolate and measure factors relating to a situation.

Construction of Hypotheses. Like the physical scientist, the historian formulates hypotheses. He also carefully collects and critically analyzes relevant evidence to ascertain whether his hypothesis gives a more satisfactory explanation for an event than any of the rival hypotheses. But the type of hypotheses and testing procedures the historian employs usually differs from that used by the physical scientist.

Because his subject matter is more complex than that of the physical scientist, a historian experiences greater difficulty in ascertaining the causes of events. As you know, scientists hold that an event is dependent upon and conditioned by its causes, that is, certain conditions must exist before an event can take place. Since the physical scientist deals with relatively stable elements solely on the physical level, he is able to speak of "the cause"—the precise and exclusive factor or factors accounting for an occurrence. When a historian attempts to select the probable antecedent conditions that precipitated an event, and to test whether one or more of them caused it, he may encounter many obstacles. Some factors that were associated with a past event may be difficult to discern, many may be unmeasurable, and some may never have been recorded, consequently, he can never be certain that he is giving consideration to all pertinent antecedent factors. Moreover, the phenomena he is studying may have a greater number of antecedents and a more complicated pattern of interaction among them than phenomena in the physical sciences.

Since no single cause satisfactorily explains most historical events, an investigator frequently resorts to multiple hypotheses—presenting a group of explanations for a given occurrence. If a historian speaks of *"the* cause," he means "not the only cause but 'the most important cause' . . . among a complex of causal conditions, or the condition which was most decisive to what occurred, or which made the difference between what occurred and what would probably have occurred in its absence" (25:111). Because of the complexity of his subject matter and the limited quantity of his data, the historian is unable to draw as conclusive and decisive conclusions about causes as his colleagues in the physical sciences.

Observation and Experimentation. Unlike physical scientists, educational historians cannot test their hypotheses by experimentation—controlled observation. They cannot deliberately recreate personalities and conditions as they once were for the purpose of further examination and manipulation. Historians cannot set up an experiment in which they control all essential factors, remove or add particular factors, and measure their effect on the situation. Each event that has occurred in the past is unique and non-repeatable under laboratory conditions. Hence, research workers have to be satisfied with examining whatever relevant data are available when they want to explain a past event. Since they cannot directly manipulate and observe their phenomena, they may attempt to gain a better understanding of it through historical comparisons and hypothetical constructs. They may compare and contrast an event with similar events in the past to detect likenesses and differences. Sometimes they visualize what would have taken place if a particular antecedent event had not occurred and give an answer, "of varying degrees of probability, in terms of approximate regularities observable in other instances" (25:113). But no matter how carefully this work is done, it is not as satisfactory as actual observation.

Since historians cannot personally view the educational practices of hundreds of years ago, they must rely on observations made by others in bygone days and on the examination of relics. Secondhand observations, of course, are not as satisfactory as the direct observations that physical scientists can make. But if investigators are fully aware of the fallibility of human observation, they can check the authenticity and credibility of testimony by subjecting it to intensive external and internal criticism. Ascertaining whether every fact is absolutely true is not possible, for the most reliable witness to an event may have erred in perception or memory. But a research worker can determine the credibility of testimony in degrees of confidence—from confidence that is approximately certain at one end of the scale to confidence that is mingled with considerable doubt on the other end. Historians can ascertain with a high degree of probabilty that some data are "true" facts. But, because the reliability of data is dependent on the character, circumstances, and competence of the creators and interpreters, they are extremely cautious about accepting any historical artifact or report.

The reliability of a historical research report is determined not only by how critically the investigator examined witnesses' observations of past events, but also by the depth and breath of his knowledge about the past and present. The historian delineates events of yesteryear in as much detail as surviving evidence permits and in terms of the general information and understandings he has acquired about occurrences, peoples, and institutions.

His interpretation of early Greek education, for example, will be conditioned by how much he knows about Grecian society, his understanding of human behavior, and his familiarity with the present as well as the past.   Block points out that "misunderstanding of the present is the inevitable consequence of ignorance of the past.   But a man may wear himself out just as fruitlessly in seeking to understand the past, if he is totally ignorant of the present" (2:43).   Limited experiences and understandings of either the past or present may cause a researcher to ignore or misinterpret important evidence and thereby to produce erroneous accounts of earlier educational events.   Although the past is viewed through the mirror of the present and not directly through the eyes of the researcher, gross distortions need not occur.   The more carefully a historian screens observers' reports and the greater effort he makes to acquire a comprehensive understanding of the past and present, the more accurately he will recreate an image of the past.

Technical Terminology.   Educational historians are handicapped because they lack the precise technical vocabulary that physical scientists possess. Many educational terms do not have clearly assigned and commonly understood meanings.   When words such as democracy, education, teaching, curriculum, school, and discipline are used by different workers in the field, they may stand for slightly or radically different things.   In contrast, the technical terms in the exact sciences, such as meter, ampere, pound, light-year, and calorie are instruments of great exactitude.   Because a "one-to-one correspondence between symbols and meanings" (21:249) exists, variations due to their use by different physical scientists are kept at a minimum. The absence of a clearly defined technical vocabulary is a distinct weakness in the discipline of educational history, for it inevitably leads to some degree of vagueness and ambiguity in the communication of ideas and information.

Generalization and Prediction.   Some historians dispute whether history can be classified as a science on another basis.   Science seeks to generalize. Both scientists and historians may start with propositions about singular, particular, unique events, but scientists' ultimate objective is to establish broad generalizations—universal laws and theories that will explain many unrelated, singular events or conditions.   Scientists strive to establish laws that have precise predictive power.

Constructing laws by generalizing about repetitive and common factors relating to past events is entirely outside the province of historical research in the opinion of some authorities.   They believe that it is their duty to acquire richly detailed knowledge of a particular event or condition that occurred at a specific time and place in the past and to trace what preceded and succeeded it.   But they are not concerned about what always, typically, or generally happens; similarities between events; or repeatable aspects of events.   The unique factors associated with a specific occurrence that differentiate it from other events are what interests them.   In their opinion, as soon as a fact becomes merely an instance of a general rule or law, it has lost its identification with the past and, therefore, is no longer a historical fact.   Historians of this school show causal relationships between parts of an event or between the conditions existing before and after it, but they do not seek to generalize about the qualities one occurrence has in common with similar ones.   They leave the establishment of generalizations or laws that will predict what inevitably will reoccur under certain conditions to sociologists and psychologists.

Vigorous opponents of the historians with a "particularist passion" contend that historians must go beyond the description and interpretation of particular events in the past.   Some men are convinced that broad generalizations or laws can be derived from a study of historical facts and, thus, they should study the past for the lessons it teaches.   Like Thucydides they want to tell "what has happened and will hereafter happen again according to human nature" (29).   They believe that historians can discover and formulate the fixed laws that govern human events just as scientists have discovered natural laws that govern phenomena in the physical world.

A more modest role is accepted by most historians.   Some believe it is their responsibility to make generalizations about *past events* but not within their power to *predict future events*.   Others contend that by drawing historical analogies and tracing historical trends they can suggest in some instances various possible outcomes "one or more of which may be anticipated with a high degree of probability" (25:139).   They attempt to provide us with a basis of knowledge for choosing alternative courses of action, but do not expect to construct comprehensive generalizations that possess the precise predictive power of laws in the physical sciences.   "Historical analogies present us most often with clues to *possible* rather than *probable* behavior, with the ability only to *anticipate* rather than to predict, to *take precautions* rather than to *control*" (12:269).

The possibility that man may someday establish historical laws continues to intrigue many scholars.   When critics attack this view as unscientific they ask whether "it is more scientific to assume that the development of man as a social being has been casual, fortuitous, uncontrolled by law?" (26:166–167).   However, entertaining the idea that constructing historical laws may be possible does not blind scholars to the overwhelming difficulties that must be surmounted.

Among the reasons that have been given for the lack of success in constructing historical laws as exact as those developed in the physical sciences are (25.138–139):

. . . (1) the apparent impossibility of using certain modern scientific methods, notably experimentation and the use of instruments to aid the senses; (2) the greater complexity of social data as compared to physical: as seen in the circumstance that history presents unique personalities who seem to affect the course of history (or events) and from time to time emergent phenomena not apparently explicable by preexisting phenomena; (3) the paucity in the social and psychological sciences of adequate generalizations which might be applied in historical studies; (4) the changing character of social phenomena from one age to the next, in comparison with the relatively constant character of the data of the physical sciences; and (5) the circumstance that many potentially pertinent data are lost beyond recall.

The compilers of this list conclude that it is questionable that these difficulties can be overcome, but some of them may be eventually. In the meantime, it is important for the historian to recognize his limitations and make his work as exact as possible.

BIBLIOGRAPHY

1. Benjamin, Harold H., *The Role of Hypothesis in Selected Histories of American Education, 1912–51.* Doctoral dissertation. Ann Arbor: University of Michigan, 1955.

2. Block, Marc, *The Historian's Craft.* New York: Alfred A. Knopf, Inc., 1953.

3. Brickman, William W., *Guide to Research in Educational History.* New York: New York University Bookstore, 1949.

4. Burt, Cyril, "Review: A Young Girl's Diary," *The British Journal of Psychology, Medical Section,* 1 (July, 1921): 353.

5. Butts, R. Freeman, *The American Tradition in Religion and Education.* Boston: The Beacon Press, 1950.

6. Chiappetta, Michael, "Historiography and Roman Education," *History of Education Journal,* 4 (Summer, 1953): 149.

7. Draper, Andrew S., *Origin and Development of the Common School System of the State of New York.* Syracuse, N.Y.: C. W. Bardeen, Publisher, 1903.

8. Fell, Sister Marie Léonore, *The Foundations of Nativism in American Textbooks, 1783–1860.* Washington, D.C.: The Catholic University of America Press, 1941.

9. Fling, Fred M., *The Writing of History.* New Haven: Yale University Press, 1920.

10. Garraghan, Gilbert J., *A Guide to Historical Method.* New York: Fordham University Press, 1946.

11. Good, Carter V., and Douglas E. Scates, *Methods of Research.* New York: Appleton-Century-Crofts, Inc., 1954.

12. Gottschalk, Louis, *Understanding History.* New York: Alfred A. Knopf, Inc., 1956.

13. Henderson, Robert W., *Ball, Bat and Bishop.* New York: Rockport Press, Inc., 1947.

14. Hockett, Homer C., *Introduction to Research in American History.* New York: The Macmillan Company, 1932.

15. Holt, Andrew D., "The Struggle for a State System of Public Schools in

Tennessee, 1903–1936," *Contributions to Education,* no. 753.   New York: Teachers College, Columbia University, 1938.

16. Hug-Hellmuth, Hermine (ed.), *A Young Girl's Diary.*   New York: Thomas Seltzer, 1923.

17. Johnson, Allen, *The Historian and Historical Evidence.*   New York: Charles Scribner's Sons, 1930.

18. Kemp, William W., "The Support of Schools in Colonial New York by the Society for the Propagation of the Gospel in Foreign Parts," *Contributions to Education,* no. 56.   New York: Teachers College, Columbia University, 1913.

19. Knox, Ronald, trans., *The Autobiography of St. Thérèse of Lisieux.*   New York: P. J. Kenedy & Sons, 1958.

20. Krug, Josef, "Kritische Bemerkungen zu dem' Tagebuch eines halbwüchsigen Mädchens," *Zeit schrift für Angewandte Psychologie,* 27 (July, 1926): 370.

21. Larrabee, Harold A., *Reliable Knowledge.*   Boston: Houghton Mifflin Company, 1945.

22. Leonard, Fred E., and George B. Affleck, *A Guide to the History of Physical Education.*   Philadelphia: Lea & Febiger, 1947.

23. McMurray, Dorothy, "Herbartian Contributions to History Instruction in American Elementary Schools," *Contributions to Education,* no. 920.   New York: Teachers College, Columbia University, 1946.

24. Mangun, Vernon L., *The American Normal School: Its Rise and Development in Massachusetts.*   Baltimore: Warwick and York Incorporated, 1928.

25. Report of the Committee on Historiography, *Theory and Practice in Historical Study.*   New York: Social Science Research Council, 1946.

26. Schlesinger, A. M., "History," in W. Gee (ed.), *Research in the Social Sciences.*   New York: The Macmillan Company, 1929.

27. Seybolt, Robert F., "The S.P.G. Myth: A Note on Education in Colonial New York," *Journal of Educational Research,* 13 (February, 1926): 129.

28. Tewksbury, Donald G., "The Founding of American Colleges and Universities Before the Civil War," *Contributions to Education,* no. 543.   New York: Teachers College, Columbia University, 1932.

29. Thucydides, *The History of the Peloponnesian War,* translated by H. Dale. London: G. Bell & Sons, Ltd., 1912.

30. Vincent, John M., *Historical Research.*   New York: Holt, Rinehart and Winston, Inc., 1911.

31. Woody, Thomas, "Of History and Its Method," *Journal of Experimental Education,* 15 (March, 1947): 175.

CHAPTER 10

Patterns of Descriptive Research

Before much progress can be made in solving problems, men must possess accurate descriptions of the phenomena with which they work. Hence, the early developments in educational research, as in other fields, have been made in the area of description. To solve problems about children, school administration, curriculum, or the teaching of arithmetic, descriptive researchers ask these initial questions: What exists—what is the present status of these phenomena? Determining the nature of prevailing conditions, practices, and attitudes—seeking accurate descriptions of activities, objects, processes, and persons—is their objective. They depict current status and sometimes identify relationships that exist among phenomena or trends that appear to be developing. Occasionally, they attempt to make predictions about future events.

GENERAL OVERVIEW OF DESCRIPTIVE STUDIES

The nature of descriptive research is easier to comprehend if one first obtains some knowledge of the various steps involved in an investigation as well as the different methods employed to collect and express data, and the general categories under which studies may be classified. Thus, the following brief overview presents skeletal information concerning these topics.

Steps in an Investigation. In descriptive studies researchers do not merely present private convictions and data based on casual or cursory observations. As in any investigation, they carefully (1) examine their problematic situation; (2) define their problem and state their hypotheses; (3) list the assumptions upon which their hypotheses and procedures are based; (4) select appropriate subjects and source materials; (5) select or construct techniques for collecting the data; (6) establish categories for classifying data that are unambiguous, appropriate for the purpose of the study, and capable of bringing out significant likenesses, differences, or relationships; (7) validate the data-gathering techniques; (8) make systematically selected, sharply discriminating, objective observations; and (9) describe, analyze, and interpret their findings in clear, precise terms. Investigators seek more than

184

bare description: they are not—or should not be—mere tabulators.   Competent researchers collect evidence on the basis of some hypothesis or theory, carefully tabulate and summarize the data, and then thoroughly analyze it in an endeavor to draw meaningful generalizations that will advance knowledge.

Collection of Data.   When conducting a descriptive study, one must identify not only the information that is needed but also the exact nature of the population from which it is to be obtained.   The population, sometimes called the universe or aggregate, is a *whole*.   The units that constitute a population may be people, or items, events, or objects; thus, all the arithmetic books published in this country between 1930 and 1940 or all the children in Haven High School may constitute a population.   After identifying the population, one must decide whether to collect data from (1) the total population or (2) a representative sample of the population.   The nature of the problem and the use to be made of the findings determine which method is employed.

Total Population.   Information can usually be obtained from every unit of a small population, but the findings cannot be applied to any population other than the group studied.   An investigator may collect information, for example, about the salary, training, age, and sex of all teachers in one school.   From these data he can draw generalizations about the average salary, training, age, and sex of that particular group, but he cannot claim that these generalizations would hold true for any other group of teachers— now, in the past, or in the future.

Sample Population.   When it is necessary to obtain information about a large population, such as all of the teachers in the state, it is often impractical, impossible, or exorbitantly costly to contact, observe, measure, or interview every unit in the group.   Moreover, the amount of time necessary to collect the information may render the data obsolete before it can be used. Hence, in many studies, one merely collects information from a few *carefully selected* units in a group.   If these sample units accurately represent the characteristics of the population, generalizations based on the data obtained from them can be applied to the entire group.   But selecting a representative sample is a difficult task as you will discover when reading this chapter and the discussion on sampling in Chapter 12.

Expression of Data.   Descriptive data not only may be collected by different methods, but also may be expressed in different forms: it may be presented (1) *qualitatively*—in verbal symbols—or (2) *quantitatively*—in mathematical symbols.   Some studies consist almost exclusively of one form, but many contain both forms.   A study comparing the guidance programs of selected schools, for example, may present qualitative data—word descriptions—concerning the administrative organization of the program, the duties of counselors, the underlying philosophy, and the board of education decisions regarding the program. But it may also include considerable quantitative data, such as the amount of money spent on guidance, number of children served by each guidance counselor, and amount of specialized training staff members have received.

Qualitative Symbols. Qualitative data[1]—word descriptions—may predominate in studies that examine the general nature of phenomena. Pioneer studies in a field, particularly, are apt to be expressed in verbal terms. The qualitative statements made by Freud, for example, laid the foundation for clinical psychology. Arnold Gesell's studies on the development of infants' motor and perceptual skills verbally described the nature of certain changes that take place as children mature. In *Changing the Curriculum,* Alice Miel presented verbal observations of the factors that hinder or foster change in the school curriculum. In the study of *The Polish Peasant in Europe and America,* W. I. Thomas and Florian Znaniecki described the adjustments people make to a new social situation. Verbal data have also been used extensively in comparative educational studies to describe objectives, administration, philosophy, and other factors.

Qualitative studies give social scientists much useful information, but verbal symbols lack precision: they do not hold the same meaning for all people, for all times, and in all contexts. Great leaps forward are not usually taken in a field until countable units of measurement are used. But qualitative studies need not be deprecated, for they help workers identify the significant factors to measure. Until these general explorations are made, measurement cannot be utilized fruitfully. After employing qualitative methods to locate the factors to measure and after devising appropriate data-gathering devices, researchers endeavor to employ numerical rather than verbal symbols when describing data. Years, decades, or a century may pass before it is possible to pass from the qualitative to the quantitative stage of research, and, at present, in some areas of the social science, this objective appears to be unattainable.

Quantitative Symbols. Characteristics and examples of quantitative studies are discussed later in this chapter and in other chapters. But a few introductory remarks may serve a useful purpose at this point. The numerical symbols used to describe data may be the products of counting or measuring. Researchers may *count* the occurrence or nonoccurrence of discernible units, items, or categories of elements. Frequency of occurrence data, for example, may reveal the number of teachers in the city schools with B.A., M.A., and Ph.D. degrees; the number of people who do and do not favor consolidating the schools in a district; or the number of guidance counselors who have or have not had specialized training. Sometimes researchers are interested in measuring amounts rather than counting items.

---

[1] Some verbal symbols, such as few, small, near, light, and seldom, possess quantitative characteristics.

They may, for example, *measure* the amount of specialized training guidance counselors have had; the weight of twelve-year-old girls; the mental age of nonreading first-grade pupils; or the amount of space devoted to playgrounds.

Types of Descriptive Research. Writers are not in agreement on how to classify descriptive studies. But it is easier for the reader to become acquainted with the numerous types of investigations if some convenient classification system is employed. Hence, the text will describe these studies under three arbitrary headings: (1) survey studies, (2) interrelationship studies, and (3) developmental studies. These are not rigid categories. Some studies fall exclusively within one of these areas, but others have characteristics of more than one.

SURVEY STUDIES

When trying to solve problems, men from many fields—government, advertising, politics, education—often conduct surveys. They collect detailed descriptions of existing phenomena with the intent of employing the data to justify current conditions and practices or to make more intelligent plans for improving social, economic, or educational conditions and processes. Their objective may not merely be to ascertain status, but also to determine the adequacy of status by comparing it with selected or established standards, norms, or criteria. Health examination procedures, for example, may be compared with "best practices" as defined by authorities, and children's reading scores may be compared with norms established for specific groups. Investigators may also survey how others have solved similar problems in order to obtain information that will help them improve their existing status. Some men collect all three types of information: (1) existing status, (2) comparisons of status and standards, and (3) methods and means of improving status; and others confine their studies to one or two of these types.

Surveys may be broad or narrow in scope. Geographically, they may encompass several countries or may be confined to one nation, region, state, city school system, or some other unit. Survey data may be gathered from every member of a population or from a carefully selected sample. Data may be collected concerning a large number of related factors or a few selected items. The scope and depth of the study depends primarily upon the nature of the problem.

Survey studies will be discussed under the following headings in this chapter: (1) school surveys, (2) job analysis, (3) documentary analysis, (4) public opinion surveys, and (5) community surveys. No presumption is made that this classification is fundamental or that a sharp dividing line exists between these types. Some studies have characteristics of more than one of these types and some authorities would not include all of these types under the heading of surveys. Since a clear-cut, universally accepted classification system has not been established, an arbitrary but reasonable selection of one is necessary.

School Surveys. Early in this century, members of the profession began to conduct school surveys. On the basis of their findings they formulated plans for improving educational efficiency and effectiveness. Down through the years, their successors have continued to gather facts through observations, questionnaires, interviews, standardized tests, score cards, rating scales, and other data-gathering and evaluating techniques. As a result of analyzing such information, they have made recommendations that have transformed many administrative, instructional, financial, and curricular practices in our schools.

Types of School Surveys. Three ways of making school surveys have evolved since 1910, when one of the first modern studies was conducted at Boise, Idaho. All three patterns—(1) the *outside expert survey,* (2) the *self-survey,* and (3) the *cooperative survey*—are still employed. But there is a definite trend away from the pioneer type of outside expert survey that is conducted exclusively by the research staff of a university or state department of education. The self-survey which is undertaken by members of the local school organization appeared more frequently in the 1920s when schools began to add research specialists to their staffs who could offer competent leadership. The self-survey remains popular today, but since 1935 the cooperative survey has been gaining ground. Cooperative surveys are of two types: outside consultants join with a local staff to conduct a study, or lay citizens and school staff members—with or without consultants—undertake the survey.

Cooperative surveys have certain advantages over one-shot or periodic surveys that are made exclusively by outside experts. Although visiting specialists may be well trained in research techniques, they can acquire only a limited knowledge of the local scene. Educators and laymen who are intimately familiar with the community can help them enlarge these understandings and assist them in designing the most appropriate survey for the particular school system. If local staff members do not participate in surveying the schools' strengths and weaknesses, they do not always understand the need for change and the means by which the experts advise that it should be effected. Consequently, they may ignore or resist placing the experts' recommendations into effect. Many schools, therefore, favor utilizing experts to guide, supplement, and stimulate the work done by the local personnel—teachers and citizens. Moreover, rather than conducting surveys at infrequent intervals they carry on more or less continuous survey activities.

Coverage of Surveys. Educational surveys have probably been the most popular form of research in the field of education. By 1938, a total of

3,022 public school surveys were listed in bibliographies prepared by Smith and O'Dell (32,33). Hundreds of others have been made for local use that were never published and since that time a multiplicity of published and unpublished reports have appeared. As one would expect, most school surveys have been done on the local level. Although they are less common-place, some state-wide surveys have been made, such as the studies done in Florida and Indiana. On the national level, a few surveys have been con-ducted, such as the Office of Education's *National Survey of Secondary Education* (36) and *National Survey of the Education of Teachers* (37).

Data Sought in Surveys. The information sought in most surveys falls into the following categories: (1) the setting of learning, (2) the educa-tional personnel, (3) the pupils, and (4) the educational process. Studies may extensively explore one or more of these areas or they may intensively examine specific aspects of one area.

1. *The setting for learning.* Some surveys are concerned with the legal, administrative, social, or physical setting for learning. They may seek in-formation about the enabling acts, charters, state regulations, local council ordinances, board of education rulings, or boards of health and recreation regulations that affect education. Studies may investigate the composition, responsibilities, authority, and interrelationships of school boards, councils, commissions, and associations that are related to educational enterprises. Questions about school finance, such as the amount of taxable wealth, pres-ent basis of taxation, bonded indebtedness, per-pupil costs, and similar items may be asked. Not uncommonly, surveys seek descriptions of various aspects of the school plant, such as the location, heating, lighting, ventila-tion, floor space per-pupil, health and safety conditions, play areas, cafeteria, and library. Questions are sometimes asked about equipment and supplies, such as the number and kinds of library books or the amount and types of laboratory, athletic, audio-visual, or other equipment. Some studies are concerned with the size, length, and frequency of classes. Other studies in-vestigate aspects of the social structure in the classroom, home, or com-munity that may influence learning.

2. *The characteristics of educational personnel.* Many surveys gather in-formation about the teachers, supervisors, and administrators who are largely responsible for the educational process. Questions may be raised con-cerning their sex, age, nationality, education, degrees, socioeconomic back-ground, group memberships, or income. An effort may be made to ascer-tain where they live; the adequacy of their dwellings; or their certification, tenure, and retirement status. Numerous surveys study the behavior of in-structional personnel in the classroom, their department, and the community with the objective of assessing or improving teaching effectiveness. De-termining the physical fitness of educators; their attitudes on various ques-tions; the nature and number of their contacts with colleagues, students, and

the community; and the levels of expectation they hold for themselves, students, the school, and the community are the objectives of some surveys. Others seek information about the various duties educators perform and the amount of time they devote to each. Studies are also made of the responsibilities, authority, and interrelationships of administrators, department heads, teachers, and nonteaching personnel.

3. *The nature of pupils.* Acquiring information about the behavior patterns of pupils in classrooms, with peers, at home, and in the community is the purpose of many surveys. Descriptions of the family's socioeconomic status may be sought. Researchers may ask questions about pupils' health, attitudes, knowledges, skills, academic achievements, intelligence, aptitudes, work or study habits, and likes and dislikes. Some studies inventory extracurricular activities, work or travel experiences, or play and recreational activities. Questions about reading habits, health practices, or diet may be asked. Some investigations are concerned with attendance and drop-out records, the number and type of handicapped or other exceptional students, or the number and nature of disciplinary or delinquency incidents.

4. *The educational process.* The educational programs, processes, and outcomes may come under the scrutiny of researchers. They may investigate what is and is not included in the curriculum. Time allotments for activities and for various aspects of each activity, such as the amount of time given to literature, grammar, and composition in the English classes may be studied. The nature and amount of various types of content in textbooks and instructional materials may be appraised. The nature and number of school services, such as health, library, guidance, research, and adult education services may be described. Some investigators seek information about the kinds and degrees of acceleration or retardation among students in various subjects and on different academic levels.

Job Analysis. Sometimes job analysis—a technique borrowed from business and government—is employed to study administrative, teaching, and noninstructional positions. In these investigations information may be collected about the general duties and responsibilities of workers, the specific activities that they engage in on a job, their status and relationships in the administrative organization, their working conditions, and the nature and type of their facilities. Descriptions of the education, specialized training, experience, and salaries of workers and the knowledges, skills, habits, health standards, and behavioral traits that they possess may also be sought. The data gathered help researchers describe the current practices and conditions of employment and the competencies and behavioral traits that personnel possess or should possess to carry out their work effectively and efficiently.

An analytical knowledge of job components can serve several useful purposes: it can help administrators and scholars (1) detect weaknesses, duplications, or inefficiency in the present work procedures; (2) establish uniform classifications for similar work; (3) determine wage or salary schedules for jobs entailing various levels of skill or responsibility; (4) identify the competencies to seek when employing personnel; (5) assign workers to jobs in a manner that will achieve the best utilization of the available manpower; (6) set up training programs and prepare instructional materials for prospective or inservice employees; (7) establish requirements for promotion; (8) make decisions concerning the transfer or retraining of personnel; and (9) develop a theoretical framework for studying administrative functions and structures.

Various procedures are employed by those who conduct job analysis studies (13:343). From personal observations and judgments obtained from authorities in the field, a researcher may compile a list of the broad functions involved in administrative, supervisory, or teaching positions. An investigator may examine documents, such as state laws, school district regulations, or court decisions, to obtain information concerning the duties, responsibilities, and rights of personnel holding a given position. By questioning workers, a researcher may try to ascertain what duties they perform. Charters and Waples (8), for example, gathered statements from about six thousand teachers and examined previous studies of teacher activity. From these data they derived a master list of about one thousand types of activities that teachers engage in on the job. Another procedure employed in job analysis consists in determining the duration of time devoted to duties. The Research Division of the NEA (25), for example, sent a questionnaire to over two thousand teachers asking them to report the number of hours given per week to various duties. Similar time studies have been made to describe the work load of principals, college teachers, and other workers.

Researchers who undertake job analysis studies should be aware of the difficulties involved in obtaining accurate descriptions. If a study breaks down a job into a multiplicity of specific kinds of activities, for example, the sum of these quantitative or mechanical considerations gives only a partial picture of the job. The qualitative or creative characteristics which are necessary for successful job performance are omitted from the description. If a study does not give consideration to the personal characteristics required of a worker, such as ideals and attitudes, resourcefulness and cooperativeness, dependability and tact, it does not produce a full job description. Yet it is difficult to obtain objective and reliable data concerning these personal characteristics which play an important part in determining the manner in which work is done. A job analysis that gives equal weight to all activities, functions, and personal characteristics associated with a particular position also presents a distorted picture, for each factor does not contribute equally to work performance. Hence, some method of weighing the relative importance of the various job components must be devised, and it is difficult to obtain an objective method of doing this.

Documentary Analysis. Documents and records may be dull reading to laymen, but researchers often unearth exciting and pertinent data from these sources. Documentary analysis—which is sometimes referred to as content, activity, or informational analysis—is closely akin to historical research. Both methods of investigation explore existing records, but historical research is primarily concerned with the more distant past and descriptive research with present status.

Types of Analyses. A wide variety of documentary surveys are made. Some scholars analyze judicial decisions, state laws, and school board rulings. They count and classify specific items included in these sources that relate to their problems, such as information about salary schedules, certification, liability for school accidents, and district organization. Researchers may also gather data describing existing school practices, processes, and conditions from administrative records, forms, and reports; committee reports and minutes of meetings; budgets and financial records; and cumulative attendance and health records.

Examining university catalogs or bulletins to obtain information about curriculum offerings, content of particular courses, entrance or graduation requirements, and tuition is the objective of some investigators. Others examine syllabuses; courses of study; reading lists; curriculum materials; school schedules; lesson plans; textbooks; or pupils' work—class papers, tests, notebooks, reports—to determine what is and is not taught, the grade placement of particular materials, and the amount of time devoted to them. When analyzing textbooks, researchers may count the kind and frequency of concepts, the errors and distortions, or the number of pictures or tables. They may measure the length of sentences, the allotment of space devoted to certain topics, or the vocabulary level. This information enables them to determine where, when, and how much is being taught about specific topics and helps them detect prejudices and beliefs of the writers. Sometimes they find that personal documents, such as diaries, autobiographies, expense accounts, and letters provide them with valuable data. Scholars may also analyze the contents of reference works, newspapers, periodicals, and cartoons, pictures, films, and photographs.

Classroom teachers often complain that, "We can't teach everything! What are the most important skills and knowledges that we should help children attain?" To answer this question, many educators have turned to documentary research. In the field of mathematics, they have conducted investigations to discover what arithmetic processes are most commonly employed in business and social usage. In one study, Wilson and Dalrymple (40) examined 102,000 uses of fractions which they obtained from business records and concluded that 90 per cent of ordinary adult usage of fractions was confined to halves, thirds, and fourths. To determine what content should be included in the curriculum, investigators have also analyzed the types of errors made by pupils in oral and written communication, arithmetic, spelling, and other subjects. Educational textbook writers have been aided by studies that have ascertained the basic vocabulary that children possess at different ages. To determine what facts, topics, issues, and generalizations are most frequently used in adult life, social scientists have tabulated the frequency of their mention in newspapers, periodicals, motion pictures, cartoons, and other sources. Studies such as these have led to many curriculum revisions.

Early documentary research was rather superficial and mechanical; it primarily consisted in reading written or printed materials and tabulating the frequency of the occurrence of items under categories that were convenient but were not designed to reveal particularly significant meanings. About mid-century, studies began to introduce more subtle and plastic methods of categorizing items so as to force significant qualitative factors to the surface. These qualitative studies were concerned with more complex themes than the quantitative studies. They asked questions such as: How are minority ethnic groups treated in elementary social studies textbooks? How do the values in Boy Scout literature in the United States differ from those in *Hitlerjungen* literature? When conducting this qualitative type of study, the researcher is "relatively less concerned with the content as such than with content as a 'reflection' of 'deeper' phenomena" (4:123). His work may be semiqualitative in nature, but it is "often based upon presence-absence of particular content (rather than relative frequencies)" (4:119). Also, it usually contains "a higher ratio of non-content to content statements than quantitative analysis" (4:122).

Advantages and Limitations. Documentary analysis can serve a number of purposes (4). It can (1) describe specific conditions and practices that exist in schools and society; (2) spot trends; (3) detect weaknesses; (4) trace the development of a student's or writer's work; (5) disclose differences in the practices of various areas, states, or countries; (6) evaluate the relationships of stated objectives and what is being taught; (7) expose biases and prejudices; and (8) detect the attitudes, interests, values, and psychological states of people.

Documentary research produces much valuable information, but the method has certain limitations and investigators can easily draw faulty conclusions from the data. An analysis of the errors made on test papers, for example, may reveal what difficulties pupils encounter, but this information is of limited usefulness for it does not reveal why they made the errors. Frequency of occurrence studies may depict existing status of interests or activities, but what they discover may be too fleeting or temporary in nature to serve as a basis for planning long-term educational policies. Counting the frequency of occurrence of particular content or activities and measuring the amount of time or space devoted to them, may not accurately reveal the cruciality or importance of the item being analyzed. The position of content in a record or document and the emotional terms with which it is described are other factors that must be considered.

Some documentary research findings are of little value because the investigators fail to analyze a representative sample of source materials. Many studies do not provide information concerning the adequacy of the sample size or the conformity of the sample to the universe. A study may, for example, report that the sample included specific newspapers, sections of certain newspapers, or topics within certain newspapers and let the matter rest. If an analysis is made of newspaper editorials concerning school segregation, reading the Bible in public schools, or teacher labor unions, for example, the reader must judge for himself whether the newspapers selected represent the opinions in different parts of the country; different-size cities; and different social, religious, economic, or political groups.

Another weakness found in some documentary studies is the failure to analyze the trustworthiness of source materials. Printed and written materials are not necessarily accurate. Sometimes clerks make errors in recording information; committee members conceal their real convictions when writing reports; official records are altered or slanted to give a better picture of conditions than actually exist; different types of data are classified under the same category by various institutions; courses listed in college catalogs are not actually taught; personal documents such as diaries, autobiographies, or letters are forgeries or attributed to the wrong author. Hence, a researcher must submit his source materials to the same careful criticism that a historian does to establish the authenticity of documents and the validity of their contents.

Public Opinion Surveys. Industrial, political, educational, and other leaders must make many decisions. Rather than formulating policies on the basis of private hunches, blind guesses, or pressure group demands, some leaders seek knowledge of the public's opinions, attitudes, and preferences. Business firms, for example, often conduct public opinion polls— market surveys—to determine what types of products, packaging, or advertising appeal to purchasers. Political pollsters attempt to ascertain how people will vote or what programs they favor. Educators conduct public opinion surveys to find out how people feel about school issues. See, for example, K. L. Massanari, "Public Opinion as Related to the Problem of School District Reorganization in Selected Areas in Illinois" (22).

Public opinion surveyors usually employ questionnaires or interviews to gather their data, and the able ones select their subjects with care so that the views of each segment of the entire population is adequately represented. To predict the outcome of a national election, for example, they first endeavor to identify the variables that will affect how individuals vote, such as economic status, religion, party affiliation, age, rural-urban residence, education, and sex.   After making these determinations, they evaluate how much weight to give each variable when selecting the sample.

Public opinion surveys have limitations; those that are not carefully structured produce unreliable knowledge. Suppose a superintendent passes out questionnaires concerning a school bond issue at all public school PTA meetings. The results of his survey probably will not correspond with the vote on election day, for PTA members are usually much more interested in obtaining new schools than retired citizens, childless couples, and people who send their children to nonpublic schools. The environment in which a poll is taken may also affect the reliability of the data. Suppose students are asked to express their attitudes toward mathematics. If they do not like their present teacher or have recently had a difficult test, they may record these reactions rather than their more permanent attitudes toward the subject.   Other questions can also arise concerning the reliability of the answers gathered in surveys.   When people have given considerable thought to an issue, they may be able to give a definite opinion about it; if they are uninformed concerning the topic, they can only give arbitrary decisions or snap judgments. Measuring the intensity or depth of opinion is also difficult.   If two women answer a questionnaire, each may indicate that she is opposed to teaching about the United Nations in the schools, but one of them may easily be convinced to change her opinion and the other may be intensely opposed and adamant in her conviction.

Community Surveys. Because of the close relationship between the schools and the community, educators often find it necessary to study the local setting and particular aspects of life in it. Sometimes they join other social scientists in fact-finding projects known as community surveys, social surveys, or field studies. These community surveys are closely akin to school surveys; they may contain data concerning the schools and conversely school surveys may analyze many aspects of the community.

History of Surveys. The "muckraking" articles that appeared at the turn of the century gave impetus to the community survey movement in this country. These dramatic descriptions of slums and sweatshops aroused a demand for social reforms and caused some social foundations and government agencies to undertake community surveys. A precedent for compiling detailed bodies of exact, verifiable facts about a community as a means of instigating social reforms had been set by men abroad. Some of the early surveyors were John Howard (1726–1790), who made a detailed study of English prisons, Frédéric Le Play (1806–1882), who studied French working people, and Charles Booth (1840–1916), who surveyed the impoverished East Side of London.

One of the first extensive community surveys in the United States was conducted by Paul Kellogg and a group of professional workers in Pittsburgh (1909–1914). Other surveys of American cities, many of which were limited to particular phases of community life, soon followed. *A Bibliography of Social Surveys* (9) listed 2,775 that were completed by the end of 1927. Not only localized, but also regional surveys were conducted. Between 1927 and 1931, *The Regional Survey of New York and Its Environs* (eight volumes) and *The Regional Plan of New York* (two volumes) were published. Other communities also initiated studies to gather data that would enable them to plan for the future development of their regions. Such surveys have been repeated at intervals or conducted on a continuing basis by some communities. For example, another *New York Metropolitan Region Study* (nine volumes) under the direction of Raymond Vernon was published in 1959–1960.

Rather than seeking social reforms or planning for the future, some researchers are interested in conducting surveys to obtain detailed scientific knowledge about community life. The pioneers in this movement, Robert S. and Helen M. Lynd, painstakingly studied and restudied Muncie, Indiana. Their sociological reports, *Middletown* (1929) and *Middletown in Transition* (1937), vividly portrayed the changing culture in an average-size Middle Western town over a period of several decades. Since the appearance of the Lynds' studies, several similar ones, such as *Plainville, USA* and *Hollow Folk* have been produced, and gradually improvements in techniques have been devised.

Scope and Depth of Community Surveys. Some community studies are sharply focused on a particular condition, such as health services, employment, juvenile delinquency, housing, or racial discrimination. Other studies present data concerning a specific segment of society, such as Puerto Ricans, Negroes, or trailer-camp residents. Comprehensive surveys, on the other hand, cover many aspects of community life and may give approximately equal weight to each phase. The nature of the investigator's problem; the amount of time, money, and qualified leadership available; and the willingness of agencies to cooperate in a community survey are factors that play a role in determining a study's scope and depth.

Investigators who make comprehensive surveys gather information concerning many factors that contribute to the character of community life. To do this, they ask questions such as the following:

1. *History.* What facts are available concerning the community's origin and early development, its first inhabitants, its early leaders and their influences, and its first institutions and economic activities? What developments have taken place since that time? What factors caused these changes?

2. *Government and law.* What is the legal or regulative basis for the existence and present operation of the community? How do enabling acts, charters, state regulations, and local ordinances define the rights, duties,

and relationships of the various agencies and officials? What political organizations exist? What factions dominate them and who are the leaders? What methods of levying taxes are employed? What laws govern the right to raise taxes? What is the taxable wealth of the community? What is the nature, quality, and extent of the services offered by governmental agencies?

3. *Geographical and economic conditions.* How does the geography of the area affect transportation, communication, business, occupations, health, land values, recreation, distribution of the population, and social history? What economic activities exist in the community? What men, cliques, or organizations represent the interests of the various business, labor, or farm groups? What influence do they have in the community? What is the economic status of the people?

4. *Cultural characteristics.* Is the community socially isolated from other communities? What are the causes and effects of this condition? Are there manifestations of cooperative efforts and group solidarity? Are there manifestations of caste, class, color, religious, or nationality cleavages and conflicts? What are the general moral standards of the community? What cultural activities, services, and facilities exist, such as churches, libraries, museums, and parks? What government and social agencies, organizations, and private enterprises provide these services and what are their relationships with one another? What antisocial activities or conditions exist, such as areas of blight, crime, and delinquency, and who is responsible for them? To what extent and how do various groups, agencies, and conditions enrich or endanger community life?

5. *Population.* What is the composition of the population on the basis of age, sex, race, color, nationality, education, occupation, home language, political affiliation, and type and location of residence? How mobile is the population? What is the size of the population? Is it increasing or decreasing and why? What do the birth, death, and disease rates reveal about the population?

From the beginning, community surveyors have employed research methods from various fields and have drawn upon many different sources of information. They have used questionnaires, interviews, direct observation, statistical, ecological, and other techniques to gather data from public officials, social agencies, ministers, children, teachers, and various documents. Their interdisciplinary approach to research has permitted them to utilize multiple, interrelated methods of ferreting out information concerning the nature and role of various social processes.

INTERRELATIONSHIP STUDIES

Some descriptive researchers are not satisfied with merely obtaining accurate descriptions of surface phenomena. They not only collect information about existing status, but also endeavor to trace interrelationships between the facts obtained to gain a deeper insight into the phenomena. Three types of these studies will be discussed in the following section: case studies, causal comparative studies, and correlation studies.

Case Study. A case study makes an intensive investigation on the complex factors that contribute to the individuality of a social unit—a person, family, group, social institution, or community. Through the use of a number of research tools, pertinent data about the unit's present status, past experiences, and relationships with the environment are gathered. After probing deeply into the factors and forces that condition its behavior and analyzing the sequences and interrelationships of those factors, one can construct a comprehensive, integrated picture of the unit as it functions in society.

Nature of Case Studies. Social workers and guidance counselors ordinarily study an individual personality with the intent of diagnosing a particular condition and recommending therapeutic measures. Their interest is confined to the individual as a unique personality. Research workers, on the other hand, are more apt to be interested in individuals as representative types. They gather data about carefully selected individuals with the intent of obtaining a more complete understanding of the group that they represent.

Case studies always probe in depth, but they may examine the total life cycle of a social unit or may focus attention on a specific phase of it. An investigation may be confined to a study of boys' relationships with members of their gang or teachers' relationships with their administrators. On the other hand, if a researcher wants to ascertain what has contributed to hardened criminals' social maladjustment or to teachers' success, he may thoroughly investigate almost every aspect of their entire lives—their childhood, home, school, work, social experiences, and many of their behavioral traits.

A case analysis is cast within an adequate social framework and the nature of the case determines the dimensions of the framework. To discover what conditions or forces cause youths to commit crimes, for example, the investigation must go beyond the incidents themselves—the time, place, nature, and immediate cause of the acts. Case studies that are confined to an isolated fragment of men's lives are likely to be superficial and meaningless; they do not produce the data necessary to probe the fundamental cause-effect relationships. Since human beings function in a dynamic social setting, a case study must include considerable information about the people, groups, and conditions that subjects contact and the nature of their relationships with them. Human beings are constantly interacting with diverse environmental factors; consequently, their behavior cannot be understood without thoroughly examining these relationships.

Case study data may come from numerous sources. An investigator may procure personal testimony from subjects by asking them to recall various past experiences or to express present wishes in interviews or questionnaires. Personal documents, such as diaries and letters and various physical, psychological, or sociological tests or measurements may yield valuable information. (These tools will be discussed in Chapter 12.) Data may also come from parents, brothers and sisters, friends, acquaintances, and various court, government, school, hospital, business, social agency, and church records.

A case study is similar to a survey,[1] but instead of gathering data concerning a few factors from a large number of social units, it makes an exhaustive study of a limited number of representative cases. Moreover, a case study is more qualitative in nature than a survey. Through word descriptions it reveals a wealth of enlightening information that a quantitative study might not be able to produce. Consequently, the case study is often used to supplement the survey method. Young claims that "the most meaningful numerical studies in social science are those which are linked with exhaustive case studies describing accurately the interrelationships of factors and of processes" (41:230). Case studies are useful to a surveyor, because they may reveal what factors are relevant in a given situation that can be measured quantitatively. Statistical surveys, on the other hand, may provide a guide for selecting representative subjects for case studies. Thus, the two methods are more or less interdependent.

Contributions and Limitations. Case studies can make useful contributions to research, but they have certain limitations that the investigator must keep in mind. The expansive, exploratory nature of a case study may give one insights that may lead to the formulation of fruitful hypotheses, for knowledge that a particular condition exists in a unique instance suggests factors to look for in other cases. But a generalization drawn from a single case or a few casually selected ones cannot be applied to all cases in a given population. If a generalization is drawn from an adequate number of representative cases, however, it can be. The difficulty, of course, lies in selecting subjects or units for a study that are representative or typical. Although evidence derived from one case study cannot be generalized to a universe, a negative piece of evidence produced in a single case will alert the investigator to the possibility that he may need to modify his hypothesis. Case study data also prove useful when the researcher needs to illustrate statistical findings, for concrete examples drawn from individual cases can help readers understand statistical generalizations more readily.

The question of objectivity also arises when evaluating the usefulness of case studies: Are case study data too subjective to be of scientific value?

[1] Some studies of communities, for example, are classified as case studies by some writers and as surveys by others.

Some data, such as those concerning height and weight, are as objective as data collected by other research methods. But elements of subjectivity can enter into a report, particularly when judgments are made about a subject's character and motives. An investigator must guard against permitting personal biases, standards, and prejudices to influence his interpretation. Facts must be reported precisely and objectively and judgments must be suspended until considerable evidence has been gathered to support a conclusion. When collecting evidence from records, documents, interviews, and questionnaires one must exercise every possible precaution to detect and avoid accepting data that are the product of errors of perception, faulty memory, deliberate deception, unconscious bias, the reporter's or subject's desire to present the "right" answer, and the tendency to overemphasize unusual events or to distort them for dramatic effect.

Causal Comparative Studies. Some descriptive studies try to discover not only *what* a phenomenon is like, but, if possible, *how* and *why* it occurs. They compare the likenesses and differences among phenomena to find out what factors or circumstances seem to accompany certain events, conditions, processes, or practices. Most descriptive studies merely uncover the fact that a relationship appears to exist, but some probe deeper with the hope of ascertaining whether this relationship may cause, contribute, or account for the surface condition.

Need for Causal Comparative Method. When scientists study causation, they prefer to employ the experimental method, but sometimes the causal comparative method[2] is the only feasible way to attack a problem. In the experimental method, investigators arrange conditions and control all factors except a specific independent variable which they manipulate to discover what takes place. A replication of the conditions under which the experiment is performed is possible; consequently, verification is relatively more exact than if other methods are employed. However, in certain circumstances experimental procedures cannot be used. In astronomy, for example, the space and time dimensions prevent the astronomer from manipulating the orbit of a planet to observe its effect. Since it is impossible to vary the orbit of a planet, the astronomer does the next best thing—he studies the planet in orbit and observes what actually happens.

In the behavioral sciences many problems cannot be solved by the experimental method. Because of the complexity and nature of social phenomena, one cannot always select and control the factors necessary to study cause and effect relations in an artificial laboratory situation. If an experimenter controls variations in all but a single independent—experimental—variable, he may prevent the simultaneous functioning of variables that normally are found operating together and thus may free the independent variable from the influence of the other variables (7:336). In

[2] Sometimes referred to, particularly by sociologists, as the *ex post facto design*.

such instances an analysis of what actually does happen in a natural situation may be a more satisfactory way to study causes.

Employing the experimental method is impractical or prohibitively costly in time, money, and effort in some instances, such as studies of riots or "life as it is lived." In other instances employing the experimental method is unethical or immoral. One cannot justify staging fatal airplane crashes to ascertain their causes or placing emotionally stable children in controlled environments to determine whether it is possible to produce various psychoses. Respect for living things thus prevents an investigator from inflicting unnecessary pain, hardship, or harm on others, or from interfering in any way with the normal growth and development of an individual. Hence, in some cases, experiments cannot be utilized to study causation; thus, one must turn to the causal comparative method.

Methods of Searching for Relationships. When using the causal comparative method, instead of arranging a controlled laboratory experiment and inducing subjects to do or become something, a researcher studies a life situation in which subjects are playing, experiencing, or being what he wants to investigate. To study school integration riots, for example, rather than setting up an experiment to test whether various factors will cause a riot, he compares a community that has experienced a riot with one that has not. After studying the likenesses and differences between the two situations, he describes the factors that appear to account for the riot in the one instance and not in the other.

Likewise, in studies of emotional instability, selected children are not placed in a situation where all factors are kept constant except one variable which is manipulated to determine what causes a particular type of emotional disturbance. Rather, children are chosen who according to a selected criterion are "disturbed," and they are compared with a group who are not. A search is made for factors or conditions which seem to be associated with one group and not the other that might serve as a possible explanation of the underlying causes of the emotional problem.

The causal comparative type of investigation stems from John Stuart Mill's method of discovering causal connections. Mill's *Method of Agreement* rules that, "If two or more instances of the phenomenon under investigation have only one circumstance in common, the circumstance in which alone all the instances agree, is the cause (or effect) of the given phenomenon" (23:224). A concrete illustration of this principle may make it more comprehensible. Suppose that six students—A, B, C, D, E, and F—went to a debating tournament and subsequently three of them—A, B, and C—became ill. To find out the cause of their illness, the doctor might question A, B, and C about what food they had eaten and find that every item they had selected differed except for strawberry cream pie. In other words, the only food consumed by all those who became ill was the pie. In conformity with the *Method of Agreement,* the doctor could conclude that the illness was caused by the pie, for it was this, and only this, item on the menu that the ill students had experienced in common.

If the doctor wished to make more certain of his diagnosis, he could have employed Mill's *Joint Method of Agreement and Difference* which rules that, "If two or more instances in which the phenomenon occurs have only one circumstance in common, while two or more instances in which it does not occur have nothing in common save the absence of that circumstance; the circumstance in which alone the two sets of instances differ, is the effect, or cause, or necessary part of the cause, of the phenomenon" (23:229). To apply this rule, the doctor would have to determine not only that strawberry cream pie was the only food that all the ill students consumed, but he also would have to question members of the group who did not become ill—D, E, and F. If he found the only item common to those who suffered no ill effects was the absence of pie, he would have strengthened his conclusion that strawberry cream pie was causally related to the illness of the students. Thus, this method gives the researcher a double check on his conclusions concerning causality. Life situations, however, are rarely as simple as this illustration.

Types of Problems. Many educational processes, practices, programs, and products have been analyzed by the causal comparative method. The problems range from relatively simple, nonmathematical designs to moderately complex studies in which control groups and some characteristics of the experimental method are employed. A few representative studies are a comparative study of delinquent and nondelinquent adolescents (6), a differential analysis of the play of adolescent boys (38), and methods of attack used by poor and good achievers in attempting to correct errors in six types of subtraction involving fractions (28). In these studies, the investigators searched for likenesses and differences among their subjects to obtain clues about what might cause or contribute to the occurrence of a particular phenomenon.

Some studies of educational systems in various countries, states, or regions also utilize causal comparative techniques. These studies do not merely report on school status, but also search for likenesses and differences in educational theories and practices in different places and analyze the interrelationships of the historical, social, economic, and philosophical forces that have operated in an effort to ascertain what caused or contributed to the conditions that exist. I. L. Kandel's two studies, *The End of an Era* (18) and *The New Era in Education* (19), for example, examined the conditions leading up to World War II, the problems stemming from the war, the challenges resulting from the clash of democratic ideals and Communist ideology, and the impact of these forces upon the European and American educational scene.

Difficulties Encountered. While the causal comparative approach to solving problems can be useful, it also has its limitations. Some of the difficulties that can be encountered when employing this method are:

1. If the relevant factor causing a particular condition is not included among the items being considered when studying the problem, the cause cannot be ascertained. But how does one determine what is relevant? If certain factors seem to accompany a certain condition, one or more of them may be the cause of it; but, on the other hand, things may go together without having a cause and effect relationship. The three ill debaters in our previous illustration, for example, may have had certain common experiences aside from eating strawberry pie—drinking coffee, taking the same type of pills, or swimming in the same pool—that did not play any part in their illness. Hence, a scholar must have considerable general knowledge of his phenomena and must plan his observational procedures with care if he is going to spot possible relevant causes and eliminate chance associative factors from his study.

2. The joint method of agreement and disagreement requires that there is a single critical factor responsible for the occurrence or nonoccurrence of the phenomenon. But this condition is rarely found when working with complex social phenomena, for events usually have multiple rather than single causes. For example, what is the decisive factor responsible for good teaching? Is it the instructor's college training, quality of scholarship, nonschool experiences, attitude toward children, or type of personality? The phenomenon of good teaching does not seem to stem from a single definable factor, but from the interaction of several relevant factors. Hence, in many instances, the causal comparative method of research arrives at only an approximation of the cause for a given phenomenon.

3. A phenomenon may result not only from multiple causes but also from one cause in one instance and from another cause in another instance. For example, the three ill debaters all experienced one factor in common—eating strawberry cream pie—but this factor may not have been the cause of their illness. It is within the realm of possibility that Student A became ill because of overexertion, B because of inhaling automobile gas fumes, and C because of overeating. Thus, sometimes searching for likenesses associated with conditions or events leads an investigator up blind alleys and prevents him from detecting the real cause involved in the situation.

4. Detecting relationships does not necessarily solve problems about the cause of a condition. As previously noted, the fact that two subjects have something in common may be a chance circumstance and not related to the cause of the phenomenon being studied. When a cause-effect relationship is discovered, it is not always easy to determine which is the cause and which is the effect. If a study notes a relationship between low grades and automobile ownership among high school boys, the question arises: Does

automobile ownership cause the low grades or do boys who get low grades feel insecure and seek status by purchasing automobiles? Even though two factors may always appear together, the one may not necessarily be the cause of the other, for both of them may be caused by a third factor or a complex of factors. Studies reveal, for example, that older women in the general population bear more intelligent children than younger women, but this is because women with high intelligence and ability tend to marry later in life and not because middle age is the best time to bear intelligent children.

5. Classifying subjects into dichotomous groups for the purpose of comparison also presents problems, for social phenomena are not alike except within broad limits. They do not automatically fall into exclusive categories. Typists, swimmers, teachers, or spellers may range from those who possess few skills to those who are highly skilled. Even the ill debaters previously mentioned may vary from one who experiences a slight headache to one who is critically ill. Comparing one vague variable with another may produce a precise statistic, but it may provide little useful knowledge about existing status. If comparisons are to be made of successful or unsuccessful students, ill or well debaters, or any other subjects to ascertain what causes the factor under consideration, the phenomena and categories must be defined with great care.

6. In comparative studies of natural situations, the researcher does not have the same careful control over the selection of subjects as he does in well-designed experimental studies. It is extremely difficult to find naturally existing groups of subjects who are similar in all respects except for their exposure to one variable. The danger always exists that the groups differ in some other way—health, intelligence, home background, previous experience—that will affect the findings of the study. For example, if one tests a hypothesis about the effects of a health textbook on specific practices of children by comparing the hygienic habits of students who have read the book with those who have not, the possibility exists that the group that did not read the book had better hygienic training at home than the former group. Or, the students who were sufficiently interested in health to enroll in the class may have possessed better health practices than nonenrollees before they read the textbook.

Causal comparative studies have many limitations, and they often do not produce the precise, reliable knowledge that can be gained through good experimental studies. But they do provide a means of tackling problems that cannot be probed in laboratory situations, and they do yield valuable clues concerning the nature of phenomena. As the techniques, tools, and controls used in conducting causal comparative studies have been improved, this method of inquiry has gained greater respect.

Correlation Studies. Some studies obtain descriptions of phenomena by employing correlation techniques. The mathematical processes involved in these procedures will be discussed in Chapter 13, but the following general explanation and illustrations will indicate how this technique helps researchers detect the magnitude of relationships between data.

Correlation techniques are used to ascertain the extent to which two variables are related, that is, the extent to which variations in one factor correspond with variations in another. Suppose that you want to know whether there was any connection—and how much—between the IQ scores and algebra marks of ninth-grade students in attendance at the Lincoln School during the last academic year. On the basis of general impressions, you may have arrived at the hypothesis that the higher the student's IQ score, the higher his algebra mark. To test this hypothesis and to determine the magnitude of the relationship, you can conduct a simple investigation.

First, obtain the IQ scores and algebra marks for the ninth-grade students from their cumulative folders. After recording the IQ scores in order of increasing size—from the lowest to the highest score—place each pupil's algebra mark beside his IQ score. Now note whether the algebra marks increase in correspondence with the IQ scores. If the two orders correspond exactly, a perfect positive correlation exists between the IQ and algebra scores. If the two orders coincide in part, some relationship between the two scores may exist, but the intensity of the relationship between the variables can only be determined by applying certain mathematical procedures.

Variables may be closely related, moderately related, or completely unrelated. In general, the magnitude of a correlation depends upon the extent to which an increase or decrease in one variable is accompanied by an increase or decrease in the other—whether in the same direction or the opposite direction. For example, a *high positive correlation* exists if, in general, a high rank in one set of scores is accompanied by a high rank in the other (high IQ—high school marks) and a low rank in one set is accompanied by a low rank in the other (low IQ—low school marks). A *high negative correlation* exists if, in general, a high rank in one set of scores corresponds with a low rank in the other (high IQ—low school marks), and if a low rank in the first set corresponds with a high rank in the other (low IQ—high school marks). *No or little correlation* exists if, in general, a high score in one set is just as likely to correspond with a low or a high score in the other set. (Students with high IQ scores, for example, are as likely to have high as low school marks.) In other words, no discernible correspondence prevails between the high and low ranks of the sets of scores. Correlations, therefore, range over a scale which extends from a perfect negative correlation, to no correlation, to a perfect positive correlation.

Correlation techniques can serve a number of different purposes. Social scientists find them particularly useful in studies of prediction and cause and effect. Researchers are often asked to find a means of predicting whether pupils or employees will be successful on the job or in mastering particular skills or subject matter. When faced with a problem of predicting scholastic success, for example, an educational research bureau may design a test to measure "academic aptitude" and administer it to all freshman students entering college in September. At the close of the academic year, they may correlate the scores on this test with the students' quality point averages. If a high positive correlation between the two variables exists and if the youths taking the "academic aptitude test" are representative of the succeeding freshman students, the researchers may assume that the test will be of value in predicting the scholastic success of future students. Consequently, they may plan to use it as a basis for screening and counseling students. Of course, there is always the possibility that the relationship found between the variables is due to mere chance or to some irrelevant factors.

In studies analyzing cause and effect, the correlation technique may be used in the following manner. Suppose that from observing typing classes you have decided that the amount of time spent in glancing away from the copy is inversely related to typing speed. To test this hypothesis, you may have all ninth-grade typing students in Jones school type the same copy. After recording the typing speed of each student and the amount of time spent in glancing away from the copy, you compare the speed scores with the glancing away time and discover that a high negative correlation exists—that is, the lower the typing speed a student achieves, the more time he spends glancing away from his copy. This correlation suggests, but does not conclusively prove, that time spent in glancing away from the copy is an important factor relating to the speed of typing. It suggests that speed of typing may be improved by decreasing the amount of time glancing away from the copy.

The correlation technique is valuable in cause-effect analysis, but it merely quantifies the extent to which two variables are related: it does not imply that a cause-effect relationship necessarily exists. Interpreting the meaning of the relationship is accomplished by logical analysis rather than statistical computation. This interpretation is subject to all of the pitfalls and limitations discussed in the previous section on causal comparative studies.

DEVELOPMENTAL STUDIES

Developmental descriptive studies are concerned not only with the existing status and interrelationships of phenomena, but also with changes that take place as a function of time. They describe variables in the course of their development over a period of months or years. In the following sections two types of developmental descriptive studies will be discussed: growth studies and trend studies.

Growth Studies. To teach effectively one must have knowledge of the nature and rate of changes that take place in human organisms. One must know what interrelated factors affect growth at various stages of development and when various aspects of growth are first observable, spurt forward, remain rather stationary, reach optimal development, and decline.

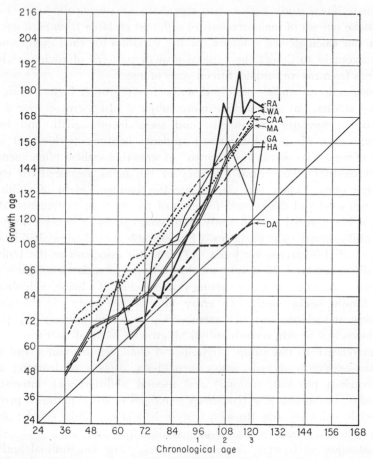

Fig. 16. Growth of a boy at a high level. Letters represent attributes of growth: (RA) reading age; (WA) weight age; (CAA) carpal age; (MA) mental age; (GA) grip age; (HA) height age; (DA) dental age. Small numbers below the base line represent growth of pubic hair: (1) first appearance; (2) pigmented; (3) pigmented and curly. (*From W. C. Olson and D. O. Hughes, "Concepts of Growth. Their Significance to Teachers," Childhood Education,* 21 (*Oct.,* 1944): 54.)

Growth Study Techniques. Human development can be studied by two methods: the longitudinal and the cross-sectional techniques. In both types of studies a series of planned and systematic observations are made. In the *longitudinal* studies, the growth states of the *same children* are measured at *different ages.* You might, for example, test and measure the same group of students on a number of variables when they are twelve, thirteen, fourteen, and fifteen years of age and plot their individual growth patterns for these factors during these years. But when conducting a *cross-sectional* study, rather than repeatedly measuring the same children, you make one set of measurements of *different children from each age level.* Then you calculate the averages for the variables for each group and plot these averages to depict the general growth patterns of each variable for children from twelve through fifteen years of age.

Cross-sectional studies usually describe fewer growth factors than longitudinal studies, but they include more subjects. In a cross-sectional study, you might measure the weight, and some length, girth, and breadth measurements of several thousand students between twelve and sixteen years of age. To obtain the "norms" of growth for these phenomena, you would calculate the central tendency of the items measured for each of the five years. Thus, you could state the average weight of children on each age level and the average for each of the other measurements taken.

In a longitudinal growth study, you would probably observe fewer subjects and measure more variables. For example, a study described in *Development of Adolescence* by Jones (17) and his associates at the University of California traced the development of a boy, "John Sanders," for a period of years. Among the many factors studied were (1) home, neighborhood, and family background; (2) entry into adolescence; (3) reactions of teachers and classmates; (4) membership in social groups; (5) physical development—health records, physical growth, skeletal maturing, growth curves relative to the group, physiological changes; (6) motor and mental abilities—strength record, achievement tests, aspects of learning ability, and various physical, manual, and mental abilities; (7) interests and attitudes; (8) underlying tendencies—analyses of drive patterns, projective materials, voice records, Rorschach records, and emotional trends; and (9) John as he saw himself and as he judged himself and others.

Evaluation of Growth Study Techniques. The longitudinal and cross-sectional techniques both possess advantages and limitations as a tool for discovering the nature of a human organism's development. The longitudinal technique is generally considered the most satisfactory method, but the cross-sectional technique is more commonly used because it is less expensive and less time consuming. When the cross-sectional technique is employed, data can be gathered and analyzed in a relatively short time; it is not necessary to test and measure the subjects year after year, or to wait until they mature before a study can be completed.

Sampling problems occur in the use of both techniques. In cross-sectional studies, the different subjects measured at each age level may not be comparable, for example, a cross-sectional study of the strength and intelligence of males between fifteen and sixty-five years of age.   The data collected for the youngest and oldest age group are not comparable for two reasons.   The older men are presumably representative of those who at fifteen possessed the physical and intellectual capacity to survive until sixty-five years of age.   The fifteen-year-old group undoubtedly contains some boys who will not survive until they are sixty-five.   Even if the age spread in a cross-sectional study is not great, errors can be made in comparing the average growth of different groups.   A researcher may want to obtain a description of the average strength and intelligence of American children between the ages six and eighteen.   But testing the students in Irontown schools between these ages will give him a distorted picture of older youths' capacities, for in this mining town many brighter students go away to school after the ninth grade and many stronger boys go to work.

Longitudinal studies also have weaknesses.   Since they are usually confined to fewer subjects than cross-sectional ones, their data do not experience the corrective influence of many samples.   When subjects are selected from a community with a stable population for the sake of keeping track of them throughout the years of the study, the low mobility of the group introduces a bias that will influence the findings.   Longitudinal studies may give accurate measurements for the growth of the individuals studied, but these descriptions are not necessarily representative of the total population.   Can findings, for example, concerning the growth and development of students in a laboratory school at the University of Michigan be applied directly to students in a rural Mississippi community or children of migrant Mexican laborers?

Another complication of the longitudinal method is that the researcher usually cannot make improvements in his techniques as his study develops without disrupting the continuity of procedures.   He may, for example, discover a new and better instrument for measuring a particular aptitude after the study has been underway for a year or two.   But, if he introduces it, he may not justifiably be able to make comparisons between the data collected by the different tests.

Longitudinal studies usually include a relatively small number of subjects from one locality.   Therefore, they are not likely to give as accurate a picture of the great range of individual differences that exist among children as cross-sectional studies do.   But individual variability of growth and development is revealed better in longitudinal than in cross-sectional studies.   At best, cross-sectional studies provide approximations about the individuality of growth with time, for they give the average growth status of an age group which tends to minimize or blot out individual variability.   Thus, the growth spurt during adolescence may not be revealed in a cross-sectional study, because the combination of late- and early-maturing subjects tends to smooth out the curve. When studying the physical growth patterns of children, for example, Shuttleworth (30) found that late- and early-maturing girls exhibited different growth curves which were not apparent when age cross-sectional data were used. Children mature at different rates, and their growth patterns reflect the influence of illness and environmental experiences that they encounter. Hence, the longitudinal method is the best way of obtaining accurate descriptions of individual growth.

When utilizing the longitudinal technique, however, a researcher may encounter difficulties. Obtaining complete data for all subjects over the years may be impossible because some of them may die, become ill, move, or lose interest in participating. Moreover, the conditions that made the subjects unavailable may have a bearing on the growth patterns being studied, which, of course, cannot be reflected in the last stages of the study results. If strength is being measured, for example, the weaker boys may lose interest in the study and "just go through the motions" or even refuse to take the tests after the first few years. If all data for subjects with incomplete measurements are discarded, as some investigators suggest should be done (1), the size of the sample may be reduced to a point of little value. The alternative, of course, is to start with a group considerably larger than will be reported in the final results. This procedure, obviously, is exceedingly costly and time-consuming.

Problem solving by the use of the longitudinal approach usually requires extensive facilities, considerable financial support, and continuity of personnel over a number of years. Hence, it is not surprising that child welfare stations connected with the larger universities have exerted practically all of the leadership in this field of research. Graduate students and individual professors usually pursue cross-sectional studies. But no real antagonism exists between cross-sectional and longitudinal methods: each method possesses value and each tends to supplement the information concerning growth and development provided by the other.

Trend Studies. Obtaining social, economic, or political data and analyzing it to identify trends and to predict what is likely to take place in the future is the objective of some descriptive studies. Researchers who engage in this work either repeat the same status study at intervals over a period of years, or gather information from documentary sources that describe present events or conditions and those that occurred at different times in the past. After comparing the data—studying the rate and direction of change—they predict the conditions or events that may prevail in the future. This type of study may combine the historical, documentary, and survey techniques.

Administrators involved in making plans for the future of an industry, community, or school system often conduct or examine trend surveys before formulating policies. Leaders from many fields undoubtedly will peruse the *New York Metropolitan Region Study* (nine volumes), which examines jobs and wages; shift of residential areas; population growth and decline; conditions affecting business, industry, and trade; transportation; finance; labor; and education. On the basis of current trends, the study projects probable developments through 1985. To plan intelligent future courses of action, school authorities must possess information such as this. Studies of home building trends in the community and the age of the new residents, for example, give them some idea of when and where to build future schools. Studies of migrations inform them of the population gains and losses to expect, so that they can adjust school budgets, instructional programs, classroom construction, and teacher recruitment programs accordingly.

Since World War II, several studies (26,27,35) have warned educators to prepare for enormous increases in secondary school and college enrollments. These predictions have been based on trend analyses that reveal a skyrocketing increase in births since 1940 and a higher proportion of students completing their high school education and going on to college. These studies have alerted college officials to the need for accelerating their building programs, attracting more youths to college teaching as a profession, and conducting vigorous campaigns for the funds needed to expand their programs.

Among other examples of educational trend studies are the interesting and complex analyses of population changes that have been reported by Edwards and Richey (10) and the Research Division of the NEA (see issues of the *Research Bulletin*). These studies raise questions about the educational implications of trends, such as the rising level of schooling attained by the population, the changing age structure of the population, and the differential fertility of the racial, socioeconomic, and educational groups in the population. For several years, R. C. Maul and others have been analyzing birth rate trends, enrollments in schools of education, and other factors to make predictions about teacher supply and demand in various fields. Studies in occupational trends have also provided school administrators with information that aids them in planning future educational programs.

Making predictions from social trend data is a precarious venture because economic conditions, technological advances, wars, personal wants, and other unforeseen events may suddenly modify the anticipated course of events. Long range population predictions, for example, have usually proved wrong. Malthus foresaw mass starvation because of overpopulation, but he did not foresee the productivity of the Industrial Revolution and the agricultural Americas. With the decrease in immigration and the decline of the birth rate during the depression years, scholars suggested that the United States should prepare for a leveling off of the population. But in recent years, the projections of the Census Bureau on population growth have been invalidated almost before their publication because of the unexpected increases. Again pundits prophesy that the population explosion will bring global misery. They predict that colleges will not be able to cope with expanding enrollments. But perhaps new techniques and resources will be discovered to solve the colleges' problems. Moreover, the anticipated increase in enrollments may not be fully realized if a war, serious depression, sharply increased tuition, or higher entrance standards prevent many youths from attaining a higher education. Because of the many unforeseeable factors that may impinge upon social phenomena, trend analyses range considerably in certainty of prediction. Generally, the long-range predictions represent mere estimates; short-term predictions possess greater certainty.

EVALUATION OF DESCRIPTIVE RESEARCH

Descriptive research is the method of investigation that has been most commonly employed by educators. Popularity, however, is not proof of worth. Some descriptive studies increase men's understanding of educational phenomena, but many are of limited value. In an attempt to place descriptive research in proper perspective, the following discussion will examine the advantages and limitations of this method of investigation.

Values of Descriptive Research. Descriptive studies that obtain accurate facts about existing conditions or detect significant relationships between current phenomena and interpret the meaning of the data provide educators with practical and immediately useful information. Factual information about existing status enables members of the profession to make more intelligent plans about future courses of action and helps them interpret educational problems more effectively to the public. Pertinent data regarding the present scene may focus attention upon needs that otherwise would remain unnoticed. They may also reveal developments, conditions, or trends that will convince citizens to keep pace with others or to prepare for probable future events. Since existing educational conditions, processes, practices, and programs are constantly changing, there is always a need for up-to-date descriptions of what is taking place.

Descriptive studies supply not only practical information that can be used to justify or improve the immediate situation, but also the factual foundations upon which higher and higher levels of scientific understanding can be built. Compared with the natural sciences, research in the field of education is of relatively recent origin. Consequently, many areas within the field have not been thoroughly explored: numerous gaps in knowledge exist. A rich reservoir of information about the nature of educational phenomena must be collected, classified, and correlated before investigators can gain insights that will enable them to "break through" to higher levels of scientific understanding.

Descriptive research is sometimes disparaged because it provides the lowest level of scientific understanding—descriptions of what exists.   It does not produce grandiose scientific theories that form the apex of our hierarchy of knowledge.   Indeed, some men classify descriptive studies as scholarly work, but do not consider them to be research.   Undoubtedly, educators have been too preoccupied with descriptive studies and there is a pressing need to move on into more fundamental probes concerning the nature of phenomena in the field.   Nevertheless, descriptive data serve a useful purpose.   Unless educators accumulate relevant facts about a situation, they cannot sense what is significant.   If they do not possess the facts, they cannot fit them into complex frames of relationships that reveal general scientific theories and laws and thus produce a more sophisticated level of knowledge.

Descriptive research is a necessary initial step for a young science to take and sometimes it is the only method that can be employed to study social situations and aspects of human behavior.   Since not all social phenomena can be subjected to laboratory experiments, studying conditions as they exist in a classroom, community, recreation center, or camp may be the only way to examine and analyze the factors involved in a given situation. Granted, descriptive research has many limitations, but as improved techniques and tools have been designed some of the weaknesses have been minimized.   The descriptive method of investigation has led to the development of many research tools and it has provided some means of studying phenomena that other methods cannot probe.

Application of the Scientific Method.   Do descriptive studies conform to the scientific method of research?   In some respects well-designed studies do, but the complex nature of social science phenomena makes the full realization of this goal unattainable.   Some of the problems that arise are concerned with (1) a critical examination of the source materials, (2) technical terminology, (3) construction of hypotheses, (4) observation and experimentation, and (5) generalization and prediction.

Critical Examination of Source Materials.   Scientific inquiry requires the presentation of accurate, precise facts that are verifiable by public tests of common perception.   Some descriptive data can measure up to this standard, but many of them cannot be established as scientifically as facts of physical science.   Social science phenomena are much more complex than physical phenomena, hence, it is more difficult to isolate relevant and representative factors in a given situation and to weigh and measure— quantify the findings—so as to establish relatively stable facts that can be confirmed by any competent observer.

Descriptive data are infinitely numerous and diverse. Unlike the physical sciences which are concerned with data on one level—the physical—descriptive studies may deal not only with physical facts, but also with social, biological, or psychological facts. Reliable, objective measurements can be ascertained for some social phenomena, such as the age and sex of pupils, the number of days they were absent from school, or times they were tardy, or how many teachers have their M.A. degrees. These facts can be checked and verified by any able observer. But some data that are of the greatest interest to educators cannot readily be isolated and precisely measured. Measuring attitudes and motives of children, opinions of community groups, and behavioral traits required for effective teaching is far more difficult than appears on the surface.

A researcher can quickly ascertain that Johnny is a 100-pound white male youth, but he may have great difficulty in obtaining accurate information about the boy's attitudes toward Negroes or why the youth prefers fattening foods. Johnny may deliberately conceal his real motives from the investigator, may give an answer that he thinks is socially acceptable, or may make a reply that he has heard repeated often. He may give answers that reflect a reaction to a recent vivid experience rather than his customary attitude. His preferences for fattening food may be conditioned by physiological conditions, family food habits, a desire to compensate for lack of success in athletics or intellectual activities, or many other factors. Attempting to isolate causal factors and to determine in what proportion each is responsible for an existing condition or event is often a difficult if not an impossible task.

Descriptive studies cannot produce significant findings if they are based on erroneous data. Yet, some researchers do not critically examine their source materials. They accept much information that appears in print or in official records at face value. This is a dangerous practice, for records may be deliberately falsified or may include unintentional errors and printed materials may reflect the author's biases or may be based on secondhand rather than firsthand observations. Some researchers also forget that data collected from different sources, by different people, by different techniques, or at different times may not be comparable.

Technical Terminology. Social scientists have not devised a universally accepted, precise vocabulary to communicate to one another. Different workers may use different terms to describe the same phenomena. The term, "descriptive research," itself, is not universally employed. Some investigators will refer to a descriptive study as survey research, a normative-survey, a status study, or a field study. When workers employ the same terms, they do not always have the same meanings in mind. If two observers are seeking data about "cooperative behavior" of pupils, one may tabulate incidents of blind obedience to authority and the other incidents of critical-constructive participation. One worker may use the term "aggressive behavior" when he is referring to antisocial or delinquent acts, while another may use the term to describe demonstrations of initiative and leadership. An absence of clearly assigned meanings for terms results in ambiguous communications, which cannot provide a solid foundation for scientific understanding.

Formulation of Hypotheses. The scientific method requires scholars to make "intelligent guesses" that will solve problems and to test whether these hypotheses present accurate explanations of phenomena. If descriptive studies present hypotheses, they are usually of a somewhat lower order than those found in explanatory studies. In the latter, the hypotheses offer general explanations of *why* certain phenomena behave as they do. Descriptive studies simply portray the facts—they describe *what* exists but rarely seek to account for *why* the present state of affairs has occurred. Descriptive studies may describe the rudimentary groupings of things by comparing and contrasting likenesses and differences in their behavior. They may classify, order, and correlate data seeking to describe relationships that are discoverable in phenomena themselves. But they do not penetrate deeply into knowledge that lies beyond that which can be gained directly from the events or conditions. They do not fully analyze and explain why these relationships exist. Seeking higher-order meanings is left to explanatory hypotheses. Of course, there is no sharp dividing line between descriptive and explanatory hypotheses. Some causal comparative studies approach the level of explanatory hypotheses.

Educational research is in an early stage of its development and naturally some of its pioneer products have been unsatisfactory. Many descriptive studies have been poorly conceived in design; they have been lacking in depth and perspective. Rather than constructing well-thought-out hypotheses and collecting pertinent data to test them, many researchers blindly have made clerical tabulations of the available data on some subject. Their neat piles of data have not solved problems, for data cannot advance knowledge very much unless they are used to confirm or disconfirm a hypothesis concerning the nature of phenomena.

Hypotheses are more commonly stated in research papers today than they were earlier in the century. Perhaps some statements taken from recent literature are the best means of illustrating the nature of descriptive hypotheses. In a study of permissiveness, permission, and aggression and the effect of adult presence or absence on aggression in children's play, Siegel and Kohn (31:134) stated, "The hypothesis is that children under the two conditions will exhibit different session-to-session changes in aggression, in that aggression of the children under the adult-absent condition will tend to decrease in comparison to the aggression of the children under the adult-present condition, which will tend to increase."

A study designed to explore the effect of personal values on pupils and teachers in the determination of school marks states that the investigator (3:28) examined the following three hypotheses:

1. Among pupils of similar aptitude, age, and sex, the value patterns of those who receive high marks in a particular subject tend to have higher correlation with pupil value patterns considered ideal by the teacher who determines the marks than do the patterns of pupils who receive low marks in the subject.

2. If aptitude, age, and sex are controlled, the value patterns of pupils with high scholarship averages in their several subjects will tend to have higher correlation with a composite value pattern determined by several teachers in the school than will patterns of pupils with low averages.

3. In a Spearman Two-Factor pattern composed of a sample of teachers, a given number of high achieving pupils, and the same number of low achieving pupils in a particular high school, the loadings on the common factor for teachers and high achieving pupils will tend to exceed loadings on this factor for low achieving pupils.

Although hypotheses appear in some recent research reports, many of them are ambiguously formulated, overgeneralized, or logically unsound. Furthermore, most research papers fail to include a thorough and comprehensive analysis of the problem and the assumptions on which it is based so that the reader can determine how the researcher came to frame the particular hypotheses. Another common weakness of reports is the omission of the deductive elaboration of the hypotheses. The reports lead one to presume that the investigators tested the hypotheses directly rather than indirectly (according to step 4 of the Dewey stages of reflective thinking), through the deduced consequences of the hypotheses.

Experimentation and Observation. Whenever possible, social scientists test their hypotheses by experimentation—controlled, direct observation. Because this method cannot be utilized to solve numerous human behavior and educational problems, researchers often must study conditions as they operate in normal situations. Making observations in a dynamic, ongoing situation, however, is much more difficult than observing a few isolated variables in rigidly controlled laboratory experiments. Workers who employ descriptive procedures may exercise every possible precaution when making observations so that irrelevant factors do not bias their results, but, at best, they can only approach experimental conditions. Moreover, in some instances, they must rely on observations made by others, which introduces the problem of checking the authenticity and credibility of the secondhand information. Hence, the findings of descriptive research are not always as decisive as necessary for scientific acceptance.

Generalization and Prediction. The goals of science are to explain, predict, and control conditions and events. Descriptive research contributes to science primarily by building a foundation of facts upon which explanatory hypotheses can be constructed and by checking the validity of existing theories. Science begins with descriptions of singular, unique events, but it does not remain on this primitive level of knowledge. Scientific workers endeavor to construct generalizations—hypotheses—that will explain why events occur. Rather than confining their attention to a particular isolated incident, they imaginatively structure broad generalizations that will account for the occurrence of many unrelated events and conditions. Their ultimate objective is to establish universal laws with predictive power that will enable man to control nature.

For the most part descriptive research is temporally localized, hence, it does not possess great predictive power. Most of its findings are applicable only within relatively short limits of time. Descriptive generalizations may help solve contemporary problems, but many of them have a limited useful life span. They do not survive because many social phenomena change from day to day and from one age to the next; they are not as stable as phenomena in the physical sciences. Some descriptive data, obviously, are more enduring than others. Data that describe certain physical conditions of the school environment—location of buildings—or physical characteristics of a child—color of eyes—are quite stable. Data concerning some behavioral phenomena, such as intelligence or authoritarianism, are relatively more enduring than descriptions of attitudes, interests, desires, or opinions, which may be rather fleeting in nature. The transitory character of much knowledge collected in descriptive studies usually limits the relevancy of the data to contemporary problems.

Most descriptive studies are spatially localized, thus, they produce limited rather than universal generalizations that possess predictive powers. If a researcher collects evidence concerning a limited range of conditions from a small segment of the population in a given culture, the hypothesis he confirms can only apply to the specific group of people that his sample represents. Since cultures differ from one another and no culture is absolutely uniform in nature, descriptive data can mirror only particular aspects of specific events or conditions in a given setting. If researchers study the same variables utilizing different populations, they often produce dissimilar results, thus, their results cannot be generalized beyond the immediate sample. Much of the descriptive research that is being done produces discrete bits of knowledge that are of local significance.

If a social scientist wishes to apply his findings to subjects or situations other than the specific ones included in a study, he must design his inquiry so that this is possible. But many workers employing the descriptive technique make no effort to obtain representative samples so that they can generalize upon their findings. They frequently study the population that is readily available, thus, their findings can only apply to the sample under consideration.

If it is possible, serious social scientists observe the niceties of sampling procedures in their inquiries, but, despite their sincerity, they cannot establish as broad generalizations as their colleagues in the natural sciences. "When social scientists seek generalizations about all human beings, rather than, say, about members of a specific culture or a specific organization, their sample is invariably nonrepresentative. No one has yet studied a representative sample of persons or behaviors from all cultures at all periods" (29:256–257). Chemists can be quite certain that one sample of pure magnesium is substantially like another, but educators can never claim that one child is exactly like all other children.

Social science workers are constantly plagued by the complexity of their phenomena. They are unable to abstract specific temporal and spatial characteristics from an event and generalize to all future occurrences of the event with any degree of preciseness. They find it almost an insurmountable task to forecast, for successful prediction rests upon the duplication of the past in the future. Rose states (29:158) that

. . . as long as social science deals with social phenomena on the level at which they can be observed directly, it cannot find cause-and-effect laws that apply universally in all known and possible cultures. The explanation of this requires no metaphysics; it is simply based on the fact that one of the determinants of an individual's behavior, when it is of the mediating type, is his "apperceptive mass," the full range of experiences that he has had since birth and that is retained in his nervous system. To predict his physical movements at these times, the predictor would have to know everything that ever happened to him, and this is impossible. Further, no two individuals have had exactly the same past experiences, and therefore knowledge of how one individual acts is no sure guide to how another will act. This is to say that we may never be able to make perfectly accurate predictions about human behavior or to make propositions about human behavior that hold good universally, as we may be able to make for the behavior of turtles or rocks.

Educational phenomena involve far too many variables for researchers to spell out detailed laws. One cannot precisely predict human behavior, but neither can one conclude that life consists of random or accidental events. By describing some of the reoccurring patterns or regularities of human behavior, some reasonably reliable, limited predictions can be made. Some descriptive studies accumulate knowledge that enables researchers to make predictions that are more accurate than chance alone would allow. But these forecasts do not possess the universality, precision, or degree of accuracy that predictions do in the natural sciences. They are likely to be stated "when this happens, this *tends* to occur" or "if this happens, we can expect that to happen in 60 per cent of the cases." Evolving universal generalizations that permit highly accurate predictions may be the ideal, but even the physical scientists are less certain today than they once were about their ability to predict in certain areas except in terms of statistical averages.

BIBLIOGRAPHY

1. Anderson, John E., and J. T. Cohen, "The Effect of Including Incomplete Series in the Statistical Analysis of Longitudinal Measurements of Children's Dental Aches," *Child Development,* 10 (June, 1939) : 145.

2. Barr, Arvil, R. A. Davis, and P. O. Johnson, *Educational Research and Appraisal.* Chicago: J. B. Lippincott Company, 1953, chaps. 5, 7, 10, and 12.

3. Battle, Haron J., "Relation between Personal Values and Scholastic Achievement," *Journal of Experimental Education,* 26 (September, 1957) : 27.

4. Berelson, Bernard, *Content Analysis in Communication Research.* Glencoe, Ill.: Free Press, 1952.

5. Best, John W., *Research in Education.* Englewood Cliffs, N.J.: Prentice-Hall, Inc., 1959, chap. 5.

6. Birkeness, Valborg, and Harry C. Johnson, "A Comparative Study of Delinquent and Non-delinquent Adolescents," *Journal of Educational Research,* 42 (April, 1949) : 561.

7. Brown, Clarence W., and E. E. Ghiselli, *Scientific Method in Psychology.* New York: McGraw-Hill Book Company, Inc., 1955, chap. 15.

8. Charters, W. W., and Douglas Waples, *The Commonwealth Teacher-training Study.* Chicago: University of Chicago Press, 1929.

9. Eaton, Allen, and S. M. Harrison, *A Bibliography of Social Surveys.* New York: Russell Sage Foundation, 1930.

10. Edwards, Newton, and H. G. Richey, "The School in American Society," *Review of Educational Research,* 28 (February, 1958) : 29.

11. Furfey, Paul H., *The Scope and Method of Sociology.* New York: Harper & Brothers, 1953, chaps. 14 and 15.

12. Good, Carter V., *Introduction to Educational Research.* New York: Appleton-Century-Crofts, Inc., 1959, chaps. 5–7.

13. Good, Carter V., and Douglas E. Scates, *Methods of Research.* New York: Appleton-Century-Crofts, Inc., 1954, chaps. 5–9.

14. Harris, Chester W. (ed.), *Encyclopedia of Educational Research.* New York: The Macmillan Company, 1960.

15. Hillway, Tyrus, *Introduction to Research.* Boston: Houghton Mifflin Company, 1956, chaps. 10, 12, and 14.

16. Jahoda, Marie, et al., *Research Methods in Social Relations.* New York: The Dryden Press, Inc., 1951, chap. 3.

17. Jones, Harold E., *Development in Adolescence.* New York: Appleton-Century-Crofts, Inc., 1943.

18. Kandel, I. L., *The End of an Era.* New York: Teachers College, Columbia University, 1941.

19. Kandel, I. L., *The New Era in Education.* Boston: Houghton Mifflin Company, 1955.

20. Keesing, Felix M., *Cultural Anthropology.* New York: Holt, Rinehart and Winston, Inc., 1958.

21. Lindquist, E. F., *A First Course in Statistics.* Boston: Houghton Mifflin Company, 1942, chap. 10.

22. Massanari, K. L., "Public Opinion as Related to the Problem of School

District Reorganization in Selected Areas in Illinois," *Journal of Experimental Education,* 17 (June, 1949) : 389.

23. Mill, John S., *A System of Logic.* New York: Harper & Brothers, 1846.

24. Monroe, Walter S. (ed.), *Encyclopedia of Educational Research.* New York: The Macmillan Company, 1950.

25. NEA, Research Division, "Teaching Assignments and Time Schedules," *Research Bulletin,* 29 (February, 1951) : 10.

26. NEA, Research Division, "Growth in School Enrollments," *Research Bulletin,* 36 (December, 1958) : 124.

27. President's Committee on Education Beyond the High School, *Second Report to the President,* Government Printing Office, 1957.

28. Ramharter, Hazel K., and Harry C. Johnson, "Methods of Attack Used by 'Good' and 'Poor' Achievers in Attempting to Correct Errors in Six Types of Subtraction Involving Fractions," *Journal of Educational Research,* 42 (April, 1949) : 586.

29. Rose, Arnold M., *Theory and Method in the Social Sciences.* Minneapolis: The University of Minnesota Press, 1954.

30. Shuttleworth, Frank K., *The Physical and Mental Growth of Girls and Boys Aged Six to Nineteen in Relation to Age at Maximum Growth.* Monograph of the Society for Research in Child Development, 1939.

31. Siegel, Alberta E., and L. G. Kohn, "Permissiveness, Permission and Aggression in Children's Play," *Child Development,* 30 (March, 1959) : 131.

32. Smith, H. L., and E. A. O'Dell, *Bibliography of School Surveys and of References on School Surveys.* Indiana University, Bulletin of the School of Education, vol. 8, nos. 1 and 2, 1931.

33. Smith, H. L., and E. A. O'Dell, *Bibliography of School Surveys and of References on School Surveys.* Indiana University, Bulletin of the School of Education, vol. 14, no. 3, 1938.

34. Travers, Robert M. W., *An Introduction to Educational Research.* New York: The Macmillan Company, 1958, chaps. 10 and 12.

35. U.S. Dept. of Commerce, Bureau of Census, *Illustrative Projections of the College-age Population, by States: 1958–1973.* Current Population Reports, ser. P-25, no. 132, Washington, Feb. 20, 1956.

36. U.S. Office of Education, *National Survey of Secondary Educatoin.* Bulletin, 1932, no. 17.

37. U.S. Office of Education, *National Survey of the Education of Teachers.* Bulletin 1933, no. 10.

38. Van Dalen, D. B., "A Differential Analysis of the Play of Adolescent Boys," Journal of Educational Research, 41 (November, 1947) : 204.

39. Whitney, Frederick L., *The Elements of Research.* Englewood Cliffs, N.J.: Prentice-Hall, Inc., 1946, chap. 7.

40. Wilson, G. M., and C. O. Dalrymple, "Useful Fractions," *Journal of Educational Research,* 30 (January, 1937) : 341.

41. Young, Pauline V., *Scientific Social Surveys and Research.* Englewood Cliffs, N.J.: Prentice-Hall, Inc., 1956.

CHAPTER 11

Patterns of Experimental Research

When one engages in experimental research, one does not merely describe a condition, determine the status of something, or chronicle past events. Instead of confining activities to observing and describing *what* exists, one deliberately manipulates certain factors under highly controlled conditions to ascertain *how* and *why* a particular condition or event occurs. "Experimentation, as distinguished from observation, consists in the deliberate and controlled modification of the conditions determining an event, and in the observation and interpretation of the ensuing changes in the event itself" (27:618–619). From the previous chapter, you recall that causal-comparative studies are concerned with causality and those that are carefully controlled approach the level of other experimental investigations. If science is to achieve its goal—to explain, predict, and control behavior and events—it is imperative that causal connections among particular phenomena be discovered. Thus, educators who design experiments that lay bare the causes producing certain events perform a service of utmost importance to society.

NATURE OF EXPERIMENTAL RESEARCH

Conducting a test to determine cause is only one task involved in experimental research. Unless all the other procedures are executed with the greatest care, the experimental testing process is valueless. Perhaps the following list will give you a more comprehensive picture of the work one may have to do when undertaking an experimental study:

1. Identify and define the problem.
2. Formulate hypotheses and deduce their consequences.
3. Construct an experimental design that represents all the elements, conditions, and relations of the consequences. This may entail: (*a*) selecting a sample of subjects to represent a given population; (*b*) grouping or pairing subjects to secure homogeneity; (*c*) identifying and controlling nonexperimental factors; (*d*) selecting or constructing and validating instruments to measure the outcomes of the experiment; (*e*) conducting pilot or "trial run"

tests to perfect instruments or design; and (f) determining the place, time, and duration of the experiment.

4. Conduct the experiment.

5. Reduce the raw data in a manner that will produce the best unbiased appraisal of the effect which is presumed to exist.

6. Apply an appropriate test of significance to determine the credence one can place on the results of the study.

The first two tasks in this process have been discussed in detail in previous chapters, and, hence, will merely be reviewed in this one. Because the last two tasks involve a knowledge of statistics, they will be discussed in Chapters 13 and 14. Nevertheless, it should be emphasized at this point that many early experiments failed to apply appropriate tests of significance and this was a grave weakness. The discussion in this chapter is primarily concerned with the third task—designing the experiment and establishing the necessary controls. But before proceeding with that discussion, let us briefly review the relationship of the experiment to the problem and hypothesis.

Bases of an Experiment. Experimental research starts where any inquiry starts, namely, with the identification and rigorous analysis of the problem. The issues involved in the problem are sharpened by formulating hypotheses and ascertaining the consequences that are logically implied by them. A test is then devised to ascertain whether the consequences that should occur if the hypotheses are to be confirmed are actually observable.

Many students are extremely enthusiastic about experimental research, but they have a rather vague concept of the precision required to analyze problems and formulate hypotheses. To them experimentation is a blind trial and error procedure: "If we try this, what will happen?" Often, they have only a nebulous notion about what they are testing and their plans for observing what happens are equally indefinite. Sometimes they stumble upon fruitful explanations of causality by this procedure, but the chance of expending an enormous amount of effort without producing significant results is great. Conducting experiments to test crudely conceived hypotheses is a waste of time.

If a hypothesis and its deduced consequences are well conceived, **two** factors are precisely identified:

(1) an independent variable and (2) a dependent variable[1]
Condition A   *causes*   *Condition B*

A hypothesis suggests that an antecedent condition (independent variable) causes another condition, event, or effect (dependent variable) to occur.

[1] Some investigators apply different names to these factors, such as (1) cause and (2) effect, (1) stimulus and (2) response, (1) antecedent and (2) consequent, (1) experimental variable and (2) behavior variable, and (1) treatment and (2) effect.

To test a deduced consequence of a hypothesis, one constructs an experiment in which he attempts to control all conditions except the independent variable which he manipulates. Then the investigator observes what happens to the dependent variable presumably because of the exposure to the independent variable. The dependent variable is the phenomenon that appears, disappears, or changes as the researcher applies, removes, or varies the independent variable. The independent variable is the factor that is manipulated to ascertain its relationship with the dependent variable under observation.

Examples of Experiments. A botanist, for example, can contend that sunlight (independent variable) has an effect on plant growth (dependent variable). To test this hypothesis, he may obtain plants of the same species, cover each with a bell jar, and place one in a shaded place and the other in the sunlight. Thus, he manipulates the amount of sunlight the plants receive. His experiment will give him direct empirical evidence that exposure to the sun results in plant growth and the absence of the sunlight retards plant growth. The botanist may wish to broaden the experiment by setting out several like plants and shading the bell jars so that various intensities of light fall upon them in order to appraise how much various light conditions affect growth.

In education, a researcher may vary some condition in the students' environment and observe its effect on achievement. An investigator, for example, may hypothesize that children will learn to spell better if spaced drill is used rather than massed drill. The independent variable that will be manipulated in the experiment is the "spacing of drill." The dependent variable that will experience the effects of this manipulation is spelling mastery. To test this hypothesis, the experimenter must attempt to control all conditions so that they are the same for the two groups of children, except that he gives one group a massed spelling drill of sixty minutes once a week and the other group a fifteen-minute drill the first four school days of each week. In other words, all conditions are held constant except the experimental variable—spacing of drill—which is manipulated. Consequently, any difference in the spelling mastery of these two groups at the close of the experiment can be attributed to the independent variable—spacing of drill.

Essential Requirement of an Experiment. Experimentation is not merely a little game of manipulating one variable to see what happens to another variable. Experimentation consists in *controlled observation.* The most important task that the researcher faces when planning an experiment is to achieve control over all factors that affect the dependent variable. Unless he identifies and controls them, he can never be certain whether it is the manipulation of the independent variable or some other factor that has caused the particular effect. Suppose, for example, that the teacher who conducted the spelling experiment did not control the selection of the spelling words, the amount of time devoted to study, and the selection of the subjects.   It is entirely possible that one group of students might have had easier words to spell, a longer total time to study, and greater spelling mastery prior to the experiment than the other group.   When assessing the results of the experiment, the investigator would have had no way of knowing whether the spacing of drill or these other factors were responsible for the difference in spelling mastery.

The quality of the experiment is determined largely by the extent to which rigid controls are introduced.   Some investigators test vaguely stated hypotheses without trying to identify and control the factors that influence the dependent variable, but their studies are not acceptable as scientific experiments.   Other researchers achieve a certain measure of control, but their results are always subject to question because of the limitations of their procedures.   Achieving adequate control of the variables is extremely difficult because of the complex nature of educational phenomena, but the most competent experimenters strive to construct research designs that will give the greatest measure of control over them.

CONTROL OF THE EXPERIMENT

To discover cause-and-effect relationships one must not only elicit and control the expression of the independent variable, but also identify and hold constant other variables or factors that affect the dependent variable.   But how does a researcher determine what variables affect his dependent variable?   Previous experience with the phenomena and a careful analysis of the problem will undoubtedly suggest some clues.   Thoroughly examining all research studies that have dealt with the same dependent variable will inform him about factors that other scholars have found to influence it. Each investigator unearths a little additional information that gives added insight into the phenomena.   Hence, the findings of one's predecessors provide the richest source of information concerning what variables it is necessary to control in an experiment.

Investigators who have studied the dependent variable sensorimotor skill, for example, have found little relationship between intelligence test scores and sensorimotor learning, but they have identified several other factors that are related to such skills: strength, speed, accuracy, endurance, agility, body size, reaction time, steadiness, balance, and control of voluntary movements.   Thus, if one wants to discover whether another factor influences sensorimotor skills, he must find some way to control these previously identified variables so that they do not also affect his results. One of the biggest mistakes a researcher can make is to rush into the construction of an experimental design before he has adequate knowledge of the relevant factors that he must control.

Types of Factors to Be Controlled.   What types of factors does the researcher attempt to control in his experiment?   In general, there are three types: (1) those arising from the population, (2) those stemming from the testing procedures, and (3) those exerting influences from external sources.

Population Variables.   Sometimes the manipulation of the independent variable appears to cause a given effect on the dependent variable when it is actually the character of the participating subjects that is responsible. In a reading experiment, for example, if students taught by method A achieve higher scores on reading tests than those taught by method B, one cannot claim that group X's higher scores were caused by the method employed.   Why?   Perhaps the pupils in group X did better on the test because they came from culturally privileged homes where many experiences were given to encourage and improve their reading while students in group Y did poorly on the test because they came from impoverished families that neglected their basic needs and gave them no academic assistance or encouragement.   Thus, in an experiment, the researchers must analyze whether there is any characteristic about the subjects that could affect the dependent variable, such as intelligence; age; sex; physical or emotional status; or previous educational, home, or cultural experiences. Until he finds some means of controlling the population variables, he cannot properly appraise the effect of the independent variable on the dependent variable.

Experimental Procedures.   The experimental procedures themselves may affect the dependent variable.   Suppose that an investigator wants to determine whether children will achieve greater mastery of fractions if taught by the "drill" or "comprehension" method.   He may take the precaution of selecting two groups of subjects who are alike in all respects so that differences in their nature cannot affect the results.   But if he fails to control his procedures, differences in them may contribute to the subjects' mastery of fractions.   If he does not give the "drill" and "comprehension" groups the same total amount or distribution of practice, does not present them with lesson plans that are equally interesting and difficult, does not select subject matter that is equally suitable for teaching by either method, does not administer tests of mastery that are equally fair for evaluating both methods of instruction, or does not give each group the same amount of time to complete the final test, these procedural differences may influence the groups' gains in achievement.   The length of the experiment may also produce variations in the results obtained.   It is conceivable that the "drill method" could produce greater gains than the "understanding method" over a brief period of time and exhibit greater losses over an extended period of time. On the other hand, the "understanding method" could show smaller initial gains, but less forgetting over a longer time interval. Thus, when determining the duration of an experiment, one may be making a decision that will influence the results obtained.

Experimental procedures may also introduce unconscious signaling which will influence the results obtained. The subjects may receive clues from the behavior of the experimenter or from the nature of the tools, tests, or questionnaires employed that enable them to surmise what hypothesis is being tested or to suspect the significance of their responses. Anything that tips off the subjects to the purpose of the study may distort their normal responses to the experimental variable. They may either try to behave as they assume the investigator expects them to act or to conceal their normal reactions to the experimental variable. Likewise, if a researcher knows which subjects have received the treatment he favors in an experiment or how well students have done on a pretest, it may influence the judgments he makes when recording observations concerning the amount or nature of change that takes place because of exposure to the experimental variable. If the same observer judges the performance of two or more groups in succession or the same subjects before and after the application of the experimental variable, his judgments may vary because he becomes more fatigued, more discriminating, or more experienced.

Sometimes the experimental procedures generate a variable that alters a subject's responses to the independent variable. Because of the practice received through more than one exposure to a test or independent variable during an experiment or because of the order in which stimuli are presented to him, a subject may acquire skill, develop speed, or even lose receptivity to a stimulus. If an investigator applies a surprise electric shock to a subject, for example, he cannot repeat the "surprise shock" too many times and expect the same psychological reaction to occur on each successive occasion. If a pretest is given in an experiment, it may actually serve as a learning experience which enables the subject to do better on the final test whether or not an experimental factor is applied. If subjects are exposed to teaching method A and tested, and then method B and tested, the results on the second test may be a product not only of the skills they acquired through teaching method B but also of those retained from method A. Thus, the changes that occur in a dependent variable may not be wholly or even partially caused by the manipulation of the independent variable, but rather by the effect of practice or fatigue factors. The researcher must be on guard concerning these possibilities and seek some means of controlling them.

External Influences. Some external influences that impinge upon the situation may have an effect on the dependent variable. In the arithmetic experiment, for example, one group of students may have been taught in a much noisier room or at a less favorable hour of the day than the other. The teacher presenting one method may have been more proficient than the one employing the other method. If the same teacher taught both groups, she may have been more enthusiastic about one method than the other. A student in one group may have been a troublemaker or a dynamic leader who motivated the whole group to do poorer or better work than they would ordinarily do. Such incidents may be multiplied many times. Thus, an able researcher carefully examines his experimental plans to ascertain whether any external influences as well as population and procedural variables might possibly affect his dependent variable and makes every effort to control those he identifies.

Purposes of Control. In an experiment one seeks to control variables for the following purposes: "(1) to isolate the determiners individually and in combinations; (2) to vary them as magnitudes either singly or in combinations; and (3) to describe quantitatively the extent of their expression and their interacting effects, again, either as single determiners or as combinations of determiners" (4:76).

Achieving Isolation. To prevent a factor other than the independent variable from affecting the dependent variable, the researcher may remove the unwanted or interfering variable or keep constant its effect. Thus, in an experiment involving touch, taste, or smell discrimination, the researcher may blindfold the subjects so that the unwanted visual stimuli do not affect what the subjects report they touch, taste, or smell. Often it is not possible to remove unwanted variables before applying the independent variable. Age, for instance, is a variable that affects many dependent variables. Since all subjects possess an age, a researcher cannot eliminate it. But one control that is available to him is to maintain constancy of condition by selecting subjects of the same age. Thus, while the factor of age will affect a dependent variable, such as reading mastery, it will have a similar effect on the test scores of the control group and the experimental group. Hence, it is possible to conclude that the differences in the test results of the two groups are due to the independent variable and not to age.

Achieving Changes in Magnitude. An investigator may strive not only to isolate the independent variable, but also to ascertain how much effect it contributes. To achieve this, he must be able to vary the magnitude of the experimental variable. In a psychological study, for example, the experimenter may make observations for each degree of change in the independent variable—intensity, pitch, or timbre of an auditory stimulus—to determine its effect on the dependent variable. In some studies, of course, he cannot seek this level of control because not enough is known about the independent variable to vary it through finely graded steps. Consequently, he investigates whether the presence or absence of a certain factor has any effect at all and leaves it for his successors to study the graduations of effect.

Achieving Quantitative Evaluation. The ultimate goal of a researcher is to express the magnitude of the variable in quantitative terms. He does not merely want to know that one expression of a variable is larger or smaller than another, but, precisely how much larger or smaller it is. If two variables are functionally related, he does not merely want to state that they are positively or negatively related, but rather the specific degree of relationship in terms of some numerical value.

Methods of Control. Researchers have devised a number of procedures to control variables. Brown and Ghiselli (4) suggest that they fall into three broad categories: (1) physical manipulation, (2) selective manipulation, and (3) statistical manipulation. Sometimes direct physical manipulation can be used to gain control with the same success in the social sciences as it is in the physical sciences. The nature of educational phenomena, however, often makes it necessary to gain control through the indirect methods of selection and statistical manipulation.

Physical Manipulation. Various means of physical manipulation may be employed so as (1) to give all subjects the same exposure to the independent variable or (2) to control nonexperimental variables that affect the dependent variable. A *mechanical means* may be devised: an experimenter may soundproof or lightproof a room to screen out unwanted stimuli; use a one-way-vision screen to observe subjects so that his presence will not change or influence their behavior; employ a tachistoscope to present each subject with a specific number of words, numbers, pictures for brief intervals of duration; or construct a maze to study an ability to learn. *Electrical means* can also be employed to effect control: an investigator may utilize constant-speed motors for driving various types of apparatus, such as the memory drum which presents materials through a slot in a machine while the drum revolves at selected speeds. *Surgical means* may be used to control: an experimenter may remove glands from the body or destroy tissue to certain parts of the brain to determine their effects on behavior. *Pharmacological means,* such as changes of diet, drugs, or gland extracts can also be used to achieve control.

Selective Manipulation. Some variables cannot be controlled by direct physical manipulation but can be by rigorous indirect manipulation. One may effect control of variables through the *selection of materials.* For example, in a study concerning the amount of time required to memorize materials of different lengths, such as a series of nonsense syllables, something other than length of materials may affect the time required for learning. If the shorter units of material are more difficult than longer units, this condition may affect the amount of time required to master them.

Hence, the experimenter controls the unwanted factor of difficulty by select-ing short and long learning units that are comparable in difficulty.

Through the *selection of subjects* it is often possible to manipulate in-directly variables that cannot be controlled by direct physical means. If one wants to know, for example, whether method A or B is the better way of teaching a particular skill, a number of things besides the method may affect the mastery of it. If the more intelligent pupils are in group X, one cannot assume that these subjects have achieved greater skill than sub-jects in group Y because of the teaching method. To gain control over this unwanted factor of intelligence, subjects of equal intelligence can be paired and randomly assigned—one student of each pair to each group. In a similar manner, control can be achieved over other unwanted factors, such as age, interests, attitudes, socioeconomic status, religion, amount of educa-tion, physical status, or previous experiences that might produce variation in the results.

Sometimes it is not possible to set up laboratory experiments in which conditions can be physically manipulated to observe their effects on human beings. Consequently, the researcher must attempt to gain control through the *selection of data*. Manipulating variables to see whether they cause suicides or juvenile crimes, for example, cannot be condoned. But one might be able to select primary data from records of institutions and governmental agencies that would provide information needed for studying factors contributing to such behavior. Of course, the only factors that can be isolated for study are those that are separately measured in the existing reports. If an investigator, for instance, wishes to study the effect of church attendance, participation in organized recreation programs, or marital status on juvenile delinquency, the project is only possible if the existing records provide such information. And the quality of control that can be achieved by this method depends upon the completeness and accuracy of the reports.

Statistical Manipulation. When variables are not amenable to physical or selective manipulation, they may be controlled by statistical techniques. Statistical controls can achieve the same precision as other methods when they are employed to evaluate a variable's effect. They are particularly useful in situations where multiple variables may be causing a particular effect, as is often the case in the social sciences.

In classical experimentation isolating and varying one variable at a time to study its effect on the dependent variable was considered an essential rule. But, if one does this when working with complex educational phenomena, he may prevent or ignore the simultaneous functioning of vari-ables with which the experimental variable interacts in normal situations. To overcome this difficulty, he can study a number of variables operating together and afterward apply statistical techniques to isolate and evaluate the effect of each of the variables. Suppose that *A, B,* and *C* act conjointly on dependent variable X. If only the relationship between A and X is obtained, the findings are spurious, for A is partly a product of its interaction with B and C. Thus, some means must be found to hold B and C constant to determine the precise relationship between A and X. Statistical procedures, which will be discussed in the next two chapters, permit one to do this and thus to approximate the relative importance of the contribution of each variable to X.

TYPES OF EXPERIMENTAL DESIGNS

Before conducting a study, researchers must select an experimental design that is suitable for testing the deduced consequences of their hypotheses. A number of types exist; some of them have already been used to illustrate points in this chapter. The following discussion will briefly explain the nature of a few traditional designs and their limitations.

One-group Method. The simplest experimental method requires only one group of subjects. The researcher observes his subjects' performances before and after he applies or withdraws an experimental variable and measures the amount of change, if any, that takes place. Thus, his first task is to obtain some measure of the average or mean attainment of the group in the characteristic that is to be influenced. After administering Test 1 (T_1 may ascertain reading speed), he exposes the same subjects to an independent variable (such as a method of training) for a reasonable interval of time and then gives a second test (T_2). Next, he finds the average or mean score of the group on a second test (T_2) to determine what influence the independent variable (IV) had on the dependent variable (reading speed). To ascertain the amount of change (difference) that has taken place as a result of the exposure to the experimental variable, he subtracts T_1 from T_2.

The following paradigm and example may help you gain a better understanding of the one-group method:

Step 1 $T_1 \ldots \ldots IV \ldots \ldots T_2$
Step 2 $T_2 - T_1 = D$ (Difference between the mean scores)

Suppose that an experimenter is interested in studying the effect of the independent variable—Diet A—on youths. On September 10, he checks the weight of each subject (Test 1 or T_1) and finds the mean weight of the group. Then, after providing them with Diet A for several months and weighing them again (Test 2 or T_2), he discovers the following:

$T_1 \ldots \ldots$ Independent Variable (IV) $\ldots \ldots T_2$

The mean weight of the group is 100 *lb*	*Diet A*	*The mean weight of the group is* 115 *lb*

With this information, he proceeds to the second step; namely, to determine the resulting change that has occurred between the administration of the two tests.

$T_2 - T_1$, that is, 115 − 100 = Difference that presumably was caused by the independent variable, Diet A.

This simple one-group method has been employed by investigators (26) who wished to determine whether placing the calf muscle of man under tension alters its readiness to respond.   First, they determined the latent time of the calf muscle under normal conditions (T_1).   (Latent time was defined as the interval elapsing between the application of the electrical stimulus to the muscle and the beginning of the response as indicated by the start of muscle thickening.)   Then, they placed the calf muscle under tension (IV) by exerting pressure on the ball of the foot and again applied the electrical stimulus (T_2) to determine the latent time of the same muscle under conditions of tension.   Afterward, the investigators compared the latent time under the normal and tension conditions.   Finally, they utilized a statistical device to ascertain whether the difference between the normal and tension latent time was significant.   Their findings revealed that tension significantly decreased the latent time of the calf muscle.   Therefore, the experiment suggested that if a runner in the start of a sprint assumes the crouch position, which places tension on the calf muscle, he will get a faster start than if the calf muscle were not under tension.

In some one-group studies, two or more independent variables are successively administered to the same subjects.   One may, for example, try to determine the effect of administering two different drugs or various dosages of the same drug on the time required to do a task.   To accomplish this, one first exposes his subjects to one drug $(T_1 \ldots IV_1 \ldots T_2)$ and then to a second one $(— \ldots IV_2 \ldots T_3)$.   By comparing the results of the final tests $(T_2$ and $T_3)$ one can make some judgment about which drug or dosage $(IV_1$ or $IV_2)$ enabled the subjects to do the task in the least time.   However, this design cannot be used unless the influence of the first independent variable is completely dissipated before the second independent variable is administered.   Otherwise, T_3 would be measuring not only the influence of IV_2 but also the carry-over effect of IV_1.   Moreover, this design usually requires that equivalent forms of the tests be used, so as to eliminate the practice effect of repeating the same test.   If one must construct equivalent test forms, he may find it a difficult and time-consuming process.

The one-group design has certain advantages and limitations.   Since it involves only one group of subjects it is simple to use.   Because the same rather than dissimilar groups of subjects is exposed to each independent variable, no part of the difference in the results can be attributed to the variability of the subjects. When employed to attack many educational problems, however, the one-group method can lead to grave errors. Since the method fails to control many nonexperimental variables, it is difficult to ascertain whether the difference between the pretest and posttest scores results from the influence of the independent variable or from other variables. The disparity, for example, may be attributable to the fact that students were older, less enthusiastic, or more fatigued when they took the second test. Perhaps the difference is a product of the extra effort that pupils exerted because they were proud of participating in the experiment. The practice that subjects received on T_1 may have enabled them to do better on T_2. The subjects' responses on the final test may have been conditioned by the carry-over effects from exposure to independent variables previously administered in the experiment. Unless the one-group design is handled with care, the experimenter may easily give undue credit to the independent variable for causing changes and overlook other conditions that actually account for the results obtained.

It has been suggested that the probability of satisfying the fundamental criteria for selecting the one-group method is increased (18:28–29):

(1) Where the EF or EF's [experimental factor or independent variable] produce a relatively drastic effect, for this tends to make the influence of irrelevant [nonexperimental] factors practically negligible.

(2) Where the experiment is of brief duration, for this abbreviates the action of large, constant, cumulative, irrelevant factors such as maturing for example.

(3) Where the trait in question does not involve purposes or methods of work, for these usually show a larger carry-over than specific information.

(4) Where the tests are scaled on the basis of the same unit for this increases probability of equality of units.

Equivalent-group Method. The equivalent-group experiment is designed to overcome certain difficulties encountered in the one-group design. To control some of the nonexperimental influences on the dependent variable that the one-group design ignores, such as maturity, this method simultaneously utilizes *two equivalent groups* of subjects. The second group, which is called the control group, serves as a reference from which comparisons are made.

When employing the equivalent-group design, an investigator first selects two groups that are as much alike as possible. Then, he introduces an independent variable to the experimental group and withholds it from the control group. Thus, the control group carries on in the customary manner, or receives no treatment, while the other group receives the experimental treatment. After a reasonable interval of time, the difference between the two groups is observed. Since the two groups are supposed to be equivalent in all respects, except for the exposure to the independent variable, the researcher assumes that any difference that exists is a result of the experimental treatment. The difference is a measure of the effect of the independent variable. The aim of this design is to treat two like groups differently so as to draw a conclusion concerning the effects of the dissimilar treatments. Without a control group the findings of many experiments are meaningless, for the possibility always exists that the same effect may have occurred without the presence of the experimental variable.

The experimenter utilizes a control group to strengthen his conviction that the independent variable actually is responsible for the change in the dependent variable. Suppose that an independent variable—a method of reading—is administered to *one group* of students and at the end of a specified time they receive much higher scores on a reading test than they did on an equivalent form of the test taken prior to the experiment. One cannot be certain whether the higher scores were caused by the independent variable (the reading method) or by the maturation of the students. But, if two equal groups were used in the experiment and only one was exposed to the reading method, both groups would have matured the same amount during the conduct of the study. Consequently, one would know that the difference in the test scores was not caused by maturity but presumably by the reading method. Thus, the control group makes the influence of the independent variable interpretable.

The following paradigm and explanation may help you gain a better understanding of the equivalent-group design:

Step 1. After equating the groups, the investigator gives all subjects an initial test (T_1) to determine their current status and finds the average or mean test score of the experimental group (T_{1_E}) and the control group (T_{1_C}). When this is completed, conditions are kept the same for the two groups except that the experimental group—but not the control group—is exposed to the independent variable (IV) for a stipulated period of time. Then both groups take a second test and the average score for each group $(T_{2_E}$ and $T_{2_C})$ is found.

Experimental Group	$T_{1E}\ldots\ldots\text{IV}\ldots\ldots T_{2E}$
Control Group	$T_{1C}\ldots\ldots\ldots\ldots\ldots T_{2C}$

Step 2. The difference between the mean scores that each group made on the first and second test is found.

Experimental Group	$T_{2E} - T_{1E} = D_E$ (Difference between mean scores on first and second tests)
Control Group	$T_{2C} - T_{1C} = D_C$ (Difference between mean scores on first and second tests)

Step 3. By comparing D_C and D_E—the mean change in scores obtained by the two groups—the investigator can determine whether the ap-

plication of the independent variable caused a significant change in the experimental group's scores as compared to the control group's scores. The chapters on statistics will explain how appropriate statistical procedures are applied to ascertain whether the difference in the scores is sufficiently great to be a real difference or whether it is only a chance occurrence.

The equivalent-group design may also be extended to permit the study of two or more independent variables or several variations of the same variable on a dependent variable.   To ascertain the effect of teaching long division by two different methods, for example, three equated groups can be selected and one method can be applied to the first group, another method to the second group, and no long division instruction to the third group as the following paradigm indicates:

First Experimental Group	T_{1E_1}......IV_1......T_{2E_1}	
Second Experimental Group	T_{1E_2}......IV_2......T_{2E_2}	
Control Group	T_{1C}..............T_{2C}	

If the researcher is merely interested in comparing the effects of two treatments, he may not use the control group, but it does give him an added measure of information for interpretive purposes.

One cannot give casual consideration to equating the experimental and control groups, for this is a matter of crucial concern.   The two groups must be as alike as possible in respect to all factors that influence the dependent variable.   If this is not done, one cannot ascertain whether the difference between the results obtained for the experimental and control groups is attributable to the independent variable or to initial differences between the groups.   Because human beings vary in a multiplicity of ways, obtaining two groups of people that are alike in all respects is impossible. But the experimenter should at least attempt to fashion groups that are equivalent in regard to the *relevant* variables—those factors that others have found influence the dependent variable under study.   To accomplish the difficult task of equating groups, a researcher may employ the co-twin, matched-pairs, matched-groups, randomized-groups, or statistical technique.

Co-twin Technique.   Because nature does an excellent job of pairing identical twins, the so-called co-twin control is one of the most accurate pairing procedures known.   It offers an unusual opportunity to study such problems as the role played by learning and maturation.   To ascertain whether maturation or training was a significant aspect of bladder control, for example, McGraw (19) selected two sets of twin boys.   She exposed one boy from each set to toilet training for several months before she exposed their brothers.   In a study concerning learning and growth, Gesell and Thompson (8) gave an experimental twin training in stair climbing six weeks before the control twin received a two-week training period. In both of these studies, the control twins quickly achieved the, proficiency of the ones who had experienced the much greater number of practice periods. Hence, the findings suggested that the development of the specified achievements was not hastened by prolonged training but was fundamentally a product of maturation—"ripeness of the neural structures."

Matched-pairs Technique. Because a sufficient number of twins is rarely available for most experimental studies, investigators often employ the matched-pairs technique. In this method, an analysis is made to determine what factors influence the dependent variable. If reading ability, IQ, sex, and socioeconomic background exert an influence, one tries to find two subjects who are alike in these respects. After selecting a sufficient number of pairs, one assigns a member of each pair—usually at random—to the experimental group and the other member to the control group. Thus, the two groups are as nearly alike as the matching procedure permits.

Finding matched pairs often proves to be an extremely difficult process. Usually one measures the relevant factors for a large number of subjects before finding a sufficient number of qualified pairs. Consequently, much time and effort is employed testing subjects who cannot be used in the study. Precise matching of more than two or three variables is rarely possible. Moreover, deciding which of the relevant variables should be given consideration in pairing often presents a thorny problem. If the remaining relevant factors—those not used as a basis for matching—are not randomized in the two groups they may bias the conclusions. Sometimes the tools used to measure the relevant factors are crude, consequently, it is questionable whether matching based on the results that they produce is accurate. The possibility of subjects dropping out of the experiment is ever present and the loss of any cases may impair the matching design.

Matched-group Technique. When it is not possible to find matching subjects, groups may be matched. To do this, one selects control and experimental groups that have the same average possession of each relevant variable—the same mean scores—and a similar distribution pattern of subjects' scores around the average. If, for example, intelligence is considered to have an effect on the dependent variable, the investigator divides his subjects into two groups and proceeds to find the average IQ of the members in each group. If one group has an average IQ of 100 and the other of 110, he shifts subjects from one group to the other until both groups have an average IQ of 105. But he cannot safely assume that the two groups are then equal, for the IQs in one group may range widely about the average (80 to 130) and those in the other group may have a narrow range of variation (98 to 115). Thus, in addition to finding the average IQ, he uses statistical procedures to ascertain the nature of the distribution of the scores. If the patterns differ in the two groups, he also tries to make them similar.

The matched-group technique is not free from disadvantages. Suppose that one is matching two groups in terms of intelligence and some skill. Even though the distribution of the IQs and skill scores is equated for the two groups, it is possible for subjects in the groups to have different combinations of these capacities as the following illustration reveals:

> Group X: Low IQs with high skills and high IQs with low skills
> Group Y: High IQs with high skills and low IQs with low skills

If these differences exist, they can affect the conclusions of the study.

Randomized-group Technique. Determining what factors to equate, precisely measuring the known relevant factors, and finding matched subjects cannot always be done. To achieve equivalency of the experimental and control groups in such instances, one may employ randomization techniques. Randomization is not a haphazard or arbitrary method of selecting subjects; it is a systematic procedure. The researcher refrains from exercising direct control over the assignment of subjects because he may consciously or unconsciously choose the better ones for the experimental group. To avoid the introduction of a bias toward the greater achievement of either group, some mechanical randomization technique is employed that gives each individual in a population an equal chance of being placed in any given group. Quite commonly the people in the population are numbered consecutively and a published Tables of Random Sample Numbers or some other chance procedure is used to assign each individual until half are placed in one group and the other half in the other group.

Statistical Techniques. Sometimes it is impossible or impractical to control variables by direct selection of subjects. A superintendent of schools, for example, may be unwilling to reorganize classes on a matched basis for experimental purposes, but he may permit an investigator to study two classes as they are constituted. If groups cannot be equalized prior to experimentation, statistical control procedures are employed. This is necessary in instances where a factor that influences the dependent variable is not observable until after an experiment is under way. In a study of the effect of different diets, for example, all subjects may be given the same amounts of food, but not every subject will necessarily eat everything he is given. If some of them do not, this may influence the results. But this factor can be observed and measured during the experiment and accounted for by statistical procedures when analyzing the results.

The most commonly used statistical control is known as the analysis of covariance. When employing this technique, the investigator observes the uncontrolled variable in the two groups during the experiment and makes appropriate adjustments for the source of variation in the analysis of the outcomes. This statistical procedure, which will be explained more fully in Chapter 14, permits an investigator to carry out an experiment with the same precision as if he had matched the experimental and control groups.

Rotation-group Method. The rotation-group method of experimental research overcomes some of the difficulties encountered in the one-group and equivalent-group methods. It is commonly employed in situations where a limited number of subjects are available or where a comparison of teaching methods is made. The first stage of a rotation-group method is the same as the equivalent-group method. Group A experiences the experimental treatment (IV_1) while group B is exposed to the traditional or other treatment (IV_2). In the second stage, the groups rotate their roles

Stage 1	*Stage 2*
Group A: IV_1	Group A: IV_2
Group B: IV_2	Group B: IV_1

Thus, when employing the rotation-group method, the researcher applies the same independent variables to different groups at different times during the conduct of the experiment. To compare the effectiveness of the textbook and field trip methods of instruction, for example, he may have subjects study units concerning two city departments: fire and police. After designing appropriate tests for each unit and selecting two groups of students that are as equivalent as possible, he exposes the two groups to the same method of instruction but at different times during the investigation. The following discussion gives a detailed explanation of what is done:

Stage 1. The two groups take pretests to ascertain what they know about the fire department and the average or mean score for each group (T_1) is found. Then group A receives textbook instruction (IV_1) on this unit while group B takes field trips (IV_2) to the fire department. Afterward both groups take a second test and the average score for each group (T_2) is found.

Group *A:* $T_1 \ldots \ldots IV_1 \ldots \ldots T_2$
fire $\ldots \ldots$ text $\ldots \ldots$ fire
Group *B:* $T_1 \ldots \ldots IV_2 \ldots \ldots T_2$
fire $\ldots \ldots$ field $\ldots \ldots$ fire

Then the difference between the mean scores that each group made on their first and second tests is found.

Group *A:* $T_2 - T_1 = D_1$
text
Group *B:* $T_2 - T_1 = D_2$
field

Stage 2. In the second stage of the experiment both groups take pre-tests on what they know about the police department and the average score for each group is found. But this time group A rather than group B goes on the field trip (IV_2), and group B receives the textbook instruction (IV_1). Afterward both groups take a second test and the mean score is found for each group.

$$Group\ A: \quad T_1\ldots\ldots IV_2\ldots\ldots T_2$$
$$police\ldots\ldots field\ldots\ldots police$$

$$Group\ B: \quad T_1\ldots\ldots IV_1\ldots\ldots T_2$$
$$police\ldots\ldots text\ldots\ldots police$$

Then the difference between the mean scores that each group made on their first and second tests is calculated.

$$Group\ A: \quad T_2 - T_1 = D_3$$
$$field$$

$$Group\ B: \quad T_2 - T_1 = D_4$$
$$text$$

Stage 3. The mean change in scores obtained by the two groups from the field trip instruction is added—$D_2 + D_3$—and the mean change obtained from textbook instruction—$D_1 + D_4$—and the results are subjected to a statistical analysis that permits one to appraise the effectiveness of the methods.

The rotation method rotates out some nonexperimental factors that influence the dependent variable. If the children in one group are more able than those in the other group, both independent variables—the field and the textbook methods—will profit equally from their superiority. If the subject matter and test used in the police unit are more difficult than those used in the fire unit, the difficulty is rotated out for both the field and, textbook methods come under these influences. When students are exposed to the second unit of work, they will be more mature and they may carry over some of the learning acquired on the first unit, which will influence their test results. But since both independent variables are exposed to these influences once during the conduct of the experiment, the effect of maturation and carry-over learning on the dependent variable tends to be minimized. However, the results obtained would be a measure of average effects which need not be the same as direct effects.

The rotation technique cannot equalize effectively all nonexperimental factors. If the carry-over learning from IV_1 to IV_2 and IV_2 to IV_1, for example, is not of the same magnitude in both instances, the carry-over factor may be minimized but it will not be equalized. Nor can the rotation technique cope adequately with factors such as bias on the part of the teacher or the tests in favor of one experimental variable. Neither is equalization achieved if subjects in one group become more fatigued or less highly motivated with the progress of the experiment than the other group.

Ideal Experimental Design.   The one-group, equivalent-group, and rotation-group designs all have limitations.   Each is useful in different situations, but no one design can be used to solve all problems.   The nature of the problem determines which design is most appropriate and how it should be tailored to meet the needs of the particular study.   Researchers have devised several variations of the traditional methods discussed in this chapter.   In more recent years they have created more sophisticated designs, some of which will be discussed in Chapter 14.

Selecting the proper design for an experiment is a challenging task because a multiplicity of factors must be taken into consideration.   An ideal design must achieve a number of objectives (4:266) :

The experimental procedures must be designed to elicit and control the expression of the variables through which the conditions of the theorem [deduced consequences] are represented.   We have called these the experimental variables.

The experimental procedures must be designed to control the expression of all other variables that are operative in the empirical situation. . . .

The experimental procedures must be designed to register all behavior that may either directly or indirectly pertain to the testing of the theorem.   This requires that procedures be used that make a faithful and permanent record of any changes reflected in behavior that result from variables operating during the empirical test.

The experimental procedures must be designed to separate the behavior changes pertinent to the theorem from all other behavior changes.   It is necessary that the behavior changes that can be used as evidence be in a form that can be analyzed independently of other behavior changes.

The experimental procedures must be designed to enable the investigator to evaluate the amount of evidence and the degree of pertinence of the evidence in relation to the theorem being tested.   This is best accomplished by quantitative description of the variables and quantitative analysis of the relationships existing among the variables.

The preceding objectives represent an ideal experimental situation.   Fully attaining these objectives in the social sciences is not always possible, but these are the goals toward which researchers strive.

EVALUATION OF EXPERIMENTAL RESEARCH

When the experimental method can be used to solve problems, it is the most satisfactory means of obtaining reliable knowledge.   The basic reasons underlying the adequacy of this method are (17:37)

. . . that it permits the repetition of observations under practically identical conditions.   This facilitates the verification of observations by many observers.

In the second place, it enables the observer to vary only one condition at a time and to maintain all other conditions rigidly constant. This allows us to analyze the relations of cause and effect with much greater speed and certainty than is possible under uncontrolled conditions. . . . Because of these tremendous advantages of the experimental method, the question as to its applicability in the social sciences becomes one of major importance. If this method is not applicable to social phenomena, it seems reasonable that the social sciences will be greatly handicapped, if not entirely thwarted, in their more exact development.

Perhaps an answer to the question can be obtained by quickly surveying educators' attempts to utilize the experimental method.

Early in this century, some members of the profession became excited about following the example of the natural scientists who had taken giant strides of progress as the result of conducting experimental research. Since that time educators have done considerable work, but much of it has been of doubtful value because of numerous procedural weaknesses and the intrinsic characteristics of the subject matter. They have found that the method is not applicable to some of their problems and when it is employed many obstacles have to be hurdled that do not hamper natural scientists. The following evaluation of how satisfactory educational experimental studies have conformed to the scientific method of solving problems will acquaint you with some of the problems and possibilities that the method presents.

Formulation of the Problem. The scientific method of research requires a thorough analysis of a problem, the precise formulation of hypotheses, and a rigorous check on the assumptions underlying experimental plans. Because these important responsibilities have often been neglected, severe attacks have been made on educational research studies. Griffiths contends, for example, (11:16) that

. . . without doubt, the greatest weakness of research in educational administration is the lack of theory. Most studies in educational administration are done at the level of "naked empiricism." By this we mean that the researcher has an idea that a vaguely defined problem needs to be solved. He collects data through a questionnaire, survey, or some other method and attempts to find an answer by "looking at the data." By following this procedure we have amassed tons of data, but have come up with very few answers. The opposite of "naked empiricism" is research based on theory. By this is meant that the researcher starts with a well defined problem, a set of clearly stated assumptions, and from these assumptions he deduces by logico-mathematical methods a set of testable hypotheses. Theory is essentially a set of assumptions from which a set of empirical laws (principles) may be derived.

Griffiths's criticism of research in educational administration is applicable to many other areas within education.

When researchers conduct experimental investigations, they are less frequently guilty of collecting data aimlessly—without a theoretical orientation—than when they employ other research methods. Most experimental workers give consideration to the analysis of the problem, the formulation of hypotheses, and check the assumptions underlying their problems, but the quality of their work varies. Sometimes mere token recognition is given to these steps in procedure.

Assumptions. Experimental studies that are based on false assumptions cannot yield valid results, yet some researchers only superficially examine the assumptions underlying their hypotheses, procedures, and methods of analyzing the results. They assume, for example, that a given test will measure a particular ability of their subjects without checking whether there is reliable evidence available to support that it will. Novice investigators often complain, "Challenging assumptions is a make-work project. Everyone knows that these assumptions are true." But researchers cannot blindly accept what "everyone knows"; they are obligated to probe more deeply. They must critically analyze the assumptions underlying every phase of their experimental plans, eliminate those they cannot defend, and recognize what implications the remaining ones have for the interpretation of their findings.

In recent years, more workers seem to be including a statement concerning the assumptions in their studies. To illustrate, one researcher (13), in "An Experiment in Developing Critical Thinking in Children," stipulates that

. . . in the endeavor to set up criteria for the selection of content material and the development of teaching methods, the following assumptions were posited. . . .

1. That thinking is critical when it is essentially logical.

2. That logical thinking is no more than the application of the rules of logic to factual data in order to arrive at valid as well as true conclusions. It follows from this assumption that an individual's growth in the ability to do logical thinking must depend upon his acquiring a working knowledge of the basic rules of logic.

3. That children in the upper grades of the elementary school are, in general, mentally capable of acquiring the necessary understanding of logic and a proficiency in the use of its rules.

4. That the most effective way of helping children to acquire the necessary working knowledge of the principles of logic is through direct instruction.

5. That this direct instruction should consist of: *a.* materials and learning content which embody the principles of logic. *b.* Teaching methods that provide full opportunity for the pupil to discover for himself these principles and to formulate them as generalizations.

Hypotheses. The heart of scientific research—the hypothesis—appears more commonly in experimental than in descriptive or historical research reports. Moreover, experimental hypotheses give educators a deeper insight into their phenomena than descriptive hypotheses, for they seek to explain why conditions or events occur—what causes certain effects—rather than merely to describe what exists.

Unfortunately, however, some investigators give insufficient attention to the analysis of problems and the construction of hypotheses. Experimental designs, procedural details, and the actual conduct of experiments completely absorb their attention. They forget that, although science makes great advances through experimental studies, the experiment itself does not provide the intellectual thrust that pushes back the frontiers of knowledge. The experiment does not initiate discoveries; it tests ideas that are already born. It merely checks hypotheses that the researcher or some other scholar has previously conceived. Thus, a brilliantly executed experiment is of little value if it tests a poorly conceived hypothesis.

All experimental hypotheses are not equal in their ability to exhibit cause and effect relationships. Many of them are rudimentary questions; they border on trial-and-error speculation. When puzzled about a phenomenon, some investigators merely ask, "What will occur if we do this?" Their poorly conceived hypotheses are usually unproductive, for they are not testing a clearly stated generalization. On the next higher level, researchers formulate hypotheses which propose that some cause and effect relationship exists, but they fail to state exactly what the relationship is or do not include the full circumstances of what is presumed to exist. If some relationship is established by testing this type of hypothesis, researchers are usually one step closer to understanding the nature of their phenomena and, thus, are in a better position to construct more complex hypotheses. The highest level hypotheses explain the specific nature of the existing cause and effect relationship. This type is the most desirable to achieve, but it is the most difficult to formulate. At present, it is used less frequently than the other types. Nevertheless, it is the goal toward which researchers strive, and the more elementary hypotheses provide useful information that enables them to reach these desired objectives.

Observation and Experimentation. Experimental research conforms to the scientific method of acquiring knowledge in that it provides for testing hypotheses by experimentation—controlled observation. One does not merely observe and describe a situation, but rather directly manipulates certain variables, attempts to control others, and then observes and interprets the changes that take place. When employing this method, social scientists must exercise the same care in controlling their experiments as physical scientists do. In some respects they are able to do this, but in many instances they encounter considerable difficulty.

Quality of Tools. Inappropriate, imprecise, or faulty apparatus and data collecting instruments can introduce inaccuracies in an experiment that render it useless. Yet some experimenters are not so meticulous as they should be about selecting and maintaining the tools that they use to measure the influence of variables, to hold factors constant, to manipulate variables in a predetermined manner, and to amplify or magnify phenomena for better observation. Consequently, they sometimes report that an independent variable has caused a particular effect that actually has been caused by the improper functioning or inadequacy of apparatus or instruments. When studying the influence of a diet on body weight, for example, an inept investigator may assume that a recorded gain in weight is attributable to the diet when it actually has been produced by the faulty operation of the scales. To avoid such foolish errors, experienced experimenters constantly check and recheck their apparatus. They calibrate timers, gauges, and similar devices in terms of some criterion and examine equipment for wear of mechanical parts, faulty electrical contacts, and adequacy of lubrication.

Developing and selecting tools is often a more difficult task than maintaining them. Sometimes investigators fail to select or cannot locate instruments that will produce the required kind and form of data. Sometimes their tools are not appropriate for testing the type of subjects participating in the experiment. Quantifying findings also presents problems: creating tools that will accurately and precisely weigh or measure the effect of the experimental variable cannot always be done. Consequently, it is difficult to establish relatively stable facts that can be confirmed by any competent observer. When data are grossly quantified or inappropriately structured, researchers are unable to make precise analyses or interpretations. Although a concerted effort has been made to develop and improve educational research tools, many are used that do not possess the required validity, reliability, and objectivity, or that do not produce sufficiently discriminating measurements. Hence, much work remains to be done, for experimental findings can be no more secure than the instruments through which data are gathered.

Degree of Control. The experimental method produces highly satisfactory results if all factors affecting the dependent variable are controlled, but this goal is not easy for social scientists to achieve. Physical scientists conduct the majority of their experiments in the laboratory where workers can eliminate many extraneous factors that influence the independent variable, control those that cannot be eliminated, manipulate the independent variable, and observe and measure the changes that take place. Whenever possible, educators also deliberately take phenomena from the natural setting and investigate them in the laboratory, where the optimum conditions of control can be maintained. But some problems, such as those concerning crowd behavior, cannot be readily re-created in the laboratory. Studying those that can be re-created sometimes proves to be a futile effort, for human beings who are exposed to an experimental variable in an artificial laboratory situation do not always react the same as they would in a normal situation. To overcome these difficulties, social scientists have devised field-type experiments in which they test hypotheses in the natural setting, such as a classroom. They introduce as many controls as possible, but, of course, the number of extraneous factors that affect the dependent variable increases in the nonlaboratory situation.

Discovering what to control and how to accomplish it is a major problem. Identifying all the nonexperimental factors that affect the dependent variable may not be possible. Moreover, because of the complexity of educational phenomena, trying to control those that are known may be difficult. Studies have found, for example, at least ten fundamental factors underlying the performance of motor skills (see page 224); at least three factors—verbal comprehension, abstract reasoning, and acquired mechanical knowledge—influence mechanical aptitude; and Burkart (5) has compiled a list of 214 abilities relating to the reading process.

Unlike the physical scientists, educators cannot physically remove many of the extraneous factors that can affect a dependent variable. Consequently, they must obtain control through the use of control groups or statistical procedures. Obviously, matching groups with respect to a large number of relevant variables is not feasible. Randomizing can be used to achieve control in such instances, but this technique also presents difficulties. A random sample is selected from a population on an unbiased basis, but a large number of subjects must be used in order to give chance differences an opportunity to nullify each other. When this is not done, the chance possibility of obtaining unequal groups remains great. Since it is not always practicable to have a large number of subjects in a single experiment, researchers must repeat experiments— perhaps many times—before they can justify applying their conclusions to the population as a whole.

Manipulating human beings to meet the requirements of the most theoretically desirable research design is not always possible or socially acceptable. Researchers may be able to equate groups for their studies, but school administrators may be unwilling to reorganize classes to meet their particular needs. Because educators work with human beings rather than inanimate elements and forces, they also face certain ethical issues when planning an experiment. For example, does the subject have a moral right to know that he is part of an experiment? Can experimenters add something to the diet or drinking water of subjects to study the effect without informing them? Do experimenters have the right to choose by a toss of a coin whether a subject receives the experimental or control treatments—especially if it is strongly suspected that the experimental treatment may save lives. If there is a possibility that the experimental treatment may physically or emotionally harm human beings, do researchers have the right to test hypotheses about learning, endurance, riots, sex, or suicides that may considerably advance knowledge?

Because of practical and ethical problems and the complexity and non-uniformity of human phenomena, the (22:228)

. . . experiment in the social sciences is not possible in the same sense that it is in physics and chemistry where an experiment may be repeated an endless number of times under controlled and practically identical conditions. The problem of control in the social sciences is almost insurmountable and it is impossible to repeat experiments under identical conditions. But it is desirable to approach the methodology of the exact sciences in every way possible, recognizing that in so far as the experimenter falls short of such standards his results are defective.

Generalization and Prediction. To advance knowledge appreciably in the field of education, researchers must understand the phenomena with which they are working. From carefully conducted descriptive studies they acquire a low level of understanding: an accurate account of what conditions, activities, and practices prevail in their field. Experimental studies are not satisfied with finding out what exists; they seek a higher level of explanation. They probe the problem of causality: Why does this condition or event occur? What causes this particular effect? Until such knowledge is obtained, educators cannot expect to predict and control phenomena in their field with great success.

A scientist considers that he understands his phenomena when he can successfully project his generalization to other situations and when his knowledge enables him to manipulate the conditions determining a phenomena in order to achieve some desired end. But the complexity and nonuniformity of social science phenomena make it difficult to test educational explanatory hypotheses and arrive at generalizations that can be projected to other situations. The basis for scientific generalizations and prediction is the controlled experiment; but because of the problems encountered in identifying and controlling all the relevant factors affecting the dependent variable, one cannot assume with full confidence that the conclusions of any one study would hold true for all similar conditions or events.

The nonuniformity of his phenomena constantly confronts the social scientist. A chemist can assume that if he applies an experimental stimulus to one pure sample of his phenomena he can be relatively certain that all like samples will react in the same way. But because of the tremendous variability of people's minds, bodies, and attitudes and their socioeconomic, educational, political, religious, and geographical backgrounds, the social scientist cannot always be certain that if a stimulus is applied to one group of human beings it will produce the same effect when applied to another group.

Except when dealing with behavior that is practically unmodifiable among humans, such as reflexes, social scientists cannot project their findings from one study to all human beings. Indeed, the haphazard method of selecting subjects for some studies makes it impossible to apply the findings to any group other than the specific one studied. If subjects are drawn at random from a defined population, the research findings can be applied to other samples of the same population, but not to any other population. If a study produces a generalization about a random sample from the male population of a Middle Western state teachers college, for example, these findings are, at best, applicable only to similar males; they are not applicable to "ivy-league," premedical, or high school males or to female college students.

In some physical sciences scholars are kept busy for years testing certain high-level hypotheses, theories, and laws; but for the most part educators have only been able to achieve low-level generalizations. Social scientists are working on a gigantic unfinished patchwork quilt. Through the replication of studies some generalizations have become rather well substantiated small patches of knowledge. Little work has been done with retesting other generalizations, or the results have been inconclusive. Some of the small patches of knowledge have been fitted into more comprehensive theoretical structures, and it may be possible to keep integrating accumulated knowledge into generalizations of higher and higher levels.

Progress in developing educational generalizations has been impeded by the inflexible demands of the classical experimental design. Isolating and varying one variable at a time while all other conditions are held constant cannot always be done in the social sciences. If it can be done successfully, researchers must exercise caution when interpreting their results, for the effect caused by an isolated factor may not be the same as when there is a normal interaction of variables. Educational phenomena are usually the product of several variables operating simultaneously and the variables may produce different effects in different combinations. Hence, investigators need to obtain information not only about the single variables but also about the interaction of variables.

Currently, critics are deeply concerned because most researchers confine their attention to main effects and ignore the possible interaction of variables. Tiedeman and Cogan point out (23:286), for example, that,

. . . in investigating the effect of the teacher or the effect of various instrumentalities upon the accomplishment of pupils, the research has produced statements such as: "Teachers who are X accomplish Y" (a learning outcome); "Procedure A accomplishes Y"; and "Pupils who are S learn Y." We do not have statements of the kind: "Teachers who are X accomplish Y through procedure A with pupils S." That is, researchers have made certain simplifying assumptions with regard to the variables of the teaching-learning process, and consequently have too often failed to investigate the interactions of the variables in this process.

Within recent years, the obstacle of the "law of the single variable" presented by the classical experimental design has been somewhat overcome. R. A. Fisher and other workers have developed statistical techniques that permit the investigator to manipulate several variables simultaneously and to determine the effect of each factor as well as the joint effect of various factors on the dependent variable. The new experimental designs which utilize these procedures will be discussed in Chapter 14. These promising designs have aroused considerable excitement for they enable men to tackle fundamental problems that previously were ignored; but, like the older designs, they also have specific limitations.

BIBLIOGRAPHY

1. American Association for Health, Physical Education and Recreation, *Research Methods in Health, Physical Education, and Recreation.* Washington, 1959, chap. 10.

2. Barr, Arvil, R. A. Davis, and P. O. Johnson, *Educational Research and Appraisal.* Philadelphia: J. B. Lippincott Company, 1953, chap. 8.

3. Best, John W., *Research in Education.* Englewood Cliffs, N.J.: Prentice-Hall, Inc., 1959, chap. 6.

4. Brown, Clarence W., and E. E. Ghiselli, *Scientific Method in Psychology* New York: McGraw-Hill Book Company, Inc., 1955, chaps. 5, 12, 13, and 14.

5. Burkart, Kathryn H., "An Analysis of Reading Abilities," *Journal of Educational Research,* 38 (February, 1945):430.

6. Carmichael, Leonard, *Manual of Child Psychology.* New York: John Wiley & Sons, Inc., 1946.

7. Doby, John T. (ed.), *An Introduction to Social Research.* Harrisburg, Pa.: The Stackpole Company, 1954, chap. 5.

8. Gesell, Arnold, and Helen Thompson, "Learning and Growth in Identical Infant Twins: An Experimental Study by the Method of Co-twin Control," *Genetic Psychology Monographs,* 6 (July, 1929):1.

9. Good, Carter V., *Introduction to Educational Research.* New York: Appleton-Century-Crofts, Inc., 1959, chap. 8.

10. Good, Carter V., and Douglas E. Scates, *Methods of Research.* New York: Appleton-Century-Crofts, Inc., 1954, chap. 7.

11. Griffiths, Daniel E., *Research in Educational Administration.* New York: Bureau of Publications, Teachers College, Columbia University, 1959.

12. Hillway, Tyrus, *Introduction to Research.* Boston: Houghton Mifflin Company, 1956, chap. 11.

13. Hyram, George H., "An Experiment in Developing Critical Thinking in Children," *Journal of Experimental Education,* 26 (December, 1957):125.

14. Jahoda, Marie, et al., *Research Methods in Social Relations.* New York: The Dryden Press, Inc., 1951, chap. 3.

15. Kingsley, Howard L., and Ralph Garry. *The Nature and Conditions of Learning.* Englewood Cliffs, N.J.: Prentice-Hall, Inc., 1957, chap. 2.

16. Linquist, E. F., *Design and Analysis of Experiments in Psychology and Education.* Boston: Houghton Mifflin Company, 1956.

17. Lundberg, George A., *Social Research.* New York: Longmans, Green & Co., Inc., 1929.

18. McCall, William A., *How to Experiment in Education.* New York: The Macmillan Company, 1923.

19. McGraw, Myrtle B., "Neural Maturation as Exemplified in Achievement of Bladder Control," *Journal of Pediatrics,* 16 (May, 1940):580.

20. Rose, Arnold M., *Theory and Method in the Social Sciences.* Minneapolis: The University of Minnesota Press, 1954, chaps. 15 and 16.

21. Rummel, J. Francis, *An Introduction to Research Procedures in Education.* New York: Harper & Brothers, 1958, chap. 8.

22. Spahr, Walter E., and Rinehart J. Swenson, *Methods and Status of Scientific Research.* New York: Harper & Brothers, 1930.

23. Tiedeman, David V., and Morris Cogan, "New Horizons in Educational Research," *Phi Delta Kappan,* 39 (March, 1958):286.

24. Townsend, John C., *Introduction to Experimental Method.* New York: McGraw-Hill Book Company, Inc., 1953.

25. Travers, Robert M. W., *An Introduction to Educational Research.* New York: The Macmillan Company, 1958, chap. 13.

26. Tuttle, W. W., and D. B. Van Dalen, "The Effect of Tension on the Latent Time of the Gastrocnemius Muscle," *Arbeitsphysiologie,* 9 (October, 1936):345.

27. Werkmeister, W. H., *An Introduction to Critical Thinking.* Lincoln, Nebraska: Johnsen Publishing Company, 1948, chap. 22.

28. Whitney, Frederick L., *The Elements of Research.* Englewood Cliffs, N.J.: Prentice-Hall, Inc., 1946, chap. 9.

CHAPTER 12

Tools of Research

Early in the research project, an investigator weighs the merits of various procedures for collecting evidence. After determining which approach will yield the form and kind of data necessary to test his hypothesis adequately, he examines the available tools and chooses the ones that are most appropriate for his purpose. If the existing apparatus or instruments do not meet his specific needs, he may supplement or modify them or construct his own.

Note that the inquiry starts with the problem and that the nature of the hypothesis governs the selection of the tools. One does not master a single method of obtaining data—such as the questionnaire—and apply it to every problem that arises. Each tool is appropriate for acquiring particular data and sometimes several instruments must be employed to obtain the information required to solve a problem. Thus, a researcher must possess considerable knowledge about a wide variety of tools, techniques, and instruments. He must be familiar with the nature of the data that they produce; their advantages and limitations; the assumptions upon which their use is based; and how reliable, valid, and objective they are. Moreover, he must be skilled in employing, constructing, and maintaining tools and interpreting the information they produce.

SAMPLING

Many problems in scientific research cannot be solved without employing sampling tools. Since most educational phenomena consist of a large number of units, it is not always possible to interview, test, or observe each one under controlled conditions. Sampling tools solve this dilemma, for they help a researcher select representative units from which he can gather data that permit him to draw inferences about the nature of the entire population. Sampling tools save an investigator time, money, and energy and enable him to probe problems that are too unwieldy to be tackled by conventional methods. Therefore, becoming thoroughly familiar with sampling procedures and the pitfalls that one can encounter when utilizing them is an essential part of a researcher's education.

Construction of Samples. Sampling does not consist in collecting data casually from any conveniently located units. To obtain a representative sample, one systematically selects each unit in a specified way under controlled conditions. Several steps are involved in the process. A researcher must (1) precisely define his population, (2) procure an accurate and complete list of the units in the population, (3) draw representative units from the list, and (4) obtain a sufficiently large sample to represent the characteristics of the population.

Define the Population. Conclusions cannot be drawn concerning a population until the nature of the units that comprise it is clearly identified. If a population is vaguely defined, it is impossible to decide what units to consider when selecting the sample. To obtain information about the average salary of university professors, for example, one must define the specific population about which he intends to draw generalizations. Does he want to include professors of all ranks, in all schools— medicine, liberal arts, law—and in administrative positions? Certainly a salary generalization drawn from a population that includes administrators will differ from one that is confined to the lower-paid liberal arts professors. People are repeatedly deceived by institutional, political, and advertisers' reports, because they assume the generalizations presented were drawn from one population when they actually were drawn from another.

List the Population. Once the population is clearly identified, the investigator obtains or constructs a complete, accurate, and up-to-date list (called a frame) of all the units in the population. This task can consume considerable time; sometimes it constitutes the greatest part of the investigative effort; sometimes it cannot be accomplished. Listing the salaries of university professors in a specific geographical area may be relatively simple, for institutions will have such records, but they may not be willing to reveal this information. "Tailor-made" lists of units in a population are not always available. Difficulties would be encountered, for example, if one wanted a list of the unemployed experienced teachers living in Ohio or the boys who "committed" crimes in New York last year. No one agency keeps a record of all unemployed teachers. The courts may have information about juveniles, but their records may include neglected as well as delinquent children, and, of course, they would not list unidentified criminals.

Many investigators produce disappointing results because they use available population frames without investigating the methods that were used to compile them, and without ascertaining whether all members of the population were included. Sometimes they select unit lists that are out of date, contain inaccuracies or duplications, or do not adequately represent the population. A classic example of this occurred in 1936 when telephone directories and automobile registrations were used to obtain a sample of how people would vote in the presidential election. On the basis of the poll's findings, the prediction was made that Alfred Landon would be elected. What went wrong? Since the telephone directories and automobile registrations did not include many voters in the lower economic groups, a sample selected from these lists did not represent all members of the voting population.

Select a Representative Sample. Once a population is defined and all units are listed, the next essential task is a relatively simple one. It involves the procedure of selecting units from the list. Despite the mechanical ease of drawing a sample, mistakes are frequently made. Some workers, for example, select any group of units that is conveniently at hand—the first twenty-five names on a list, the people who live in one block, the parents who happen to attend a meeting, or the first four rows of students in the auditorium. If these particular units are quite similar in nature and differ considerably from the remaining units, they are unrepresentative of the population. All the slum dwellers living in one New York block are units in the city's population, but generalizations derived from data concerning their health, salaries, and dwellings certainly are not applicable to all citizens in the city. A good sample must be as nearly representative of the entire population as possible.

Obtain an Adequate Sample. Some samples are too small to represent the characteristics of the population. The IQ scores of two students selected as a sample from a population of 100 children, for example, are not likely to represent the average IQ of that group. But, how large must a sample be to achieve an acceptable degree of reliability? There are no specific rules on how to obtain an adequate sample, for each situation presents its own problems. If the phenomena under study are homogeneous, a small sample is sufficient. A few centimeters from a 1,000-gallon container of a particular chemical may be adequate. But, if the units under study are variable, as much educational phenomena are, a much larger sample is necessary. The greater the variability of the phenomena, the more difficult it is to get a good sample. Increasing the size of the sample is of little value, of course, if units are not selected by a means that ensures representativeness of the sample. In general, three factors determine the size of an adequate sample: the nature of the population, the type of sampling design, and the degree of precision desired. The researcher gives careful consideration to these factors and then selects the sampling design that will provide the desired precision at minimum cost.

Types of Sampling Designs. Several methods have been devised to select representative samples. The following discussion briefly describes random, stratified, double, and cluster sampling. Detailed explanations of these and other sampling techniques can be found in texts that are devoted to the subject (2,6,10,14,19).

Random Sampling. The purpose and mechanics of drawing a random sample from a known population were discussed in Chapter 11. This method is reconsidered here merely for the sake of completeness and to refresh your memory. In random sampling, carefully controlled conditions are created to insure that each unit in the population has an equal or known chance of being included in the sample. To prevent the investigator from biasing the results by exercising direct control over the choice of units, some mechanical device is employed to draw the sample. The names of all units may be placed in a fish bowl or on cards and shuffled thoroughly before the desired number of slips is drawn. If a small group is involved, a coin may be flipped to select the sample. Perhaps the best method is to employ a table of random numbers, such as those prepared by Fisher and Yates, Tippett, or Kendall and Babington-Smith. After assigning consecutive numbers to units of the population, one starts at any point on the table of random numbers and reads consecutive numbers in any direction (horizontally, vertically, or diagonally). When a number is read that corresponds with that written on a unit card, that unit is chosen for the sample. One continues to read until a sample of the desired size is obtained.

A random sample does not necessarily represent the characteristics of the total population, but it does leave the choice of subjects to chance and thus reduces the possibility of bias entering the selection of the sample. By chance, of course, one could select a sample that does not accurately represent the total population. The more heterogeneous the units are and the smaller the sample, the greater is the chance of drawing a poor sample.

Stratified Sampling. Since a random sample may by chance have an undue proportion of one type of unit in it, it is sometimes advisable to use stratified random sampling to get a more representative sample. When employing this technique, the researcher divides his population into strata by some characteristic and from each of these smaller homogeneous groups draws *at random* a predetermined number of units. To ascertain how people may vote on a public school issue, for example, one may subdivide a population into groups on the basis of known voting behavior—perhaps age, income, educational levels, or religion. Stratified sampling, of course, is no better than simple random sampling unless it is known that there is a high correlation between certain groups of people and their voting behavior. *Proportional sampling* enables one to achieve even greater representativeness in the sample. This technique requires one to select units at random from each stratum in proportion to its actual size in the total population. Hence, if 10 per cent of the voting population are college graduates, 10 per cent of the sample is taken from this stratum. Because proportional sampling improves representativeness, it enables one to use a smaller sample and thereby reduce the cost.

Double Sampling. When employing a mailed questionnaire, double sampling is sometimes used to obtain a more representative sample. This is done because some randomly selected subjects who are sent questionnaires may not return them. Obviously, the missing data will bias the results of the study, if the people who fail to reply to the query differ in some fundamental way from the others in respect to the phenomena being studied. To eliminate this bias, a second sample may be drawn at random from the nonrespondents and the people interviewed to obtain the desired information. This double sampling technique enables one to check on the reliability of the information obtained from the first sample. Double or multistage sampling can also be used to "spot-check" data. After a simple inexpensive survey is made of a large sample, another sample can be selected from this group for a more comprehensive investigation.

Systematic Sampling. When a frame of a given population is available, a sample is sometimes drawn from fixed intervals on the list. Suppose that an investigator wants to select a sample of 50 names from a list of 500 school children, social agency cases, or factory workers. First, he divides 50 into 500 to determine what size of interval to use (in this case 10). Then, he picks a starting number at random from 1 to 10 (assume the number is 9) and selects each tenth name thereafter (thus, 9, 19, 29, . . .) until he has drawn the desired 50 names. If the names on the list are randomized at the beginning, this method is equivalent to the random sampling technique.

But one must be wary of certain departures from randomness, such as a "trend." Suppose that children are listed by age in years and months and sample units are drawn at fixed intervals of ten. The estimated mean age of the group would vary from sample to sample depending on the beginning number selected at random. A group selected from intervals beginning at 2 would have a different mean age from one beginning with unit 10 on the list, for in the latter sequence each child would be older than his counterpart in the other sequence by 8 ranks. Cyclical fluctuations are another factor that one must be on the alert to detect. If a list is kept of the number of college students utilizing the library each day, a biased sample will probably be obtained if every seventh day is chosen as a sample unit, for fewer students probably study in the library on Sundays than on weekdays.

Cluster Sampling. In cluster sampling the sample unit contains groups of elements (clusters) instead of individual members or items in the population. Rather than listing all elementary school children in a given city and randomly selecting 15 per cent of these students for the sample, a researcher lists all of the elementary schools in the city, selects *at random* 15 per cent of these clusters of units, and uses all of the children in the selected schools as the sample.   Rather than listing all of the dwellings in a city, one may list all the blocks in the city, select *at random* 7 per cent of these clusters of units, and include all of the dwellings in the selected blocks in the sample.   Cluster sampling is economical, for it is much easier and less expensive to observe clusters of units in a few schools than randomly selected students scattered in many schools throughout the city. On the other hand, a cluster sample usually produces a larger sampling error than a simple random sample of the same size, for each cluster—such as a block in a given neighborhood—may be composed of units that are like one another, which reduces the representativeness of the sample.

QUESTIONNAIRES

The questionnaire is an instrument that is widely used by educational workers to obtain facts about current conditions and practices, and to make inquiries concerning attitudes and opinions. For some studies or certain phases of them, it may be the only practical device available for presenting respondents with carefully selected and ordered stimuli that will elicit the data required to confirm or disconfirm a hypothesis.

Isolating and precisely identifying specific items for respondents to consider in a questionnaire tends to objectify, intensify, and standardize their observations.   But these favorable features do not ensure that the subjects will provide reliable data, for human beings often cannot or will not supply accurate answers.   Some people suffer from faulty perception or memory or are unable to express their impressions and ideas adequately in words.   Respondents who are not free, willing, or qualified to divulge information may ignore certain questions or falsify their answers.   Many people do not give thoughtful consideration to questionnaires; they fill out the forms carelessly or report what they assumed took place.   Not uncommonly respondents tailor replies to conform with their biases, to protect their self-interests, to place themselves in a more favorable light, to please the researcher, or to conform with socially accepted patterns.   Thus, while the questionnaire is a useful method of acquiring data, it is not an "all purpose" tool for cutting through to the truth.   Moreover, it must be handled adroitly to obtain reliable data.

Methods of Presentation.   Questionnaires can be presented to respondents in two ways: through the mails or in a face-to-face situation.   In the latter case, a questionnaire is sometimes called a schedule, particularly if it is filled out by the interviewer rather than by the subject.   Advantages and disadvantages are associated with both methods of contacting subjects.

Direct Contact. When the researcher personally presents the questionnaire to respondents, he can explain the purpose and significance of the study, clarify points, answer questions that arise, motivate respondents to answer questions carefully and truthfully, and obtain fewer partial responses and refusals to reply. But bringing a group together to fill out a questionnaire is often difficult and meeting members individually may be excessively costly and time-consuming, hence, it is often necessary to send questionnaires through the mails.

Mailed Questionnaires. Mailed questionnaires can quickly and easily reach many people in widely scattered areas at a relatively low cost. Unfortunately, the returns do not bound back with equal celerity, and partial returns can introduce a bias that will render the obtained data useless. If nonrespondents are quite different from the respondents—less educated or less interested in the issue—they may not hold the same views as those who do answer the questions. Thus, their missing data might substantially change the findings of the study. The mailed questionnaire has another limitation: it cannot obtain a representative sample of data from a population that includes some nonreaders.

Forms of Questionnaires. A researcher can cast questions in a closed, open, or pictorial form and can utilize one type exclusively or a combination of them when structuring his questionnaire. The nature of the problem and the character of the respondents determine which form or forms will most likely supply the desired data.

Closed Form. Closed-form or structured questionnaires usually consist of a prepared list of concrete questions and a choice of possible answers. To indicate his reply, a respondent marks *yes* or *no;* checks, circles, or underscores one or more items from a list of answers; or ranks a series of statements in the order of their importance (1,2,3, . . .). Sometimes he is asked to insert brief statements into blank spaces or on empty lines (How old were you on your last birthday?——).

Closed-form questionnaires are easy to administer and fill out, help keep the respondent's mind riveted on the subject, and facilitate the process of tabulation and analysis. But they often fail to reveal the respondent's motives (why he answers as he does), do not always yield information of sufficient scope or depth, and may not discriminate between fine shades of meaning. Fixed alternative responses may make respondents take a stand upon issues about which they have no crystallized opinion or may force them to give answers that do not accurately express their ideas. The listed alternative answers may be placed in an order that encourages the respondent to reply in accordance with the researcher's wishes. These weaknesses can be somewhat overcome, however, if proper precautions are taken in constructing the questionnaire. To avoid biasing the results by placing the desired answers in the most conspicuous place, items in a check list may be randomized.   Yes-no and true-false questions may be improved upon by inserting a third choice (undecided, don't know, or no opinion).   When it is impossible to provide a full range of choices in a check list, the difficulty may be resolved by adding the statement "None of the above descriptions apply" or leaving a blank in which the respondent can clarify, amplify, or qualify his answer.

Open Form.   Rather than forcing respondents to choose between rigidly limited responses, the open-form questionnaire permits them to answer freely and fully in their own words and their own frame of reference.   It gives them an opportunity to reveal their motives or attitudes and to specify the background or provisional conditions upon which their answers are based.   On the other hand, this data gathering device has some disadvantages.   When respondents answer general questions and have no clues to guide their thinking, they may unintentionally omit important information or fail to note sufficient details.   If subjects are not highly literate and willing to give considerable time and critical thought to questions, they cannot provide useful data.   If they are capable of providing a wealth of pertinent information, their many different, detailed, and complex answers may create problems.   The task of categorizing, tabulating, and summarizing the data may be extremely difficult and time-consuming.

Pictorial Form.   Some questionnaires present respondents with drawings or photographs rather than written statements from which to choose answers; they may also provide oral rather than written directions.   This form of questionnaire is a particularly suitable tool for gathering data from children and adults with limited reading ability.   Pictures often capture the attention of respondents more readily than printed words, lessen subjects' resistance to responding, and stimulate their interest in the questions. Sometimes they clearly depict situations that do not lend themselves readily to verbal descriptions, and sometimes they make it possible to detect attitudes or gather information that could not be obtained by other procedures.   Pictorial techniques, however, possess at least two limitations: (1) their use must be restricted to situations involving distinguishable and understandable visual characteristics, and (2) they are difficult to standardize, particularly when the pictures are photographs of human beings.

Construction of Questionnaires.   Questionnaires are a popular research tool because every individual assumes that he knows how to ask questions. But asking questions that will obtain the precise, reliable data required to test a hypothesis is no easy task.   A researcher is often amazed when respondents draw many different meanings from questions that he thought were perfectly clear.   And he may prickle with resentment when colleagues point out biases in the wording or structuring of his questionnaire, which seems absolutely objective to him.

If a researcher wants data about income, marital status, or age of teachers, he must ask specific rather than "shotgun" questions to elicit the information required. Does he want to know the respondent's age on his last birthday or in years and months at the present time? Does he want to know total income from all sources or only from teaching? Does he want to obtain salary information for the regular school session or also for summer school and evening classes? A question that merely asks a respondent to check whether or not he is married may need to be recast to obtain more specific information. One might ask: Are you at present: Married_____ Single_____ Widowed_____ Divorced_____? Framing questions to obtain honest answers is an art. Note the difference in the following questions: Did you cheat on your school examinations? Did you ever engage in the commonplace practice of cheating on school examinations? Ever_____ Always_____ Never_____. Do you believe in the communistic policy of providing free college education for everyone? Should we provide everyone with a free college education? Did you exercise your American right to vote in the last school election? Did you vote in the last school election or for some reason were you unable to vote? Did_____ Did not_____.

Questionnaires have been subject to severe criticism, but many common weaknesses in them can be avoided if they are carefully structured and effectively administered to qualified respondents. Some factors that should be given careful consideration are brought out by the following questions and others are listed in the evaluation of questionnaires presented in Chapter 16.

Establishing Rapport. Is the study of sufficient importance to warrant asking busy people to answer the questions? Has permission to contact respondents been obtained from the highest authorities in the school, organization, or governing unit? Does the questionnaire or an accompanying letter clearly explain the purpose of the study, indicate that it is sponsored by a reputable institution, arouse interest in contributing accurate information, and offer to provide respondents with a summary of the findings? Are respondents asked for any information that the researchers can easily obtain elsewhere?

Framing of Questions. Has the researcher thoroughly explored his hypotheses, experiences, the literature, and other questionnaires so as to frame questions that probe the crucial issues in depth? Are the questions stated in crystal-clear, simple language and sharply focused in meaning? Are subordinate questions asked or is an exhaustive list of alternative choices provided so as to explore various aspects of a decision and probe beneath vague, stereotyped, "don't know," or evasive answers? Are questions framed to elicit specific answers (if possible, quantified answers—number of times per week rather than sometimes, often, or always) ?

Ordering of Questions. Are items placed in a psychologically or logically sound sequence—simple, interesting, neutral questions preceding more difficult, crucial, or personal ones and those that establish a frame of reference or provide keys to recall before those asking for details? Is a smooth transition made from one group of questions to the next?

Designing the Directions and Format. Are clear, complete directions given concerning the type and scope of information that is wanted, where it is to be placed, and in what form? Are the categories, format, and directions designed to elicit accurate, unambiguous answers; to require a minimum of the respondent's time; to facilitate the tabulation and interpretation of data; and, if possible, to permit the quantification of results?

Eliciting Honest Replies. Are directions and questions worded and ordered so as to allay any fears, suspicions, embarrassment, or hostility on the part of the respondent?   If personal questions are asked, is a guarantee of anonymity given or assurance that the responses will be held in strict confidence?   Are any questions colored or phrased so as to elicit replies that will support the researcher's beliefs?   Are respondents asked for information concerning subjects about which they have little or no knowledge?   Are specific questions asked in order to check the truthfulness of answers to general questions?   Are parallel questions asked in order to check consistency of answers?

INTERVIEWS

Many people are more willing to communicate information verbally than in writing and, therefore, will provide data more readily and fully in an interview than on a questionnaire. Indeed, several advantages accrue from the friendly interaction in an interview that cannot be obtained in limited, impersonal questionnaire contacts. In a face-to-face meeting, an investigator can constantly encourage subjects and help them probe more deeply into a problem, particularly an emotionally laden one. Through respondents' incidental comments, facial and bodily expressions, and tone of voice, an interviewer can acquire information that would not be conveyed in written replies. These auditory and visual cues also help him key the tempo and tone of the private conversation so as to elicit personal and confidential information and to gain knowledge about motivations, feelings, attitudes, and beliefs. Presenting questions orally is a particularly appropriate means, of course, for gathering information from young children and illiterates.

Interviews vary in purpose, nature, and scope.   They may be conducted for guidance, therapeutic, or research purposes.   They may be confined to one individual or extended to several people who are closely associated with him as in a case study.   To solve some problems, a number of people with similar or different backgrounds are questioned once briefly or several times intensively.   Sometimes interviews are repeated at intervals to trace the development of behavior, attitudes, or situations.   Repeated interviews have been used, for example, to study the progressive reactions of voters toward presidential candidates during an election year.   The following discussion describes several types of interviews.

Individual and Group Interviews.   Most interviews are conducted in a private setting with one person at a time so that the subject will feel free to express himself fully and truthfully.   Sometimes, however, group interviews produce more useful data.   When qualified individuals with common or divergent backgrounds are brought together to explore a problem or to evaluate the merits of a proposition, they can present a wide range of information and varied viewpoints.   They can also help one another recall, verify, or rectify items of information.   Subjects may refrain from expressing some points before a group, however, that they might reveal in a private interview.   Moreover, one person (and not necessarily the best-informed one) may dominate the discussion so that the viewpoints of other participants are not explored thoroughly.

Structured Interviews.   The structure of interviews varies as much as the number of participants.   Some interviews are rigidly standardized and formal: the same questions are presented in the same manner and order to each subject and the choice of alternative answers is restricted to a predetermined list.   Even the introductory and concluding remarks are systematically stated.   These structured interviews are more scientific in nature than unstructured ones, for they introduce the controls that are required to permit the formulation of scientific generalizations.   But they also have certain limitations, because the necessity of collecting quantified, comparable data from all subjects in a uniform manner introduces a rigidity into the investigative procedures that may make it impossible to probe in sufficient depth.

Unstructured Interviews.   Unstructured interviews are flexible; few restrictions are placed on respondents' answers.   If preplanned questions are asked, the queries are altered to suit the situation and subjects.   Sometimes subjects are encouraged to express their thoughts freely and only a few questions are asked to direct their discourse.   In some instances, the information is obtained in such a casual manner that the respondents are not aware that they are being interviewed.

In an informal unstructured interview, one can penetrate behind initial answers, follow up unexpected clues, redirect the inquiry on the basis of emerging data into more fruitful channels, and modify categories to provide for a more meaningful analysis of data.   Quantifying the accumulated qualitative data may be difficult, however, and the nonuniform tactics employed in collecting it may introduce irrelevant variables.   Consequently, it is usually impossible to compare data from various interviews and to derive generalizations that are universally applicable.

Nonstructured interviews are not ordinarily used when one is testing and verifying hypotheses, but they are valuable instruments in the exploratory stage of research. When an investigator is uncertain about what questions to ask or how to ask them, an informal interview may uncover the essentials of the problem and help him select and formulate questions for standardized questionnaires and interviews. An unstructured interview may also provide insights into human motivation and social interaction that enable him to formulate fruitful hypotheses.

A researcher must be familiar with both structured and unstructured interview techniques, for he is apt to employ both types during an investigation. Since many of the rules that apply to the formulation of questionnaires also apply to structured interviews, additional examples of them are unnecessary. Because the methods of conducting the more informal interviews vary considerably, it may be well to describe two specific types: the nondirective depth interview and the focused interview.

Nondirective Depth Interview. An unguided interview, which is almost psychoanalytical in character, is sometimes the most appropriate method for obtaining insights into hidden or underlying motivations; unacknowledged attitudes; personal hopes, fears, and conflicts; and the dynamic interrelatedness of responses. Rather than asking a number of direct or predetermined questions to obtain specific items of information, an investigator permits the subject to talk freely and fully concerning a particular issue, incident, or relationship. While the subject unfolds his story, the interviewer serves as a good listener who unobtrusively inserts a judicious "hmmm," "that is interesting," "go on," or generalized question to stimulate the flow of conversation. When the interview is drawing to a close, he may ask some direct questions to fill in the gaps and round out the discussion. By placing few restrictions on the direction of the discussion and encouraging a wide range of responses, the interviewer gets a natural and representative picture of the subject's behavior and gains an insight into the character and intensity of his attitudes, motives, feelings, and beliefs.

Focused Interview. A focused interview is less diffused than a depth interview. It "focuses" attention upon a concrete experience that the informant has had. If he has seen a movie or read a book, for example, an effort is made to ascertain the specific effects that this experience has had upon him. To probe the attitudes and emotional responses of the subject, the interviewer thoroughly analyzes the movie or book prior to meeting him; prepares appropriate questions to serve as a framework for the discussion; and during the interview, confines the conversation to these relevant issues. The respondent is permitted to express himself completely, but the interviewer directs the line of thought.

Conduct of an Interview. A good interview is more than a series of casual questions and generalized replies; it is a dynamic, interpersonal experience that is carefully planned to accomplish a particular purpose. Creating a friendly, permissive atmosphere; directing the discourse in the desired channels; encouraging the respondent to reveal information; and motivating him to keep presenting useful facts require a high degree of technical skill and competence. To evaluate the effectiveness of an interview, one must keep in mind many of the questions that were raised concerning questionnaires as well as the following factors.

Preparing for the Interview. Did the interviewer decide what areas of information to cover, and did he prepare appropriate questions to extract the desired data? Did he insert comments that made the respondent feel at ease and stimulated the flow of conversation? Did he find out as much as possible about the interests, beliefs, and background of the subjects so that he could gain their confidence, avoid antagonizing them, and "draw out" their experiences and special areas of knowledge? Did he obtain sufficient information to understand their frame of reference and interpret their replies as they were intended? When it was advisable, did he make a definite appointment for the interview at a time that was convenient for the subject? Did he conduct the interview in an environment in which the subject was at ease (usually in private) and in a setting where the most fruitful information could be obtained? Did he conduct a few preliminary interviews to detect weaknesses in his methods, manner, questions, or recording system?

Establishing Rapport. Was the interviewer pleasant, efficient, straightforward, and poised? Did he refrain from assuming an overly sentimental, solemn, or sympathetic attitude? Did he avoid adopting a superior, patronizing, clever, cunning, or "third degree" manner? Did he dress appropriately? Did he use a suitable vocabulary and approach for working with the particular respondent?

Eliciting Information. Was the interviewer an attentive, analytical listener who discerned when it was necessary to repeat or explain a question? Did he detect when answers were vague, contradictory, evasive, or deceptive? Did he skillfully introduce alternative or more penetrating questions to help respondents recall information, amplify statements, clarify their thinking, rectify facts, or give more concrete evidence? Did he pace the questions at the proper speed for the respondents? Did he ask general questions first and then sharpen the focus of succeeding questions? Did he follow up crucial clues provided by responses and stay with fruitful lines of questioning until he had extracted all of the useful information? Did he inject courteous comments to redirect the interview into channels that were more pertinent to the inquiry? Did he sense when it was best to approach delicate matters and probe for "depth materials"? Did he carefully plan the wording of these questions? Did his tone of voice, facial expression, or phrasing and timing of questions imply what answers he preferred?   Did he avoid blaming or censuring the respondent and refrain from revealing that an answer shocked, annoyed, or displeased him?   Did he seek the same information in different ways during the interview to check the honesty of responses?   Did he check some replies against official records to determine whether they were accurate?   Did he terminate the interview before the subject became tired?

Recording Data.   Did the interviewer use some schedule, structured format, or system that enabled him to record notes quickly and accurately? Did he legibly record the exact (nonedited) words of the respondent at the time they were spoken or immediately after the interview?   Did he consider using a tape recorder that would free him during the interview; provide a means of verifying responses later; preserve the emotional and vocal character of replies; and help him avoid the omissions, distortions, modifications, and errors that sometimes are made in written accounts of an interview?   Did the interviewer make notes concerning any behavior or conditions that he observed which did not conform with the respondent's replies?   Did he make a record of significant emotional displays, hesitations, stammering, sudden silences or transitions, quickly corrected words, and obvious omissions?

APPRAISAL INSTRUMENTS

In addition to interviews and questionnaires, researchers employ tests, scales, inventories and other tools to obtain data.   Hundreds of these instruments have been devised, and others are constantly being constructed. Some of them provide for a self-appraisal, others require that the assessments be made by an expert.   Excellent descriptions and evaluations of many tests can be found in *Mental Measurements Yearbook* and research journals.   Usually these sources also give the names of the publishers, the prices, and the grade level for which the tests are designed.   Explanations of the techniques employed in constructing and evaluating tests appear in several measurements and evaluation texts.   Because of the extensive literature in the field this chapter can give only a brief description of some types of tools.

Instruments have been designed to measure many different things. Some appraise the *performances* and *potentialities* of subjects.   (1) Intelligence tests, for example, measure the general mental abilities and certain specialized tests assess a limited range of abilities, such as those required in mechanical comprehension or in the judgment of spatial relations.   (2) Information and achievement tests measure the present level of mastery in a subject or skill that a person has attained as a result of specific instruction.   These include typing, spelling, reading, and arithmetic proficiency tests; educational achievement batteries that measure performance in several areas; and similar types of tests. (3) Aptitude tests predict the subject's ability to improve his performance with additional training in some particular academic or vocational field. Although these tests are based on present performance, they usually measure some areas in which the subject has not received specific training. They may appraise factors such as mechanical skill, motor coordination, musical or artistic potential, or aptitude for medicine, engineering, languages, algebra, or stenography.

Tools are also available that measure the *preferences* and *behavior* of individuals. (1) Some of them inventory the interest that subjects have in particular occupations or activities. (2) Others ascertain the nature and dimensions of the attitudes and beliefs that individuals or groups hold concerning issues, activities, institutions, and segments of society. (3) A variety of tools assess emotional and social factors—the adjustment of a person to himself and to others. (4) Somewhat similar tests appraise aspects of a subject's behavior and conduct, such as his moral conduct, cooperativeness, friendliness, or leadership qualities.

Various techniques have been devised to determine the *environmental* and *physical* status of people and institutions. Some measure aspects of the home: the family's socioeconomic status or the parent-to-parent, child-to-child, or parent-child relationships. Various survey instruments evaluate factors in a school, institution, or community, such as the number and quality of facilities; leadership services; programs and practices; and cohesiveness. Medical and physical fitness tests assess the health status of individuals.

Appraisal instruments vary not only in respect to what they measure, but also in respect to how they obtain data. They may acquire information through performance tests, inventories, or scales, or they may utilize some of the newer sociometric and projective techniques. Hence, the following discussion will briefly describe these methods.

Tests. Pencil and paper tests and other special performance tests are commonly employed to measure subjects' abilities and many considerations must be kept in mind when constructing them. In the beginning, one identifies the population for which the test is intended, defines the precise ability—breadth and depth—that is to be tested, and carefully analyzes all the factors that contribute to it. Then, he selects test items to cover them and keeps the number in proper proportion to each factor's contribution to the ability. When constructing test items, he carefully observes the rules for selecting appropriate performance tasks or for formulating various types of questions (multiple choice, matching, etc.) and makes certain that each item is of suitable difficulty for the subjects. In addition, he may establish time limits for various phases of the test. When he has written all the directions and test items in clear, concise language and has developed a format that makes it easy to read the questions, to answer them, and to tabulate the results, the researcher administers his preliminary test draft to a group of subjects.

Afterward he examines the student's responses and revises the directions that have caused confusion, corrects weaknesses revealed in the format, and eliminates or revises poor test items.   When he has completed his corrections, he rechecks to make certain that all aspects of the ability to be measured are still represented in proper proportion and applies tests of objectivity, validity, and reliability.   The test constructor may also prepare norms to help users interpret whether their pupils are average, above average, or below the average level of ability.   To do this, he draws a sample from the population for whom the test is intended, administers the final form of the test to these subjects, and from the data collected constructs the norms.

The preceding discussion has indicated that the determination of a test's objectivity, validity, reliability, and practicality is of paramount importance.   Since these evaluative criteria are also applied when one selects or constructs any other type of appraisal tool, they will be discussed before proceeding to the description of inventories, scales, and other measuring instruments.

Objectivity.   A test or scale is objective if it produces the same score regardless of who marks it.   Thus, the best testing instruments are designed so that the score can be obtained without involving the subjective judgment of the examiner.   When a true and false key is provided for a test, for example, subjective judgments are not required for scoring it.   If no guide is given for evaluating an essay test, the personal values and emphases of the examiner influence the marks that subjects receive.   The greater the degree of subjectivity that is involved in making judgments about the level of performance, the less objective is the test.   Thus, to improve the objectivity of their tests, competent workers write specific directions to the observer or scorer and furnish scoring keys that allow no room for disagreement among scorers.

Validity.   An appraisal instrument is valid if it measures what it claims to measure.   The need for this quality is obvious.   Because validity is of primary importance, researchers present evidence to support claims concerning the characteristics that their tests measure.   A number of validation techniques are used to do this.   Logical or curricular validity is obtained when the investigator analyzes the particular ability, skill, or course content that he intends to appraise and structures an instrument to measure the various aspects of that factor.   To design a standardized algebra test, for example, he may examine many textbooks in the field and the courses of study and objectives prepared by the state departments of education and professional bodies.   From these materials he can determine what the test should cover and the proportion of it that should be devoted to various aspects of algebra. The method of "jury validation" is similar to logical validation except that the items to be included on the test are submitted to qualified experts who rate them as to their importance in contributing to the factor being measured. If the literature and the judges indicate that certain aspects of algebra are important, the investigator demonstrates curricular or logical validity when he includes items relating to them in his test.

Designers of appraisal instruments also endeavor to establish empirical validation which embraces (1) the method of internal consistency and (2) the method of outside criteria. The method of internal consistency attempts to determine whether the test has the power to discriminate between subjects of varying abilities. A test item is said to discriminate if the pupils who answer it correctly receive higher scores on the total test than those who do not. Thus, to ascertain the discriminating power of test items, the investigator correlates each item score with the total test score, or uses an equivalent method. Items that fail to meet standards of discrimination are screened out of the final form of the test, but a recheck must then be made to ascertain whether all aspects of the factor being measured are still covered in the test and in the proper proportion.

Appraisal instruments are also validated by various external criteria. Scores on tests that predict academic or vocational success, for example, are often checked against the subsequent performances of the subjects as revealed by their school grades or job productivity. Thus, to validate an algebra aptitude test one might correlate subjects' test scores with the grades that they later receive in algebra courses. If one test has been validated and a cheaper or more convenient one is designed to measure the same factor, the scores on the two tests can be correlated to determine the validity of the new test. If a test measures a certain aspect of behavior, the scores that the subject receives can be correlated with ratings made by several associates or experts (teachers, friends, and supervisors) who know him well.

Validity is sometimes established by the "known group" technique. This method involves administering the test to two groups already known to differ on the factor being measured. A scale measuring attitudes toward the United Nations, for example, can be given to some subjects who are known to be enthusiastic supporters of the institution and to others who are known to be extremely hostile. If the test fails to discriminate sharply between these two groups, it does not measure what it claims to measure; it is not valid.

Reliability. The reliability of appraisal instrument measurements must be considered. A test or scale is reliable if it consistently yields the same results when repeated measurements are taken of the same subjects under the same conditions. If a student receives a score of 110 on an intelligence test, for example, he should receive approximately the same score when an equivalent form of it is given several weeks later. Three methods of measuring reliability are used: (1) the test-retest, (2) parallel forms, and (3) split-half methods. In the first method, the test is given to the same subjects twice and their resultant scores are correlated. If it is possible that recall or the effect of practice will carry over from one testing to another, parallel or equivalent forms of the evaluation device are constructed. When this is done, the two forms are administered to the same subjects and the agreement between the two test scores is determined. When the split-half method is used, the test is given only once, but items in it are divided randomly into halves, and the scores tabulated for each half are correlated.

Practicality. When selecting a test, scale, or inventory, one must determine whether it is a practical instrument for his purpose. Will it obtain the type of data that he needs? Will it produce measurements that are sufficiently precise for his purposes? Will it be suitable for the age and type of subjects and the time and locality in which he intends to use it? If two tests are equally reliable and valid, the one that is the less expensive, more easily and quickly scored, available in alternative forms, and accompanied by norms, is usually preferable to its counterpart. Most publishers print manuals that give detailed information about the construction, reliability, and validity of standardized tests as well as the nature of the population upon which the norms are based. A prudent researcher carefully examines these explanations when he is searching for appropriate testing instruments. When conducting an investigation, he also remembers that the best tests available cannot yield reliable data if they are administered improperly or under undesirable and distracting conditions, scored incorrectly, or interpreted inaccurately.

Inventories. Inventories are instruments that attempt to "take stock" of one or more aspects of an individual's behavior rather than to measure in the usual sense. Unlike tests, they do not require subjects to perform at their maximum level, but merely ask for information about their typical behavior. An inventory presents subjects with a list of items relating to the factor being appraised and requests them to indicate preferences or to check items that describe their typical behavior. Later the responses are evaluated to obtain descriptions of certain fundamental predispositions of the subjects. Hundreds of inventories have been constructed to obtain information about interests, personality traits, social attitudes, social adjustments, study habits, and similar factors. Some commonly employed ones are the SRA Youth Inventory, Bernreuter Personality Inventory, Minnesota Multiphasic Personality Inventory, and Washburne Social Adjustment Inventory.

Items cannot be placed in an inventory merely because the investigator strongly believes that they reflect the factor being measured. To validate an inventory, one must demonstrate that the scores obtained on it agree highly with some other reliable device for measuring the factor under study. To measure interest in the teaching profession, for example, one may first list the various ways in which interests in teaching are expressed and then present these statements to successful teachers and people in other fields. The items upon which the teachers score high and other vocational groups score low can then be retained in the inventory.

Valid measurements, of course, are not obtained from an inventory if a subject gives false answers to make a desired impression or if he lacks sufficient insight into himself to report certain dimensions of his behavior objectively. Some procedures have been devised to detect dishonest answers and sometimes faking can be kept under control by using items that do not readily reveal the nature of the factor being measured. The difficulty of validating inventories, however, limits their use as scientific instruments.

Scales. Many social science data cannot be measured in inches, grams, or similar standardized units that convey the same meaning to all people. Since this is a major stumbling block to scientific advancement, workers in the field have been searching diligently for tools that will enable them to assign numerical values to their estimates of the magnitude of variables. Several scaling techniques have been devised to do this, but many of them are characterized by certain limitations and inadequacies. Progress is being made in finding methods to transform qualitative data into quantitative measures that are more amenable to analysis and interpretation, but the work is still in a pioneer stage of development.

To construct valid, reliable, and objective scales, a researcher must overcome many obstacles. Difficulty may be encountered when he attempts to describe the precise character of the factor to be rated and to identify the characteristics that contribute to it. Without a full knowledge of the field, he cannot select representative items from the universe of items that contribute to a factor being measured and cannot judge what items to eliminate because they are not logically related to it. A scale constructor must not only define the factor to be evaluated, but also clearly differentiate between various degrees of that factor so that the rater will know specifically what to evaluate when making each judgment. In some scales the question of giving the proper weight to items also arises.

Furthermore, the effectiveness of rating scales depends in part upon the qualifications of the raters. Some people may not have sufficient knowledge about a factor to make discriminating observations and judgments. Not uncommonly, individuals check scale choices on the basis of inadequate evidence or merely "guess" if they have had little or no opportunity to observe the factor being evaluated. Raters often suffer from a halo effect—

they carry over a general impression gained from rating one factor to all factors that they rate. Some people rate everyone too severely or too leniently or refrain from checking items at either extreme of the scale. Because each rater tends to make judgments upon the basis of a slightly different frame of reference, pooled ratings are sometimes preferred.

Not all scales produce the same precision of measurement. Some of them are too primitive to be considered scientific instruments. In general, there are four levels of scales. In *nominal scales*—the lowest type of scale—entities are placed in two or more different categories which for the sake of convenience may be given identifying numbers, but these categories do not have an ordered relationship to one another. Not uncommonly, however, it is important to know whether factors vary in degree rather than just in kind. By constructing an ordinal scale, this goal can be achieved. *Ordinal scales* place entities in a clearly defined rank order, but the distance between the successive entities is unknown and not necessarily equal. If A, B, and C receive leadership scores of 15, 10, and 5, respectively, on an ordinal scale, one can say that A is superior to B in leadership and B is superior to C. One cannot say, however, that A is *as much* superior to B as B is to C—that is, that the interval 10-15 is equal to the interval 10-5. To be able to state the latter, one must employ an interval scale.

An *interval scale* not only places entities in a clearly defined order, but also utilizes some means of attaining equidistant intervals of measurement. While this scale permits one to say that the distances between A and B and between B and C are equal, it does not permit one to say that A with a score of 15 is thrice as superior as C with a score of 5 and that B with a score of 10 is twice as superior as C. To do this, one must employ a ratio scale. A *ratio scale*—the highest type of scale—possesses all the characteristics of an interval scale and in addition is characterized by an absolute zero which offers a consistent starting point for measurement. With such a scale, it is possible to speak of relative amounts as well as difference in amount of any property or characteristic.

Many different methods of constructing scales have been devised to obtain more precise and reliable data for the solution of educational problems. Only through considerable concentrated study can one become thoroughly familiar with them and learn how to construct them. The following discussion merely provides a brief introduction to some of these techniques.

Rating Scale. A rating scale ascertains the degree, intensity, or frequency of a variable. To construct one, an investigator identifies the factor to be measured, places units or categories on a scale, to differentiate varying degrees of that factor, and describes these units in some manner. No established rule governs the number of units that should be placed on a scale, but having too few categories tends to produce crude measures that have little meaning, and having too many makes it difficult for the rater to discriminate between one step and the next on the scale.

The description of the scale units may consist of points, numbers, or general descriptive phrases placed along a line:

   | | | | | or   1 2 3 4 5

or *almost always, frequently, occasionally, rarely, almost never.*

Since these points, numerical symbols, and generalized terms do not necessarily carry the same measurement meaning to all people, more specific descriptive phrases may be presented to give the rater a clearer standard for judgment. In a Bogardus-type social distance scale, for example, a subject does not merely check a number of vague phrases to indicate how closely he is willing to associate with members of different ethnic groups. Rather, he examines and checks specific statements that describe varying degrees of acceptability. He may indicate, for example, whether he would be willing to have an average member of various groups (1) as a mate, (2) as a personal friend, (3) as a neighbor, (4) as a fellow employee, (5) as a citizen of his country, (6) as a visitor to all parts of his country, (7) as a visitor restricted to a limited area of his country.

Sometimes specimens of work are used to describe units on a scale. Samples of handwriting that represent various levels of merit, for example, may be placed on a continuum according to values determined by a jury. To rate a product, one matches it with the scale specimen that it most nearly resembles. Man-to-man scales are similar to product scales, except that the bench marks on them are names of about three to five men. These men are known to the judges, and they possess varying degrees of a particular trait, say, leadership. Subjects are rated by matching them with the men on the scale that they most nearly resemble.

Score Card. A score card, which is frequently called a numerical rating scale, provides for the appraisal of a large number of items that contribute to the status or quality of some complex entity. Score cards have been developed, for example, to evaluate school facilities, institutional programs, communities, textbooks, and the socioeconomic status of families. Each item on a score card is assigned a predetermined numerical value, and ratings are made by awarding all of the points or some fraction thereof for the amount of the factor judged to be present. By combining all the ratings, one obtains a total score that indicates the over-all evaluation of the object or condition observed. This technique is rather satisfactory when used to appraise physical facilities. It is less effective, however, when used to evaluate the program or quality of an institution, for there are some intangibles in group activities that seem to defy quantitative appraisal.

Rank-order Scale. Rather than rating subjects, objects, products, or attributes on an absolute scale, a rank-order scale compares them with one another. This technique is especially useful for handling in a quantitative manner data that have not been precisely differentiated. Suppose an educator wishes to rate twelve teachers in respect to leadership ability. On a rank-order scale, he does not check a numerical symbol or descriptive phrase to indicate the degree of this quality that each possesses. Rather, he gives the teachers serial numbers to indicate how they rank in leadership in comparison with their colleagues. Thus, the teacher with the highest leadership qualities receives serial number 1, the next highest, serial number 2, and the lowest, serial number 12. Since there are apt to be more average teachers than extremely good or poor ones, it is usually more difficult to detect degrees of difference between the average teachers. Thus, rank-order scales are apt to give a more reliable measure at the extremes of the scale than in the central portion.

Paired Comparisons. In the method of paired comparisons, the subject is presented with a list of items, such as different ethnic groups, occupations, or recreational activities, and is asked to judge each item in turn with every other item in terms of which he prefers. A subject, for example, may be asked to underline which activity of the following pairs of activities he enjoys participating in the most:

football-tennis   baseball-tennis
baseball-checkers   pingpong-football
tennis-pingpong   tennis-checkers
football-baseball   pingpong-baseball
checkers-pingpong   checkers-football

The judgments of the subjects can be manipulated so that each activity can be assigned a scale value. This method, which may give more accurate results than the rank-order approach, is satisfactory when a small number of items must be compared, but it is time consuming and laborious when a large number of comparisons is required.

Equal-appearing Intervals Scale. The technique of equal-appearing intervals, which Thurstone utilized to establish attitude scale units, has become widely employed. In this method a hundred or more separate statements expressing various degrees of intensity of feeling toward a group, institution, object, or issue may be given to between fifty and one hundred judges. Each judge is asked to arrange the statements as objectively as possible into piles (usually seven to eleven) that appear to him to be equally spaced psychologically and to order the piles so that statements in the first pile represent the most favorable attitude toward the factor being evaluated, those in the center pile represent a neutral attitude, and those in the last pile represent the most unfavorable attitude. Afterward, the number of times that each statement is included in the several piles is tabulated, and each statement is assigned a score value based on the median position given to it by the judges. Statements that are too broadly scattered by the judges are discarded as ambiguous or irrelevant. To construct the final scale, somewhere between fifteen and forty of the remaining statements are selected to represent the different intensities of the attitude in question, and they are arranged in a random order. When taking the test, the subject checks only those statements with which he agrees, and his score is the median of the scale values for the statements.

Method of Summated Ratings. This method, which dispenses with judges, was introduced by Likert. It is as reliable as the Thurstone technique and somewhat simpler. The trial Likert test contains a large number of statements which indicate clearly a position for or against a particular issue. After each statement, subjects check one of several alternative answers, such as *strongly approve, approve, neutral, disapprove, strongly disapprove.* The "arbitrary" or "sigma" methods may be used in scoring. The former, which is sometimes preferred, will be explained because it is simpler. This method arbitrarily gives a weight of 1 to 5 to the alternative answers, and the same numerical values are always given to the responses that show the greatest favorableness toward the phenomena, for example:

"Exclude all Negroes from the city."   *strongly disapprove*—weight of 5.
"Appoint a Negro to the school board."   *strongly approve*—weight of 5.

Although the answers differ, they receive the same weight because they both reveal a favorable attitude toward Negroes. The total score for each subject is the sum of the values assigned to each item that he checked. Before constructing the final test, the investigator applies techniques that help him identify weak items. If an item fails to exhibit a substantial correlation with the total score or does not possess the power to discriminate consistently between people who receive high and low scores on the scale, he eliminates it.

Sociometric Technique.   In recent decades workers have been developing sociometric methods to obtain data regarding social interaction among group members. In its simplest form, this technique involves asking each person in a group to express which other member he would prefer to associate with in a particular relationship or activity, for example, as a roommate or coworker on a project. Sometimes subjects are asked to select second and third choices and to list the persons that they would reject. The choices may be plotted on a sociogram which presents each student's name within a circle or triangle and utilizes connecting lines (solid for acceptance and broken for rejection) and arrows to show the flow of interpersonal relationships. This network of acceptances and rejections reveals the star and mutual attractions in the group as well as the fringers and isolates; it depicts social subgroupings, social cleavages, and the cohesiveness of the group. Sociometric data may also be presented on a matrix chart upon which all pupils' names are listed horizontally and vertically; first, second, third, and rejection choices (given and received) are plotted in the proper squares or cells; and the total acceptances and rejections for each is tabulated below.

A "guess who" test is another device for detecting how persons in a group regard one another. The test consists of a series of statements describing hypothetical people—"He is always cheerful and enthusiastic." "He is usually gloomy and complaining about something." Subjects are asked to write after each statement the name of the member in their group to whom it applies. The status of each member of the group can be judged by counting the frequency with which he is mentioned for various favorable and unfavorable descriptions.

Projective Techniques. When a subject is asked for information about himself, he may deliberately conceal his real attitudes, lack sufficient insight into his own motives to discuss them, or be unable to give accurate and objective verbal descriptions of his reactions and experiences. Consequently, workers have devised projective techniques to probe areas that cannot be reached easily by other means or areas in which direct questions are apt to elicit distorted data. Instead of asking a subject for specific information, an investigator has him interpret or respond freely to ambiguous stimuli, such as inkblots, pictures, unfinished sentences, word associations, or lifelike dramatic roles. Through self-structured, spontaneous responses, the subject unconsciously reveals manifestations of his personality characteristics and organization. Only highly trained workers can interpret the implications of these responses, however, and scoring them is laborious. Projective techniques are difficult to validate, and many of the tools have not been standardized. Some weaknesses in them are gradually being overcome, but much work remains to be done.

OBSERVATION

Interviews, questionnaires, and documentary sources are the only tools that can be used to obtain data concerning some incidents. This is particularly true when one needs information about the personal lives of subjects, group activities from which outsiders are barred, and events that have occurred in the past. Whenever direct observation is possible, however, this is the preferable method to use. The researcher cannot observe in a casual or haphazard manner; however, he must know precisely what to focus his attention upon and how to report accurately what he sees, hears, and smells. Various tools have been devised to aid him in making more objective and reliable observations and to systematize the collection of data.

In addition to the score cards, rating scales, and various tests that have already been discussed, some of the following techniques are commonly employed.

Check Lists and Schedules. Researchers often construct check lists or schedules to facilitate the recording of data. These instruments list items (carefully defined, observable factors) that are relevant to the problem and, if possible, group them into categories. After each item they provide a space for the observer to write in a few descriptive words or to indicate the presence, absence, or frequency of the phenomenon's occurrence. These guides enable investigators to record many different observations rather quickly and rapidly and ensure that they do not overlook relevant evidence. They also tend to objectify the observations and provide for a uniform classification of data. Some check lists are designed so that the researcher can arrive at a score that enables him to make comparisons with other data or to determine the general condition of an object or facility.

Time Sampling. The time sampling technique requires that one record the frequency of observable forms of occurrences during a number of definite time intervals that are systematically spaced. Let us consider an uncomplicated example to illustrate this technique. If a teacher desires to ascertain the types of activity engaged in by John Adams, he records observable forms of behavior that this pupil exhibits during a specified five-minute interval in a history class each school day for a two-week period. Rather than recording everything the boy does, the teacher may wish to tabulate the occurrence or nonoccurrence of one objectively defined form of behavior, such as "the frequency of class participation." To obtain such data, he would observe John Adams for a definite number of class periods spaced over several days or weeks and record each time that John contributed to the class discussion. The length of the observation interval depends upon the nature of the problem and such practical considerations as the availability of the subjects for the duration of the observation period. In general, research reveals that several short, well-distributed observations provide a more typical picture of behavior than a few long periods of observation.

Time sampling is a valuable technique, because it permits observable instances of behavior to be quantified directly. By making a series of observations on the same day, on successive days, or at any other stated intervals of time, a score can be obtained that shows the number of times that the subject exhibited a particular form of behavior during each period and during the total number of periods. These obtained scores lend themselves readily to statistical treatment.

Behavioral Diaries and Anecdotal Records. Sometimes rather informal methods are employed to collect data. When a pupil is involved in a significant incident in the classroom, hall, lunchroom, or some other concrete situation, an investigator may write a factual statement about what the subject said or did, note the date of the incident, and describe the situation in which it occurred. After accumulating a series of these direct observations of significant behavior over a period of time, he may have sufficient data to gain considerable insight into the growth, development, and adjustment of the subject.

Anecdotal records are of little value, however, if observers are not able to report the relevant facts objectively. Some investigators make the mistake of accumulating only negative data; others record vague generalizations about the incident or a subjective interpretation of it rather than stating exactly what the subject said or did. Sometimes investigators generalize about the behavior of a subject before they have collected sufficient data. The greatest liability of the anecdotal technique is that considerable time is required to record, analyze, and interpret the data.

Mechanical Instruments. When several observers describe the same incident, their reports often vary because of their personal biases, selective perceptions, emotional involvements, or capricious memories. Because mechanical instruments are unaffected by such factors, they can often obtain a more accurate record of an event. Motion pictures and sound recordings, for example, preserve the details of an incident in a reproducible form so that the full account of the occurrence can be studied repeatedly and intensively by the investigator and also can be checked by other research workers. Films have been used to analyze audience reactions, to make slow-motion analyses of complex activities that could not have been studied under normal conditions, and to serve many other purposes. Some mechanical instruments not only give a reliable account of what happened, but also report it in a quantified form. Dynamometers, for example, measure the strength of the hand grip, and electromyographs record the frequency, intensity, and duration of the activity of a muscle. Rather than measuring the responses of subjects, some instruments control the stimulus source in an experiment. The episcotister, for example, regulates the intensity of light emanating from a source. Hundreds of mechanical instruments have been constructed, and the research worker should become familiar with those that are used in his field.

Although mechanical devices may produce more refined and reliable data than human observers, they are subject to certain limitations. They can be employed more easily in carefully controlled laboratory experiments than in studies conducted in a natural setting, such as a classroom. The presence of the instrument sometimes alters the behavior of the subjects and as a consequence the investigator does not get an accurate measure of their typical behavior. The money and time required to construct, utilize, or maintain an instrument may be prohibitive. Both crude and complicated instruments present problems, and, of course, well-designed, precise instruments cannot yield reliable data if they are not properly employed and maintained. Furthermore, it is no easier to classify data collected by mechanical instruments in a manner that will reveal meaningful relationships than it is to categorize data obtained from less sophisticated tools.

BIBLIOGRAPHY

1. American Association for Health, Physical Education and Recreation, *Research Methods in Health, Physical Education, and Recreation*. Washington, 1959, chaps. 4 and 5.

2. Barr, Arvil, R. A. Davis, and P. O. Johnson, *Educational Research and Appraisal*. Philadelphia: J. B. Lippincott Company, 1953, chap. 6.

3. Best, John W., *Research in Education*. Englewood Cliffs, N.J.: Prentice-Hall, Inc., 1959, chap. 7.

4. Brown, Clarence W., and E. E. Ghiselli, *Scientific Method in Psychology*. New York: McGraw-Hill Book Company, Inc., 1955, chap. 14.

5. Doby, John T. (ed.), *An Introduction to Social Research*. Harrisburg, Pa.: The Stackpole Company, 1954, chaps. 6, 8, and 9.

6. Festinger, Leon, and Daniel Katz, *Research Methods in the Behavioral Sciences*. New York: The Dryden Press, Inc., 1953, chaps. 5, 6, and 8.

7. Furfey, Paul Hanly, *The Scope and Method of Sociology*. New York: Harper & Brothers, 1953, chaps. 12 and 18.

8. Good, Carter V., *Introduction to Educational Research*. New York: Appleton-Century-Crofts, Inc., 1959, chap. 5.

9. Good, Carter V., and Douglas E. Scates, *Methods of Research*. New York: Appleton-Century-Crofts, Inc., 1954, chaps. 6 and 7.

10. Goode, William J., and Paul K. Hatt, *Methods in Social Research*. New York: McGraw-Hill Book Company, Inc., 1952, chaps. 11-17.

11. Harris, Chester, W. (ed.), *Encyclopedia of Educational Research*. New York: The Macmillan Company, 1960.

12. Hillway, Tyrus, *Introduction to Research*. Boston: Houghton Mifflin Company, 1956, chap. 12.

13. Jahoda, Marie, et al., *Research Methods in Social Relations*. New York: The Dryden Press, Inc., 1951, chaps. 5–7.

14. Johnson, Palmer O., "Development of the Sample Survey as a Scientific Methodology," *Journal of Experimental Education*, 27 (March, 1959):167.

15. Larson, Leonard A., Morey R. Fields, and Milton A. Gabrielsen, *Problems in Health, Physical and Recreation Education*. Englewood Cliffs, N.J.: Prentice-Hall, Inc., 1953, chap. 10.

16. Rummel, J. Francis, *An Introduction to Research Procedures in Education*. New York: Harper & Brothers, 1958, chaps. 6 and 9.

17. Townsend, John C., *Introduction to Experimental Method*. New York: McGraw-Hill Book Company, Inc., 1953, chap. 10.

18. Travers, Robert M. W., *An Introduction to Educational Research*. New York: The Macmillan Company, 1958, chaps. 10 and 14.

19. Werkmeister, W. H., *An Introduction to Critical Thinking*. Lincoln, Nebr.: Johnsen Publishing Company, 1948, chap. 18.

20. Young, Pauline V., *Scientific Social Surveys and Research*. Englewood Cliffs, N.J.: Prentice-Hall, Inc., 1956, chaps. 7 and 8.

CHAPTER 13

Descriptive Statistics

BY WILLIAM J. MEYER

The purpose of this chapter and the one which follows is to acquaint the student with some of the basic terms, arithmetical operations, and concepts involved in the use of statistics. It is hoped that this overview will motivate the beginning student to go further on in his study of statistics and, in addition, will provide sufficient familiarity with the more commonly employed procedures to permit a better understanding of his own professional literature. In a way, it is unfortunate that these chapters appear separate from the material on descriptive and experimental methodology, for it is our feeling that statistics are not a separate and distinct aspect of research but rather that they are integral to the planning of sound research. Indeed, some of the material to be presented in the next chapter will seem meaningless unless the reader has already grasped the issues involved in the design of experiments. It is our hope that the student will attempt to relate the materials presented in these chapters back to the issues raised earlier.

ORGANIZING THE DATA

After the data have been collected, the first task is to organize the material so that some intelligibility can be derived from it. Suppose the research problem called for the administration of an intelligence test to 100 eighth-grade pupils. Recording each score as it happens to appear would certainly lead to chaos. What is needed is some conventional system for ordering the data.

The Frequency Distribution. The conventional schema is to place the highest score at the top of the distribution and then, in intervals of one, to place every other possible score that could exist, from the top score to the bottom, down the column. After the total range has been recorded, it is a relatively simple matter to record the tally marks next to the appropriate score. Table 1 illustrates a typical frequency distribution where X

is the notation for the raw score and f is the symbol for frequency.   Though the arrangement of the data on the left-hand side of Table 1 is easier to conceptualize than if the data were presented in random fashion, it is still difficult to grasp.   The next section describes a technique for improving the presentation of the data.

The Class Interval. It is possible to present data in a more concise way by organizing them into intervals of a size greater than 1 and tallying the scores falling within the limits of each interval.   The data in Table 1

TABLE 1. FREQUENCY DISTRIBUTION OF ACHIEVEMENT TEST SCORES
OF 92 ELEVENTH-GRADE PUPILS

X	f	X	f	X	f	X	f
86	1	56		26		85–89	1
85		55	1	25		80–84	2
84		54	1	24		75–79	3
83		53	2	23	1	70–74	
82	1	52	1	22		65–69	4
81		51	1	21		60–64	10
80	1	50	1	20		55–59	5
79		49	1	19		50–54	6
78		48	1	18	1	45–49	8
77		47	1		92	40–44	13
76	2	46	3			35–39	16
75	1	45	2			30–34	15
74		44	1			25–29	7
73		43	3			20–24	1
72		42	2			15 19	1
71		41	4				92
70		40	3				
69	1	39	6				
68	1	38	5				
67	1	37	2				
66	1	36	1				
65		35	2				
64	1	34	3				
63	3	33	3				
62	1	32	3				
61	2	31	1				
60	3	30	5				
59	2	29	4				
58	1	28	3				
57	1	27					

have been reorganized into a class interval of size 5 which gives a fairly adequate picture of the distribution of scores.   Of course, the width of the class interval can assume any value dependent upon the purposes of the investigator.   However, too coarse a grouping (large class interval) tends to mask the essential nature of the distribution and is a source of error in subsequent computational procedures. On the other hand, too fine a class interval often does not give the economy of space desired and does not reduce the labor involved in preparing the distribution over what would exist if a class interval of size 1 were employed. A useful though arbitrary rule of thumb is to fix the number of intervals at some figure between 12 and 16, usually 15, and then determine the size of the class interval. This operation simply requires that the range be divided by the number of class

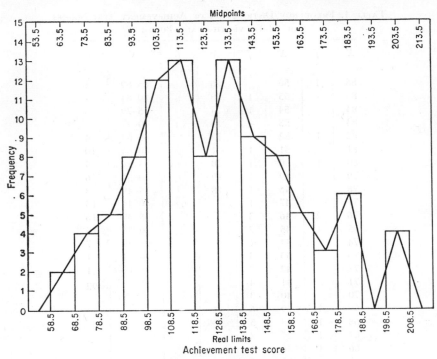

Fig. 17. Frequency polygon and histogram.

intervals desired. The resulting dividend will, when rounded to the nearest whole number, give the interval size.[1]

One additional assumption is pertinent to the present discussion of class intervals. In using numbers in statistics, we assume that each number represents a continuum. Such an assumption implies that the quantitative measures we make of any attribute can assume an infinite number of values. Sometimes this assumption leads to rather silly statistical statements, such as that the average American family produces 2.15 children. Obviously,

[1] For the sake of consistency among investigators, a general rule to follow is to set the value of the lower limits of the interval as a multiple of the interval size. For example, in Table 1 the lower limits are 15, 20, 25, etc.

we cannot always meet the requirements of a continuous series, but if it is assumed that any number is actually a point on a continuum, each number takes on a range of values. For example, take the number 5. Actually, the *real limits* of this number are from 4.5 to 5.4999, or 5.5. Applying the same principle to a class interval such as 45 to 50 would mean that the real limits of the interval are 44.5 to 50.5.

Graphic Presentation of a Frequency Distribution. It is often helpful to present a frequency distribution in graphic form. There are at least two types of such graphs: the *frequency polygon* and the *histogram*. Examination of Figure 17 shows the basic difference in the construction of these graphs. The points marked off along the horizontal axis, or *abscissa,* for the histogram are the upper and lower limits of each class interval. The points along the abscissa for the frequency polygon are the mid-points of each class interval. Frequencies are denoted on the vertical scale, or *ordinate,* and are identical for each type of graph. Each interval on the ordinate scale is actually one unit of frequency with a width equal to one interval on the abscissa. The area under the histogram or polygon represents the total frequency. The student should be sure he understands the interpretation of these methods of graphically presenting data in terms of area rather than heights of ordinates. The decision as to which approach to use is arbitrary; however, the polygon will generally yield a clearer picture when more than one distribution is to be plotted on the same set of axes.

DESCRIBING SAMPLE ATTRIBUTES

Before describing the uses and arithmetical manipulation necessary in computing descriptive statistics, it is necessary to review the properties of the typical educational and psychological scales on page 268. Although the typical scales technically restrict the statistical procedures that can be employed in analyzing data, they are nevertheless used [see Stevens (3), Chapter 1].

Measures of Central Tendency. One of the responsibilities of the careful research worker is to report as completely and meaningfully as possible the attributes of his sample. We have already examined some of the important issues involved in sampling procedures (see Chapter 12). Our concern now is with the techniques for statistically describing the sample. The three techniques to be described in this section are known as the mode, median, and mean, each of which yields information about the "typical" person in a frequency distribution.

The Mode. The measure or score which occurs most often in a frequency distribution is called the mode. When grouped data are being considered, the mode is the mid-point of the interval with the largest number of cases. Sometimes it will occur that two or more adjacent intervals will have the same frequency, which also happens to be the largest in the distribution. Determination of the modal value of such a bimodal distribution is accomplished by determining the mid-point of the entire interval.

Of the three measures of central tendency, the mode is perhaps the easiest to determine, involving for the most part merely inspection of the distribution. Unfortunately, it is also the least reliable technique in the sense that with successive samplings from the same population the magnitude of the mode tends to fluctuate a great deal more than does the median or mean. This point may be somewhat clearer if it is understood that a change in the magnitude of the group intervals could bring about a fairly substantial change in the magnitude of the mode.

TABLE 2. COMPUTATION OF THE MEDIAN

X	f	Cf
85–89	1	92
80–84	2	91
75–79	3	89
70–74		86
65–69	4	86
60–64	10	82
55–59	5	72
50–54	6	67
45–49	8	61
40–44	13	53
35–39	16	40
30–34	15	24
25–29	7	9
20–24	1	2
15–19	1	1

The Median. The point on a distribution below which 50 per cent of the cases fall is called the median (Mdn.). The median is particularly useful when describing a frequency distribution that has extreme scores and on this dimension is superior to the mean. In terms of its sampling stability, the median is superior to the mode but less efficient than the mean. Ease of computation makes the median a convenient technique to employ; it is not used more frequently because most statistical techniques have been derived for use with the mean.

We shall turn now to the computational procedures for determining the median.

1. Determine the appropriate class intervals for the data and set up a frequency table (see Table 2).

2. Next to the frequency column make another column and label it *Cf* (cumulative frequency). Starting at the bottom, add the frequencies for each class interval, placing each successive sum in the next row.

3. Since our concern is with the fiftieth percentile, we need to determine that score below which 50 per cent of the cases fall. To determine the exact number of cases up to the centile desired, multiply *N*, which is 92, by the value of the centile. In this case, 50 per cent of 92 is 46.

4. Examination of the *Cf* column reveals that by the time we get to the top of the 35 to 39 interval, we have 40 cases, but adding the frequency in the next step interval gives a sum greater than 46. Therefore, we know immediately that the desired score is somewhere in the interval 40 to 44. Now the problem is to determine what proportion of the cases in that interval will give us the required 46.

5. We need 6 cases from the next interval 40 to 44; the desired 46 less the 40 cases included below this interval. Since the frequency in the next interval is 13, we need $\frac{6}{13}$ or 0.46 of these cases.

6. The proportion of cases determined in step 5 is based on an interval width of 1, whereas our interval size is 5. Therefore, we must convert this proportion into units equal to the class size by multiplying it by $0.46 \times 5 = 2.30$.

7. Adding this figure to the bottom real limit of the interval, $39.5 + 2.30$ gives the desired median or fiftieth centile, 41.80.

$$\text{Mdn.} = 39.5 + \frac{6}{13}(5)$$
$$= 41.80$$

The Mean. The sum of all the separate scores divided by the total number of scores, denoted *N*, is the mean (*M*). The mean, in most situations, is the best measure of central tendency. It tends to fluctuate least from sample to sample and is used most frequently with other statistical techniques. One of the disadvantages of the mean is that it is influenced by extreme scores and may, if used without caution, suggest misleading generalizations. However, this disadvantage is outweighed by its advantages.

Computation of the mean or average is relatively straightforward and can be accomplished by means of the formula

$$M = \frac{\Sigma fX}{N} \tag{1}$$

where ΣfX = sum of the products of each score multiplied by the frequency with which it occurs

N = number of cases

When a calculator is not available and the number of cases is large, it is more convenient to compute the mean by means of coded scores. The formula for this technique is

$$M = AO + i\frac{\Sigma fx'}{N} \qquad (2)$$

where AO = arbitrary origin
$\quad\quad i$ = class interval
$\quad\quad \Sigma fx'$ = sum of the frequencies times coded score
$\quad\quad N$ = number of cases

The procedures implied by the formula first require the determination of an arbitrary origin which may be any class interval in the distribution. For the distribution shown in Table 3, the class interval 15 to 19 was selected as the arbitrary origin. On the assumption that the mean of the class interval approximates the mid-point of the interval, the value of AO would be 17. We can now deal with the distribution by giving each class interval from AO a coded score, ranging in this case from 0 to 14, and multiplying by the appropriate frequency. Dividing the sum of the coded scores by N and multiplying the result by 5 (the size of the class interval) gives us the mean of the coded scores in class interval units. Adding the AO to this value gives us the mean in the original score units.

$$M = 17 + 5\frac{525}{92}$$
$$= 17 + 28.55$$
$$= 45.55$$

The use of coded scores does not introduce any error into the final value of the mean, although some error will occur because of the class interval.

Measures of Variation. A description of any distribution requires some measure of the degree of dispersion or variability in that group. A teacher confronted with a group of children all of whom have the same IQ will be able to conduct her class quite differently from the teacher who has an IQ range in her class from, say, 80 to 140. Usually an investigator will attempt to minimize the degree of variability in his samples for those variables which are important to his results, but which, at the time, are of little interest. Generalizations must then, of course, be made only for other similar groups.

The Range. The range of scores in a distribution yields certain information about variability. However, this technique is quite unreliable since a change of performance of just one person can have a sizable effect on the magnitude of the range.

The Semi-interquartile Range. The semi-interquartile range, defined as $C_{75} - C_{25}/2$, is frequently reported as an index of dispersion. This measure, however, does not take into account the value of individual scores and completely overlooks those scores falling beyond the chosen centile points. For these reasons, this technique yields a less reliable measure of variability than the indices to be described below.

The Average Deviation. The average deviation *(AD)* is a more reliable estimate of variation than the foregoing procedures because its computation depends upon the deviation of all individual score values from the mean. An *AD* can be defined as the mean of the absolute deviations of each score around the mean of the distribution.

$$AD = \frac{\Sigma x}{N} \tag{3}$$

where x = deviation around the mean, regardless of direction or algebraic sign

TABLE 3. COMPUTATION OF THE MEAN AND STANDARD DEVIATION
USING CODED SCORES

X	f	x'	fx'	fx'²
85–89	1	14	14	196
80–84	2	13	26	338
75–79	3	12	36	432
70–74	0	11	00	000
65–69	4	10	40	400
60–64	10	9	90	810
55–59	5	8	40	320
50–54	6	7	42	294
45–49	8	6	48	288
40–44	13	5	65	325
35–39	16	4	64	256
30–34	15	3	45	135
25–29	7	2	14	28
20–24	1	1	1	1
15–19	1	0	0	0
	92	..	525	3,823

This technique is useful and meaningful in those situations where interest lies only in the numerical value and where no further statistical analysis involving other statistical techniques is desired. Careful examination of the definitional formula will reveal the reason for this serious limitation. Note that in determining Σx, no attention is paid to the direction of the deviations, which, of course, divests the *AD* of important algebraic properties.

The Standard Deviation. The standard deviation *(S)*, like the *AD*, is a stable estimate of the degree of variation, and its computation also includes all of the scores in the distribution. The standard deviation is defined as the square root of the mean of the squares of the deviations from the mean. Stated in symbolic form:

$$S = \sqrt{\frac{\Sigma x^2}{N - 1}} \qquad (4)$$

The essential term in formula (3) is Σx^2, which is the sum of the squared deviations around the mean and is usually referred to as the sum of squares. In contrast with the average deviation, the algebraic sign of the deviation (x) is maintained in computing S. Since the algebraic sum of the deviations around the mean is zero, these deviations are first squared and then summed. Such a procedure maintains the algebraic properties of S, permitting it therefore to enter into valid relationships with other statistics.

The most obvious approach to computing S would be to take each score, subtract it from the mean and square the difference. These squared deviations would then be summed, divided by $N - 1$, and the square root taken. There are fortunately several less tedious approaches which we shall now examine. If a calculator is available, the following formulas provide an efficient method of computation:

Step 1.   Compute the sum of squares:

$$\Sigma x^2 = \Sigma X^2 - \frac{(\Sigma X)^2}{N} \qquad (5)$$

where ΣX^2 = sum of squared scores
    $(\Sigma X)^2$ = sum of scores squared
Step 2.   Compute S:

$$S = \sqrt{\frac{\Sigma x^2}{N - 1}}$$

When a calculator is not available, it is more convenient to group the data in class intervals and work with coded scores as we did in the computation of the mean (see Table 3).

Step 1. Compute the sum of squares:

$$\Sigma x^2 = \left[\Sigma fx'^2 - \frac{(\Sigma fx')^2}{N} \right] i^2 \qquad (6)$$

where $\Sigma fx'^2$ = sum of the products of fx' multiplied by x'
    $\Sigma fx'$ = sum of the frequencies times the deviation from the arbitrary origin
    i^2 = square of the class interval size
Step 2. Compute S:

$$S = \sqrt{\frac{\Sigma x^2}{N - 1}}$$

The following computation is based on the distribution shown in Table 3.

Step 1

$$\Sigma x^2 = 3823 - \frac{(525)^2}{92} (5)^2$$
$$= 827.08 (25)$$
$$= 20677.00$$

Step 2

$$S = \sqrt{\frac{20677.00}{92 - 1}}$$
$$= 15.07$$

It should be noted that a correction term for coding and for the fact that the deviations were computed from the AO rather than the mean is included in formula (6).

In working with the standard deviation, it is possible to add or subtract a constant from all the scores without changing the magnitude of S. This holds true because the addition of a constant to every score not only increases each score but also increases the mean by the value of the constant. Under these conditions the magnitude of the deviation of any score from the mean remains unchanged. Such is not the case, however, when a constant is multiplied or divided into each score. The student should reason why the effect of multiplying would be to increase the size of S by the size of the multiplier.

The standard deviation is preferred over the other indices of variation because it has algebraic relationships with other statistical methods and with the normal probability curve, because it gives extra weight to extreme scores, and because it gives a stable estimate of the population variation.

Transformation of Scores. One important application of the standard deviation is related to the problem of determining relative position. Suppose a sixth-grader obtains a raw score of 70 on both an arithmetic test and a vocabulary test. In addition, assume that the means of the two distributions are 50, with a standard deviation of 10 for arithmetic and 15 for vocabulary. In order to determine relative standing on the two tests, the scores could be converted into standard deviation units; i.e., put the original raw scores on a scale wherein the means and standard deviations are identical. The resulting scores are called Z scores, and are computed as follows:

$$Z = \frac{X - M}{S} = \frac{x}{S} \tag{7}$$

where X = raw score
M = mean
S = standard deviation
x = deviation of score from its mean
Z = deviation of score from its mean in standard deviation units

A Z score or standard score has a mean of 0 and a standard deviation of 1. The solution to our hypothetical problem, following formula (7), would lead to the conclusion

Arithmetic	*Vocabulary*

$$Z = \frac{70 - 50}{10} = 2.00 \qquad\qquad Z = \frac{70 - 50}{15} = 1.33$$

that the child's relative standing was superior in arithmetic. It can be seen that any raw score above the mean of its distribution will have a positive value and any score below the mean will have a negative value.

A variation of the Z score, designed to overcome the negative scores, is a technique called the T score. The T score is simply another transformation of the original scale, this time to one with a mean of 50 and an S of 10. The formula for computing the T score is

$$T = \frac{X - M}{S}(10) + 50 \qquad\qquad\qquad (8)$$

In terms of the foregoing problem, the student would have a T score of 63.33 in vocabulary and 70 in arithmetic.

SCALE VALUES FOR VOCABULARY TEST

Original scores	5	20	35	50	65	80	95
Sigma scores	−3	−2	−1	0	1	2	3
T scores	20	30	40	50	60	70	80

Centiles. Centiles provide a technique for those situations where rankings are sufficient but where the distances between ranks are of no concern. A centile or percentile is a point on a distribution of scores below which a certain percentage of cases fall. The symbol for centile is a large C with a subscript to denote the specific point; i.e., C_{52} is the fifty-second centile; C_{90} the ninetieth centile, etc. Some centiles are given special labels. C_{25} is referred to as the first or lower quartile; C_{75} as the third or upper quartile. C_{50} may be called the second quartile, the fifth decile, the median, or the fiftieth centile. (The logic underlying these various terms is left to the student.) The important point is that a centile is a point on a distribution above or below which a certain proportion of area or cases lie.

The Unit Normal Curve. The normal probability curve, or bell-shaped curve, is a theoretical frequency distribution derived from the laws of chance. Many, though by no means all, of the attributes measured in education and psychology approximate the normal curve distribution. The unit normal curve has a mean of zero and a standard deviation of 1. From this bit of information it should be clear that the curve is actually made up of the theoretical frequencies with which various values of Z will occur in the population.   The student should note that the scale along the abscissa is in sigma units identical to those discussed earlier in this section.   Since there exists a known theoretical relationship between these points along the abscissa and frequency, it is reasonable to expect that specific statements can be made concerning the proportion of cases to be expected above or below a specific ordinate.   Table A (Appendix A) consists of the relative frequencies to be expected for each sigma value (column labeled ordinate) and also the proportion of cases to be expected between the mean and the Z score (column labeled area).   The proportion of cases beyond the Z-score value is given in column 3.

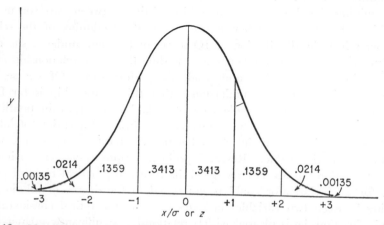

Fig. 18. Normal curve showing areas between ordinates at different values of *x/σ* or *z. From George A. Ferguson, Statistical Analysis in Psychology and Education, New York: McGraw-Hill Book Company, Inc., 1959, p.* 81.

If the researcher is interested in determining the proportion of cases to be expected between the mean and one sigma, he would enter Table A and find the number 1.00 in the first column and then, under column A, he would see 0.341, which is the expected proportion of cases.   We can also reason that a person 1 standard deviation above the mean exceeds 84.1 per cent of the cases since the proportion of cases below the mean must be 50 per cent.   Since the curve is symmetrical, it is obvious that the same area relationships exist for scores below the mean.   Hence, a Z score of —2.70 would include 49.6 per cent of the area between M and x/S.   When normal curve properties are used in this way, centile ranks can be estimated, as well as expected proportions between ordinates (see Figure 18).

The student who attempts to test some of the foregoing assertions concerning area relationships in the normal curve is apt to be disturbed by the discrepancies between his data and those protected by the normal curve.

However, it must be remembered that the theoretical proportions are derived on the assumption that N is extremely large and that the shape of the distribution is normal or nearly so. With small samples, these conditions cannot be met. Nevertheless, the foregoing discussion about the normal curve is essential if the student is to understand the notions underlying statistical inference, a topic to be discussed in detail in the following chapter.

MEASURES OF RELATIONSHIP

Our discussion to this point has been concerned exclusively with the distribution of a single variable. Very frequently, however, there is interest in examining the degree of relationship existing between two (or more) variables. For example, when a teacher, at the beginning of the school year, examines the distribution of IQ scores of her new students, she does so with the more or less implicit understanding that some relationship exists between intellectual ability and academic performance. Of course, the more sophisticated teacher understands that this relationship is far from perfect and that an innumerable array of variables enter into the prediction of academic performance. Such problems as this, and a variety of others, which commonly appear in the educational literature, have a certain practical utilitarian value. Research problems appropriately employing indices of relationship are not restricted, however, to practical types of problems, for an investigator could be interested in the degree of relationship existing between two variables in terms of some theoretical consideration. In this situation, he is pleased with a relationship significantly greater than zero, though he would not be willing to make predictions of individual behavior on the basis of the correlation. Rather, having found the relationship to exist, he would follow through with an experimental investigation in an effort to examine the properties of the variable under more rigorous conditions.

The Product Moment Correlation Coefficient r. When an investigator is concerned with the degree of relationship existing between *two continuous essentially normally distributed variables,* the product moment correlation, denoted by the letter r, is usually the best statistic to employ. An r can be defined as the mean of the cross products of the standard scores; in symbols this would be

$$r = \frac{\Sigma Z_x Z_y}{N} \tag{9}$$

The magnitude of r ranges from a perfect negative relationship ($r = -1.00$) or positive relationship ($r = +1.00$) to no relationship at all ($r = 0.00$). Since it is extremely rare that an r ever reaches unity, the student is probably wondering what magnitude of r can be considered adequate. This question, however, requires an understanding of the interpretations and assumptions underlying the technique and will be postponed until the more basic issues are presented.

Computation of r. A variety of formulas exist for the computation of r, each of which will appear rather forbidding to the beginning student. An attempt will be made here to demonstrate that these formulas are all derived from the basic definition given in formula (9). These derivations involve relationships already known to the reader and can be reviewed as necessary. Nevertheless, in order that the student understand correlation, he must apply himself most rigorously to this next section.

The numerator term of formula (9) contains standard scores for the X and Y variables. Though this formula can be used in computing r, computing two Z scores for each individual is quite tedious. However, we already know that $Z_x = (X - \overline{X})/S_x$ and that $Z_y = (Y - \overline{Y})/S_y$. Substituting these terms we obtain

$$r = \frac{\Sigma(X - \overline{X})(Y - \overline{Y})}{NS_xS_y}$$

$$r = \frac{\Sigma xy}{NS_xS_y} \tag{10}$$

Substituting already known expressions for S_x and S_y in the denominator and combining terms results in

$$r = \frac{\Sigma xy}{\sqrt{\Sigma x^2 \Sigma y^2}}$$

where it can be shown that

$$\Sigma xy = \Sigma XY - \frac{(\Sigma X)(\Sigma Y)}{N}$$

$$\Sigma x^2 = \Sigma X^2 - \frac{(\Sigma X)^2}{N}$$

$$\Sigma y^2 = \Sigma Y^2 - \frac{(\Sigma Y)^2}{N}$$

Finally, taking advantage of the relationships described above, we arrive at the commonly used formula for computing r on the basis of *raw scores:*

$$r = \frac{\Sigma XY - (\Sigma X)(\Sigma Y)/N}{\sqrt{\Sigma X^2 - (\Sigma X)^2/N} \ \sqrt{\Sigma Y^2 - (\Sigma Y)^2/N}} \tag{11}$$

which is merely another form of formula (9).

If a calculating machine is not available, the arithmetical operations required in formula (11) will be prohibitive. Fortunately, procedures have been worked out for computing r using coded scores similar to that used for computation of the standard deviation and the mean. Indeed, careful examination of the procedures described below will immediately show that only one new operation is required in computing an r, i.e., the numerator, $\Sigma x'y'$. An example problem using real data is presented below.

Scores obtained by 92 students on the Verbal Scale of the Primary Mental Abilities (PMA) and their performance on an achievement test some three and one-half years later have been recorded in Table 4, which is called

TABLE 4. BIVARIATE FREQUENCY

Intervals	5–6	7–8	9–10	11–12	13–14	15–16	17–18	19–20	21–22	23–24	25–26	27–28	29–30	31–32	(1) f	(2) y'	(3) fy'	(4) fy'^2	(5) $\Sigma x'y'$	(6) $y'\Sigma x'y'$
85–89													/		1	14	14	196	12	168
80–84								/						/	2	13	26	338	21	273
75–79									/	/				/	3	12	36	432	34	408
70–74															0	11	0	0	0	0
65–69						//			//						4	10	40	400	32	320
60–64			/		/	//		/	/		/	/	/	/	10	9	90	810	77	693
55–59						//	//				/				5	8	40	320	32	256
50–54	/				/	/	/	/						/	6	7	42	294	35	245
45–49					/			//	/				/	//	7	6	42	252	64	384
40–44		//	//	/	//	//	//	//			/				14	5	70	350	77	385
35–39		//	/	/// /	/		/// /	/	/	/					16	4	64	256	71	284
30–34	/		//	//	/	/// //	//		//						15	3	45	135	67	201
25–29	///	/	/					/	/						7	2	14	28	16	32
20–24		/													1	1	1	1	1	1
15–19					/										1	0	0	0	4	0
$f(1)$	4	5	7	7	10	12	11	11	7	1	5	3	5	4	92		524	3,812	543	3,650
$x'(2)$	0	1	2	3	4	5	6	7	8	9	10	11	12	13			$\Sigma y'$	$\Sigma y'^2$		$\Sigma x'y'$
$fx'(3)$	0	5	14	21	40	60	66	77	56	9	50	33	60	52	543 $\Sigma x'$					
$fx'^2(4)$	0	5	28	63	160	300	396	539	448	81	500	363	720	676	4,279 $\Sigma x'^2$					
$\Sigma y'x'(5)$	9	18	31	28	46	66	65	56	35	13	49	26	49	33	524					
$x'\Sigma y'x'(6)$	0	18	62	84	184	330	390	392	280	117	490	286	588	429	3,650 $\Sigma x'y'$					

X = Verbal ability

Y = Achievement

a *bivariate frequency distribution.* The coded score formula for computing *r* is

$$r = \frac{\Sigma x'y' - (\Sigma x')(\Sigma y')/N}{\sqrt{[\Sigma x'^2 - (\Sigma x')^2/N][\Sigma y'^2 - (\Sigma y')^2/N]}} \qquad (11a)$$

for which we shall now derive the necessary values. Note that columns 1 through 4 in this table are those already familiar from our discussion of the standard deviation and are used here in precisely the same manner. To compute the numerator terms, $\Sigma x'y'$, we first need to determine the values in column 5 and row 5. Each entry in the column is the sum of x' values for a constant value of y'; each row entry is the sum of the y' values for a constant value of x'. Thus for a y' value of 12, the sum of the x' values would be $13 + 11 + 10 = 34$. For an x' value of 11, the sum of the y' values would be $12 + 9 + 5 = 26$. The entries in column and row 6 are the products of columns or rows 2 and 5, the summation of which yields the required term. Substituting this number in formula (11a) we obtain

$$r = \frac{3,650 - (543)(524)/92}{\sqrt{[4,279 - (543)^2/92][3,812 - (524)^2/92]}}$$
$$r = .58$$

Interpretations of *r.* Galton observed that when he plotted the medians of the columns and rows of his bivariate distribution, they formed essentially straight lines, which he labeled *lines of regression.* Regression lines may be defined as the rate of change in one variable as the other varies. Here then is one of the important interpretations of *r*, *rate of change,* which shall now be considered.

Rate of Change. Unfortunately, Galton's row and column medians did not produce a perfect straight line, the degree of variation being dependent upon sampling errors and the linearity of relationship existing between the variables. This latter restriction, linearity, must be assumed in working with the product moment *r*, and specific tests exist by which the assumption can be tested (3:268–275). Sampling fluctuations, however, must be dealt with in some systematic way so that the determination of regression lines will be consistent among investigators.

Line of Best Fit. Logic argues that the best positions of the lines of regression are such that the sums of squares (Σx^2) of the errors (residuals) around the lines are a minimum. On the basis of our assumption of linearity of regression, we know that the basic equation of regression lines takes the form

$$X = BY + A$$
$$Y = BX + A$$

where X or Y = predicted score
$\qquad B$ = slope of the regression line
X or Y = score for which a prediction is to be made
$\qquad A$ = a constant

or in deviation units, where the constant is no longer required because the origin of the regression lines is at the point where the X and Y axes meet,

$$\bar{x} = by \qquad \bar{y} = bx$$

for which we need to determine the equation for determining the value of the slope of the regression line. Recall that we want the slope of this line to be such that it minimizes errors of prediction. The derivation stems from the calculus and results in the equation

$$b_{yx} = r\frac{s_y}{s_x} \qquad (12)$$

for the slope of the line of y on x. Similarly

$$b_{xy} = r\frac{s_x}{s_y} \qquad (12a)$$

which is the equation for the slope of the line of x on y. By simple algebraic manipulation, we can rewrite formulas (12) and (12a) in a form already familiar to the reader from his computation of r:

Substituting in (12) the following value of r:

$$r = \frac{\Sigma xy}{Ns_x s_y}$$

we obtain

$$b_{yx} = \frac{\Sigma xy}{Ns_x s_y}\frac{s_y}{s_x}$$

Multiplying the two terms, we have

$$\frac{\Sigma xy}{Ns^2x}x \qquad \text{where } S_x{}^2 = \frac{\Sigma x^2}{N}$$

Dividing by N,

$$b_{yx} = \frac{\Sigma xy}{\Sigma x^2}x$$

and in similar fashion

$$b_{xy} = \frac{\Sigma xy}{\Sigma y^2}y$$

Substituting the appropriate values from the problem in Table 4, the slope of the line of y on x is 0.67 and of x on y is 0.52.

$$b_{yx} = \frac{\Sigma xy}{\Sigma x^2} x = \frac{\Sigma x'y' - (\Sigma x')(\Sigma y')/N}{\Sigma x'^2 - (\Sigma x')^2/N} x = \frac{557.26}{827.14} x = 0.67x$$

$$b_{xy} = \frac{\Sigma xy}{\Sigma y^2} y = \frac{\Sigma x'y' - (\Sigma x')(\Sigma y')/N}{\Sigma y'^2 - (\Sigma y')^2/N} y = \frac{557.26}{1073.87} y = 0.52y$$

Once the slopes of the regression lines are determined, points on the surface of the bivariate plot can be determined by which the individual lines of regression are drawn. Each of these points is actually a predicted score. The formulas for predicted scores, in raw score form, are

$$Y = \bar{Y} + b_{yx}(X - \bar{X})$$
$$X = \bar{X} + b_{xy}(Y - \bar{Y})$$

Several such points can be determined in Table 4 and the regression lines drawn. In order to understand better the concept of regression, it would be helpful to plot several of these points on your own.

Accuracy of Prediction. In predicting any score in that situation where these correlations are less than unity, it should be obvious that errors in prediction will be made. Assessment of the magnitude of such expected errors is the problem discussed in this section.

Suppose you were called on to predict a child's Arithmetic Achievement score from a knowledge of his aptitude score. Further let us imagine that the correlation is zero. The best prediction you could make under these conditions would be the mean of the Achievement scores where the amount of variation due to errors in prediction would be the standard deviation. As the magnitude of r increased, there would be less dependence on the mean, less error in prediction, and consequently, the degree of variation attributable to error would be smaller. When r achieves unity, no error in predictions could be made.

Since we are making predictions on the basis of the regression line, it is reasonable that we can determine the magnitude of our expected deviation (error) from this line of "best fit." This statistic is called the *standard error of estimate.* The manipulation requires the assumptions of linearity of regression—that the variation around the regression line is essentially equal (the term to describe this condition is homoscedasticity), and that the scores are normally distributed around the lines of regression. When these assumptions are met, it can be shown that the standard error of estimate for predicting Y from a knowledge of X is

$$S_{yx} = \sqrt{\frac{\Sigma(y - \bar{y})^2}{N - 2}}$$
$$S_{yx} = S_y \sqrt{1 - r^2}$$

(13)

and that the standard error of estimate for predicting x from a knowledge of y is

$$S_{xy} = \sqrt{\frac{\Sigma(x - \bar{x})^2}{N - 2}}$$

$$S_{xy} = S_x \sqrt{1 - r^2}$$

(13a)

In the problem presented in Table 4, the S_{yx} for a predicted Y score would be

$$S_{yx} = 15.16 \sqrt{1 - (.58)^2}$$

$$= 12.28$$

The interpretation of the standard error of estimate is similar to that of the standard deviation. For example, in the present problem if a Y score of 41.66 had been predicted, then 68 times in 100, the actual score would be within the limits 41.66 ± 12.28.

A final note concerning the standard error of estimate. The term $\sqrt{1 - r^2}$ in formulas (13) and (13a) obviously reduces the magnitude of S; the greater the r, the greater the reduction in S. This term is called the *coefficient of alienation* and plays an integral role in the interpretation of r. Of note is the fact that an r of .866 is required before the error-of-estimate is reduced by half.

Variance. In many correlational problems we are interested in the degree to which a knowledge of a person's performance on variable X is related to his performance on variable Y. It has already been demonstrated that when r is less than unity, errors in prediction will occur. The total amount of variation in the criterion variable (Y) may be thought of as including not only the variance unaccounted for, $S_{yx}{}^2$, but also the variance $S_{y'}{}^2$ which is accounted for from a knowledge of X. Dividing both sources of variation by the total variation and assuming linearity of regression, we obtain

$$\frac{S_{yx}{}^2}{S_y{}^2} + \frac{S_{y'}{}^2}{S_y{}^2} = 1$$

(14)

Recall that

$$S_{yx}{}^2 = S_y{}^2 (1 - r^2)$$

which becomes

$$\frac{S_{yx}{}^2}{S_y{}^2} = 1 - r^2$$

and when we substitute this value in (14), we have

$$1 = S_{y'}{}^2 + 1 - r^2$$

$$r^2 = \frac{S_{y'}{}^2}{S_y{}^2}$$

(15)

Stated in words, the correlation coefficient squared gives the proportion of the total variation in Y which is attributable to variation in X. For example, in our problem, the r of .58 permits the conclusion that 34 per cent of the variation in either variable is accounted for from a knowledge of the other variable. Caution needs to be exercised here concerning interpretations of cause and effect. It would seem to make good sense in our problem to state that of the total variation on the achievement test, 34 per cent of it is attributable to variation on the Verbal Scale of the PMA. However, another equally logical possibility is that variation in verbal abilities is attributable to variation on the achievement score. Another source of concern in making too glib interpretations of cause and effect is the possibility that variation in both X and Y can be attributed to still a third variable. The student should carefully think through the logic of his correlation problem rather than have his thinking guided by the magnitude of the statistic.

OTHER MEASURES OF RELATIONSHIP

In certain situations, the investigator may have reason to suspect that a third variable, related to both X and Y, is influencing the magnitude of an obtained r. For example, he may have found a surprisingly high r between aptitude and achievement. Examination of the sample suggests that age may be the variable which is spuriously raising the magnitude of the r. What is needed is a product moment r from which the effect of a third variable has been removed or partialed out.

Partial r. If the assumption of linearity of regression of X_1 on X_3 and X_2 on X_3 is tenable, then it can be shown that formula (16) will give us the required r.

$$r_{12.3} = \frac{r_{12} - r_{13}r_{23}}{\sqrt{1 - r_{13}^2}\ \sqrt{1 - r_{23}^2}} \qquad (16)$$

The $r_{12.3}$ is read as the correlation between variables one and two with the effect of three held constant, i.e., partialed out. The foregoing formula is not as simple to understand as the familiar symbols may lead one to believe. Actually, this formula is the same as expressing each individual's X_1 and X_2 score as a deviation from the mean of the X_3 variable; the effect of X_3 does not enter into the computations. For example, if we are interested in the correlation between verbal ability and achievement with the effect of age partialed out, we would need to determine the deviation of each verbal ability score and each achievement score from the mean of the respective age group and then correlate the pairs of deviations.

Obviously, when the effect of X_3 is positive and large, the resulting partial r will be reduced, whereas if the X_3 has little effect on X_1 and X_2, the partial

r will be of approximately the same magnitude as r_{12}. However, when the relationship between X_3 and either X_1 or X_2 is negative, the resulting partial r will be larger than the zero-order r.

Multiple R. We saw earlier in the discussion of the product moment r that verbal ability as measured on the PMA does a fair job in predicting performance on an achievement test. However, a more accurate prediction would be possible if another test score were used in combination with verbal ability. Actually, the foregoing assertion is tenable under certain conditions which unfortunately are not easily attained. Putting these required conditions aside for the moment, however, our problem is to place the predictor variables in combination such as to minimize the errors of predicting performance on the criterion variable.

The procedures involved in the multiple R, $R_{1.23} \cdots n$ serve to maximize predictive power by the assignment of optimal weights. In the notation used in this presentation, X_1 is the criterion variable; X_2, X_3, $\ldots$, n are the predictor variables. Defining the problem in symbolic form,

$$X_1' = B_2 X_2 + B_3 X_3 + \cdots + B_N X_N + A$$

and in deviation units,

$$X_1' = b_2 x_2 + b_3 x_3 + \cdots + b_n x_n$$

In these equations, the B or b represents the slope which a plane makes with its individual axis. Concerning ourselves for the moment with a three-variable problem, the student should attempt to visualize a cube through which a plane with slope B_2 and B_3 passes, cutting the X_2 axis and the X_3 axis. The required slope of this plane is readily derived if we work with standard scores

$$Z_1' = \beta_2 Z_2 + \beta_3 Z_3$$

wherein β is a beta weight and is identical in meaning to B or b. In order to get the optimal weighting for Z_2,

$$\beta_2 = \frac{r_{12} - r_{13} r_{23}}{1 - r^2_{23}} \qquad (17)$$

and for Z_3,

$$\beta_3 = \frac{r_{13} - r_{12} r_{23}}{1 - r^2_{23}} \qquad (17a)$$

With these terms we can now define $R_{1.23}$:

$$R_{1.23} = \sqrt{\beta_2 r_{12} + \beta_3 r_{13}} \qquad (18)$$

The interpretations permitted with $R_{1.23}$ are identical to those with the product moment r. With respect to accuracy of prediction, the standard error of estimate for a predicted score is

$$S_{1.23} = S_1 \sqrt{1 - R^2_{1.23}} \qquad (19)$$

A brief numerical example should help to point up some of the logic underlying the use of multiple predictors. Recall that an r of .58 was reported between verbal ability and achievement. Suppose now that we were to include reasoning ability score from the same PMA in our prediction of achievement. The relevant terms are X_1 = achievement score, X_2 = verbal ability score, X_3 = reasoning ability score. The following correlations were obtained:

$$r_{12} = .58 \qquad r_{13} = .36 \qquad r_{23} = .42$$

The required beta weights are computed below:

$$\beta_2 = \frac{.58 - .36(.42)}{1 - (.42)^2} = .52$$

$$\beta_3 = \frac{.36 - .58(.42)}{1 - (.42)^2} = .15$$

When the beta weights are known, the value of $R_{1.23}$ is

$$R_{1.23} = \sqrt{.52(.58) + .15(.36)}$$
$$= .59$$

Unfortunately, the additional labor seems to have added very little to our ability to predict achievement. Why? Inspection of the r's suggests that the overlap between the two predictors is greater than the relationship between X_1 and X_2; i.e., X_3 accounts for little, if any, of the variance in X_1 which has not already been accounted for by X_2. Suppose, however, that r_{23} were only .10. Then β_2 would be .55 and β_3 would be .30, resulting in an R of .65. Suppose in the first problem $r_{23} = .42$, what effect would this have on $R_{1.23}$? Why?

Multiple R's can be worked out for any number of predictor variables, though the increase in precision is usually not sufficiently large to warrant the great effort required in adding several variables. Basically, the same problem of determining beta weights holds for the solution of a multiple R when there are more than three variables. However, the solution is not achieved as readily as with the three-variable problem, since it requires the solution of simultaneous equations. (For a discussion of this solution the student should see 3:178–185.) However, interpretations remain the same for the three-variable problem.

The interpretation and uses of a multiple R are dependent upon the investigator's purposes and the logic underlying the problem. There are however, several potential pitfalls in the use of the multiple R. For example, suppose an investigator has as many as ten possible predictors and decides to use only those five which correlate highest with the criterion. This procedure is not legitimate because the magnitude of the five correlations may have occurred by chance alone, so that repetition of the study, using a different sample, would likely produce a different set of variables.   It is important, therefore, that any multiple prediction equation be cross-validated on at least two additional samples in an effort to determine the consistency of the beta values. This step is often discouraging because consistency is difficult to achieve.   Nevertheless, the step is crucial if any real confidence can be achieved in the results and their general application.

Biserial r.   Many times in the development of a test, the investigator wishes to determine if a specific item discriminates between high and low performers on the over-all test score.   In other words, what we want to know is the degree of relationship existing between performance on a particular item and performance on the test as a whole.   If the assumption that continuity underlies the division between passing and failing an item is met, then the biserial *r*, r_b, can be used to assess the relationship.   Actually r_b is an estimate of *r* for the situation where one variable is continuous and the second is dichotomized.   The formula for computing r_b is

$$r_b = \frac{M_L - M_S}{S_t} \frac{pq}{y} \tag{20}$$

where M_L = mean of the group who passed the item
   M_S = mean of the group who failed the item
   S_t = standard deviation of the entire distribution of scores
   p, q = proportion of subjects either passing (p) or failing (q) the item
   y = height of the ordinate on the normal curve at p or q

In addition to the assumption of underlying continuity in the dichotomized variable, the data for an r_b should meet the usual assumptions for the product moment correlation *r*.   Fairly good estimates of *r* can be achieved if these assumptions are met and if the proportions (p and q) are not more extreme than .10 or .90.

Point Biserial r.   The point biserial r_{b_p} is designed for those situations in which the assumption of underlying continuity in the dichotomized variable is not tenable.   Computation of r_{b_p} requires the following formula:

$$r_{b_p} = \frac{(M_2 - M_1)\sqrt{P_1 P_2}}{S_y} \tag{21}$$

Point biserial *r*'s are smaller than the corresponding biserial, with the least difference occurring when P_1 and P_2 are .50.   The assumptions required for r_b, except for underlying continuity, are required for r_{b_p}.

Tetrachoric r.   In the brief discussion of the biserial *r*, it was assumed that one of the variables was continuous, and the second variable, though dichotomized, had underlying continuity.   Sometimes it develops that both variables have been dichotomized and that the assumption of underlying continuity is reasonable for both variables.   When this situation exists, and when all of the usual assumptions of product moment r are met, the degree of relationship can be assessed by means of the tetrachoric r, r_t.

Situations in which r_t would be appropriate are rare. In addition, if it is at all feasible to use the product moment r, one should do so because the sampling errors involved in r_t are much larger than for r; hence, one can place far more confidence in a product moment r than tetrachoric r computed from the same data.

TABLE 5. FOURFOLD CONTINGENCY TABLE

A	B
C	D

Phi Coefficient. Recall that the point biserial does not require the assumption of underlying continuity in the dichotomized variable. The phi coefficient is designed for those situations where both variables have been dichotomized and for which the assumption is made that these are points in a situation without underlying continuity. For example, one might be interested in knowing if a relationship exists between two items on a test, where the items are arbitrarily scored 0 or 1. A contingency table could be set up as shown in Table 5 and appropriate entries made. Then substituting in formula (22), an estimate of the relationship could be obtained. The most frequent use of phi coefficient is the statistical analysis of tests.

$$\phi = \frac{BC - AD}{\sqrt{(A + B)(C + D)(A + C)(B + D)}} \tag{22}$$

The Correlation Ratio Eta.   One of the basic assumptions underlying the use of the correlational techniques already described is that of linearity of regression.   The line of least squares provides the best estimate of predicted scores even though the column (row) means diverge somewhat from this line.   Actually, we ascribe such discrepancies to chance errors.   However, if one were interested in the correlation between speed of reaction and chronological age, where age is taken over a large range, the array means would probably not even approximate a straight line.   In this situation, the use of regression lines derived from the assumption of linearity would fail to give a valid estimate of the degree of correlation present between the variables.   Rather than making use of the regression lines, the means of the arrays are employed and the standard errors of estimate are derived from the means.

In computing eta (η), the assumption that the errors of estimate for both variables are equal is not valid.   Hence, it is necessary to compute two etas, one describing the relationship of X to Y and the other of Y to X. Eta square, descriptive of the prediction of X from Y, is given in formula (23) and the eta square for predicting Y from X is given in (23a).

$$\eta_{xy}^2 = 1 - \frac{S_{ax}^2}{S_x^2} \tag{23}$$

$$\eta_{yx}^2 = 1 - \frac{S_{ay}^2}{S_y^2} \tag{23a}$$

From these formulas it can be seen that eta square is defined as the ratio of the variance of each array mean about the mean of the arrays to the total variance.

The foregoing abbreviated discussion should suggest to the reader the importance of determining the kind of relationships, linear or other, existing between the variables under consideration.   Perhaps the easiest way to do this is to plot the data on a bivariate distribution.   More precise statistical techniques exist, however, to determine if departure from linearity is greater than chance (2:268–275).

RANK CORRELATION METHODS

Many times in educational research it is not possible to obtain scores as such on one or more of the attributes of concern, although it may be possible to order the attributes in terms of rankings.   When such a procedure is feasible, one of the several rank correlation procedures may be applicable (3).

Spearman's Rho. As an example of a rank correlation procedure, we have chosen Spearman's rank-difference correlation technique, rho, as defined in formula (24).

$$\rho = 1 - \frac{6 \Sigma D^2}{N(N^2 - 1)} \tag{24}$$

The only new term in this formula is *D*, which signifies the difference between an individual's ranking on the two variables.   The data in Table 6

TABLE 6. RANK ORDER CORRELATION OF PERFORMANCE
ON TWO CHILD PSYCHOLOGY EXAMINATIONS *

Student	X_1	X_2	Rank 1	Rank 2	D	D^2
A	20	53	7.5	11.0	−3.5	12.25
B	17	33	3.5	3.0	.5	.25
C	10	28	1.0	1.5	− .5	.25
D	11	28	2.0	1.5	.5	.25
E	27	60	12.5	13.0	− .5	.25
F	19	52	6.0	10.0	−4.0	16.00
G	20	47	7.5	7.0	.5	.25
H	24	40	10.5	4.0	6.5	42.25
I	27	44	12.5	6.0	6.5	42.25
J	18	43	5.0	5.0	0.0	0.00
K	21	54	9.0	12.0	−3.0	9.00
L	24	51	10.5	9.0	1.5	2.25
M	17	48	3.5	8.0	−4.5	20.25
					0.0	145.50

* These are error scores; therefore a low score indicates good performance.

are ranks based upon the scores achieved by thirteen students in a child psychology course.   Substituting in formula (2) we obtain

$$\rho = 1 - \frac{6(145.50)}{13(169 - 1)}$$
$$= 1 - .40$$
$$= .60$$

Note that the algebraic sum of the differences between ranks is zero and therefore provides a check on arithmetic.   The obtained rho of .60 is comparable in meaning and magnitude to *r*, although rho is usually somewhat smaller.   Even though the interpretation of rho and *r* is comparable, rho does not possess the mathematical properties of *r* and hence is limited in its usefulness.

Rank data do not necessarily have to be derived from scores; rankings of judges are also permissible. In either event, the problem will arise where a discrimination between two or more people is deemed impossible. When such ties in ranking occur, the standard procedure is to average the successive ranks involved. For example, in the case of subjects A and G on Examination I, the rank of 7.5 is the average of ranks 7 and 8. A three-way tie, say for rank 6, would be $6 + 7 + 8 \div 3$; or 7. An excessive number of ties tends to distort the magnitude of rho, though procedures for correcting the effect are available (1:25–36).

Spearman's rho is most often employed in those situations where N, the number of pairs, is less than 30. Though rho cannot be used in place of the product moment r in the mathematical determination of accuracy of prediction, line of best fit, or variance, rho does provide a convenient estimate of the product moment r.

BIBLIOGRAPHY

1. Kendall, M., *Rank Correlation Methods,* 2d ed. London: Charles Griffin & Co., Ltd., 1948.

2. McNemar, Q., *Psychological Statistics.* New York: John Wiley & Sons, Inc., 1955.

3. Stevens, S. S. (ed.), *Handbook of Experimental Psychology.* New York: John Wiley & Sons, Inc., 1951, chap. 1.

CHAPTER 14

Inferential Statistics

BY WILLIAM J. MEYER

In the preceding chapter the procedures for describing the attributes of a sample were presented. However, for most research purposes, if not all, the investigator is concerned with the generalizability of the data beyond that of the immediate sample. Stated somewhat differently, the investigator does not make inferences from the sample data to an entire population with the assertion that *all* the members of the population will conform exactly to the sample. In general, he asserts that they will be similar to the sample, as in terms of the mean and standard deviation. The problems examined in this chapter are concerned primarily with the degree to which such inferences from samples to populations are appropriate and with the degree of error that can be expected when such inferences are made.

SAMPLING THEORY

On the assumption that the purpose of a particular study is to draw inferences of the kind described above, certain important theoretical issues must be considered. If all the members of a *population* (*universe, aggregate*), defined as all the members belonging to a specified group, were included in a study, there would be no need for statistical inferences because the mean of this group would be the population value.[1] Typically it is impossible to have available all members of a population, so that one is forced to draw *random samples* from the population and, on the basis of these samples, estimate the population value. Samples and sampling then assume important roles in research and statistical analysis. A random sample is one in which each member of the defined population has an equal chance of being selected, and the selection of one member in no way influences the selection of another.

---

[1] Technically this statement is not correct because the presence of unreliability in the measuring instrument, intrasubject variability, etc., will affect the mean.

The Standard Error of a Statistic. Having drawn a random sample and computed the desired descriptive statistics, it is possible to determine the stability of the obtained sample value, i.e., accuracy in the estimate of the population value.[2] The primary question here concerns the amount of fluctuation of the statistic to be expected from sample to sample and is dependent upon such factors as the sample size (the larger the sample, the less fluctuation); the statistic employed, (the mean being the most stable measure of central tendency); the degree of variation of the attribute measured existing in the population (the greater the interindividual variation, the greater the probability that extreme cases will occur in any particular sample). The amount of fluctuation or variation of a sample statistic is called the *standard error of the statistic.* Actually the standard error of a statistic is the standard deviation of the distribution of sample statistics.

The Standard Error of a Proportion and a Frequency. One of the difficulties in understanding the concept of the standard error is the fact that in most instances it is not possible to observe directly the distribution of the statistic. This is not the case with respect to proportions or frequencies because, on the basis of knowing the population values of the proportion P and the number of observations included in the sample, it is possible to describe the expected frequency distribution by means of the binomial distribution. For example, in a coin-tossing experiment the proportion P of heads expected by chance is .50, and, of course, the proportion Q of tails expected by chance is also .50, so that $P + Q = 1.00$. Defining a single sample as five tosses of the coin, the binomial distribution $(P + Q)^n$ would be

$$\left(\frac{1}{2}+\frac{1}{2}\right)^5 = \left(\frac{1}{2}\right)^5 + 5\left(\frac{1}{2}\right)^4\left(\frac{1}{2}\right) + \frac{5\cdot4}{1\cdot2}\left(\frac{1}{2}\right)^3\left(\frac{1}{2}\right)^2 + \frac{5\cdot4\cdot3}{1\cdot2\cdot3}\left(\frac{1}{2}\right)^2\left(\frac{1}{2}\right)^3$$

$$+\frac{5\cdot4\cdot3\cdot2}{1\cdot2\cdot3\cdot4}\left(\frac{1}{2}\right)\left(\frac{1}{2}\right)^4 + \frac{5\cdot4\cdot3\cdot2\cdot1}{1\cdot2\cdot3\cdot4\cdot5}\left(\frac{1}{2}\right)^5 = 1.00$$

$$= \tfrac{1}{32} + \tfrac{5}{32} + \tfrac{10}{32} + \tfrac{10}{32} + \tfrac{5}{32} + \tfrac{1}{32} = 1.00$$

which is the frequency of occurrence of all possible events. In Table 7 are the theoretical frequencies with which five heads in five tosses of the coin should occur, the frequency with which four heads should occur, etc. The remaining columns are concerned with the computation of the mean and standard deviation of the distribution. Focusing on the standard deviation, it should be understood that in the case of the data in Table 7 the value of the standard error of the statistic (frequency) is the population

[2] The student must keep in mind that the procedures and theory to be described below are limited to the degree to which the initial sampling procedures and methodology are reliable and free from error. Statistical procedures can never counteract poor methodology and planning.

TABLE 7. THEORETICAL FREQUENCY DISTRIBUTION OF FIVE TOSSES OF A COIN

(1)	(2)	(3)	(4)
X	f	fX	fX^2
5	1	5	25
4	5	20	80
3	10	30	90
2	10	20	40
1	5	5	5
0	1	0	0
	32	80	240

$$\bar{X}_f = \frac{fX}{N} = \frac{80}{32} = 2.50$$

$$\sigma_f = \sqrt{\frac{\Sigma fX^2 - (\Sigma fX)^2/N}{N}}$$

$$= \sqrt{\frac{240 - (80)^2/32}{32}}$$

$$= 1.11$$

standard error, because *all* possible sample values along with their frequency of occurrence are present in the distribution.   Note that the symbol σ is used here rather than S to denote the fact that the variation is around the population mean and not the sample mean.   Similarly, the mean in this case is the population mean and is denoted $\bar{X}$.   The computations required for the analysis in Table 7 can become quite tedious as the size of the sample increases.   Fortunately it has been shown that the mean and sigma can be computed directly by substituting the appropriate values in formulas (1) and (2):

$$\bar{X}_f = nP$$
$$= 5(\tfrac{1}{2}) = 2.5 \tag{1}$$

where n is the sample size and P is the proportion of successes;

$$\sigma_f = \sqrt{nPQ}$$
$$= \sqrt{5(\tfrac{1}{2})(\tfrac{1}{2})} \tag{2}$$
$$= 1.11$$

where Q is the proportion of failures (tails).

Making use of the same relationships described for frequencies, it is also possible to compute a mean proportion and the standard error of a proportion.

$$\bar{X}_p = \frac{nP}{N} = \frac{5(\tfrac{1}{2})}{5} = 0.5 \tag{1a}$$

$$\sigma_P = \sqrt{\frac{PQ}{N}} = \sqrt{\frac{(\tfrac{1}{2})(\tfrac{1}{2})}{5}} = 0.223 \tag{2a}$$

The Standard Error of the Mean. As was the case with frequencies and proportions, our problem with the mean is to develop a way in which the standard deviation of a distribution of means can be determined. Recall that each time a sample statistic is computed we are estimating a population value. If successive samples of the same size N were drawn from the same population the resulting distribution of means would have a standard deviation which could be approximated by substituting the following in formula (3):

$$S_m = \frac{S}{\sqrt{N}} \tag{3}$$

where S = unbiased estimate of the population standard deviation
$\quad\quad N$ = sample size.

which is called the *standard error of the mean.* Note that the standard deviation in formula (3) is an estimate of the population value because the deviations are taken around the sample mean. For the same reason the standard error term can then be only an estimate of the variation among sample means. It is absolutely crucial that the best estimate of the population standard deviation be obtained.

Examination of the components of formula (3) is consistent with our previous discussion of the factors which influence the magnitude of any standard error term. For a constant sample size it is clear that as the variation among individuals increases, so will the variation among sample means and thus the standard error. This is entirely logical in that the greater the magnitude of the deviations from the mean, the greater the chances of their influencing the value of the sample mean. The denominator term shows that as the sample size increases, the variation of successive sample means will decrease. Obviously this is the case, because larger samples incorporate more members of the population, whereas smaller samples permit greater sampling errors.

The Standard Error of the Product Moment Correlation (S_r). An obtained correlation between two variables derived from a particular sample represents an estimate of the population value of the correlation (r). Successive samples of the same size N drawn from the same population will vary around this population value. Estimates of the degree of variation are not as easily derived for r's because, depending upon the sample size and population value of r, the resulting distribution may be a serious departure from normality. Unless N is large (at least 30) and the population value of r is .50 or less, the sampling distribution will be skewed. If the foregoing conditions prevail it is possible to estimate the standard error of an $r(S_r)$ by formula (4).

$$S_r = \frac{1}{\sqrt{N-1}} \tag{4}$$

When either one or both conditions are not present, an alternative equation is required which will minimize the effects of nonnormality. In order to understand this equation, it will first be necessary to understand why distributions of r's around a large population r are skewed. Essentially the issue rests on the fact that a product moment r has a fixed maximum value, so that for an r of .90 the *possible* sample values can extend downward to negative values but up only to 1.00. It should be obvious that with this fixed value, successive sample r's will pile up between .90 and 1.00, thus producing a positively skewed distribution. The problem is to normalize the distribution by transforming it in such a way that the resulting values are essentially normal. Professor R. A. Fisher has performed this valuable service, resulting in what is called the *r to z transformation* and is presented in Table B (Appendix A). The standard error of z has been shown to be

$$S_z = \frac{1}{\sqrt{N - 3}} \tag{5}$$

HYPOTHESIS TESTING

Having explored the meaning of the concept of the standard error, we are now ready to examine several applications. Our primary concern in this section will be with testing statistical hypotheses by means of the normal probability curve.

The Unit Normal Curve and Probability. As a way of aiding our understanding of probability we shall examine the logic underlying a simple problem. Suppose some self-styled expert claims that he can with great consistency distinguish between brand A and the illustrious brand X. An experimental situation is arranged in which the expert tastes A and X, without the presence of any identifying cues. Ten attempts to identify the brand are made, resulting in eight correct responses. Two questions may be asked: (1) What is the probability of this occurring by chance, and (2) Can the expert really tell the brands apart?

TABLE 8. EXPANSION OF THE BINOMIAL $(\frac{1}{2} + \frac{1}{2})^{10}$

Successes	0	1	2	3	4	5	6	7	8	9	10
Probability	$\frac{1}{1024}$ +	$\frac{10}{1024}$ +	$\frac{45}{1024}$ +	$\frac{120}{1024}$ +	$\frac{210}{1024}$ +	$\frac{252}{1024}$ +	$\frac{210}{1024}$ +	$\frac{120}{1024}$ +	$\frac{45}{1024}$ +	$\frac{10}{1024}$ +	$\frac{1}{1024}$

There are two solutions to the foregoing questions, one of which involves the binomial distribution and the other the unit normal curve. Of the two approaches, the binomial expansion is the most direct and the most accurate. Expanding the binomial expression $(\frac{1}{2} + \frac{1}{2})^{10}$ is the first step.

From Table 8 it can be seen that the probability of obtaining exactly eight successes in the ten events is $\frac{45}{1024}$. Our concern must be with the probability of obtaining at least eight successes, which would be the sum of the probabilities of eight, nine, and ten successes:

$$\frac{45}{1024} + \frac{10}{1024} + \frac{1}{1024} = \frac{56}{1024} \quad \text{or} \quad .0547$$

Notice that the probability is the ratio of the number of successes to the total number of possible events, which is consistent with the definition of probability. In this case the chances are slightly better than 5 in 100 that the expert could have had eight or more successes by chance alone.

We shall now examine the problem in terms of the normal curve. In the problem as stated, *a priori* logic indicates that the population frequency of successes is 5 for samples of $N = 10$ when $p = \frac{1}{2}$. As shown in Figure 19, we need to determine the proportion of area that lies to the right of the

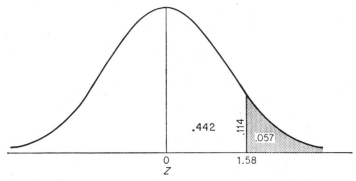

Fig. 19. Normal curve showing area relationships.

ordinate at $Z = 1.58$, to the total area.[3] The reader will recall that the third column of Table A (Appendix A) corresponds to the shaded area of Figure 19. In order to make use of the normal probability table it is necessary to convert the deviation of the observed frequency from the theoretically expected frequency into standard score form, or x/s, which happens to be column 1 of Table A (Appendix A).

$$Z = \frac{x}{s} = \frac{\hat{F} - F}{\sqrt{NPQ}} \tag{6}$$

The required statistic is obtainable from formula (6) where $x = \hat{F} - F$, and $S = \sqrt{NPQ}$. The denominator is the familiar standard error of a frequency. Substituting in formula (6) we have

$$Z = \frac{8 - 5 - .5}{\sqrt{10\ (\frac{1}{2})(\frac{1}{2})}} = \frac{2.50}{1.58} = 1.58$$

---

[3] Since the normal curve is a continuous function and data with small N's are discrete, a correction of .5 for continuity is made.

which is the magnitude of the deviation between the expected and theoretical frequencies expressed in standard deviation units. Entering column 1 of Table A (Appendix A) with the value of 1.58 and reading across to column 3, we note that the corresponding area is .0571. This value compares favorably with the exact probability of .0547, the discrepancy occurring because of the smallness of the sample size.

Employing identical logic, the probability of an observed discrepancy between the value of a sample statistic and some theoretically expected value of that statistic can be determined for the mean, the correlation coefficient, or any other statistic where the sampling distribution of the statistic is known. For the mean the formula would be

$$Z = \frac{x}{s} = \frac{x - M}{s/\sqrt{N}} \tag{7}$$

The formula for a correlation would be

$$Z = \frac{x}{s} = \frac{Z_{pop} - Z}{1/\sqrt{N - 3}} \tag{8}$$

The Z values required in the numerator of formula (8) represent the transformations mentioned earlier and can be obtained from Table B (Appendix A).

Hypothesis Testing. An understanding of hypothesis testing is to a great extent dependent upon a thorough understanding of probability and its relationship to the normal curve. Let us restate the problem about the expert's ability to discriminate between brands A and X to read: The expert for certain reasons can discriminate between brands A and X. It is now possible using formula (6) to determine the validity of the new hypothesis according to the principles of probability.

The Null Hypothesis. (H_0). The positive statement made above concerning the outcome of the experiment is sometimes called the research hypothesis. In most cases the experimenter has such a hypothesis, based perhaps on theoretical grounds, *a priori* hunches, or previous research, usually predicting that one group or another will be superior (inferior) in performance on some task. In order to test the hypothesis statistically, it is necessary also to set up a statistical hypothesis, which most often states that no differences exist between a sample statistic and a population value or that no differences exist between two or more sample statistics. This type of hypothesis is called the *null hypothesis*. In the present problem the null hypothesis would state that the expert is unable to discriminate between the two brands except by chance; i.e., any observed differences can be attributed to chance.

It would be worthwhile to see exactly what has been implied by statements which fit the definition of the null hypothesis. Recall that any sample statistic, which we will call for convenience θ, is an estimate of some population value (θ_{pop}). These sample statistics will vary around the population value with a variability equal to the standard error of the statistic. The null hypothesis implies that any observed discrepancy $\theta_{pop} - \theta$ is a chance occurrence and that the sample really is from a population where the value is θ_{pop}. However, as the magnitude of Z increases, the probability of the observed discrepancy being a chance departure decreases. As this occurs we become increasingly less confident that the sample was drawn from the population, θ_{pop}.

At what point can we no longer accept the hypothesis that a particular deviation can be attributed to chance alone? The answer to this question is to a certain extent a matter of individual taste, but it is generally agreed that when the probability of an event occurring is as small as 5 times in 100 ($p = .05$) or smaller, the null hypothesis is rejected or no longer acceptable. Obviously the smaller the level of significance accepted by the investigator, the less the chances are that in reality he should have accepted it. Sometimes it happens that the null hypothesis is rejected when it should have been accepted. This is called a *Type I error*. Obviously Type I errors are more likely to occur when the level at which H_0 will be rejected (this is most frequently called the level of significance) is $p = .05$ than when the level of significance is set at $p = .01$. One would suspect, however, that if a Type I error can occur, then errors in the opposite direction can also occur. A *Type II error* is said to occur whenever the null hypothesis is accepted when in fact it should have been rejected. Clearly, the lower the acceptable level of significance, the greater is the probability of making a Type II error.

Returning to the restated problem, we must now decide whether to accept or reject the null hypothesis. The Z in this case was 1.58, which from the normal curve table we found has a probability of occurrence of .0571. According to the arbitrarily stated criterion for rejection of H_0 this p value does not permit us to reject. The results of the analysis can be interpreted as meaning that the discrepancy between the expert's performance (sample frequency) and the population frequency can be attributed to chance. An alternative interpretation would state that the sample proportion (frequency) represents a chance deviation from the population value (θ_{pop}) of .50. Since the p value in this case is so near the required .05 value for rejection, one might wish to replicate the experiment. Naturally, when the p value turns out to be just below .05, the investigator should also replicate his findings.

One-tailed Test versus Two-tailed Test. In determining the probability that the expert's performance was a chance departure from the population value, only one extreme (tail) of the normal curve was used. Most of the time, however, both tails of the curve must be considered; i.e., we must double the probability value found in column 3 of the table. A one-tailed test was sufficient for this problem because the direction of performance had been specified. Had the expert only made the correct response 30 per cent of the time, we would have known without any analysis that the null hypothesis could not be rejected. In most programs it is difficult to specify direction, the experimenter being content to say only that "differences" will be found. As will be seen shortly, this situation arises most frequently when a study involves two or more sample statistics.

As an example of the use of formula (7), suppose we want to determine whether a particular sample of 100 eleventh graders who achieved a mean IQ of 105 is from a population whose IQ is 100. The standard deviation is 16.00. Substituting in formula (7) we obtain

$$Z = \frac{100 - 105}{16/\sqrt{100}} = \frac{-5}{1.60} = 3.12$$

Entering Table A (Appendix A) with $Z = 3.12$, we find that the probability of obtaining a difference as large or larger is .01 for a two-tailed test. We can thus reject the null hypothesis and conclude that this sample is from a population whose IQ is something other than 100.

We shall now briefly consider the arithmetic involved in the solution of problems for which formula (8) is appropriate. Suppose a sample r is .75 and on the basis of *a priori* reasoning we believe the population r is zero. The sample size in this case is 52. Recall that in working with sampling distributions of r it is usually best to convert the r to Z. Examination of Table B shows that for $r = 0.75$, Z is 0.973. We are now ready to substitute in formula (8) since when $r = 0$, Z also is zero.

$$Z = \frac{0.973 - 0}{1/\sqrt{52 - 3}} = \frac{0.973}{0.143} = 6.80$$

The Z in this case is clearly significant, permitting the rejection of the null hypothesis.

Confidence Limits. In the foregoing problems we found that each sample statistic, M and r, probably was not from populations wherein M equaled 100 or r equaled zero. We cannot, on the basis of this analysis, conclude that the population value is identical to the sample value, but it is possible to determine the interval of scores within which the population value is likely to fall. The assertion is *not* that this *is* the interval containing the population mean or r, but that at a certain level of confidence, defined in terms of probability, the interval does include it. For example, suppose in the case of our sample mean of 105 we wish to determine the 95 per cent confidence limits. In terms of the unit normal curve we want the interval which cuts off 2.5 per cent on each tail; i.e., 5 per cent of the time sample values will be outside of the 95 per cent confidence limits.

Entering column 2 of Table A (Appendix A), we find that the Z value for the area from M to Z which, when doubled to include the area on both sides of the mean, comes closest to 95 per cent is 1.95. The computation of the confidence interval is

$$M \pm 1.95(S_M)$$
$$105 \pm 1.95(1.60)$$
$$105 \pm 3.12$$

Thus it can be concluded that 95 per cent of subsequent sample values of the same size N drawn from the same population will fall within the limits 101.88 to 108.12. These procedures, it should be understood, hold for large samples.

We can also determine the 95 per cent confidence interval for the product moment r. The first step is to transform the r to Z as we did for our earlier problem and then determine the standard error of the r. The computations are as follows:

$$Z \pm 1.95(S_z)$$
$$.973 \pm 1.95(0.143)$$
$$.973 \pm .278$$

The confidence interval for Z would be 1.251 to .695 which now must be transformed back to an r. From Table B (Appendix A), we see that for a Z of 1.251, r is approximately .85, and for a Z of .695, r is approximately .60. The meaning of this interval is similar to that given for the confidence interval of a mean.

COMPARING TWO SAMPLE STATISTICS

A cursory examination of the research literature should reveal that the majority of studies involve a comparison of two (or more) sample means. These sample means may result from two randomly selected samples, each of which has been subjected to different experimental treatments. (The student might find that a review of the section on Types of Experimental Designs would be of help in understanding this material.) The purpose of this section is to introduce the student to the statistical concepts and techniques appropriate to the randomized design involving two independent samples, as well as statistical techniques for treating data derived from the test-retest or matched-pairs types of experimental designs.

Differences between Independent Means. Suppose an investigator is interested in the differential effectiveness of two combinations of verbal reinforcers, Right-Wrong and Right-(Nothing), on the discrimination learning of third-grade pupils. He draws a sample of fifty subjects (S's) and randomly assigns them to one of the two groups so that he has twenty-five S's in a group. The problems are presented to the children for a maximum of forty trials, or until they respond correctly on ten consecutive trials or problems.   The following data are the number of correct responses for the forty trials:

TABLE 9. NUMBER OF CORRECT RESPONSES IN FORTY TRIALS

Right-Wrong		Right-(Nothing)	
25	23	16	19
26	24	21	19
17	25	11	18
19	15	24	16
26	21	15	16
17	17	16	16
15	22	15	18
17	24	28	19
15	15	26	20
16	22	10	15
13	26	15	14
21	15	11	15
	27		13

The mean performance of the Right-Wrong (RW) group is 20.12 and that of the Right-(Nothing) group is 17.04, the difference being 3.08.   The problem is to determine whether this difference occurred by chance alone or whether it is reasonable to conclude that the reinforcements had a differential effect.

An extension of the sampling theory discussed earlier will provide an understanding of the issues involved here.   Recall that in estimating the probability that a sample statistic is a chance departure from some hypothetical population value, the sampling distribution of that statistic was required.   In the present situation there are two sample statistics, each representing an estimate of a population value.   Stated in terms of the null hypothesis it is assumed that no difference exists, which would mean, if true, that a distribution of differences between two statistics would have a mean of zero and a standard deviation equal to the standard error of the difference between the two statistics, S_{D_m}.   It should be clear that as soon as the standard error term is known it is possible to determine Z, since

$$Z = \frac{x}{s} = \frac{M_1 - M_2}{S_{D_m}} \tag{9}$$

The present problem involves estimates of differences between population means, and therefore it requires a term called the *standard error of differences between means,* given in formula (10).   Note that formula (10),

$$S_{D_M} = \sqrt{\frac{S_1^2}{N_1} + \frac{S_2^2}{N_2} - 2r_{12}S_1S_2} \tag{10}$$

includes a correlation term and represents the degree of relationship exist-ing between pairs of subjects, one from each group. In the present ex-periment the S's were randomly assigned to the groups so that no logical way exists for pairing the S's; therefore the correlation term would be zero, reducing the equation to

$$S_{D_M} = \sqrt{\frac{S_1^2}{N_1} + \frac{S_2^2}{N_2}} \tag{11}$$

as the formula for the standard error of the difference between two *inde-pendent means*.

In order to determine S_{D_M}, the variance S^2 for each group is required:

$$\Sigma x_1^2 = \Sigma X_1^2 - \frac{(\Sigma X_1)^2}{N_1} \qquad \Sigma x_2^2 = \Sigma X_2^2 - \frac{(\Sigma X_2)^2}{N_2}$$

$$= 10605 - \frac{(503)^2}{25} \qquad = 7720 - \frac{(426)^2}{25}$$

$$= 484.64 \qquad\qquad = 460.96$$

$$S_1^2 = \frac{\Sigma x_1^2}{N_1 - 1} \qquad\qquad S_2^2 = \frac{\Sigma x_2^2}{N_2 - 1}$$

$$= \frac{484.64}{25 - 1} \qquad\qquad = \frac{460.96}{25 - 1}$$

Substituting in formula (11) we obtain

$$S_{D_M} = \sqrt{\frac{20.19}{25} + \frac{19.21}{25}} = 1.26$$

And from formula (9) it is possible to determine Z:

$$Z = \frac{20.12 - 17.04}{1.26}$$

$$= 2.44$$

Entering the normal probability table we find that the probability of a dif-ference as large as 2.44 or larger occurring by chance alone is .0073 for a one-tailed test. However, in this study no direction was predicted, there-fore a two-tailed test is called for, making the probability .0146. Since $p = .01$ is smaller than the acceptable for rejecting the null hypothesis, we can reject the null hypothesis and conclude that the samples are from dif-ferent populations. It can also be stated that the population value of the differences between means drawn from the same population with same size N's is something other than zero. Stating our conclusions in terms of the experiment, rejecting the null hypothesis permits the conclusion that the re-inforcement combinations are differentially effective with Right-Wrong be-ing superior to Right-(Nothing).

Differences between Nonindependent (Correlated) Means. There are some experiments where the investigator attempts to reduce the magnitude of the standard error term by matching the S's on some relevant variable (s). (See pages 234–237 for a discussion of these designs.) The more commonly used of these experimental designs is the *matched-pairs* approach, wherein each subject in one group is matched as closely as possible with a subject in the second group. Obviously the better the match and the more variables the pairs are matched on, the greater the reduction in variation among S's. It should be kept in mind, however, that the estimate of the standard error term involved here is a function of N. The more matching variables added, the more difficult it becomes to obtain adequate sample sizes.

Another type of experimental design for which the statistical procedures described below are appropriate occurs when the experimenter wishes to determine if any learning (or change) has taken place as a result of some specific experience. In this case the optimum in matching is achieved because the performance of each subject is compared with his own prior performance. Using this type of design as a basis, we shall now examine the issues involved in the appropriate analysis. Suppose in the experiment described above the investigator wants to know if any learning took place at all in the Right-(Nothing) group, even though he already knows that the degree of learning is less than for the Right-Wrong group. He decides to compare the number of correct responses made on the first twenty trials with those on the last twenty trials. For the sake of convenience the sample size is 10. The following data are obtained:

TABLE 10. NUMBER OF CORRECT RESPONSES MADE ON THE FIRST BLOCK OF TWENTY TRIALS AND ON THE SECOND BLOCK OF TWENTY TRIALS

Subject no.	Trials 1–20	Trials 21–40
1	16	20
2	11	8
3	8	9
4	12	13
5	7	10
6	14	17
7	9	11
8	13	15
9	10	12
10	15	18

Computing the mean for each block of trials in the usual way gives $M_{1-20} = 11.5$ and $M_{21-30} = 13.3$, the difference equaling 1.80. The problem stated in terms of the null hypothesis, H_o, is to determine if the observed difference between means is a chance departure from zero. Following the procedures indicated by formula (11), we obtain

$$\Sigma x_1^2 = 1405 - 1322.50 \qquad \Sigma x_2^2 = 1917 - 1768.90$$
$$= 82.5 \qquad\qquad\qquad = 148.10$$
$$S_1^2 = \frac{82.5}{9} \qquad\qquad S_2^2 = \frac{148.10}{9}$$
$$= 9.16 \qquad\qquad\qquad = 16.46$$

$$Z = \frac{13.3 - 11.5}{\sqrt{9.16/10 + 16.46/10}}$$
$$= \frac{1.80}{1.60}$$
$$= 1.12$$

Entering the normal curve table with a $Z = 1.12$ we find that the probability of obtaining a value as large or larger is .26, which does not permit rejection of the null hypothesis.

In assessing the results of the foregoing analysis it should be noted that the correlation term of formula (10) was assumed to be zero. However, such an assumption is necessarily unjustified because the scores being compared are based on the *same* S's. The product moment correlation between the two sets of scores is .89. At this point the reader might well ask himself, what is the effect on the standard error term of knowing that a correlation exists between pairs of scores? Inspection of formula (10) clearly denotes that the error term will be smaller to a degree dependent upon the magnitude of r. This makes sense because now we can account for a part of the variation in the scores from a knowledge of the person's prior performance. In the case of matched pairs, where the matching variable is, for example, IQ, it is known that the variation between people will be reduced, hence reducing the magnitude of the error term. Perhaps the simplest way to think about this is to remember that the effect of matching is to reduce the magnitude of the variance of the differences.

Keeping in mind now that the two sets of scores in the present problem are based on the same S's, the appropriate analysis following formula (10) would be

$$Z = \frac{13.30 - 11.50}{\sqrt{(9.16/10 + 16.46/10) - 2(.89)(.96)(1.29)}}$$
$$= \frac{1.80}{.61}$$
$$= 2.95$$

Entering the normal table, the probability of obtaining a Z as large as 2.95 or larger is .01, permitting rejection of the null hypothesis.

The formula for the standard error of differences between correlated groups in its present form [formula (10)] is rather cumbersome. Fortunately there is an alternative approach which is more direct and yields identical results. From Table 11 it can be seen that the difference between the means (M_D) is identical to the mean of the differences $(\bar{D})$. It can be

TABLE 11. ANALYSIS OF MATCHED-PAIRS DATA

Subject no.	Trials 1–20	Trials 21–40	Diff.	D^2
1	16	20	+4	16
2	11	8	−3	9
3	8	9	+1	1
4	12	13	+1	1
5	7	10	+3	9
6	14	17	+3	9
7	9	11	+2	4
8	13	15	+2	4
9	10	12	+2	4
10	15	18	+3	9
			18	66

shown that the standard error of the difference between correlated means derived from a distribution of difference scores is identical to formula (10). Restated in statistical symbols already familiar to the reader, we have for the necessary sum of squares for the distribution of differences

$$\Sigma d^2 = \Sigma D^2 - \frac{(\Sigma D)^2}{N}$$

The standard deviation of this distribution is given by

$$S_d = \sqrt{\frac{\Sigma d^2}{N-1}}$$

which when divided by $\sqrt{N}$ gives the standard error of the difference

$$S_{D_M} = \frac{S_d}{\sqrt{N}} \qquad (12)$$

between correlated means. The numerical solution becomes

$$\Sigma d^2 = 66 - \frac{(18)^2}{10} \qquad S_d = \sqrt{\frac{33.6}{9}} \qquad S_{D_M} = \frac{1.93}{\sqrt{10}}$$
$$= 33.6 \qquad\qquad = 1.93 \qquad\qquad = .61$$

To obtain Z:

$$Z = \frac{\bar{D}}{S_{D_M}}$$
$$= \frac{1.80}{.61}$$
$$= 2.95 \tag{13}$$

Note that this analysis gives results identical with our earlier solution.

SMALL SAMPLE THEORY

This discussion so far has been based on statistical procedures appropriate to the normal curve function. However, a precise use of the normal curve requires the variables to be normally distributed in the population. It follows that if the foregoing assumption is met, then the distribution of sample means will also be normally distributed. However, the degree of normality of this distribution of means is dependent in part upon the sample size. As the sample size decreases, the approximation to a normal curve similarly decreases, the discrepancy becoming quite serious when N is 30 or less. Actually as the sample size decreases, the curve becomes more peaked (leptokurtic) and the tails of the curve become somewhat higher than in the normal curve. In effect this means that as the sample size decreases, the magnitude of the ratio M_D/S_{M_D} increases for the same level of probability. Implicit in this statement is the fact that for each sample size there will be a different curve. Procedures appropriate for those situations in which the sample size is small will now be described.

The t Test of Significance. A statistical test of significance which overcomes to a large degree the problems brought about by small samples is the t Test developed by R. A. Fisher. It should be clearly understood from the outset that this test is interpreted in precisely the same way as the Z, and that the standard error terms involved have precisely the same meaning as those discussed earlier. The major difference, as shown in Figure 20, is the fact that there are separate curves for each n where n denotes degrees of freedom (df). Disregarding the df for the moment, the student should examine carefully the table of t (see Table C, Appendix A) to satisfy himself that, as the df decreases, the magnitude of t required for significance at any level of probability increases. If an obtained t for a specific n exceeds the tabled value, then the null hypothesis can be rejected. The formula for the t Test between independent means is

$$t = \frac{M_1 - M_2}{\sqrt{[(\Sigma x_1{}^2 + \Sigma x_2{}^2)/(N_1 + N_2 - 2)](1/N_1 + 1/N_2)}} \tag{14}$$

and the formula for the t Test between correlated means is

$$t = \frac{\bar{D}}{\sqrt{\Sigma d^2/[N(N-1)]}} \qquad (14a)$$

Degrees of Freedom. In the most general case, df refers to the number of scores or frequencies which can vary around some constant or parameter. For example, suppose there are ten scores in a distribution for which the mean is known. Knowing that the sum of the deviations around the mean must equal zero, it follows that any nine of the scores are free to vary in value but the tenth score is not. From this reasoning, then, the number of degrees of freedom involved in any distribution of scores which vary around the mean of that distribution would be equal to $N-1$.

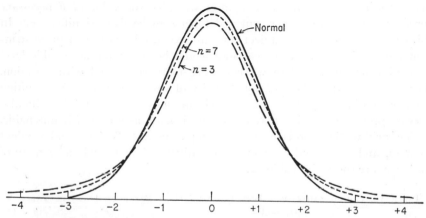

Fig. 20.   Normal compared with t distribution for $n = 3$ and $n = 7$.

The degrees of freedom involved in formula (14) are determined by $N_1 + N_2 - 2$. Two degrees of freedom are lost because two distributions varying around independent means are involved. In formula (14a), only one degree of freedom is lost because only a single mean is involved, the mean of the differences score.

Homogeneity of Variance. Note in the denominator term of formula (14) that the sums of squares have been pooled. This has been done because when working with small samples, estimates of the population variance are seriously biased. Recall that in Chapter 13, in computing S^2 the sums of squares (Σx^2) were divided by $N-1$, or, as we now call it, the degrees of freedom. In dividing by $N-1$ an unbiased estimate of the population variance is obtained. Pooling of the sums of squares represents a further attempt to obtain a better estimate of the population variance, but this procedure rests on the assumption that the variances of the samples are from the same population.

The statistical test for homogeneity of variance involves the ratio of the larger variance to the smaller variance, resulting in a statistic known as the F Test. Stated symbolically,

$$F = \frac{\Sigma x^2/(N-1)}{\Sigma x^2/(N-1)} = \frac{S_L{}^2}{S_S{}^2} \qquad (15)$$

where $S_L{}^2$ is the larger of the two variance estimates. To evaluate the F resulting from formula (15), you must enter the F table (Table E, Appendix A) with two sets of degrees of freedom, one for each variance estimate. The df for the larger variance should be located on the horizontal axis and the df for the smaller variance on the vertical. Reading across until the column and row meet will give the value of F necessary for significance at the 5 per cent and 1 per cent levels of significance. In this case we prefer not to reject the null hypothesis, so that a more stringent test for homogeneity of variance would be to set the acceptable level of significance higher than when we are more concerned with rejection. The degree to which lack of homogeneity of variance distorts the resulting probabilities has been discussed by Cochran and Cox (1:100–102) who also present procedures which may be followed if the assumption is untenable.

The arithmetical procedures for computing a t Test for independent samples, and correlated samples along with the F Test for homogeneity of variance, are shown in Table 12.

TABLE 12. COMPUTATION OF t TEST AND AN F TEST BASED ON DATA IN TABLE 9

$$t = \frac{M_1 - M_2}{\sqrt{[(\Sigma x_1{}^2 + \Sigma x_2{}^2)/(N_1 + N_2 - 2)](1/N_1 + 1/N_2)}}$$

$$= \frac{20.12 - 17.04}{\sqrt{[(484.64 + 460.96)/(25 + 25 - 2)](1/25 + 1/25)}}$$

$$= 2.44$$

$df = 48$

$p = .02$

$$F = \frac{\Sigma x^2/(n-1)}{\Sigma x^2/(n-1)}$$

$$= \frac{484.64/24}{460.96/24}$$

$$= \frac{20.19}{19.21}$$

$$= 1.05$$

$df = 24, 24$

$p > .05$

COMPUTATION OF DATA BASED ON TABLE 10

$$t = \frac{\bar{D}}{\sqrt{\Sigma x_1{}^2/[n(n-1)]}}$$

$$= \frac{1.8}{\sqrt{33.6/10(9)}}$$

$$= \frac{1.8}{.61}$$

$$= 2.95$$

$df = 9$

$p = .05$

The Use of Z as Contrasted with the t Test.   The curious student may wonder just when he should use Z or t to test the differences between means.   Before giving a specific answer to this question it might be well to review briefly the entire approach taken in the previous chapter as well as the present one in terms of estimating variance and standard error terms.   Recall that in the discussion of variance the position taken was that the best estimate of the population variance would be obtained by dividing the sum of squares by $N - 1$.   However, it should now be clear that the improvement in the variance estimate will be greater as the sample size decreases but that for N's of over 50, the difference between dividing by $N - 1$ and N is negligible.   In precise terms the use of Z wherein the variance estimates were derived from the use of $N - 1$ is technically incorrect and should not be used, although when the sample size is large the effects on the magnitude of the Z will be slight.   We can see in light of this argument that the t Test can be used with any sample size, and thus should be thought of as the general technique for testing the significance of differences between means, either independent or correlated.

The foregoing discussion should clarify some issues raised in the previous chapter with respect to standard scores and correlation.   In each of these situations estimates of the variance were made by dividing the sum of squares by $N - 1$.   In the traditional use of standard scores the variance is determined by dividing the sum of squares by N, but this is appropriate only when interest is centered on the sample itself and one is concerned only with questions of relative position.   Our purpose in dividing by $N - 1$ was somewhat broader in that we were attempting to estimate in the best manner possible population values, as well as relative position with respect to the population.   The same holds true for correlation in that the concern has been with the estimation of population values.   Of course, if the size of the sample is large these restrictions would not be valid, which should serve to show the importance of using adequate size samples.

ANALYZING MULTIPLE-GROUP SAMPLE STATISTICS

A logical extension of the study used to illustrate testing the differences between independent means would be the addition of a third group, (Nothing)-Wrong.   It is, of course, possible to analyze the data by performing three t Tests, but this procedure would violate certain principles of probability, and in addition it becomes cumbersome when the number of groups involved is large.   Analysis of variance procedures allows one to test for differences among several groups simultaneously.   Extension of the basic procedures permits the analysis of several variables as well as the interaction among the variables.   The basic procedures are usually referred to as factorial designs which can also be used in a variety of ways.   The materials to be presented below are concerned only with a simple between-methods or between-treatments analysis and one type of factorial design. An understanding of the issues involved in these types of analysis should help the student, upon consulting other references such as Edwards (2), to understand extensions of the examples given in this chapter.

Simple Between-treatments Analysis.   The basic notion underlying analysis of variance is the fact that sums of squares are additive.   Consider Table 13, in which each entry is a score made by a subject in a particular

TABLE 13. ENTRIES IN A SIMPLE ANALYSIS OF VARIANCE FOR THREE GROUPS

A	B	C
X_{1_a}	X_{1_b}	X_{1_c}
X_{2_a}	X_{2_b}	X_{2_c}
X_{3_a}	X_{3_b}	X_{3_c}
.	.	.
.	.	.
.	.	.
X_{n_a}	X_{n_b}	X_{n_c}
M_A	M_B	M_C

treatment; M_A, M_B, M_C are the means of each group, and M is the grand mean or the mean of the entire group.   The sum of the deviations squared of each score around the grand mean divided by N gives the *total sum of squares*.   It is possible to break this total sum of squares down into two parts, each of which is independent of the other.   Notice in Table 13 that the scores of each group vary around their own means, whereas each of the group means varies around the grand mean.   By means of algebraic manipulation, it can be shown that the total sum of squares is equal to the sum of squares

$$\text{Total} \quad = \quad \text{within} \quad + \quad \text{between}$$

$$\Sigma(X - M)^2 = \sum_{1}^{n}\sum_{a}^{c}(X - M_i)^2 + \Sigma n_i(M_i - M)^2 \tag{16}$$

attributable to variation among S's treated in the same way (within-groups sum of squares) plus the sum of squares attributable to variation among the three groups (between-groups sum of squares).

Since the within-groups and between-groups sums of squares are independent, it is possible to obtain two estimates of the population variance by dividing each source of variation by its appropriate degrees of freedom. The appropriate degrees of freedom have been shown to be

$$\text{Total} \quad = \text{between} + \text{within}$$
$$N - 1 = r - 1 \quad + N - r$$

Dividing each sum of squares by its degrees of freedom gives the *mean square*, that is, estimates of the population variance.[4]

When the n samples are drawn from a common population, and when variable (s) is normally distributed, the two variance estimates under the terms of the null hypothesis may be thought to differ by chance alone. It has been shown by R. A. Fisher that the ratio of the mean square between groups to the mean square within groups follows a specific distribution, F. The between-groups mean square is in the numerator because we are interested in determining if the experimental treatments have contributed more to the total variance than the variation among S's in the same treatment groups. In these terms the mean square within groups is usually referred to as the error term.

The probability values for F have been tabulated by Snedecor as shown in Table E in Appendix A. After determining F you enter Table E with the degrees of freedom for the larger mean square along the horizontal axis and the degrees of freedom for the smaller mean square along the vertical axis. If the obtained F is larger than the one required for the 5 per cent level of significance, then the null hypothesis is rejected, permitting one to conclude that the treatments are different.

Returning to the study concerned with the three pairs of verbal reinforcements, we shall now work through the necessary computations. Recall that the analysis requires our computing the total sum of squares, the sum of squares within groups (the error term), and the sum of squares between groups. The data in Table 14 are the number of correct re-

TABLE 14. NUMBER OF CORRECT RESPONSES MADE
BY THREE DIFFERENT TREATMENT GROUPS

Right-Wrong	Right-(Nothing)	(Nothing)-Wrong	
25	16	25	
26	11	15	
17	11	21	
19	18	17	
26	15	22	
23	16	24	
24	15	15	
25	20	22	
17	16	26	
19	10	15	
$\Sigma X = 221$	148	$202 =$	571
$\Sigma X^2 = 5{,}007$	2,284	$4{,}250 =$	11,541

[4] The assumption of independent variance estimates is violated when the sample variances are unequal, i.e., not from the same population. Bartlett's test for homogeneity of variance for three or more groups is described in (2:195–198).

sponses made by each subject in each of the three groups on the discrimination learning task.

1. Total sum of squares:

$$\Sigma x_t^2 = \Sigma X^2 - \frac{(\Sigma X)^2}{N}$$

$$(25)^2 + (26)^2 + (17)^2 + (19)^2 + \cdots + (15)^2 - \frac{(571)^2}{30} = 672.97$$

2. Between-groups sum of squares:

$$\Sigma x_b^2 = \frac{(\Sigma X_A)^2}{N_A} + \frac{(\Sigma X_B)^2}{N_B} + \frac{(\Sigma X_C)^2}{N_C} - \frac{(\Sigma X)^2}{N}$$

$$= \frac{(221)^2}{10} + \frac{(148)^2}{10} + \frac{(202)^2}{10} - \frac{(571)^2}{30}$$

$$= 286.87$$

3. Within-groups sum of squares:

$$\Sigma x_W^2 = \Sigma X_A^2 - \frac{(\Sigma X_A)^2}{N_A} + \Sigma X_B^2 - \frac{(\Sigma X_B)^2}{N_B} + \Sigma X_C^2 - \frac{(\Sigma X_C)^2}{N_C}$$

$$= 5{,}007 - \frac{(221)^2}{10} + 2{,}284 - \frac{(148)^2}{10} + 4{,}250 - \frac{(202)^2}{10}$$

$$= 386.10$$

A more convenient approach to the computation of the within-groups sum of squares is to subtract the sum of squares between groups from the total sum of squares:

$$672.97 - 286.87 = 386.10$$

The results of the analysis of variance are presented in Table 15. Allocation of degrees of freedom follows the model presented earlier in this

TABLE 15. SUMMARY OF THE ANALYSIS OF VARIANCE
OF THE THREE TREATMENT GROUPS

Source of variance	Sum of squares	df	Mean square	F
Between treatments.........	286.87	2	143.43	10.03
Within groups (error).......	386.10	27	14.30	
Total...............	672.97	29		

chapter. The total number of degrees of freedom available is equal to $N - 1$ or $30 - 1 = 29$; degrees of freedom attributed to the between-groups sum of squares is $r - 1$ or $3 - 1 = 2$; and the within-groups degrees of freedom is equal to $N - r$ or $30 - 3 = 27$. Dividing the sums of squares by their appropriate degrees of freedom results in the required variance estimates or mean squares. Dividing the mean square between groups by the mean square within groups results in an F of 10.03, which is the last entry in

Table 15. Entering the F table with 2 and 27 degrees of freedom we find that the required F for significance at the 5 per cent level is 3.35. Since our F is larger than the requirement we can reject the null hypothesis. On the basis of this analysis it can be concluded that the treatments produced differences among the three groups. When the analysis of variance is significant, it is permissible to compare groups by means of the t Test by first taking the largest difference and proceeding along with each successively smaller difference between means until a nonsignificant difference occurs. For a fuller discussion of the issues involved in this procedure the student would do well to consult Ryan (4).

Simple Factorial Design. Suppose an experimenter, in addition to being interested in the verbal reinforcement treatments, was also concerned about

TABLE 16. NUMBER OF CORRECT RESPONSES MADE
ON A DISCRIMINATION LEARNING TASK

Right-Wrong		Right-(Nothing)		(Nothing)-Wrong	
Boys	Girls	Boys	Girls	Boys	Girls
25	27	16	13	25	25
26	27	11	12	15	27
17	34	11	13	21	18
19	35	18	10	17	28
26	33	15	16	22	18
23	36	16	19	24	24
24	29	15	14	15	20
25	29	20	21	22	25
17	36	16	18	26	21
19	35	10	14	15	16
$\Sigma X =$ 221	321	148	150	202	222 = 1,264
$\Sigma X^2 =$ 5,007	10,427	2,284	2,356	4,250	5,084 = 29,408

the presence of sex differences in learning. If he should randomly assign to each of the treatment groups a sample of males and a sample of females he would meet the requirements of a factorial design. A factorial design exists when all the variables in a single experiment are studied in all possible combinations. An experiment involving two variations of two variables is referred to as a 2 by 2 (2×2) factorial design. The present problem involves three variations of one variable and two variations of the second, in all combinations, and would therefore be known as 3×2 factorial design. Data derived from this design have been arranged in Table 16 to show how the combinations are worked out.

In order that the student will understand the logic underlying the analysis of the data presented in Table 16, he should first consider the six groups involved in the study regardless of the treatment they may have received. Obviously, differences among these groups can be evaluated by means of the procedures considered in the previous section. The following computations are required:

1. Total sums of squares:

$$(25)^2 + (26)^2 + (17)^2 + \cdots + (16)^2 - \frac{(1{,}264)^2}{60} = 2{,}779.73$$

2. Between-groups sums of squares:

$$\frac{(221)^2}{10} + \frac{(321)^2}{10} + \frac{(148)^2}{10} + \frac{(150)^2}{10} + \frac{(202)^2}{10} - \frac{(1{,}264)^2}{60} = 2{,}009.13$$

3. Within-groups sums of squares:

$$5{,}007 - \frac{(221)^2}{10} + 10{,}427 - \frac{(321)^2}{10} + 2{,}284 - \frac{(148)^2}{10} + 2{,}356 - \frac{(150)^2}{10}$$
$$+ 4{,}250 - \frac{(202)^2}{10} + 5{,}084 - \frac{(222)^2}{10} - \frac{(1{,}264)^2}{60} = 770.60$$
$$\text{Total} - \text{between} = \text{within}$$
$$2{,}779.73 - 2{,}009.13 = 770.60$$

The results of this analysis are summarized in Table 17, from which it can be seen that the differences between the groups are significant ($F = 28.16$). Our concern, however, is not with the existence of differences between the over-all groups but rather with the differences between

TABLE 17. SUMMARY OF THE PRELIMINARY ANALYSIS
OF VARIANCE OF THE DATA IN TABLE 16

Summary	Sums of squares	df	Mean square	F
Between groups...........	2,009.13	5	401.83	28.16
Within groups (error)......	770.60	54	14.27	
Total..............	2,779.73	59		

treatments and between sexes. In factorial designs the over-all between-groups sums of squares can be broken down into as many parts as there are degrees of freedom available. In this case we have five degrees of freedom, two of which can be assigned to the treatments effect and one to the sex variable, leaving two degrees of freedom unassigned. The remaining two df belong to the sum of squares derived from the interaction of the treatments and the sexes, denoted as treatments × sex interaction. We shall delay for the moment the precise meaning and interpretation of the interaction and consider first the computation of the sum of squares for this analysis.

As we consider the procedures for analysis it would be helpful to keep in mind the purposes of the study. In the first place we are concerned with the differences between the treatment groups regardless of the sex of the S's; secondly we are interested in sex differences regardless of treatment received; and finally we are interested in the interaction of the two variables. It follows, then, that computation of the between-treatments sum of squares involves combining the sum of scores for the sexes within each treatment.

Between treatments:

$$\frac{(221 + 321)^2}{20} + \frac{(148 + 150)^2}{20} + \frac{(202 + 222)^2}{20} - \frac{(1264)^2}{60} = 1488.93$$

Similarly in determining the sum of squares for sexes, we combine the sum of scores for treatments within each sex.

Between sexes:

$$\frac{(221 + 148 + 202)^2}{30} + \frac{(321 + 150 + 222)^2}{30} - \frac{(1,264)^2}{60} = 248.06$$

The remaining degrees of freedom are attributable to the interaction of the two variables. Computation of the sum of squares for the interaction rests on the same principle applied to the determination of the degrees of freedom for the interaction term. Recall that the first step in analyzing the data for this problem involved our computing the sum of squares between all six groups, which was found to be 2009.13. Of this total amount the sum of squares for treatments plus the sum of squares for sexes has accounted for 1,736.99, leaving a remainder of 272.14, the sum of squares for the interaction.

TABLE 18. SUMMARY OF THE ANALYSIS OF VARIANCE OF THE DATA IN TABLE 16

Source	Sum of squares	df	Mean square	F
Between treatments (T)	1488.93	2	744.46	52.17
Between sexes (S)	248.06	1	248.06	17.38
T × S interaction	272.14	2	136.07	9.54
Within groups (error)	770.60	54	14.27	
Total	2779.73	59		

Dividing the sum of squares by the appropriate degrees of freedom as shown in Table 18 results in the mean squares. Dividing the mean squares for treatment, sexes, and the treatments × sexes interaction by the mean square for within groups yields the required F Tests. From Table E we find that for two and four degrees of freedom an F of 3.06 is required for significance at the 5 per cent level and an F of 4.75 for significance at the 1 per cent level. Table 18 can be interpreted as meaning that significant differences exist among the three experimental treatment groups ($F = 52.17$) and between sexes ($F = 17.38$) in terms of performance on the dependent variable. The statistically significant interaction ($F = 9.54$) can be interpreted as meaning that the reinforcement treatments are differentially effective according to the sex of the subject. We shall now turn to a more detailed explanation of the interpretation of an interaction.

The Meaning of an Interaction. Inspection of Table 16 shows that the female S's in the $R\text{-}W$ reinforcement group performed better on the task than the female S's in any of the other reinforcement groups. In order to see just how this fact contributes to the interaction sum of squares, let us simplify the problem by dropping one of the treatment groups, resulting in a 2 by 2 factorial design. Attention should now be focused on Table 19, in

TABLE 19. SUMS FOR ANALYSIS OF TREATMENTS AND SEXES

	Right-Wrong	(Nothing)-Wrong	Diff
Girls..........	321	222	99
Boys..........	221	202	19
Diff	100	20	

which have been placed the sum of scores for the four groups involved. Note that the difference between boys and girls for the $R\text{-}W$ treatment is $321 - 221 = 100$ and that the difference between the sexes on the (Nothing)-Wrong treatment is $222 - 202 = 20$. The fact that these difference scores are not similar indicates the presence of an interaction. Note that the female S's in the Right-Wrong condition clearly get more correct responses than any of the other groups including the females in the (Nothing)-Wrong treatment. Also note that the difference between the treatment groups for the female S's is $321 - 222 = 99$, whereas the difference between treatment groups for the male S's is $221 - 202 = 19$. This lack of correspondence between difference scores points up the superiority of the females' performance in the Right-Wrong treatment.

Additional Comments on the Analysis of Variance. Space does not permit our examining any additional analysis of variance techniques here, but the student should be aware that many additional procedures exist which are merely extensions of the theory and procedures presented in the foregoing pages. For example, it is possible to have very complex factorial designs involving four variations of one variable, three variations of another, and perhaps two variations of a third. Such a design gives 24 groups so that 24 S's are required to have just one subject in a cell. Defining each of the variables as A, B, and C and assuming the total N to be 48 (2 S's in a cell) the summary of the analysis would be as shown in Table 20.

In this case, along with testing for differences on each of the variables we can also test for three simple interactions and one triple interaction. The triple interaction gives information on the effects of all three variables on the performance of the S's.

Mention should also be made of another useful technique known as the analysis of covariance. Recall for a moment the problem presented earlier when we were concerned with the significance of change from the first block of twenty trials to the second block of twenty trials. In this analysis we accounted for the magnitude of the correlation between performance at the initial stages of learning and performance at the later stages of learning. The net effect of this procedure was to reduce the magnitude of the error term. It is also possible to use more than two groups in such an experimental design wherein all S's in a particular row are matched, say, in terms

TABLE 20. SUMMARY OF AN ANALYSIS OF VARIANCE
OF A 4 × 3 × 2 FACTORIAL DESIGN

Source of variation	Degrees of freedom
A	3
B	2
C	1
A × B	6
A × C	3
B × C	2
A × B × C	6
Within groups (error)	24
Total	47

of initial ability. The resulting analysis of variance will increase in sensitivity to the degree that the S's have been well matched. In each of the foregoing designs, equating on some variable, usually initial ability, has taken place prior to the running of the experiment itself, but this is not always feasible. For instance, it might not be possible to see the S's more than once, so that the investigator would not have time to assign his S's to groups such that optimal matching would be present. Sometimes it also becomes apparent during the running of the experiment that some seemingly extraneous variable is really contributing substantially to the outcome of the study, therefore making it necessary to take the variable into account. In any of these situations the analysis of covariance is useful.

As the label suggests, analysis of covariance incorporates the procedures of analysis of variance and correlation, particularly regression. Suppose in a particular experiment we have scores on initial performance which are found to correlate with performance on the experimental task. In the straight analysis of variance our objective would be to test for differences between the means on the experimental task, but these means would be contaminated by the influence of initial performance. By the procedures of analysis of covariance we can adjust the means of the experimental variable by regressing the scores in terms of initial performance. In addition to adjusting the means, these procedures also reduce the magnitude of the error term by taking into account variation attributable to differences in initial performance.

THE CHI-SQUARE TEST OF SIGNIFICANCE

There are many research situations in which the experimenter is interested in the frequency or proportion of people in a population who fall into certain defined categories. For example, he might be interested in the attitudes of people, classified according to level of education, on some issue in which their responses could be categorized. In another situation there might be a feeling that a certain test item favors one sex or another, and so we might count the number of males and the number of females who pass and fail the item. In still another situation we might wish to determine if a particular frequency distribution is truly a normal distribution, in which case our concern would be focused on the frequencies in the class intervals. Any of the foregoing situations are amenable to analysis by means of the chi-square (χ^2) technique.

The basic notion underlying the chi-square technique, stated in terms of the null hypothesis, is that the observed frequencies in a category are a chance departure from the hypothetical or expected frequencies for the category. These expected frequencies are derived from any definition one might want to give the null hypothesis. For example, in a two-category problem such as that involving the expert we met earlier in this chapter (see page 307), we might state that the observed frequencies in each category should be in a ratio of one to two or one to three. The next step is to compute the χ^2, which can be done by means of formula (17).

$$\chi^2 = \sum \frac{(O - E)^2}{E} \qquad (17)$$

where O = observed frequency in the category

E = expected frequency

In the case of the expert, recall that he was able to make eight correct responses out of a possible ten. Assuming the expected frequency to be 5, it is obvious from formula (17) that χ^2 is equal to $\frac{9}{5} = 1.80$. However, this is a *two*-category problem, so we must compute another chi-square for the second category. The value of χ^2 here will also be 1.80, and summing both chi-squares gives a total of 3.60. It is important to remember that a chi-square must be computed for each category in the problem.

In order to interpret the meaning of this χ^2 it is necessary to consult

Table D (Appendix A), which is the chi-square table. Note that the values of χ^2 necessary for significance at the 5 per cent or 1 per cent levels vary according to the number of degrees of freedom available. In our discussion of degrees of freedom in terms of the t Test, you will recall that the number of degrees of freedom available in a particular problem was dependent upon the number of scores that were free to vary. The same holds true for chi-square except that our concern is with the number of categories that are free to vary. In the present problem we have only one degree of freedom because knowing that the total number is 10, and that 8 of these are in the "correct" category, we automatically know that a frequency of 2 is in the "incorrect" category. Significance at the 5 per cent level, with one df, requires a χ^2 of 3.84 which is larger than our value. Therefore we fail to reject the null hypothesis and conclude that the expert's performance is a chance departure from a ratio of one out of two correct responses.

The alert student may be suspicious that some relationship exists between the chi-square computed above and the Z Test described at the beginning of this chapter. The relationship is that a chi-square with one degree of freedom is equal to Z^2. The Z obtained for the problem involving the expert was 1.58, which when squared is 2.50. This latter value does not agree with our χ^2 because we did not include a correction for continuity, a procedure which should be followed when only one df is available. Recomputing the χ^2 we obtain

$$\chi^2 = \sum \frac{(8 - 5 - .5)^2}{5} + \frac{(2 - 5 - .5)^2}{5}$$
$$= \sum \frac{6.25}{5} + \frac{6.25}{5}$$
$$= 2.50$$

and this value is exactly Z^2.

Fourfold Classification. One application of the chi-square technique is the situation in which there are two variables, each categorized in two ways. An example of a typical problem is that of determining the presence of sex differences in attitudes toward prohibition. We might ask a sample of sixty men and forty women if they are for or against prohibition. The resulting data might be summarized in a form modeled after Table 21. Our first problem is that of determining the expected frequencies, but now we have no *a priori* reason for suspecting any specific ratio of proportion. Therefore the best thing we can do, under the terms of the null hypothesis, is to pool the total frequency of *yes* responses $(B + D)$ and divide this sum by the total sample size (N), which gives an estimate of the population proportion (p) favorable to prohibition. Similarly the sum $A + C$ divided

TABLE 21. A FOURFOLD CONTINGENCY TABLE

	No	*Yes*	
M	*A*	*B*	$A + B = n_1$
W	*C*	*D*	$C + D = n_2$
	$A + C$	$B + D$	*N*

$$p = \frac{B + D}{N}$$

$$q = \frac{A + C}{N}$$

by N gives an estimate of the population proportion (q) unfavorable to prohibition. This latter computation could have been more easily performed from the relationship $q = 1 - p$. Having determined these proportions we can now, by means of formula (18), compute the expected frequencies.

$$E_A = \frac{A + C}{N} = q(n_1)$$

$$E_B = \frac{B + D}{N} = p(n_1)$$

$$E_C = \frac{A + C}{N} = q(n_2)$$

$$E_D = \frac{B + D}{N} = p(n_2)$$

(18)

To see how this problem is worked out, we shall now supply some hypothetical data to the fourfold contingency table just discussed.

TABLE 22. SEX DIFFERENCES IN ATTITUDES TOWARD PROHIBITION
(Numbers in parentheses are expected frequencies)

	No	Yes	Σ
Men............	40 (30)	20 (30)	60
Women..........	10 (20)	30 (20)	40
Σ	50	50	100

Computation of the expected frequencies is as follows:

$$E_A = \frac{40 + 10}{100} = 0.5(60) \qquad E_B = \frac{20 + 30}{100} = 0.5(60)$$
$$= 30 \qquad\qquad\qquad = 30$$
$$E_C = \frac{40 + 10}{100} = 0.5(40) \qquad E_D = \frac{20 + 30}{100} = 0.5(40)$$
$$= 20 \qquad\qquad\qquad = 20$$

Computation of χ^2 now follows in the usual way according to formula (17), with the modification of the correction for continuity required whenever one degree of freedom is available.

$$\chi^2 = \frac{(40 - 30 - 0.5)^2}{30} = 3.01 \qquad \chi^2 = \frac{(10 - 20 - 0.5)^2}{20} = 4.51$$
$$\chi^2 = \frac{(20 - 30 - .5)^2}{30} = 3.01 \qquad \chi^2 = \frac{(30 - 20 - .5)^2}{20} = 4.51$$
$$\Sigma\chi^2 = 15.04$$

The resulting χ^2, with one degree of freedom, is larger than that required for significance at the 5 per cent level, so we may reject the null hypothesis and conclude that sex differences exist in attitudes toward prohibition. Examination of the contingency table indicates that men are unfavorable, whereas women tend to be more favorably inclined.

An alternative approach to analyzing data from a fourfold table is given by formula (19):

$$\chi^2 = \frac{N(AD - BC)^2}{(A + B)(C + D)(A + C)(B + D)} \tag{19}$$

Chi-Square for k by l Tables. It is, of course, possible to use chi-square when there are more than two categories for each variable, and the procedures described below are applicable for most of these situations. As an example we shall examine one aspect of a study in which the investigator (3) was concerned with the stability of performance on each of the five primary mental abilities relative to performance on the over-all examination over a 3½-year period. The distributions of subscores and the total distribution were converted to stanines and then the S's were categorized for each ability separately in one of three ways: (1) a plus group, comprised of those S's whose ability score was at least one stanine higher than their total score at both grade levels; (2) an equals group, comprised of those S's whose ability score was at the same stanine level as their total score on both occasions; and (3) a minus group, comprised of those S's whose ability score was at least one stanine below the total score on both occasions. This procedure yielded five 3×3 contingency tables, one for each ability, as shown in Table 23.

TABLE 23. RELATIONSHIPS BETWEEN PATTERNS OF HIGH AND LOW SCORES
AT EIGHTH- AND TWELFTH-GRADE LEVELS

		V			S			N			R			WF		
							Twelfth grade									
Eighth grade		+	=	−	+	=	−	+	=	−	+	=	−	+	=	−
	+	23	9	2	26	11	3	21	8	8	28	14	4	25	6	8
	=	9	7	13	6	5	8	10	10	8	9	10	6	5	6	12
	−	10	8	19	8	8	25	4	12	19	3	12	14	11	4	23
		$x^2 = 21.48$			$x^2 = 27.78$			$x^2 = 17.88$			$x^2 = 23.82$			$x^2 = 18.73$		
		$df = 4$			$df = 4$			$df = 4$			$df = 4$			$df = 4$		
		$p = 0.001$			$p = 0.001$			$p = 0.001$			$p = 0.001$			$p = 0.001$		

For the sake of convenience only the chi square for the Numerical Ability (N) Test is examined in detail. Computation of the expected frequencies is accomplished in the same way as with the 2×2 table and with the same underlying assumption regarding the null hypothesis. Once the expected frequencies are determined, we can proceed with the computation of the chi square.

$$\frac{35}{100} \times 37 = 12.95 \qquad \frac{30}{100} \times 37 = 11.10 \qquad \frac{35}{100} \times 37 = 12.95$$

$$\frac{35}{100} \times 28 = 9.80 \qquad \frac{30}{100} \times 28 = 8.40 \qquad \frac{35}{100} \times 28 = 9.80$$

$$\frac{35}{100} \times 35 = 12.25 \qquad \frac{30}{100} \times 35 = 10.50 \qquad \frac{35}{100} \times 35 = 12.25$$

$$x^2 = \frac{(21 - 12.95)^2}{12.95} \qquad x^2 = \frac{(8 - 11.10)^2}{11.10} \qquad x^2 = \frac{(8 - 12.95)^2}{12.95}$$

$$x^2 = \frac{(10 - 9.80)^2}{9.80} \qquad x^2 = \frac{(10 - 8.40)^2}{8.40} \qquad x^2 = \frac{(8 - 9.80)^2}{9.80}$$

$$x^2 = \frac{(4 - 12.25)^2}{12.25} \qquad x^2 = \frac{(12 - 10.50)^2}{10.50} \qquad x^2 = \frac{(19 - 12.25)^2}{12.25}$$

$$\Sigma x^2 = 17.88$$

In order to assess the probability of obtaining a chi-square of this magnitude we necessarily need to know the number of degrees of freedom available. Remember, as you examine Table 23, that the number of degrees of freedom in chi-square is a function of the number of cell entries that are free to vary. In the present problem it can be seen that no more than four cells can vary, hence, for this 3×3 table there are four degrees of freedom available. A rule of thumb for determining df is the product of the number of columns (k) minus 1 and number of rows (r) minus 1: $df = (k-1)(r-1)$.

The results of this analysis can now be evaluated. Entering Table D (Appendix A) we note that for four degrees of freedom a χ^2 of 9.488 is required for significance at the 5 per cent level, which is smaller than the value of our chi-square. Therefore we can reject the null hypothesis and conclude that performance in grade 8 is consistent with performance in grade 12. This interpretation implies the existence of a relationship, and that is what it is meant to do. However, this is a somewhat different interpretation than has heretofore been given. Actually it is possible to state that significant differences exist among the groups, but the precise meaning of this may be somewhat obscure. Remember that in computing the expected frequencies we assumed that the proportion of S's in each of the three categories in the twelfth grade were the same. If this had indeed been correct, the chi-square would not have been significant because the frequencies would have been distributed proportionately throughout the three categories, independent of eighth-grade performance. What happened, however, was that the people who were in a specific category in grade 8 tended to remain in the category in grade 12. This leads to disproportionately larger frequencies in the plus-plus, equals-equals, and minus-minus categories, thus permitting the interpretation of significant differences. However, in terms of the purpose of the analysis, an interpretation in terms of relationship seems more appropriate.

NONPARAMETRIC TECHNIQUES

The statistical tests of significance, such as t, Z, and F, discussed in the earlier sections of this chapter, are based on the assumption that the variables are normally distributed. A moderate violation of this assumption when the sample size is large does not produce serious consequences, particularly with respect to probability statements. Nonnormal distributions do raise problems when the sample size is small and frequently require the use of tests of significance which are not restricted by assumptions of trait normality. These techniques are known as nonparametric statistics. Since these techniques do not require the assumption of trait normality, the student may wonder why they are not used regardless of the nature of the distribution.   The answer is that these tests are not as efficient as the t or F Tests; i.e., there is more likelihood that we will fail to reject the null hypothesis when indeed it is incorrect (Type II error).   Most investigators prefer to use statistics which maximize the likelihood of rejecting the null hypothesis.

The Median Test.   As we noted earlier, certain statistical tests were appropriate for independent samples and certain appropriate for cor-

TABLE 24. RESULTS OF ANALYZING DATA BY MEANS
OF THE SIGN TEST OF DATA BASED ON TABLE 3
(Numbers in parentheses are expected frequencies)

(13.5) 17	(11.5) 8	25
(13.5) 10	(11.5) 15	25
27	23	

related (matched-pairs) samples.   The same holds true for nonparametric tests.   In this case the median test is a sign test for two independent samples. An example of the procedures will make apparent the meaning of the term "sign" just mentioned.   If we were to take the data of Table 9 and combine the two distributions of scores, the median of this total distribution would be 17.5. We then tabulate the number of scores, for each distribution separately, that are above and below the median, arranging them in a 2 × 2 contingency table as shown in Table 24. Computation of χ^2 in the usual way results in a χ^2 of 4.02, which for one degree of freedom is statistically significant. It can therefore be concluded that the samples came from populations with different medians.

The median test can be generalized for more than two groups, using the same procedures described above. All the distributions are combined, and then the number of cases above and below the median for each group taken separately and tabulated, resulting in a 2 × k table.

The Mann-Whitney U Test. This test can be used when working with two independent samples, and it involves the sum of rank orders determined by combining both distributions and computing the sum of ranks for each group separately. For example, the data in Table 25 are the scores of a

TABLE 25. SCORES AND RANKS MADE BY MALES AND FEMALES
ON A TEST OF MATHEMATICAL REASONING

Males		Females	
Score	Rank	Score	Rank
28	20	24	18
27	19	20	14
23	17	19	13
22	16	16	10
21	15	15	9
18	12	14	8
17	11	12	7
10	5	11	6
8	3	9	4
6	1	7	2
	119		91

sample of males and a sample of females on a particular test. The sum of ranks for the males is 119 and for the females 91. On the assumption that the samples are from the same population, the expected sum of ranks R_1 is given by

$$ER_1 = \frac{N_1(N_1 + N_2 + 1)}{2}$$
$$= \frac{10(10 + 10 + 1)}{2}$$
$$= 105 \qquad\qquad (20)$$

and the expected sum of ranks R_2 is

$$ER_2 = \frac{N_2(N_1 + N_2 + 1)}{2}$$

$$= 105 \tag{21}$$

The sampling distribution of deviations from the expected sum of ranks follows the normal curve when the N in each sample is 8 or more. The formula for Z is

$$Z = \frac{R_1 - E(R_1)}{\sqrt{N_1 N_2 (N_1 + N_2 + 1)/12}}$$

$$= \frac{119 - 105}{\sqrt{10(10)[10 + 10 + 1]/12}}$$

$$= 1.06$$

From the magnitude of Z, we are unable to reject the null hypothesis.

When the size of the samples is less than 8, one must compute the U Test [see formulas (22) and (23)] and consult the U tables which have been reproduced by Siegel (5:273).

$$U_1 = N_1 N_2 + \frac{N_1(N_1 + 1)}{2} - R_1 \tag{22}$$

$$U_2 = N_1 N_2 + \frac{N_2(N_2 + 1)}{2} - R_2 \tag{23}$$

The values of U_1 and U_2 will not be equal, and you enter the U table with the smaller value.

The Mann-Whitney U Test is more sensitive than the Sign Test and is therefore preferred. Its major limitation appears when a large number of tied ranks occur.

The Sign Test. The Sign Test is used to determine significance of differences between two correlated samples. This test is based on the notion that when considering matched pairs, half of the differences between pairs will be positive and half will be negative. Consider the data in Table 11. If we subtract performance on the first 20 trials from performance on the second 20 trials we find that 9 out of 10 of the signs are positive. In terms of the null hypothesis of a 50–50 split, we can determine the exact probability of obtaining at least 9 heads from the binomial expansion $(\frac{1}{2} + \frac{1}{2})^{10}$ which is 0.02 for a two-tailed test. (Of course for N's larger than 10 the normal curve approximation or χ^2 can be used, as discussed earlier.) In this case we can reject the null hypothesis.

BIBLIOGRAPHY

1. Cochran, W. G., and Gertrude M. Cox, *Experimental Designs.* New York: John Wiley & Sons, Inc., 1950.

2. Edwards, A. L., *Experimental Designs in Psychological Research.*   New York: Holt, Rinehart & Winston, Inc., 1950.

3. Meyer, W. J., "The Stability of Patterns of Primary Mental Abilities among Junior High and Senior High School Students," *Educational and Psychological Measurements,* 24 (Winter, 1960): 795.

4. Ryan, T. A., "Multiple Comparisons in Psychological Research," *Psychological Bulletin,* 56 (January, 1959): 26.

5. Siegel, S., *Nonparametric Statistics.*   New York: McGraw-Hill Book Company, Inc., 1956.

CHAPTER 15

Writing the Research Report

Although you may never conduct a scientific investigation and write a doctoral dissertation, you will benefit from studying how to write a research report. A knowledge of the rules and principles involved will help you write better term papers and professional articles and will enable you to read research publications more easily and discriminatingly. Because a lack of these skills will handicap your professional growth and development, it is only prudent to master them. A lifetime can, of course, be devoted to perfecting them, for they are acquired only through persistent practice.

FORMAT OF THE REPORT

Because research papers are read by busy professional people, a rather formal and uniform method of presenting them has evolved. Most graduate schools, research institutions, and professional journals publish a report format that they expect investigators to follow. To avoid having a report rejected or returned for extensive revisions because of improper make-up, a researcher should carefully examine and meticulously adhere to the required format. Although formats at various institutions differ in some details, they are all somewhat similar to the following outline, which embraces three main divisions: the preliminaries, the body of the report or text, and the reference matter. Each main division may consist of several sections.

I. Preliminary Materials
    A. Title Page
    B. Approval Sheet (if any)
    C. Preface and Acknowledgments
    D. Table of Contents
    E. List of Tables (if any)
    F. List of Figures (if any)
II. Body of the Report
    A. Introduction
        1. Statement of the Problem
        2. Analysis of Related Studies
        3. Assumptions Underlying the Hypotheses

4. Statement of Hypotheses
5. Deduced Consequences
6. Definition of Terms
B. Method of Attack
1. Procedures Employed
2. Sources of Data
3. Data-gathering Instruments
C. Presentation and Analysis of Evidence
1. Text
2. Tables (if any)
3. Figures (if any)
D. Summary and Conclusions
1. Brief Restatement of Problem and Procedures
2. Findings and Conclusions
III. Reference Materials
A. Bibliography
B. Appendix (if any)
C. Index (if any)

Preliminary Materials. Several pages of preliminary material are presented prior to the body of a report in a dissertation. The title page, which appears first, contains the following information: (1) title of the study, (2) full name of the candidate and his previous academic background, (3) name of the faculty and institution to which the report is submitted, (4) degree for which the report is presented, (5) year when the degree is to be conferred. These items, which are illustrated in the sample title page shown on page 342, are centered between the margins of the page and no terminal punctuation is used. The title is typed in capital letters, but usually only the initial letters of principal words are capitalized in other items. If the title extends beyond one line, it is double-spaced and placed in an inverted pyramid style. Vague or broad generalizations and ambiguous or unnecessary words are not acceptable in titles. A good title gives a clear and concise description of the scope and nature of the report. It contains descriptive key words or phrases that can be placed in a bibliographical index to inform the reader whether the report is useful for his purpose.

If the institution requires an approval sheet, a page of the dissertation allots space for the adviser's signature and his name is typed below. Sometimes the names of all faculty committee members are presented on this page. If a preface is included, it usually contains a brief statement of the purpose and scope of the report and other remarks that are not particularly germane to the study. In addition, thanks may be expressed to those who gave the writer substantial guidance or assistance, but a long list of effusive acknowledgments is not in good taste.

TITLE OF THE DISSERTATION

by
Candidate's Full Name

Previous Degrees, Institutions, and Years of Graduation
A.B., University of California, 1954
M.A., University of Wisconsin, 1957

Submitted to the Graduate School of the University
of Pittsburgh in partial fulfillment of the
requirements for the degree of
Doctor of Philosophy

Pittsburgh, Pennsylvania
1961

TABLE OF CONTENTS

LIST OF TABLES*

* The list of tables always begins on a new page.

LIST OF ILLUSTRATIONS*

* The list of illustrations always begins on a new page.

The table of contents, which occupies a separate page or pages, gives the reader a bird's-eye view of the report and enables him to locate quickly each section of it. It lists the chapter headings usually in capital letters and their subdivisions in small letters with capitalized principal words. These headings appear in the exact words and order that they are in the report, and each is followed by the correct page citation. The relationship between main headings and subtopics is shown by proper indentation and capitalization. If possible, the headings are confined to one line of space, and parallel grammatical structure is used for the same value of headings. Following the table of contents are separate pages for the list of tables and the list of illustrations. The information for each item in these lists includes (1) number, usually arabic, of the table or figure, (2) exact title, and (3) number of page on which it appears in the body of the report. These preliminary materials are illustrated on the sample pages shown on pages 343 and 344.

Body of the Report. The kernel of the study, the data and their analyses, follows the preliminary materials. This body of the report contains four logical divisions: (1) an introduction, (2) the method of attack, (3) the presentation and analysis of evidence, and (4) the summary and conclusions.

Introduction. The first chapter serves as an orientation to the investigation. In it the researcher states and analyzes the nature of the problem and reviews the related studies. His résumé of the literature does not consist of a chronological list of abstracts that the reader must dissect to discover how they relate to the present problem. Rather, it is an integral part of the report that points up the issues involved in the investigation and reveals the importance of the undertaking. The review of the previous studies brings together the results of the existing research, shows how the studies are related, what they have contributed to the present investigation, and where gaps or weaknesses exist that have given rise to the present study. The significance of the problem and the need for investigating it become evident when it is placed in this wider framework of knowledge.

After reviewing the background of the problem, the writer presents his hypotheses, their deduced consequences, and the assumptions on which the hypotheses are predicated. He then defines the terms that are essential to the study or are used in a restricted or unusual manner. This information gives the reader a clear concept of the scope and limits of the investigation, the precise solution or explanation offered for the problem, and the evidence sought to test it.

Method of Attack. When describing the procedures employed in the investigation, the researcher does not merely state whether the historical, experimental, or descriptive method was used. Rather, he gives an accurate, detailed description of how the work was done as well as all of the information that the reader needs to judge the validity, adequacy, and suitability of the methods and instruments employed. His objective is to provide an explanation that will enable the reader to repeat the investigation—reproducing the exact conditions of the original study—to check the findings. Generally speaking, this explanation is rather extensive, and thus it is placed in a chapter by itself. Since the findings of a study can be no better than the tools and methods used to solve it, scholars are extremely critical when they examine this section of the report.

The kinds of procedural information presented depend on the nature of the study. They may be: types of data gathered; number and kinds of subjects—sex, age, size, previous experience, or any distinguishing characteristics that could affect the results of the investigation; how and on what basis the subjects were selected; when, where, and how the data were collected; number of subjects who did not complete or did not participate in all parts of the study, and why; exact method of executing the experiment—experimental controls, how variables were changed and manipulated, uncontrolled factors that may have affected the results and their possible implications; verbal or written directions given to subjects; pretests; and pilot studies. To assist other investigators, the researcher also explains any methods that were employed and abandoned because they proved to be inadequate or valueless.

Well-known data-gathering instruments and readily available apparatus are described briefly and references are listed to reveal where more detailed discussions can be found. But if new apparatus or instruments or variations of an old one are employed, detailed descriptions and drawings of them and clear explanations of how they were used are given. After describing the investigative instruments, the researcher explains the procedures employed to calibrate those that require it and tells what was done to determine the validity and reliability of the tools. Upon completing the introduction to the report, he rereads all the materials to make certain that nothing has been omitted that the reader must know to follow and comprehend the rest of the report.

Presentation and Analysis of Evidence. The presentation and analysis of the data constitute a vital part of the report; this is the researcher's contribution to the advancement of knowledge. No specific directions can be given for organizing these materials because of the wide variety of studies and kinds of data that exist. Tables, figures, and discussion can be used to present the information. The analysis of the data can be covered in one chapter, or separate chapters can be devoted to each major issue or part of the investigation. Raw data can be recorded in the most convenient form for collecting them, but in the body of the report, these data are classified in ways that reveal the pertinent information required to confirm or disconfirm the deduced consequences of the hypothesis. In some studies, not only the raw evidence but also the values of the statistical computations are presented. If the chapters are long, a short summary may be written for each one.

The analysis of the data points out the important facts that the collected evidence reveals and notes their relationships. It does not repeat all the detailed information that is in the tables and graphs, but rather interprets what the facts mean—their causes and effects and whether they confirm or disconfirm the hypothesis. Extracting the meaning from the data is one of the most difficult and delightful phases of an investigation. If more than one explanation can be given for a particular fact, the researcher discusses all explanations, not merely the one he favors. After drafting an explanation, he examines the data for exceptions, tries to account for them, and restates his explanation if necessary. Any uncontrollable factors that may have affected the results, and their possible implications, are discussed. If the results of the investigation are in agreement or disagreement with other studies, this is pointed out and possible explanations are given for any differences. When stating the results of the study, careful qualifications are included that stipulate the precise condition or limits to which the conclusions apply.

When presenting and analyzing data, the researcher exercises caution. To check his work, he asks questions, such as the following: Are these data a product of any errors in observations or computation? Have I confused facts with opinions and inferences? Have I drawn a conclusion from unrepresentative data? Have I omitted or ignored evidence because it did not conform to my hypothesis? Have I assumed that B is the effect of A merely because it follows A? Have I assumed that because A and B resemble each other in some respects they must resemble each other in another respect? Have I assumed that something is true merely because an important man has said it is? To what extent could chance factors have influenced my results?

Summary and Conclusions. In the summary, the researcher briefly reviews the procedures, findings, and entire evolvement of the problem. Since the evidence and the test results for the various parts of the problem are given in the presentation and analysis of the data, the important points are merely brought together in the summary—a repetition of all the evidence on which they were based is unnecessary. The precisely stated conclusions clearly relate to the original questions the problem raised and the solution proposed. They reveal whether the conditions that were deduced to be observable if the hypothesis offers an adequate explanation were observable when tested. The conclusions announce whether the findings of the study confirmed or disconfirmed the hypothesis. If the conclusions modify any existing hypothesis or theory, this fact is discussed. If any problems were raised by the investigation that require further research, they are sometimes listed.

The summary and conclusion chapter is the most widely read part of a dissertation. Since it briefly recapitulates the information presented in the previous chapters, this chapter provides the reader with the most significant details and accomplishments of the study. Hence, most readers scan the summary of a report first to obtain an overview of the problem and to determine its usefulness to them. If the study is pertinent for their purposes, they examine the other chapters before accepting the conclusions.

In addition to the summary, some institutions require a candidate to submit an abstract of about five hundred words to fulfill requirements for a degree. This abstract may be included in the formal report or may be subsequently published in *Dissertation Abstracts* or some other source. Some research journals also print a brief abstract in distinctive type at the beginning of each report. An abstract is not a substitute for the summary and conclusion chapter. It merely gives pertinent information that enables a scholar to judge whether he wishes to read the complete work.

Reference Materials. The bibliography, which will be discussed in detail later in this chapter, follows the main body of the report. If an appendix is included, it follows the bibliography. The appendix presents supporting materials that are too unwieldy to be placed in the body of the dissertation, such as questionnaires, form letters, evaluation sheets, check lists, courses of study, long quotations, raw data, documents, and interview forms. The appendix is not a dumping ground for leftover products of the study. It contains only relevant items that because of their length would break the continuity of thought if they were placed in the body of the report. The items in the appendix are grouped, labeled, lettered, and listed in the table of contents. Preparing an alphabetized index to insert after the appendix is a responsibility that the researcher assumes if his study is complex, of major importance, or to be published in book or monograph form.

STYLE OF WRITING

Writing a report in any fashion that occurs to a researcher may later make him do time-consuming revisions. Before doing any writing, therefore, he should carefully study not only the report format but also the style manual recommended by his professor, institution, or editor. If a writer is specifically granted the right to select a style, he can find several manuals available to serve as guides (3,4,10,13,19,21). After adopting a style, he must adhere to it throughout the report, for switching from one acceptable style to another is not permissible.

Mastering the methods of reporting research is important, for an outstanding scientific investigation is of little value if the findings are not effectively communicated to others. Accomplishing this feat is somewhat different from writing a nontechnical composition. A researcher does not try to entertain, amuse, or persuade the reader, nor does he merely discuss his opinions concerning a problem or suggest solutions and argue on the basis of general observations. Rather, he presents a hypothesis, explains the procedures employed to test it, cites the factual data collected, and announces whether they confirm or disconfirm the hypothesis. A clear, objective, logical presentation and analysis of the evidence rather than an emotionalized argument or diverting descriptions are required in a scientific report.

Since a report is not ordinarily read by laymen but by well-informed individuals with more than a passing interest in the topic, it is critically and systematically scrutinized. Reviewers will be skeptical of any assertions unless demonstrated evidence is presented; they may challenge the writer's reasoning processes, the interpretation placed upon the data, the accuracy of the footnotes, or they may even repeat the experiment to check the results. Hence, a research report must be able to stand the test of critical scholarship supplied by other investigators.

Organization.   Spewing a disordered jumble of raw facts into a report form not only fails to convey information to the reader, but usually indicates that the author has not grasped the significance of his materials.   Meaning cannot be derived easily from chaotic masses of isolated items.   Data must be grouped and ordered into logical, attractive patterns before they can convey clear messages.   Only through arduous intellectual effort can a researcher organize facts so that they deliver precise ideas he has in mind.

A writer does not insert a blank sheet of paper in a typewriter and compose a report as he would a family letter.   The final draft of a report is the end product of a process that begins in the initial stages of an investigation. When first exploring the literature and pondering about his potential problem, a researcher notices that certain topics recur and seem to be related to it.   If he jots down several of these, the relationship between a few isolated items may suddenly snap into focus and enable him to group them under one heading.   After scanning sufficient source materials to identify the major topics, he can organize them into a crude outline and thereafter file his notes under these categories.   While refining his hypothesis and doing more reading and observing, he may note and correct weaknesses in his outline, such as gaps that exist, materials that are not in the most logical order, topics that are in poor proportion, or items that need to be combined or omitted.   The outline is continuously remolded; it is not a rigid instrument that is constructed accurately in one draft.   Rather, it is an imperfect map that is useful even in its crudest stage, but becomes a more reliable instrument as it is improved upon during the investigation.

What dictates the items and the order in an outline?   The report format required by the institution provides the general framework.   The hypotheses serve as guides for structuring the specific arguments—the procedures employed, the evidence collected, and the conclusions reached.   But within each argument materials must be ordered in terms of importance, time, place, cause and effect, similarities and contrasts, or on some other basis. After all the arguments are structured, they must be placed in a logical order.

Hence, before writing a word of his dissertation; a researcher once again reviews the institutional format requirements and remodels sections of his outline that do not conform to it.   He also makes certain that there is a direct relationship between the items in the outline and the hypotheses, and checks whether the items are placed in the most logical order. After extending the outline so that it includes both the main topics and subtopics, he may also write topic sentences for the paragraphs that will come under them. When the outline seems satisfactory, he asks competent colleagues and his adviser to examine it critically for weaknesses.

Although most researchers obtain the best results by making a detailed outline before they write, some find that they can write more quickly and spontaneously if they do not. This type of worker immerses himself in his subject, takes notes, and mentally structures information into orderly patterns as he reads and observes. After getting a good grasp of the materials, he swiftly records his ideas. But afterward, he may outline these written materials to check whether the topics appear in the most logical order and are given proper emphasis.

A good outline guides the researcher not only in preparing the dissertation but also in constructing chapter titles and section headings. The choice of words is an important task, for carefully composed headings can give readers an overview of the materials, help them find their way around in the report, and make it easier for them to grasp meanings. Headings cannot accomplish these objectives, of course, unless they are sufficiently specific to suggest the contents of the succeeding paragraphs. Moreover, headings on the same level are expected to have the same grammatical structure and style of capitalization.

Right:	*Wrong:*
Chapter	Chapter
I. Format of the Report	I. Format of the Report
II. Style of the Report	II. Style manuals are selected with care
III. Typing of the Report	III. Typing

Language.   Words—the writer's communication tools—are selected and ordered to inform the reader about the investigation rather than to impress him with rhetorical flourishes. Encrusting a report with polysyllabic words, technical jargon, involved sentences, and profuse quotations tends to smother the reader's interest and to prevent him from receiving the intended message. It blocks rather than increases understanding. Instead of baffling the reader with a pompous, pedantic presentation, an able writer gives a simple, straightforward, and dignified account of what took place in his study. Through a careful and correct use of language, he constructs plain, precise explanations that prevent misinterpretations from arising. Whenever a researcher uses unfamiliar terms, he defines them or uses them in a context from which their meaning can be inferred. He also gives brief descriptions of any obscure theories that are mentioned in his report. Before using a term he checks its meaning, and he refrains from employing it in one sense at one point in his argument and in a different sense in another.   If a graph or drawing will make it easier to understand the written discussion, he constructs one.

A formal rather than a colloquial style is employed in research reports. But formal writing need not drain all spontaneity and individuality from ideas and press them into prim, plodding prose passages.   Lucid, lively writing is the goal.   To attain it, a writer rigorously prunes hackneyed, extraneous, and vague words from his report and diligently searches for vivid, varied, and accurate means of expression.   To hold the reader's interest and arouse clear mental images, he uses familiar, concrete nouns. Whenever possible, he employs brisk, active verbs rather than the passive voice.

Proportion and Emphasis.   To achieve proper proportion and emphasis in a report, a writer repeatedly revises an outline until he has all topics of equal importance placed on the same level.   Because his objective is to help readers identify and grasp the main ideas, he refrains from stating them in a few terse sentences and from elaborating upon minor points for several paragraphs.   When revising a report, he courageously deletes treasured words, sentences, and paragraphs that give too much weight to minor topics and carefully expands underdeveloped major topics by adding supporting evidence and illustrations.   Instead of burying significant ideas under masses of rhetorical trivia, an author skillfully spotlights them by utilizing special techniques.   He places topic sentences where they will quickly capture the reader's attention; he puts key words or phrases at the beginning or end of sentences; and he signalizes that the ideas are important by placing them in italics, numbering them, or utilizing warning words to announce that the following statements are significant.

Unity and Clarity.   To achieve unity and clarity in his report, a researcher selects homogeneous items from his notes, states the ideas in simple, coherent sentences, places them in a logical sequence, and weaves them into paragraphs that in turn are logically related.   Again and again he examines sentences, paragraphs, and chapters to determine whether like things have been placed as close together as possible and whether one idea naturally leads to the next.   After transposing misplaced items, combining similar ideas, culling unnecessary and repetitive materials, and correcting vague or weak reference of pronouns to their antecedents, he again checks the flow of his manuscript.   He asks: "Have I shown the connection between ideas, so that the reader can easily follow the arguments?   Have I used transitional words, sentences, and paragraphs that will alert the reader to changes in the road ahead and that will gently lead him from point to point?"

Other Style Problems.   Many other questions concerning style arise during the writing of a report.   This text cannot cover all of them, but the following paragraphs discuss some common ones. Since a research report is a formal and objective account of an investigation, it is written in the third person. Personal pronouns—I, me, we, you, our, and us—are not used. Although there are a few exceptions, abbreviations are not usually employed *in the textual materials*, but they are used in footnotes, bibliographies, appendixes, and tables. In dissertations "per cent" is spelled out, but some journals permit the use of the symbol % in tables and even in the textual discussion.

Numbers of less than one hundred, round numbers, and numbers that begin sentences are spelled out; fractions are spelled out unless they are part of a longer number. If small and large numbers appear in a series, figures are used for all of them. Although there are some exceptions, numbers of four digits or more usually have commas to point off thousands. The letters or numbers that enumerate items in a paragraph are enclosed in parentheses; either letters or numbers may be used, but not both forms in the same report.

Simplified spelling is not acceptable in research reports. Punctuation should conform to good usage and be consistent. A report is written in the past tense when referring to what the researcher or other investigators have done. The present tense may be used, however, when referring the reader to tables that are presently before him and when mentioning general truths and well-established principles. All style books do not present exactly the same rules, but, as has been previously stated, after a style has been selected, it must be followed consistently throughout the report.

CONSTRUCTION OF TABLES AND FIGURES

Tables and figures sometimes convey information about the investigation more effectively than the best written descriptions. Graphic illustrations are "worth more than ten thousand words," but this is true only if they are accurately compiled, properly arranged, easily read, and correctly interpreted. Since a large number of graphic procedures have been devised, the following discussion can only point out some general rules governing their construction. More detailed explanations can be found in textbooks devoted to the subject (3,10,12,15,19,21).

Tables. When collecting data, the researcher may use the most convenient method of recording information. He may list pupils' names alphabetically, for example, and place varied information about them in columns bearing the appropriate labels. But to obtain the precise information needed for his study, he may have to reorder these data so as to make comparisons on the basis of sex, age, schools, or geographical areas. Of course, an investigator studies the deduced consequences of his hypothesis and, if possible, devises a plan to collect the original data in a tabular form that will force the desired answers into clear focus.   Learning how to pattern data so as to bring out significant information is of utmost importance to a researcher.   Through a table he can often help readers spot important details, see relationships, get a concise overview of the findings, or grasp the significance of data much more quickly and easily than through many pages of prose explanation.

Content.   Simplicity and unity are essential in the construction of tables. A complex table followed by an explanation which extends for several pages may confuse rather than enlighten the reader.   The thread of an argument can easily be lost while flipping back and forth from pages of discussion to the table.   If several comparisons of distinctly different kinds are incorporated in one table, or if like comparisons are separated into many different tables, a reader can become bewildered.   A good table is similar to a well-written paragraph; it consists of several related facts that are integrated to present *one main idea.*

A well-constructed table is self-explanatory; it is complete and sufficiently clear to be understood without reading the textual explanation.   Conversely, the written discussion explains the generalizations that can be derived from the table and the relevancy of the information in a manner that enables the reader to grasp the main ideas without examining the table. In the textual discussion, the writer refers to the table by number (and page if necessary) rather than the less specific phrase, "see the following table."

All statistical materials are not placed in formal tables.   A simple statistical statement such as the following, for example, may be inserted directly in the body of a paragraph: "Of the 376 children, 120 had received no Salk vaccine shots, 136 had received one, and 120 had received two."   A few facts may be organized into an informal pattern and woven into the textual material by an introductory sentence followed by a colon, for example:

The teachers were about evenly divided in their choice of retirement plans:

	Women	*Men*	*Total*
Plan A	20	19	39
Plan B	16	18	34
Total	36	37	73

The table of contents in the dissertation does not list these informally presented statistical statements.

Placement.   A table never precedes, but rather follows, as closely as possible, the first reference to it in the report.   If a table will not fit into the remaining space on the page, it is placed on the next page at the end of the first paragraph.   If a table covers more than a half page, it usually is centered on a page by itself.   Long, detailed tables that interrupt the continuity of the discussion may be put in the appendix, and shorter tables that summarize the information may be used in the body of the text. It is advisable to type all tables on separate pages to avoid recopying them during each revision of the report; when the final draft is assembled, they can be inserted in the proper places.

Numbers and Captions. Tables are numbered consecutively throughout the report, including those that appear in the appendix. Many styles of constructing tables are acceptable, but consistency of style is required. One style that can be used conforms to the following pattern. The word "Table," followed by its number, is placed alone on the first line and the heading or title two lines below it. Both items are typed in full capital letters, arabic numerals are used, and no end punctuation is necessary. A title more than one line long is single-spaced and typed to form an inverted pyramid. A good heading describes precisely what the table contains, and in order to aid the reader, the key descriptive word is placed near the beginning of the title. The unit of measurement (thousands of dollars) or source of data (1962 Budget of Pittsburgh Public Schools) may be placed in parentheses below the title so that the reader has the information before he scans the data. Sometimes the source is placed just beneath the table as it is in Figure 21, which presents a slightly different but equally acceptable style.

In tables, the captions (column headings) and stubs (labels for rows) should be brief yet accurate and complete. Captions should be parallel in grammatical structure; common abbreviations can be used, but others are avoided if possible. Long captions may be typed broadside so as to be read up from the bottom of the page. Writers employ different capitalization styles; some capitalize only the initial letter in the first word, and proper nouns and adjectives.

To facilitate locating items referred to in the table, the columns may be numbered (sometimes in parentheses) below the column captions (see Figure 21). Units of measurement may be given following the column caption or below the horizontal line beneath the caption. Figure columns are aligned on the right, but if decimals are used, these must be aligned. When no data are available, the omission is indicated by dots or dashes, or by leaving the space blank, rather than by a zero—which represents a value of zero rather than an omission. Table footnote references are noted by standard typewriter characters—*, **, ***—or by superscript lower-case letters—[a,b,c]. Table footnotes are placed just below the horizontal line at the bottom of the table rather than at the bottom of the page.

Size. Tables should be no larger than the pages of the manuscript or publication. Folding tables into the copy is usually unsatisfactory and should be avoided if possible. If tables will not fit into the normal pages— lengthwise, crosswise, or spread across two facing pages—they may be reduced in size by photostating them or using smaller print. If a table extends beyond a page in length, the word "Table" and the number are repeated, followed by the word "Continued," at the top of the succeeding pages. (For example, Table 3—Continued.) The title is omitted on the continued table, but all other captions are repeated. If a table covers two facing pages, the full heading is placed on the top of the first page and only the word "Table" and the number, followed by the word "Continued," appear on the top of the opposite page.

Rulings. Rulings or lines are used only if they make it easier to read the table. A double or heavy horizontal line may be placed above the column captions, a single one below them, and another below the last row

TABLE 3.—NUMBER OF PUBLIC ELEMENTARY- AND SECONDARY-SCHOOL TEACHERS IN SERVICE, 1947-48 THRU 1956-57 [a]

Year	Number of elementary-school teachers	Percent change from previous year	Number of secondary-school teachers	Percent change from previous year	Total	Percent change from previous year
1	2	3	4	5	6	7
1947–48	578,226[b]	...	319,746[b]	...	897,972[b]	...
1948–49	594,047[b]	+2.7%	330,289[b]	+3.3%	924,336[b]	+2.9%
1949–50	586,276	−1.3	318,163	−3.7	904,439	−2.2
1950–51	604,131	+3.0	323,486	+1.7	927,617	+2.6
1951–52	627,285	+3.8	329,173	+1.8	956,458	+3.1
1952–53	653,573	+4.2	339,010	+3.0	992,583	+3.8
1953–54	661,900	+1.3	·362,848	+7.0	1,024,748	+3.2
1954–55	690,987	+4.4	389,342	+7.3	1,080,329	+5.4
1955–56	718,772	+4.0	408,329	+4.9	1,127,101	+4.3
1956–57	751,490	+4.6	426,560	+4.5	1,178,050	+4.5
Change from 1947–48 to 1956–57	+173,264	+30.0%	+106,814	+33.4%	+280,078	+31.2%

Source: Columns 2, 4, and 6 from: National Education Association, Research Division. *Advance Estimates of Public Elementary and Secondary Schools for the School Years,* 1947-48 thru 1956-57.
[a] See footnote to Table 2.
[b] Includes principals and supervisors.

Fig. 21. A table. *From Research Division, National Education Association, "The Postwar Struggle to Provide Competent Teachers," Research Bulletin, 35 (October, 1957), 107.*

of items in the table. Vertical rules and additional horizontal ones may be added if they break up the data into logical groups or make the arrangement simpler to use. Rulings are not made on the sides of tables.

Figures. Some ideas may be communicated more quickly and clearly by figures than by written or tabular presentations. A good drawing of a piece of apparatus or a flow chart that traces channels of authority may clarify points that would otherwise require several pages of textual explanation. By presenting certain aspects of data in a graph or chart form, one may dramatically reveal important trends or relationships that a reader could not easily grasp when examining complex statistical data. Figures do not replace word descriptions, but they sometimes make it easier to explain and interpret complicated instruments and data to the reader.

Types. The commonest forms of figures used in reports are the line graphs, bar graphs, pie charts, area or volume charts, component or belt charts, pictorial charts, flow charts, maps, diagrams of apparatus, and photographs. A number of reference books explain in detail the methods of presenting these figures, the advantages and disadvantages of utilizing each type, the pitfalls to avoid, and the rules governing their construction (3,6,7,8,10,15,18,19,20). The following discussion merely suggests some general rules for constructing figures.

Purpose. Figures are not introduced merely to convey simple concepts or to make the report more interesting. A drawing or graph is used only if it can snap important ideas or significant relationships into a sharp focus for the reader more quickly than other means of presentation. Complex, confused, or carelessly prepared figures can be less effective communicators than words. A good figure weaves a few pertinent related facts together to present one main idea. It is simple, uncluttered with unnecessary and confusing details, and it presents a limited number of symbols. Concise captions, labels, and legends are placed on figures to describe the nature of the data and to interpret the information presented.

Number and Captions. Illustrative materials are labeled with the word "Figure" or "Fig." and numbered consecutively throughout the report with arabic numbers. The word "Figure" and its number are usually placed below the illustration. The title for the illustration may be placed either (1) after the figure number, (2) at the top of the illustration, or (3) within the figure. The caption can be typed or lettered in full capital letters and in an inverted pyramid form with no terminal punctuation, or as an ordinary sentence in paragraph, underhung, or block form. The advice previously given about the placement of tables in the text and references to them in the written discussion also applies to figures.

ACKNOWLEDGMENT OF INDEBTEDNESS

Acknowledgments of indebtedness to other authors are included in a report not only as a matter of honesty and courtesy, but also as a means of confirming one's work and indicating the quality and thoroughness of the investigation. To many readers, the footnotes and bibliography in a report, which give them clues concerning the related literature in the field, are as important as the textual materials. Thus, when writing a doctoral dissertation, an article for a professional journal, or even a term paper, one should include all the information that readers will need to locate the source materials with a minimum of effort. Sources of all quoted materials and other works that were of significant value in preparing the report must be unmistakably and fully identified in accordance with the style rules that have been designed to help transmit such information. Mastering these rules is one more basic skill that a writer must add to his technical equipment.

Quotations. Laymen often joke about the array of quotations and footnotes found in research reports, and their barbs are not always unwarranted. Indiscriminately interlarding a report with quotations and footnotes is a cultural affectation that some inexperienced writers assume to conceal shoddy workmanship. Pasting numerous quotations into an authority-laden mosaic does not create an acceptable research report, for strings of these passages are dull and difficult to read. Moreover, they reveal that the author is little beyond the note-taking stage of his work. Research is a creative endeavor; a good report presents a synthesis of what the investigator has read, observed, thought, and mentally ordered into new patterns rather than a mere compilation of other men's work. Quotations are to be used sparingly and purposively rather than as a crutch for a lazy mind.

Art of Quoting. By paraphrasing rather than quoting materials, one can usually make a discussion move more directly and forcefully toward his objective. To credit the original author of an idea that is borrowed but not quoted directly, one places a footnote superscript at the end of the statement and the appropriate documentation in the footnote. If it is impossible to rephrase information as concisely, accurately, or effectively as the original source, it can be quoted directly. This is done, for example, when presenting laws and formulas or aptly expressed ideas by respected authorities that point up an argument.

Whenever possible, it is best to select a short quotation or to strip the chaff from a longer one and plant the kernel in one's own sentence. To avoid introducing all quotations that are presented as separate sentences with "Mr. X says," the introductory phrase may be placed within or at the end of the quotation. Because short quotations can be woven into a discussion more easily than long ones, they are preferred. But a particularly pertinent long quotation can be used if extraneous portions are deleted.

Mechanics of Quoting. The rules for presenting short and long direct quotations differ. A short quotation is enclosed in quotation marks, double-spaced, and incorporated in the paragraph. If another quotation appears within a short quotation, it is enclosed in single quotation marks. The arabic reference numeral to the footnote is typed one-half space above and after the phrase or sentence quoted, and after the punctuation mark if it comes at the end of the sentence. Long quotations—usually more than four typewritten lines—are usually set off in separate single-spaced paragraphs that are indented in their entirety, and no quotation marks are necessary. Quotations within long quotations are set off by full quotation marks. Exceptionally long quotations may be placed in the appendix. When a quotation occurs in a footnote it is single-spaced, enclosed in quotation marks, and indented in paragraph style.

In the previous discussion on taking notes (see Chapter 6), the text stressed the importance of checking for accuracy when duplicating quoted material. It also explained the method writers use to denote omissions in a quotation—ellipses—and to introduce corrections or explanations—brackets. Perhaps mention should be made of some other mechanics. If the first word of a quotation is grammatically linked to what preceded it in the sentence, it is not capitalized even though it was in the original sentence. For example: (1) We agree with Dr. Jones that "measurement is essential in research." (2) Dr. Jones stated, "Measurement is essential in research." End punctuation in quotations also may raise questions. Only one punctuation mark accompanies the terminal quotation marks: (1) a period or comma is placed inside closing quotation marks, (2) a colon or semicolon is placed outside quotation marks, (3) an interrogation or exclamation point is placed inside the quotation marks if it belongs to the quoted matter and outside if a part of the whole sentence.

Footnotes. Footnotes serve various purposes: (1) Some give source references for direct quotations or paraphrased material, (2) some provide cross references to materials appearing in other parts of the report, (3) some indicate sources that contain substantiating evidence, and (4) some explain or elaborate a point in the textual discussion. The last type should be kept to a minimum.

Citation of Footnotes. Several methods for inserting footnotes have been devised. The most common one is to place at the bottom of the page all footnotes for citations appearing on that page. When this method is employed, the footnotes are separated from the text by a short line—twenty spaces—drawn from the left margin one space below the written discussion. Beneath this line a double space is left before the first footnote is typed; the footnotes are single-spaced with double spaces between them. Each footnote is indented as in a paragraph and preceded by a superscript numeral that corresponds to the reference numeral used in the textual material. The first word of the footnote follows the reference superscript numeral; no punctuation or space is necessary (see page 359). If the text consists of tables, mathematical materials, or formulas, an asterisk or some symbol other than a number is selected to identify a footnote. The writer either numbers footnotes consecutively throughout the report, or begins anew on each page or in each chapter, depending upon the institutional requirements.

If a report is to be published, authors may employ other methods of inserting footnotes. To facilitate the work of the printer, they may place the footnote immediately following the textual reference on the page and separate the source information from the rest of the paragraph by typing unbroken lines above and below it. Some publishers prefer a third method of identifying source materials, i.e., the one that is used in this text. In this method, a bibliographical reference and page number are placed in parentheses immediately after a direct quotation or textual reference and in alignment with it. For example, a quotation is followed by the coded message (16:24–25).   Since all sources are cited in the bibliography, this method conserves space and cuts printing costs.

Abbreviations in Footnotes.   To save time and space, full bibliographical information about a source is presented in the footnotes the first time a reference is made to it; thereafter, abbreviations are used to identify it.   The abbreviation *ibid.* is employed when the succeeding references to a work *immediately* follow the first full citation (see sample footnotes 16 to 18).   If references to *other works intervene* between the first and later citations to the same work, the abbreviations *loc. cit.* or *op. cit.* are used.   If the reference is to the same page, *loc. cit.* is used; otherwise *op. cit.* and the volume, if necessary, and page number are given (see sample footnotes 20 and 22). The author's last name precedes these abbreviations, but his first name is added if more than one author cited in the report has the same last name. After the second work by the same author is cited, an abbreviated or full title must be given in each subsequent citation to make it unmistakably clear which of his works is meant (see sample footnote 24).   Some writers always use the abbreviated title instead of *op. cit.* and *loc. cit.*   The terms *ibid., op. cit.,* and *loc. cit.* are followed by periods to denote that they are abbreviations and underscored to indicate italics.   The following samples of footnotes illustrate the use of these abbreviations:

[16] Alice W. Heim, "Adaptation to Level of Difficulty in Intelligence Testing," *British Journal of Psychology,* 46 (August, 1955), p. 211.

[17] *Ibid.*   [same work, same page as above]

[18] *Ibid.,* p. 214.   [same work as 16, but page 214]

[19] Robert A. Jackson, "Prediction of the Academic Success of College Freshmen," *Journal of Educational Psychology,* 46 (May, 1955), p. 296.

[20] Heim, *loc. cit.*   [refers to 16, exactly the same page]

[21] Samuel F. Klugman, "Agreement between Two Tests as Predictors of College Success," *Personnel and Guidance Journal,* 36 (December, 1957), p. 255.

[22] Heim, *op. cit.,* p. 220.   [refers to 16, but page 220]

[23] Alice W. Heim, *The Appraisal of Intelligence.*   London: Methuen and Co., 1954, p. 169.   [second work by Heim is introduced]

[24] Heim, "Adaptation in Intelligence Testing," *op. cit.,* p. 223.   [repetition of title indicates which Heim work is meant]

A number of other abbreviations appear in research reports.   Many of them are in Latin, although some are now being replaced by English terms. If a researcher is not familiar with these abbreviations, he cannot interpret the footnotes in many source materials and cannot utilize these shorthand devices when writing his report.   Thus, it is wise for him to master the common communication symbols that follow:

anon.   anonymous
Bk., Bks.   book(s)
c. or *ca.*   about (approximate date, *c.* 1245)
cf.   compare (cf. *ante* p. 16, compare above; cf. *supra,* compare any proceeding

material; cf. *post* p. 26, compare below; cf. *infra*, compare any subsequent material)

Ch., Chap., Chaps.   chapter(s)

col., cols.   column(s)

e.g.   for example

ed., edd.   edition(s)

ed., eds.   editor(s); edited by

et al.   and others (author Jones *et al.* stated)

et seq., et seqq.   and the following (16 *et seq.*, page 16 and the following page)

f., ff.   and the following page(s)   (pp. 3 f., page 3 and the following page; pp. 3 ff., page 3 and the following pages)

i.e.   that is

id., idem   the same as before (the same person)

l., ll.   line(s)   (ll. 8–12, lines 8 through 12)

mimeo.   mimeographed

MS, MSS   manuscript(s)

n., nn.   footnote(s)   (n. 10, nn. 1–6)

N.B.   please note; mark well

n.d.   no date (given for a publication)

n.n.   no name

n.p.   no place

N.S.   New Series; New Style (of dating, since 1752)

No., Nos.   number(s)

O.S.   Old Series; Old Style (of dating, before 1752)

p., pp.   page(s)

passim   here and there (discussed in various places in the work)

Pt., Pts.   part(s)

q.v.   (quod vide) which see (used to suggest consulting a work, now replaced by English "see")

rev.   revised, revision

Sec., Secs.   section(s)

trans.   translator, translated by

viz.   namely

Vol., Vols.   volume(s)

vs., vss.   verse(s)

Bibliography.   The bibliography should give a clear, complete description of the sources that were used when preparing the report. Some bibliographies classify entries under headings such as Books, Periodicals, Newspapers, Reports, Public Documents, and Miscellaneous, but most of them arrange items in a single alphabetized list. The latter method must be adopted and items must be numbered consecutively if, instead of page footnotes, the cross-reference system of citations from the body to the bibliography of the report is used as it is in this text.

Style of Citing.   Bibliographical items usually are listed alphabetically by authors' surnames, but a chronological arrangement is used in some studies.

When the author's name is not given, the work is listed under the name of the school system, institution, or agency that prepared the report (see Bibliography 21). When there is no clue of authorship, the work is listed under the first important word of the title (see Bibliography 10). To make the author's name stand out, the first line of each entry is typed flush with the margin and the remaining lines are indented. Double spacing or single spacing with double spaces between entries is used.

No universally accepted style for constructing a bibliography exists. The researcher adopts one that is approved by his advisor or publisher and uses it consistently. The following samples present a simple and workable style:

1. *For a book*

Surname of author, given name or two initials, *Title Taken from Title Page* [underlined]. Edition if more than one, volume if more than one, place of publication: publisher, date on title page or copyright date.

2. *For an article*

Surname of author, given name or two initials, "Title of Article," *Name of Periodical* [underlined]. Volume of periodical (month, day, year), beginning page.

3. *For a newspaper*

Name of Paper [underlined], month, day, year, section of paper, page. [If author and title are given, they precede name of paper.]

4. *For unpublished materials* [speeches, letters, mimeographed materials, etc.]

Surname of author, given name or initials, "Title of Material," nature of material and where it is available or was presented,[1] date.

Sometimes this bibliographical style is also used for footnotes, except that the regular paragraph indention rather than the underhung style is employed and the exact page of the quotation is given. But most institutions require further changes in footnotes; they stipulate that the author's given name must appear first, and some recommend a different form for the punctuation and placement of items (see page 359). Additional information may also be required in the bibliography. As the last item in each entry, the total number of pages in the source may have to be listed to give the reader some concept of the comprehensiveness of the source. A brief annotation summarizing the viewpoint, contents, strengths, weaknesses, bias,

---

[1] For example; Unpublished Ph.D. dissertation, University of Pittsburgh.
Paper read before the annual convention of the Educator's Club, New York City.
Minutes of the Wayne Township Board of Education, Wayne, Michigan.
Letter to the writer from Dr. John Dewey, Teachers College, Columbia University.

or unique contribution of the source may also be required.   If annotations are added, they are single-spaced and separated from the rest of the entry by a double space.

Aids for Citing.   A researcher must use the same style for like items throughout his bibliography and recheck each item in every entry for accuracy and completeness.   Different types of bibliographical entries, of course, present different problems.   When puzzled about how to write an entry, one can turn to a style book for help.   An examination of the bibliographies in this text and the following general rules will answer some common questions.

1. When two or more works by the same author are listed, an unbroken line about six spaces in length, followed by a comma, is sometimes substituted for his name after the first entry.   The titles of his works are alphabetized under his name.   Publications of which he is coauthor follow those of which he is sole author.

2. If a book has two or three authors, the second and third authors' names are written in the normal order (see Bibliography 1, 4, 20).   If there are more than three authors, the name of the first is given, followed by *et al.* or "and others" (see Bibliography 9).

3. An editor or compiler is indicated by placing the proper abbreviations in the parentheses following the name (see Bibliography 11).

4. When identifying the place of publication, the name of the city is sufficient if it is well known, otherwise the name of the state or the complete address is added.

PREPARATION OF THE REPORT

Having reviewed the report format and style requirements, we can now consider the general procedures to be followed when preparing a report.   A writer adopts the patterns of working that are most suitable for him.   However, acquiring knowledge of how others have solved some writing, revising, and typing problems that commonly arise may help him improve his system.

Drafting and Revising the Report.   Some parts of a report, such as the review of the literature, may be written fairly early in an investigation, but most of the work is done after the hypotheses have been tested.   The researcher collects the data, organizes them into tables, graphs, or some other form that brings out relationships, classifies his notes, and places them in the order that they appear in his outline.   Then, while carefully examining them, he writes paragraphs of explanation and interpretation for each section of the report, composes transitional statements or paragraphs that lead the reader from one point to the next, and drafts the conclusions.

Even at this stage of the work, an investigator may reorder points in the outline to achieve a more logical presentation or smoother transitions.

Thus, in all but the final copy of a report, one should type each paragraph on a separate page so that there is sufficient room to make corrections or revisions. By doing this, it is possible to rewrite and add paragraphs or shift them from one section of the report to another without copying entire pages of contiguous materials.

Writing is arduous work. It is a prolonged process of composing, reordering, adding, deleting, and polishing. Successful writers redraft their reports many times before they are satisfied with the results. When they submit their reports to faculty advisors or editors, they receive additional suggestions for improvements. Hence, making revisions may consume more hours than writing the original draft.

A beginner usually has much to learn before he can write effectively, but by forming good work habits he can improve the quality of his work and hasten his progress. Experienced writers have the following advice to offer:

1. Set aside regular hours for writing and observe that schedule faithfully.

2. Choose an environment that is conducive to work and make certain that the necessary reference books, dictionaries, and files are at hand.

3. To overcome the difficulty of getting started at each writing session, stop writing early each day, and spend a few minutes organizing materials and listing the things to do the following day.

4. After working on a draft for a few days, set it aside and return later to read it critically.

5. Since items in a report do not have to be written in a consecutive order, compose a rough draft of a section whenever sufficient insight into the materials has been gained.

6. Concentrate on communicating information when writing. Do not let minor problems interrupt the flow of thought and block progress—skip over them and return later to find the proper word, devise a deft transition, check a fact, or insert an illustration.

7. When bogged down in a particular paragraph or section of a report, reread the preceding materials and the outline to regain perspective.

8. Ask colleagues to read the report and point out any gaps, weaknesses, or ideas that are not clearly communicated.

9. Allot generous amounts of time for making unhurried, thorough revisions.

Typing the Report. Before typing the report, the researcher should reread the institutional requirements. The style manual usually stipulates that white bond paper of the proper size and weight be used; quite commonly $8\frac{1}{2}$ by 11 inches and a 20-pound-weight stock is required for the first copy and a lighter-weight stock for the carbon copies. The style manual gives special directions for the headings, tables, figures, footnotes, quotations, bibliography, and appendix. It also states the regulations for spacing, indention, alignment of numbers, and margins (left $1\frac{1}{2}$ inches, right 1 inch, top and bottom 1¼ inches is common). A typewriter with large (pica) type is usually recommended, and the same one, or at least the same style and size of type, should be used throughout the report. The use of an electric typewriter or Varityper is permissible in some institutions. A nongreasy, fresh, black carbon paper, a medium-inked typewriter ribbon, and clean type are necessary to produce a clear, dense copy.

Before typing the final draft of a report, the researcher reads the manuscript critically, searching for inaccurate statements, ambiguous passages, omissions, and inconsistencies. After making an exacting examination to locate errors in quotations, footnotes, tables, figures, paragraphing, sentence structure, headings, mathematics, spelling, style, proper names, or bibliography, he marks the copy to provide the typist with the necessary directions for producing a satisfactory typescript. The time spent in checking the above details is well invested, for ultimately the researcher alone—and not the typist, the sponsor, or the publisher—is held responsible for the contents of the report.

A term paper or a master's thesis may be typed personally, but for a doctoral dissertation it is wiser to select a professional typist who has had considerable experience in doing such work. When the final typed copy of the report is completed, it must be proofread with the greatest care. Unnoticeable corrections can be made more easily if each page is proofread before it is removed from the typewriter. A few erasures may be made to correct a copy, but crossing out or inserting words or sentences and typing over letters are not permissible. If revisions necessitate retyping, care should be taken to equalize the materials which are inserted and deleted so that the last line on the page comes out even. If this is not done, one may have to retype the rest of the chapter and renumber the remaining pages of the report.

Every page in a report receives a number. Small Roman numerals are placed in the center and at the bottom of the preliminary pages, except on the title page, where the number "i" counts as a page but does not appear. Hence, the numbering begins with "ii" on the next page. Arabic numerals are placed on the top right-hand corner of all other pages, with the exception of the first one in each new chapter, which is numbered in the center at the bottom.

When typing any draft of an investigation, a researcher should consider making one or two carbon copies. The second copy is valuable if he loses the first, wants to use copies both at home and at the office, or has to refer to the manuscript while his adviser or colleagues are examining the original draft. Filing the duplicate and first copies in separate places gives added protection against loss through fire and other means. Making duplicate copies of the early drafts of a report is a matter of personal choice, but many publishers and all dissertations committees require that at least two copies of the final draft be submitted.

BIBLIOGRAPHY

1. Barzun, Jacques, and Henry F. Graff, *The Modern Researcher.* New York: Harcourt, Brace & World, Inc., 1957, chaps. 11–15.

2. Best, John W., *Research in Education.* Englewood Cliffs, N.J.: Prentice-Hall, Inc., 1959, chap. 10.

3. Campbell, W. G., *Form and Style in Thesis Writing.* Boston: Houghton Mifflin Company, 1954.

4. Cordasco, Franesco, and Elliott S. M. Gatner, *Research and Report Writing.* New York: Barnes & Noble, Inc., 1955.

5. Dale, Edgar, and Hilda Hager, "How to Write to Be Understood," *Educational Research Bulletin,* 27 (November 10, 1948): 207.

6. Good, Carter V., *Introduction to Educational Research.* New York: Appleton-Century-Crofts, Inc., 1959, chap. 9.

7. Good, Carter V., and Douglas E. Scates, *Methods of Research.* New York: Appleton-Century-Crofts, Inc., 1954, chap. 10.

8. Hillway, Tyrus, *Introduction to Research.* Boston: Houghton Mifflin Company, 1956, chap. 16.

9. Hopper, Robert L., et al., *Interdisciplinary Research in Educational Administration.* Bulletin of Bureau of School Service, vol. 26, no. 2. Lexington: University of Kentucky, December, 1953.

10. *A Manual of Style,* revised and enlarged. Chicago: University of Chicago Press, 1949.

11. Mawson, C. O. S. (ed.), *Roget's International Thesaurus of English Words and Phrases: A Complete Book of Synonyms and Antonyms.* New York: Thomas Y. Crowell Company, 1940.

12. Modley, Rudolf, *How to Use Pictorial Statistics.* New York: Harper & Brothers, 1937.

13. *Prentice-Hall Author's Manual.* Englewood Cliffs, N.J.: Prentice-Hall, Inc., 1952.

14. Rummel, J. Francis, *An Introduction to Research Procedures in Education.* New York: Harper & Brothers, 1958, chaps. 11 and 12.

15. Schmid, Calvin F., *Handbook of Graphic Representation.* New York: The Ronald Press Company, 1954.

16. Souther, James W., *Technical Report Writing.* New York: John Wiley & Sons, Inc., 1957.

17. Travers, Robert M. W., *An Introduction to Educational Research.* New York: The Macmillan Company, 1958, chap. 15.

18. Trelease, Sam F., *How to Write Scientific and Technical Papers.* Baltimore: The Williams & Wilkins Company, 1958.

19. Turabian, Kate L., *A Manual for Writers of Term Papers, Theses, and Dissertations.* Chicago: University of Chicago Press, 1955.

20. Tuttle, Robert E., and C. A. Brown, *Writing Useful Reports: Principles and Applications.* New York: Appleton-Century-Crofts, 1956.

21. *U.S. Government Style Manual,* rev. ed. Government Printing Office, 1959.

CHAPTER 16

Evaluation and Publication of Research

The preceding chapters have acquainted you with the objectives of researchers, some of the skills and knowledges they must acquire, and their methods of locating and tackling problems. Gaining an insight into the intricacies of scientific investigations is important, for society cannot make the most satisfactory progress if time, money, and energy are expended on faulty work. Neither can society advance if reliable findings concerning education are not widely disseminated to scholars and the general public for critical examination and appropriate application. This chapter, therefore, will discuss the evaluation and publication of research reports.

EVALUATION

Because an educator cannot possibly read the hundreds of studies that appear in print each year, and certainly does not want to apply the findings of faulty investigations, he must learn how to screen out unworthy ones. When engaging in research himself, he must be able to evaluate not only every aspect of his predecessor's investigations, but also his own study. No universally accepted yardstick has been designed for measuring research reports, but the following questions suggest some items to check before undertaking a study, during the investigation, and when the study is completed.

Title of the Research Project

1. Does the title precisely identify the area of the problem?
2. Is the title clear, concise, and adequately descriptive to permit indexing the study in its proper category?
3. Are superfluous words such as "a study of" or "an analysis of" and catchy, misleading, and vague phrases avoided?
4. Do nouns serve as the key words in the title?
5. Are the principal words placed at the beginning of the title statement?

Preliminary Materials

1. Does the report contain a title page, approval sheet, preface or acknowledgments, table of contents, list of tables, and list of figures?

2. Are the mechanical features of the above materials in accord with the required style manual?

3. Are all necessary items included in each section and proper headings provided where necessary?

4. Do the captions that appear in the table of contents and list of tables and figures correspond exactly with the captions and page citations they refer to in the text?   Is the same grammatical structure and style of capitalization used for captions on the same level?

Statement of the Problem

1. Has a thorough analysis been made of all the facts and explanations that might possibly be related to the problem?

2. Have the relationships between the facts, the explanations, and the facts and explanations been thoroughly explored?

3. Have the pertinent facts and explanations relating to the problem been isolated?

4. Is the logic of the problem analysis sound?

5. Is the problem precisely, accurately, and clearly stated?

6. Does the statement of the problem encompass and agree with all of the relevant facts, explanatory concepts, and relationships that the analysis indicated had a bearing on the problem?

7. Are all of the problem elements expressed in an orderly system of relationships?

8. Does the statement of the problem appear early in the study and is it clearly labeled?

9. Are unnecessary words, such as "the purpose of this study," avoided?

10. Is the problem statement expressed in grammatical and correct interrogative or declarative sentences?

Review of the Literature

1. Has a thorough review been made of all the literature dealing with the variables under investigation?

2. Have previous studies been evaluated in regard to the adequacy of their sample, faulty techniques, and unwarranted conclusions?

3. Has the background of the earlier studies been developed to show that the existing evidence does not solve the immediate problem adequately?

4. Does the review of the literature merely present studies in chronological order, forcing the reader to assimilate the facts and to draw the relationships existing between the cited studies and the problem?   Or does it bring together pertinent facts and theories and weave them into a meaningful network of relationships, revealing gaps in knowledge, pointing up the issues involved in the investigation, and preparing the way for the logical leap to hypothesis construction?

5. Is the review of the literature properly labeled and inserted in the introductory part of the report?

Hypotheses

1. Are the assumptions on which the hypotheses are predicated made clear
to the reader?
2. Do the hypotheses offer adequate explanations for the solution of the
problem?
3. Are the hypotheses in agreement with all the known facts and compatible
with well-attested theories?
4. Do they explain more facts that are relevant to the problem than any
rival hypotheses?
5. Are the hypotheses testable?
6. Are the deduced consequences logically implied by the hypotheses?
7. Are the hypotheses and their deduced consequences expressed in clear,
precise terms so that they leave no question about the factors to be
tested?
8. Are they clearly labeled and placed early in the report?
9. Will the hypotheses aid in the prediction of facts and relations that were
previously unknown?

Scope and Adequacy of the Problem

1. Does the problem meet the scope, significance, and topical requirements
of the professor, institution, or periodical for which it was prepared?
2. Is the problem sufficiently delimited to permit an exhaustive treatment,
yet sufficiently significant to warrant investigating it?
3. Does the problem possess significance for education? Will it present
original data that explain previously unexplained facts? Will it organize
old data into new forms and relationships to provide a more adequate
interpretation? Will it verify the findings of other researchers by repeating their studies in new situations or by utilizing improved methods
and techniques? Will the study serve as a point of departure for further
investigations?
4. How pivotal or strategical is the investigation in terms of crucial issues
in education today?

Definition of Terms

1. Have important terms and concepts used in the study been adequately
analyzed?
2. Are clear and unequivocal definitions given for these terms and concepts?
3. Have the terms from special fields been checked in proper technical
dictionaries or by authorities in the field?

4. Are commonplace words of importance in the study assigned precise meanings?

5. In the body of the report, are the terms and concepts consistently used as defined?

6. Is the "definition of terms" section of the report clearly labeled and placed early in the study?

7. Is unnecessary technical jargon avoided?

Method of Attack. There are a number of things a researcher considers when planning and carrying out a study. Since each problem is unique, the ways and means of attacking investigations vary accordingly. Consequently, it is possible only to mention procedures that are common to many problems in the following pages.

General Considerations

1. Is it better to utilize direct or indirect means to obtain data? Is it possible to collect the quantity and quality of data necessary to investigate the problem? Are the necessary tools, techniques, and subjects available? Does any known source of data exist, and can the researcher gain access to it? Are the data sufficiently precise to be of value? Does the researcher possess the language, mathematical, and specialized skills necessary to obtain the data?

2. Is an accurate, detailed explanation of the method, techniques, and tools used to test the deduced consequences given early in the report? Are the reasons for choosing them made clear? Is this information brought together in one section of the report and properly labeled?

3. Are these procedures the most appropriate for testing the particular consequences? Do they test what they claim to test? Do they adequately and correctly represent the particular factors, conditions, and relationships of the consequences to be tested?

4. Do these procedures collect the evidence with a minimum of effort or are equally good but simpler ones available?

5. Will these methods, tools, and techniques produce relevant, reliable, valid, and sufficiently refined data to justify the inferences drawn from them?

6. Is it necessary to locate or devise more refined data-gathering techniques to obtain deeper insights into the phenomena?

7. Are the assumptions that underlie the use of the data-gathering devices fully met in this study?

8. Have the procedural errors and inadequacies that existed in previous studies been eliminated, the weaknesses of the present study been pointed out, and the procedures employed and abandoned because they proved worthless been discussed?

9. Does the report accurately describe where and when the data were gathered?
10. Does it describe precisely the number and kind of subjects, objects, and materials used in the investigation and indicate whether and why any of them did not participate in all parts of the investigation?
11. If a pilot study or pretest was conducted, is it explained and the reason given for refining it?
12. Are copies of the oral and written directions and the printed forms and questionnaires used in the investigation included in the report?

General Considerations in Descriptive Studies

1. Is the research design adequate in scope, depth, and precision in order to obtain the specific data required to test the hypothesis, or will it produce a haphazard, superficial, indiscriminate collection of data?
2. Has every possible precaution been taken to establish observational conditions, frame questions, design observation schedules, record data, and check the reliability of witnesses and source materials so as to avoid collecting data that are the product of perceptual errors, faulty memory, deliberate deception, and unconscious bias?
3. Are the specific items the observer is to note when describing a condition, event, or process clearly identified, and is a uniform method provided for recording precise information?
4. Are the standards employed to classify, compare, and quantify the data valid?
5. Are the categories for classifying data unambiguous, appropriate, and capable of bringing out likenesses, differences, or relationships?
6. Does the report honestly admit instances encountered where the elusive quality of descriptive phenomena makes it difficult to obtain and interpret data?
7. Does the study reflect a superficial analysis of surface conditions, or does it probe into interrelationships or causal relationships?

General Considerations in Historical Studies

1. Is most of the report based upon primary sources? If some secondary sources are used, do they contribute the less significant data rather than the crucial evidence for the solution of the problem?
2. Has more than one independent, reliable eyewitness been found to support the alleged facts?
3. Has an investigation been made to check the witnesses' trustworthiness, competence, biases, motives, and position at the time of observation, as well as how and when they recorded their observations?
4. Have the source materials been examined critically for authenticity and credibility?

5. Are words and statements from earlier documents correctly interpreted? Is there any evidence to indicate that conceptions of later times have been read into them?
6. When necessary, has advice been sought from experts in auxiliary fields to determine the authenticity of data?
7. Have the sources been assigned to a particular author, time, or place?

General Considerations in Experimental Studies

1. Has the possibility of hidden factors, other than the experimental variable, that might influence the results of the investigation been considered?
2. What procedures, other than the manipulation of the experimental variable, have been proposed to control and/or eliminate the subjects' experiences during the investigation?
3. Is the investigator in a position where he actually can control the experimental variable?
4. Has he randomized the variables that he does not want to influence the results?
5. Is it better to gain control of the variables by statistical, physical, or selective manipulation?
6. Has the investigator considered the possibility of unconscious signaling or of previous practice influencing the results?
7. Can the investigator assume that there is constant motivation of the subjects?
8. Has he taken into account all the significant characteristics necessary to obtain equivalence of groups?
9. Has the law of the single variable been obeyed in the traditional designs?
10. Have all assumptions underlying the use of statistical techniques been met in the statistical experimental designs?
11. Are there any conditions biasing the experimenter or the subjects of the experiment?

Sampling

1. Is the sample sufficiently representative of the population to permit the investigator to generalize his findings?
2. Is the sample adequate in kind and number? Is it appropriate for the purpose of the study?
3. Are there any conditions biasing the selection of the sample?
4. Is the control group as representative as the experimental group?
5. Are the techniques of pairing or matching the subjects valid?
6. Does the sample satisfy the assumptions underlying the use of the statistical procedures?

Tests and Measures

1. Is the investigator familiar with the rules to be observed, conditions to be met, and operations to be performed when utilizing the various measures, scales, and types of tests?
2. Are the tests employed appropriate for the abilities of the subjects, time limits, sex, social classes, etc.?
3. When analyzing test data, is it better to use single, composite, or total scores?
4. Is it necessary to compare the findings for the group tested with those of other groups? Are there available norms?
5. When selecting men to rate phenomena, were qualified judges chosen? How much reliance can be placed upon their evaluations?
6. Are there any items or factors in the tests or measures that might limit the extent or type of the subject's responses?

Questionnaires and Interviews

1. Content of Questions.
   a. Is each question necessary?
   b. Is each question sharply delineated to elicit the specific responses required as data?
   c. Do the questions adequately cover the decisive features of the needed data?
   d. Are any questions asked that the respondents do not possess the information to answer?
   e. Do more concrete questions need to be incorporated to obtain an accurate description of the respondent's behavior?
   f. Do more general types of questions need to be asked to elicit general attitudes or over-all facts?
   g. Are the questions colored by personal or sponsorship biases, loaded in one direction, or asked at the improper time?
   h. Does each question afford a sufficient number of alternative answers to permit the respondent to express himself properly and accurately?
2. Wording of Questions
   a. Is the wording of each question in clear, understandable, and non-technical language?
   b. Is the sentence structure short and simple?
   c. Are any questions misleading because of the absence of important alternative choices, poorly constructed alternatives, improper order, or an inadequate frame of reference?
   d. Are stereotyped, prestige-carrying, or superlative words and phrases used that bias the response?

e. Are questions framed so that they annoy, embarrass, or anger the respondents and cause them to falsify their answers?

f. Would a more or less personalized wording of the questions better elicit the desired information?

3. Sequence of Questions

   a. Do initial questions "set the stage" for those that follow and aid in the recall of ideas, or do they make subsequent topics inappropriate and embarrassing?

   b. Are the questions grouped to hold the respondent's train of thought?

   c. Are the questions strategically located to arouse interest, to maintain attention, and to avoid resistance?

   d. Are follow-up questions or "probes" necessary?

4. Form of Responses

   a. Is it best to obtain the responses in a form requiring a check, word or two, number, or free answer?

   b. What is the best type of check question to ask—dichotomous, multiple-choice, or scale?

   c. Is it desirable to make a distinction of degree when rating items by employing an ordinal, interval, or ratio scale?

   d. Are the directions concise and clear, located next to the point of application, and made easy to follow by including properly placed blank spaces, columns, or boxes? Are any illustrations necessary?

   e. Is the instrument structured to permit ease and accuracy in tabulating the data?

   f. Are the multiple-choice responses randomly arranged to reduce the likelihood of systematic errors?

5. Pretesting the Instrument

   a. Was a clear explanation of the purpose of the study and the specific intent of each question given during the pretesting period?

   b. After redrafting the wording of the proposed instrument, was the reliability of the responses checked?

Presentation of Data

1. Are the numbers and kinds of evidence collected adequate and appropriate? Are any unnecessary data presented?

2. Is the evidence merely enumerated in the form in which it was collected, or is it organized so as to extract the information relevant to the hypothesis being tested?

3. Were precautions taken to collect and record data accurately and to recheck procedures and results for errors?

4. Were errors made when observing phenomena, making mathematical computations, selecting or carrying out experimental or statistical procedures, or copying quotations, dates, names, or any data?

5. Are source materials accurately interpreted and paraphrased?
6. Are drawings, charts, diagrams, graphs, tables, or photographs used when they can convey ideas most effectively?
7. Do the tables and figures conform to the rules for constructing good ones? Do they present the evidence accurately—without distortion or misrepresentation?
8. Are line symbols rather than variations in color used to identify lines on a graph if the report is going to be reproduced by photographic processes?
9. Does the textual presentation conform to the prescribed style and form? Is the report properly subdivided into sections? Are the sections appropriately labeled? Are the sections logically related? Is there a continuous and logical sequence in the development of the problem solution?
10. When facts from other investigations are used in the report, are the source references given so that the reader can examine the evidence for himself?
11. Are transitional words, sentences, and paragraphs inserted to clarify the relationship between items and to make it easier to follow the presentation?
12. Is the report characterized by the use of good English—style, rhetoric, and mechanics?
13. Are the statements phrased with a precision which leaves them free from ambiguity?

Analysis of Data

1. Is the evidence collected to test each deduced consequence of a hypothesis adequately and logically analyzed?
2. Is the analysis objectively stated and free from mere opinion and personal prejudices?
3. Have broad generalizations been made without sufficient evidence to support them? Are the generalizations carefully qualified?
4. Are the methods of organizing and treating the data appropriate and accurate?
5. Are more facts, illustrations, detailed explanations, or transitional statements needed to make the analysis clear to the reader?
6. Does the analysis contain any contradictions, inconsistencies, or misleading, vague, or exaggerated statements?
7. Does the researcher confuse facts with opinions and inferences?
8. Does the researcher omit or ignore evidence that does not agree with his hypothesis?
9. Are uncontrollable factors that may have affected the results discussed?

10. Have the source materials been examined critically for authenticity and credibility?
11. Are there any weaknesses in the data?   Have they been honestly faced, admitted, and discussed?

Summary and Conclusions

1. Are the summary and conclusions concisely and precisely stated?
2. Are the conclusions justified by the data gathered?
3. Are the conclusions based on insufficient or faulty evidence?
4. Are the conclusions qualified to show the limits within which they apply?
5. Do the summary and conclusions recapitulate the information presented in previous sections of the report, or has the mistake been made of introducing new data?
6. Are the conclusions stated in terms that make them capable of verification?
7. Does the researcher specifically state what empirically verifiable evidence has been produced to confirm or disconfirm the hypothesis?
8. Does the study suggest related problems that need to be investigated?

Bibliography and Appendix

1. Do the style, content, and arrangement of the bibliography meet the requirements of the audience for which it is written?
2. Are all entries in the bibliography placed in the proper order?
3. Does each entry contain all the necessary items of information, and are they placed in the proper order and correctly spelled and punctuated?
4. Is all cumbersome or voluminous supporting material—test forms, raw data, personal communications—relevant to the study located in the appendix?   Has any unnecessary material been placed in the appendix?
5. Are the items in the appendix grouped in homogeneous sections with appropriate headings?

Report Format and Style

1. Is the report neat, attractive, and divided into appropriate sections or chapters?
2. Is it ordered according to the format required by the professor, institution, or periodical?
3. Are concise, descriptive headings used?
4. Is the report free from padding with irrelevant words, phrases, quotations, statistics, examples, and other data that are not essential for accuracy, clarity, or completeness?
5. Are concrete familiar words, short direct sentences, and the active voice used whenever possible?

6. Has an approved style been followed consistently throughout the report? Has a careful check been made of spacings, margins, quotations, footnotes, tables, figures, bibliography, appendixes, headings, abbreviations, capitalization, punctuation, indentions, and the enumeration of items?
7. Are the drawings and graphs prepared in the proper manner to ensure satisfactory reproduction?
8. Are major topics insufficiently developed or minor ones overexpanded?
9. Does the complexity of the report or the use to be made of it require an index?

Abstract

1. Does an abstract accompany the presentation of the report?
2. Is the abstract prepared in accordance with the institution's or periodical's standards for style and form?
3. Does the abstract cover the principal points: statement of problem and/or hypotheses, procedures, results, and conclusions?
4. Is the abstract under the maximum number of words in length?

PUBLICATION

Researchers must not only know how to evaluate reports, but also how to get them published. After devoting months to investigations and accepting the assistance of faculty members, librarians, and colleagues, they are professionally obligated to observe the academic tradition of publishing their findings. This is necessary, because discoveries that are not made available to other scholars cannot possibly benefit mankind. Aside from research reports, educators often have other important ideas, data, questions, criticisms, and problems that should be communicated to others for the betterment of the profession. But they cannot get any article printed in professional journals and books unless they know something about publishers and the procedures involved in preparing manuscripts for them.

Types and Standards of Publishers. Various agencies publish the work of researchers. Professional associations print a large number of studies in their journals every year, most of them, however, in an abstract form. Some professional organizations and philanthropic foundations produce monographs of outstanding scientific investigations, and university presses print a few studies of special merit. In *Dissertation Abstracts,* The University Microfilms, Ann Arbor, Michigan, compiles the doctoral dissertation abstracts that many universities require candidates to submit. From time to time, other public and private agencies publish pertinent reports in their area of interest.

Most of these publishers do not offer any remuneration for reports; indeed, some journals require a payment for publication privileges. Because an increasing number of investigations are undertaken each year, journal space is at a premium today.   Moreover, the rising costs of publication prohibit the reproduction of many studies in their entirety.   One attempt to solve this problem has been made by establishing a private nonprofit organization, the American Documentation Institute.   After depositing the basic study data with the ADI, a researcher can write a report for a journal without including the long tables and other items on which his analysis is based.   In a footnote of his report, he can indicate that a microfilm or photographic copy of the complete material can be obtained from the ADI for a nominal fee.

Since the nature, style, and quality of reports accepted by various journals differ, a researcher carefully evaluates the journals to determine which one publishes the type and level of study he has to submit.   After selecting a reputable journal, he becomes thoroughly familiar with the editors' manuscript criteria.   These criteria may be printed on the back pages of the journal periodically, but if they are not, an examination of a few issues will reveal the editors' preferences in regard to the nature, length, and organization of articles as well as footnotes and bibliographical style.   These manuscript requirements cannot be ignored.   Writing a thousand-word report for a journal that limits articles to six hundred words or neglecting to follow the required organizational pattern can lead only to a rejection slip or a request for drastic revisions.

Preparation for Publication.   Writing for publication sometimes requires considerable work in addition to the preparation of the original dissertation. A candidate does not have many prepublication duties if his study is reproduced on microfilm or microcards, which is a common practice.   He may have to recast it somewhat before publishing it—in monograph form, which is sometimes done, or in book form, which is rarely done.   If he writes an abstract of his study or presents his findings in a journal article, he has to compress the contents of his entire report into relatively few pages.

An abstract, for example, may be limited to five hundred words.   Thus, a researcher must strip the key ideas from his original manuscript—largely from the summary and conclusions, express them in clear, crisp sentences, and revise his format and style to conform with the publisher's requirements. Preparing a report for a journal involves somewhat similar tasks, but more pages may be devoted to the discussion.   Because a doctoral dissertation contains considerable substance, its contents may be divided to produce two or more journal articles of eight to fifteen double-spaced pages in length. Descriptions of masters' theses are usually confined to a single journal article a few pages in length.

After pruning and polishing a report to meet the exacting requirements of editors, the author numbers the pages consecutively from start to finish and fastens them together with paper clips.   Then he slips them unfolded into an envelope and sometimes adds a piece of cardboard that is slightly larger than the material for protection—particularly if photographic prints or drawings intended for halftone reproductions are included. After inserting a letter in the envelope which explains that the article is being submitted for possible publication, he mails it to the editors. To protect himself against loss, he insures the mailed manuscript and places a carbon copy of it in his files.

Before a report is published it may be necessary for the author to obtain written permission to use quotations, graphic materials, and speeches from the copyright holders—the publisher, author, photographer, or issuing institution. His letters requesting authorization to reproduce material must identify each item precisely and explain how it is to be employed. Replies to these letters must be kept in the author's or publisher's files for later reference in case questions arise. A copyright may also have to be obtained for the report itself, particularly if it is in book form. This is a task that publishers usually perform, but an author may reserve the right to apply to the Register of Copyrights, Library of Congress, Washington, D.C., and obtain it for himself.

Reviews and Revisions. When editors receive a manuscript, they may send the author a brief note or acknowledgment, but aside from that they do not communicate with him for several weeks. In the interim, qualified specialists review the article and decide whether to accept it, reject it, or request that certain revisions be made. A manuscript may be rejected for several reasons—because it lacks merit, is unsuitable for the particular journal, or is similar to a backlog of articles previously accepted by the publisher. If a report is rejected for the last reason, it may be submitted to another publisher. If a manuscript contains fundamental weaknesses, however, no editor will accept it.

A conditionally accepted report is returned to the author with suggestions for improvements. The editors may recommend that certain points be expanded or omitted, question the accuracy of statements, point out passages that need to be clarified, suggest changes in organization and literary form, or note inconsistencies in style. Requests for revisions should challenge rather than discourage the author. Learning to write requires a long apprenticeship, and continuous criticism by qualified men is a prod that stimulates progress. All of the editor's suggestions do not have to be accepted, but each should be given serious consideration.

When making changes in the manuscript, it is important to print or write legibly and to refrain from writing insertions in the margin, for they are reserved for instructions to the printer. To indicate an insertion, a caret ($\wedge$) is placed at the proper point in the copy and the additional material is written in the space above—never below—the caret. Long insertions may be typed on small slips of paper and taped to the margin of the copy near the line containing the caret.   If a paragraph is to be transferred to another page, it may be crossed out, retyped, and inserted where it belongs or it may be circled and labeled "tr. to p. 16."   If the latter is done, the place where it belongs is indicated on page 16 by inserting a caret in the proper place and above it the note, "tr. from p. 5."   When material is to be deleted and none added, the unwanted characters are merely crossed out. Revisions of a few sentences in length may be typed on small slips of paper and pasted over deleted materials in the copy.

Galley and Page Proofs.   After the revised manuscript is returned to the editor, several months may elapse before the author receives the galley proofs of his article and the cut dummies (if any) of the engraver's proofs, The galley proofs are long sheets of paper that contain about three normal pages of print and no illustrations or page numbers.   The author is expected to compare the galley proofs with his manuscript and to correct any errors. This proofreading task is exacting work that must be done with scrupulous care.   It does not consist merely in scanning the article to make certain that the copy makes sense.   To detect inaccuracies or omissions, a competent author checks each character, letter, word, and line.   If possible, he follows the galley proof as someone slowly reads aloud from the manuscript.   The reader spells out all proper names and technical terms and reads out punctuation marks, italics, paragraph breaks, decimal points, prime marks, and other departures from ordinary type.   Particular attention is given to tables, figures, dates, and quotations.   Proofreading is done twice if time permits, for the second reading is almost certain to reveal additional errors.

Because a printer does not look for corrections in the body of the galley proof unless he sees a proofreader's mark in the margin, an author must study these standard symbols until he can automatically apply and interpret them.   When correcting a galley proof, he must be able to communicate his ideas to the editor and printer by placing the appropriate symbol in the left or right margin, whichever is nearer the error, and on the same line as the error.   When more than one error appears on a line, the corrections are written consecutively from left to right and separated one from another by a slanted line. All notes or queries to the editor or printer are circled to indicate that they are not to be set in type.   To restore something that has previously been crossed out, a row of dots is placed under the deletion and in the margin the delete sign is crossed out and "stet" (let it stand) is added.   When proofreading, the writer utilizes a number of other symbols in much the same manner.   Some of the standard ones are given below.

When checking the cut dummies of the engraver's proofs, an author makes certain that no figure has been placed upside down and that no items have been omitted.   In the margin of the galley proof, he indicates near which

Insertions, Deletions, Spacing

ʃ//	Delete words or ~~the~~ letters mar/ked.
the/h	Insert the word or ^ letter in t^e margin.
#	Insert space between^words.
⁀	Close up sp ⁀ ace.

Paragraphing and Punctuation

¶	^Make new paragraph.
No ¶	No paragraph—run in or on.
⊙	Insert period. (Sixty children participated^)
,//	Insert comma. (Smith^John^and Valois, Jean)
"/"	Insert quotation marks. (Explain the^mechanism^of the mind.)
'	Insert apostrophe. (The teacher^s equipment was good.)
-/or =/	Insert hyphen. (ten^volume encyclopedia)

Type

2	Insert inferior figure or letter subscript. (H^SO$_4$)
2	Insert superior figure or letter superscript. (Lee[1] and Ogg^ conducted studies.)
Caps	SET IN capitals.
Cap	capital letter required.
lc	Use lower-Case letter.
ital.	Set in italic type.
9	Tur^u a reversed letter.
X	Replace broken ty^pe.
lf	Set in lightface type.
bf	Set in boldface type.

Position

tr //	Transpose of order words or lettres.
⌐¬	Elevate letters or words. (John and Mary)
⌊⌋	Lower letters or words. (John and Mary)
ctr	]Center on page or line.[
]	Move to right.]
[	[Move to left.
//	Align type vertically.
=	Straighten line horizontally. (He greeted the crowd.)

Miscellaneous

1942 / ?	Query to author. (In 1952 Hitler delivered the speech.)
stet	Let all words above dots ~~in sentence~~ stand as they are.
sp	Spell out. (Tests were given to (20) children.)
⊥	Push down a space that prints.
_⌐	Mark-off or break; start new line.

passage the printer is to place a figure. (For example, he writes in the margin of galley 5, "Insert Fig. 2 here" and then jots the number of that galley, "gal. 5," below Fig. 2 in the cut dummy.) Before returning the galley and engraver's proofs to the publisher, the writer must answer all of the printer's and editor's queries and supply any missing materials, captions, or credit lines. An editor usually writes a lengthy query on a small colored piece of paper and attaches it to the side of the galley. He writes a brief query in the margin of the galley and after the suggested change places a slanted line and circled question mark. To accept a change, the author crosses out the question mark; to reject it, he crosses out the whole query.

Making alterations in the galley proofs other than the correction of printer's errors is extremely expensive. Merely inserting a word may require resetting the type for the rest of the paragraph. Because the writer may have to pay the charges for these alterations, he should endeavor to submit a perfect manuscript. If changes in the galley proof are necessary, costs can be held to a minimum by making deletions and additions so that they fill the same amount of space as the original materials. If a red pencil is used to correct printer's errors and a black one for author's changes in the copy, it is easier to place the responsibility for the charges.

After the editor and author have carefully checked the galley proofs, they return them to the printer. He corrects all the marked items and then breaks the type into page lengths, inserts the footnotes, places the illustrations where they belong, and adds the chapter titles, running heads, and page numbers. Copies of the page proofs and the dead galley proofs are then sent to the editor, who examines them to determine whether all the errors have been corrected and no new errors introduced as a result of the resets or addition of new materials. Journal page proofs are not usually sent to the author for an additional check, but book page proofs are. Some duties, such as inserting the page numbers for cross-reference citations and preparing an index, cannot be performed until one has the page proofs. Upon receiving either the galley or page proofs, the author should give them immediate attention and return them promptly, or he will upset the production schedules of editors and printers.

The rewarding moment comes when a researcher first reads his report in print! It climaxes a prolonged period of cooperative effort on the part of the author, editors, and printers. After an article is submitted, several months may pass before it is published, and a book may be in production for a couple of years. Because many would-be authors do not realize how much work is involved in transforming a manuscript into print, they fail to allot sufficient time for it. Consequently, when manuscripts are returned to them, they resent reviewers' criticisms, are reluctant to make revisions, and may become too discouraged to continue writing. If their articles are accepted, they often do a superficial job of proofreading and disregard the editors' concern about meeting deadlines and printing schedules.

The exacting process of preparing a manuscript for publication may seem burdensome, but these revisions and careful checks are essential for the production of a good report. Maintaining a high level of performance in this final stage of one's work is of utmost importance, for a carefully conducted investigation may be disregarded by other scholars if the public account of it is poorly prepared. Since one is judged for years by the quality of his printed report, it is only prudent to master the skills and expend the effort necessary to publish one that meets the highest standards of scholarship.

BIBLIOGRAPHY

1. Barzun, Jacques, and Henry F. Graff, *The Modern Researcher.* New York: Harcourt, Brace & World, Inc., 1957, chap. 16.

2. Best, John W., *Research in Education.* Englewood Cliffs, N.J.: Prentice-Hall, Inc., 1959, chap. 10.

3. Campbell, W. G., *Form and Style in Thesis Writing.* Boston: Houghton Mifflin Company, 1954.

4. Cordasco, Franesco, and Elliott S. M. Gatner, *Research and Report Writing.* New York: Barnes & Noble, Inc., 1955.

5. Dale, Edgar, and Hilda Hager, "How to Write to Be Understood," *Educational Research Bulletin,* 27(November 10, 1948):207.

6. Good, Carter V., and Douglas E. Scates, *Methods of Research.* New York: Appleton-Century-Crofts, Inc., 1954, chap. 10.

7. Hillway, Tyrus, *Introduction to Research.* Boston: Houghton Mifflin Company, 1956, chap. 17.

8. *A Manual of Style,* Revised and enlarged. Chicago: University of Chicago Press, 1949.

9. *Prentice-Hall Author's Manual.* Englewood Cliffs, N.J.: Prentice-Hall, Inc., 1952.

10. Rummel, J., Francis, *An Introduction to Research Procedures in Education.* New York: Harper & Brothers, 1958, chaps. 11 and 12.

11. Travers, Robert M. W., *An Introduction to Educational Research.* New York: The Macmillan Company, 1958, chap. 15.

12. Trelease, Sam F., *How to Write Scientific and Technical Papers.* Baltimore: The Williams & Wilkins Company, 1958.

13. Turabian, Kate L., *A Manual for Writers of Term Papers, Theses, and Dissertations.* Chicago: University of Chicago Press, 1955.

14. Tuttle, Robert E., and C. A. Brown, *Writing Useful Reports: Principles and Applications.* New York: Appleton-Century-Crofts, Inc., 1956.

15. *U.S. Government Style Manual,* rev. ed. Government Printing Office, 1953.

16. Van Dalen, D. B., "A Research Check List in Education," *Educational Administration and Supervision,* 44(May, 1958):174.

Appendixes

Appendix A

TABLE A. NORMAL CURVE FUNCTIONS

z or x/σ	Area: m to z	Area: q smaller	y or ordinate
0.00	0.00000	0.50000	0.3989
0.05	0.01994	0.48006	0.3984
0.10	0.03983	0.46017	0.3970
0.15	0.05962	0.44038	0.3945
0.20	0.07926	0.42074	0.3910
0.25	0.09871	0.40129	0.3867
0.30	0.11791	0.38209	0.3814
0.35	0.13683	0.36317	0.3752
0.40	0.15542	0.34458	0.3683
0.45	0.17364	0.32636	0.3605
0.50	0.19146	0.30854	0.3521
0.55	0.20884	0.29116	0.3429
0.60	0.22575	0.27425	0.3332
0.65	0.24215	0.25758	0.3230
0.70	0.25804	0.24196	0.3123
0.75	0.27337	0.22663	0.3011
0.80	0.28814	0.21186	0.2897
0.85	0.30234	0.19766	0.2780
0.90	0.31594	0.18406	0.2661
0.95	0.32894	0.17106	0.2541
1.00	0.34134	0.15866	0.2420
1.05	0.35314	0.14686	0.2299
1.10	0.36433	0.13567	0.2179
1.15	0.37493	0.12507	0.2059
1.20	0.38493	0.11507	0.1942
1.25	0.39435	0.10565	0.1826
1.30	0.40320	0.09680	0.1714
1.35	0.41149	0.08851	0.1604
1.40	0.41924	0.08076	0.1497
1.45	0.42647	0.07353	0.1394

TABLE A. NORMAL CURVE FUNCTIONS (*Continued*)

z or x/σ	Area: m to z	Area: q smaller	y or ordinate
1.50	0.43319	0.06681	0.1295
1.55	0.43943	0.06057	0.1200
1.60	0.44520	0.05480	0.1109
1.65	0.45053	0.04947	0.1023
1.70	0.45543	0.04457	0.0940
1.75	0.45994	0.04056	0.0863
1.80	0.46407	0.03593	0.0790
1.85	0.46784	0.03216	0.0721
1.90	0.47128	0.02872	0.0656
1.95	0.47441	0.02559	0.0596
2.00	0.47725	0.02275	0.0540
2.05	0.47982	0.02018	0.0488
2.10	0.48214	0.01786	0.0440
2.15	0.48422	0.01578	0.0396
2.20	0.48610	0.01390	0.0355
2.25	0.48778	0.01222	0.0317
2.30	0.48928	0.01072	0.0283
2.35	0.49061	0.00939	0.0252
2.40	0.49180	0.00820	0.0224
2.45	0.49286	0.00714	0.0198
2.50	0.49379	0.00621	0.0175
2.55	0.49461	0.00539	0.0154
2.60	0.49534	0.00466	0.0136
2.65	0.49598	0.00402	0.0119
2.70	0.49653	0.00347	0.0104
2.75	0.49702	0.00298	0.0091
2.80	0.49744	0.00256	0.0079
2.85	0.49781	0.00219	0.0069
2.90	0.49813	0.00187	0.0060
2.95	0.49841	0.00159	0.0051
3.00	0.49865	0.00135	0.0044
3.25	0.49942	0.00058	0.0020
3.50	0.49977	0.00023	0.0009
3.75	0.49991	0.00009	0.0004
4.00	0.49997	0.00003	0.0001

TABLE B. TRANSFORMATION OF r TO z_r*

r	z_r	r	z_r	r	z_r	r	z_r	r	z_r
0.000	0.000	0.200	0.203	0.400	0.424	0.600	0.693	0.800	1.099
0.005	0.005	0.205	0.208	0.405	0.430	0.605	0.701	0.805	1.113
0.010	0.010	0.210	0.213	0.410	0.436	0.610	0.709	0.810	1.127
0.015	0.015	0.215	0.218	0.415	0.442	0.615	0.717	0.815	1.142
0.020	0.020	0.220	0.224	0.420	0.448	0.620	0.725	0.820	1.157
0.025	0.025	0.225	0.229	0.425	0.454	0.625	0.733	0.825	1.172
0.030	0.030	0.230	0.234	0.430	0.460	0.630	0.741	0.830	1.188
0.035	0.035	0.235	0.239	0.435	0.466	0.635	0.750	0.835	1.204
0.040	0.040	0.240	0.245	0.440	0.472	0.640	0.758	0.840	1.221
0.045	0.045	0.245	0.250	0.445	0.478	0.645	0.767	0.845	1.238
0.050	0.050	0.250	0.255	0.450	0.485	0.650	0.775	0.850	1.256
0.055	0.055	0.255	0.261	0.455	0.491	0.655	0.784	0.855	1.274
0.060	0.060	0.260	0.266	0.460	0.497	0.660	0.793	0.860	1.293
0.065	0.065	0.265	0.271	0.465	0.504	0.665	0.802	0.865	1.313
0.070	0.070	0.270	0.277	0.470	0.510	0.670	0.811	0.870	1.333
0.075	0.075	0.275	0.282	0.475	0.517	0.675	0.820	0.875	1.354
0.080	0.080	0.280	0.288	0.480	0.523	0.680	0.829	0.880	1.376
0.085	0.085	0.285	0.293	0.485	0.530	0.685	0.838	0.885	1.398
0.090	0.090	0.290	0.299	0.490	0.536	0.690	0.848	0.890	1.422
0.095	0.095	0.295	0.304	0.495	0.543	0.695	0.858	0.895	1.447
0.100	0.100	0.300	0.310	0.500	0.549	0.700	0.867	0.900	1.472
0.105	0.105	0.305	0.315	0.505	0.556	0.705	0.877	0.905	1.499
0.110	0.110	0.310	0.321	0.510	0.563	0.710	0.887	0.910	1.528
0.115	0.116	0.315	0.326	0.515	0.570	0.715	0.897	0.915	1.557
0.120	0.121	0.320	0.332	0.520	0.576	0.720	0.908	0.920	1.589
0.125	0.126	0.325	0.337	0.525	0.583	0.725	0.918	0.925	1.623
0.130	0.131	0.330	0.343	0.530	0.590	0.730	0.929	0.930	1.658
0.135	0.136	0.335	0.348	0.535	0.597	0.735	0.940	0.935	1.697
0.140	0.141	0.340	0.354	0.540	0.604	0.740	0.950	0.940	1.738
0.145	0.146	0.345	0.360	0.545	0.611	0.745	0.962	0.945	1.783
0.150	0.151	0.350	0.365	0.550	0.618	0.750	0.973	0.950	1.832
0.155	0.156	0.355	0.371	0.555	0.626	0.755	0.984	0.955	1.886
0.160	0.161	0.360	0.377	0.560	0.633	0.760	0.996	0.960	1.946
0.165	0.167	0.365	0.383	0.565	0.640	0.765	1.008	0.965	2.014
0.170	0.172	0.370	0.388	0.570	0.648	0.770	1.020	0.970	2.092
0.175	0.177	0.375	0.394	0.575	0.655	0.775	1.033	0.975	2.185
0.180	0.182	0.380	0.400	0.580	0.662	0.780	1.045	0.980	2.298
0.185	0.187	0.385	0.406	0.585	0.670	0.785	1.058	0.985	2.443
0.190	0.192	0.390	0.412	0.590	0.678	0.790	1.071	0.990	2.647
0.195	0.198	0.395	0.418	0.595	0.685	0.795	1.085	0.995	2.994

* Reprinted, by permission, from Allen L. Edwards, *Statistical Methods for the Behavioral Sciences*, New York: Holt, Rinehart and Winston, Inc., 1954.

TABLE C. CRITICAL VALUES OF t*

df	Level of significance for one-tailed test					
	0.10	0.05	0.025	0.01	0.005	0.0005
	Level of significance for two-tailed test					
	0.20	0.10	0.05	0.02	0.01	0.001
1	3.078	6.314	12.706	31.821	63.657	636.619
2	1.886	2.920	4.303	6.965	9.925	31.598
3	1.638	2.353	3.182	4.541	5.841	12.941
4	1.533	2.132	2.776	3.747	4.604	8.610
5	1.476	2.015	2.571	3.365	4.032	6.859
6	1.440	1.943	2.447	3.143	3.707	5.959
7	1.415	1.895	2.365	2.998	3.499	5.405
8	1.397	1.860	2.306	2.896	3.355	5.041
9	1.383	1.833	2.262	2.821	3.250	4.781
10	1.372	1.812	2.228	2.764	3.169	4.587
11	1.363	1.796	2.201	2.718	3.106	4.437
12	1.356	1.782	2.179	2.681	3.055	4.318
13	1.350	1.771	2.160	2.650	3.012	4.221
14	1.345	1.761	2.145	2.624	2.977	4.140
15	1.341	1.753	2.131	2.602	2.947	4.073
16	1.337	1.746	2.120	2.583	2.921	4.015
17	1.333	1.740	2.110	2.567	2.898	3.965
18	1.330	1.734	2.101	2.552	2.878	3.922
19	1.328	1.729	2.093	2.539	2.861	3.883
20	1.325	1.725	2.086	2.528	2.845	3.850
21	1.323	1.721	2.080	2.518	2.831	3.819
22	1.321	1.717	2.074	2.508	2.819	3.792
23	1.319	1.714	2.069	2.500	2.807	3.767
24	1.318	1.711	2.064	2.492	2.797	3.745
25	1.316	1.708	2.060	2.485	2.787	3.725
26	1.315	1.706	2.056	2.479	2.779	3.707
27	1.314	1.703	2.052	2.473	2.771	3.690
28	1.313	1.701	2.048	2.467	2.763	3.674
29	1.311	1.699	2.045	2.462	2.756	3.659
30	1.310	1.697	2.042	2.457	2.750	3.646
40	1.303	1.684	2.021	2.423	2.704	3.551
60	1.296	1.671	2.000	2.390	2.660	3.460
120	1.289	1.658	1.980	2.358	2.617	3.373
∞	1.282	1.645	1.960	2.326	2.576	3.291

* Abridged from Table III of R. A. Fisher and F. Yates, *Statistical Tables for Biological, Agricultural, and Medical Research*, published by Oliver & Boyd, Ltd., Edinburgh, by permission of the authors and publishers.

TABLE D. DISTRIBUTION OF χ^{2*}

n	$P = 0.99$	0.98	0.95	0.90	0.80	0.70	0.50
1	0.00016	0.00063	0.0039	0.016	0.064	0.15	0.46
2	0.02	0.04	0.10	0.21	0.45	0.71	1.39
3	0.12	0.18	0.35	0.58	1.00	1.42	2.37
4	0.30	0.43	0.71	1.06	1.65	2.20	3.36
5	0.55	0.75	1.14	1.61	2.34	3.00	4.35
6	0.87	1.13	1.64	2.20	3.07	3.83	5.35
7	1.24	1.56	2.17	2.83	3.82	4.67	6.35
8	1.65	2.03	2.73	3.49	4.59	5.53	7.34
9	2.09	2.53	3.32	4.17	5.38	6.39	8.34
10	2.56	3.06	3.94	4.86	6.18	7.27	9.34
11	3.05	3.61	4.58	5.58	6.99	8.15	10.34
12	3.57	4.18	5.23	6.30	7.81	9.03	11.34
13	4.11	4.76	5.89	7.04	8.63	9.93	12.34
14	4.66	5.37	6.57	7.79	9.47	10.82	13.34
15	5.23	5.98	7.26	8.55	10.31	11.72	14.34
16	5.81	6.61	7.96	9.31	11.15	12.62	15.34
17	6.41	7.26	8.67	10.08	12.00	13.53	16.34
18	7.02	7.91	9.39	10.86	12.86	14.44	17.34
19	7.63	8.57	10.12	11.65	13.72	15.35	18.34
20	8.26	9.24	10.85	12.44	14.58	16.27	19.34
21	8.90	9.92	11.59	13.24	15.44	17.18	20.34
22	9.54	10.60	12.34	14.04	16.31	18.10	21.34
23	10.20	11.29	13.09	14.85	17.19	19.02	22.34
24	10.86	11.99	13.85	15.66	18.06	19.94	23.34
25	11.52	12.70	14.61	16.47	18.94	20.87	24.34
26	12.20	13.41	15.38	17.29	19.82	21.79	25.34
27	12.88	14.12	16.15	18.11	20.70	22.72	26.34
28	13.56	14.85	16.93	18.94	21.59	23.65	27.34
29	14.26	15.57	17.71	19.77	22.48	24.58	28.34
30	14.95	16.31	18.49	20.60	23.36	25.51	29.34

* Table D is abridged from Table IV of Fisher and Yates, *Statistical Tables for Biological, Agricultural, and Medical Research*, Oliver & Boyd, Ltd., Edinburgh, by permission of the authors and publishers.

TABLE D. DISTRIBUTION OF χ^2 (*Continued*)

n	0.30	0.20	0.10	0.05	0.02	0.01	0.001
1	1.07	1.64	2.71	3.84	5.41	6.64	10.83
2	2.41	3.22	4.60	5.99	7.82	9.21	13.82
3	3.66	4.64	6.25	7.82	9.84	11.34	16.27
4	4.88	5.99	7.78	9.49	11.67	13.28	18.46
5	6.06	7.29	9.24	11.07	13.39	15.09	20.52
6	7.23	8.56	10.64	12.59	15.03	16.81	22.46
7	8.38	9.80	12.02	14.07	16.62	18.48	24.32
8	9.52	11.03	13.36	15.51	18.17	20.09	26.12
9	10.66	12.24	14.68	16.92	19.68	21.67	27.88
10	11.78	13.44	15.99	18.31	21.16	23.21	29.59
11	12.90	14.63	17.28	19.68	22.62	24.72	31.26
12	14.01	15.81	18.55	21.03	24.05	26.22	32.91
13	15.12	16.98	19.81	22.36	25.47	27.69	34.53
14	16.22	18.15	21.06	23.68	26.87	29.14	36.12
15	17.32	19.31	22.31	25.00	28.26	30.58	37.70
16	18.42	20.46	23.54	26.30	29.63	32.00	39.25
17	19.51	21.62	24.77	27.59	31.00	33.41	40.79
18	20.60	22.76	25.99	28.87	32.35	34.80	42.31
19	21.69	23.90	27.20	30.14	33.69	36.19	43.82
20	22.78	25.04	28.41	31.41	35.02	37.57	45.32
21	23.86	26.17	29.62	32.67	36.34	38.93	46.80
22	24.94	27.30	30.81	33.92	37.66	40.29	48.27
23	26.02	28.43	32.01	35.17	38.97	41.64	49.73
24	27.10	29.55	33.20	36.42	40.27	42.98	51.18
25	28.17	30.68	34.38	37.65	41.57	44.31	52.62
26	29.25	31.80	35.56	38.88	42.86	45.64	54.05
27	30.32	32.91	36.74	40.11	44.14	46.96	55.48
28	31.39	34.03	37.92	41.34	45.42	48.28	56.89
29	32.46	35.14	39.09	42.56	46.69	49.59	58.30
30	33.53	36.25	40.26	43.77	47.96	50.89	59.70

TABLE E

5 PER CENT (ROMAN TYPE) AND 1 PER CENT (BOLD-FACE TYPE) POINTS FOR THE DISTRIBUTION OF F*

Each cell shows the 5 per cent point (roman type) over the 1 per cent point (bold-face type).

Degrees of freedom for greater mean square

Degrees of freedom for lesser mean square	1	2	3	4	5	6	7	8	9	10	11	12	14	16	20	24	30	40	50	75	100	200	500	∞
1	161 / 4052	200 / 4999	216 / 5403	225 / 5625	230 / 5764	234 / 5859	237 / 5928	239 / 5981	241 / 6022	242 / 6056	243 / 6082	244 / 6106	245 / 6142	246 / 6169	248 / 6208	249 / 6234	250 / 6258	251 / 6286	252 / 6302	253 / 6323	253 / 6334	254 / 6352	254 / 6361	254 / 6366
2	18.51 / 98.49	19.00 / 99.01	19.16 / 99.17	19.25 / 99.25	19.30 / 99.30	19.33 / 99.33	19.36 / 99.34	19.37 / 99.36	19.38 / 99.38	19.39 / 99.40	19.40 / 99.41	19.41 / 99.42	19.42 / 99.43	19.43 / 99.44	19.44 / 99.45	19.45 / 99.46	19.46 / 99.47	19.47 / 99.48	19.47 / 99.48	19.48 / 99.49	19.49 / 99.49	19.49 / 99.49	19.50 / 99.50	19.50 / 99.50
3	10.13 / 34.12	9.55 / 30.81	9.28 / 29.46	9.12 / 28.71	9.01 / 28.24	8.94 / 27.91	8.88 / 27.67	8.84 / 27.49	8.81 / 27.34	8.78 / 27.23	8.76 / 27.13	8.74 / 27.05	8.71 / 26.92	8.69 / 26.83	8.66 / 26.69	8.64 / 26.60	8.62 / 26.50	8.60 / 26.41	8.58 / 26.35	8.57 / 26.27	8.56 / 26.23	8.54 / 26.18	8.54 / 26.14	8.53 / 26.12
4	7.71 / 21.20	6.94 / 18.00	6.59 / 16.69	6.39 / 15.98	6.26 / 15.52	6.16 / 15.21	6.09 / 14.98	6.04 / 14.80	6.00 / 14.66	5.96 / 14.54	5.93 / 14.45	5.91 / 14.37	5.87 / 14.24	5.84 / 14.15	5.80 / 14.02	5.77 / 13.93	5.74 / 13.83	5.71 / 13.74	5.70 / 13.69	5.68 / 13.61	5.66 / 13.57	5.65 / 13.52	5.64 / 13.48	5.63 / 13.46
5	6.61 / 16.26	5.79 / 13.27	5.41 / 12.06	5.19 / 11.39	5.05 / 10.97	4.95 / 10.67	4.88 / 10.45	4.82 / 10.27	4.78 / 10.15	4.74 / 10.05	4.70 / 9.96	4.68 / 9.89	4.64 / 9.77	4.60 / 9.68	4.56 / 9.55	4.53 / 9.47	4.50 / 9.38	4.46 / 9.29	4.44 / 9.24	4.42 / 9.17	4.40 / 9.13	4.38 / 9.07	4.37 / 9.04	4.36 / 9.02
6	5.99 / 13.74	5.14 / 10.92	4.76 / 9.78	4.53 / 9.15	4.39 / 8.75	4.28 / 8.47	4.21 / 8.26	4.15 / 8.10	4.10 / 7.98	4.06 / 7.87	4.03 / 7.79	4.00 / 7.72	3.96 / 7.60	3.92 / 7.52	3.87 / 7.39	3.84 / 7.31	3.81 / 7.23	3.77 / 7.14	3.75 / 7.09	3.72 / 7.02	3.71 / 6.99	3.69 / 6.94	3.68 / 6.90	3.67 / 6.88
7	5.59 / 12.25	4.74 / 9.55	4.35 / 8.45	4.12 / 7.85	3.97 / 7.46	3.87 / 7.19	3.79 / 7.00	3.73 / 6.84	3.68 / 6.71	3.63 / 6.62	3.60 / 6.54	3.57 / 6.47	3.52 / 6.35	3.49 / 6.27	3.44 / 6.15	3.41 / 6.07	3.38 / 5.98	3.34 / 5.90	3.32 / 5.85	3.29 / 5.78	3.28 / 5.75	3.25 / 5.70	3.24 / 5.67	3.23 / 5.65
8	5.32 / 11.26	4.46 / 8.65	4.07 / 7.59	3.84 / 7.01	3.69 / 6.63	3.58 / 6.37	3.50 / 6.19	3.44 / 6.03	3.39 / 5.91	3.34 / 5.82	3.31 / 5.74	3.28 / 5.67	3.23 / 5.56	3.20 / 5.48	3.15 / 5.36	3.12 / 5.28	3.08 / 5.20	3.05 / 5.11	3.03 / 5.06	3.00 / 5.00	2.98 / 4.96	2.96 / 4.91	2.94 / 4.88	2.93 / 4.86
9	5.12 / 10.56	4.26 / 8.02	3.86 / 6.99	3.63 / 6.42	3.48 / 6.06	3.37 / 5.80	3.29 / 5.62	3.23 / 5.47	3.18 / 5.35	3.13 / 5.26	3.10 / 5.18	3.07 / 5.11	3.02 / 5.00	2.98 / 4.92	2.93 / 4.80	2.90 / 4.73	2.86 / 4.64	2.82 / 4.56	2.80 / 4.51	2.77 / 4.45	2.76 / 4.41	2.73 / 4.36	2.72 / 4.33	2.71 / 4.31
10	4.96 / 10.04	4.10 / 7.56	3.71 / 6.55	3.48 / 5.99	3.33 / 5.64	3.22 / 5.39	3.14 / 5.21	3.07 / 5.06	3.02 / 4.95	2.97 / 4.85	2.94 / 4.78	2.91 / 4.71	2.86 / 4.60	2.82 / 4.52	2.77 / 4.41	2.74 / 4.33	2.70 / 4.25	2.67 / 4.17	2.64 / 4.12	2.61 / 4.05	2.59 / 4.01	2.56 / 3.96	2.55 / 3.93	2.54 / 3.91
11	4.84 / 9.65	3.98 / 7.20	3.59 / 6.22	3.36 / 5.67	3.20 / 5.32	3.09 / 5.07	3.01 / 4.88	2.95 / 4.74	2.90 / 4.63	2.86 / 4.54	2.82 / 4.46	2.79 / 4.40	2.74 / 4.29	2.70 / 4.21	2.65 / 4.10	2.61 / 4.02	2.57 / 3.94	2.53 / 3.86	2.50 / 3.80	2.47 / 3.74	2.45 / 3.70	2.42 / 3.66	2.41 / 3.62	2.40 / 3.60

df																								
12	4.75 / 9.33	3.88 / 6.93	3.49 / 5.95	3.26 / 5.41	3.11 / 5.06	3.00 / 4.82	2.92 / 4.65	2.85 / 4.50	2.80 / 4.39	2.76 / 4.30	2.72 / 4.22	2.69 / 4.16	2.64 / 4.05	2.60 / 3.98	2.54 / 3.86	2.50 / 3.78	2.46 / 3.70	2.42 / 3.61	2.40 / 3.56	2.36 / 3.49	2.35 / 3.46	2.32 / 3.41	2.31 / 3.38	2.30 / 3.36
13	4.67 / 9.07	3.80 / 6.70	3.41 / 5.74	3.18 / 5.20	3.02 / 4.86	2.92 / 4.62	2.84 / 4.44	2.77 / 4.30	2.72 / 4.19	2.67 / 4.10	2.63 / 4.02	2.60 / 3.96	2.55 / 3.85	2.51 / 3.78	2.46 / 3.67	2.42 / 3.59	2.38 / 3.51	2.34 / 3.42	2.32 / 3.37	2.28 / 3.30	2.26 / 3.27	2.24 / 3.21	2.22 / 3.18	2.21 / 3.16
14	4.60 / 8.86	3.74 / 6.51	3.34 / 5.56	3.11 / 5.03	2.96 / 4.69	2.85 / 4.46	2.77 / 4.28	2.70 / 4.14	2.65 / 4.03	2.60 / 3.94	2.56 / 3.86	2.53 / 3.80	2.48 / 3.70	2.44 / 3.62	2.39 / 3.51	2.35 / 3.43	2.31 / 3.34	2.27 / 3.26	2.24 / 3.21	2.21 / 3.14	2.19 / 3.11	2.16 / 3.06	2.14 / 3.02	2.13 / 3.00
15	4.54 / 8.68	3.68 / 6.36	3.29 / 5.42	3.06 / 4.89	2.90 / 4.56	2.79 / 4.32	2.70 / 4.14	2.64 / 4.00	2.59 / 3.89	2.55 / 3.80	2.51 / 3.73	2.48 / 3.67	2.43 / 3.56	2.39 / 3.48	2.33 / 3.36	2.29 / 3.29	2.25 / 3.20	2.21 / 3.12	2.18 / 3.07	2.15 / 3.00	2.12 / 2.97	2.10 / 2.92	2.08 / 2.89	2.07 / 2.87
16	4.49 / 8.53	3.63 / 6.23	3.24 / 5.29	3.01 / 4.77	2.85 / 4.44	2.74 / 4.20	2.66 / 4.03	2.59 / 3.89	2.54 / 3.78	2.49 / 3.69	2.45 / 3.61	2.42 / 3.55	2.37 / 3.45	2.33 / 3.37	2.28 / 3.25	2.24 / 3.18	2.20 / 3.10	2.16 / 3.01	2.13 / 2.96	2.09 / 2.89	2.07 / 2.86	2.04 / 2.80	2.02 / 2.77	2.01 / 2.75
17	4.45 / 8.40	3.59 / 6.11	3.20 / 5.18	2.96 / 4.67	2.81 / 4.34	2.70 / 4.10	2.62 / 3.93	2.55 / 3.79	2.50 / 3.68	2.45 / 3.59	2.41 / 3.52	2.38 / 3.45	2.33 / 3.35	2.29 / 3.27	2.23 / 3.16	2.19 / 3.08	2.15 / 3.00	2.11 / 2.92	2.08 / 2.86	2.04 / 2.79	2.02 / 2.76	1.99 / 2.70	1.97 / 2.67	1.96 / 2.65
18	4.41 / 8.28	3.55 / 6.01	3.16 / 5.09	2.93 / 4.58	2.77 / 4.25	2.66 / 4.01	2.58 / 3.85	2.51 / 3.71	2.46 / 3.60	2.41 / 3.51	2.37 / 3.44	2.34 / 3.37	2.29 / 3.27	2.25 / 3.19	2.19 / 3.07	2.15 / 3.00	2.11 / 2.91	2.07 / 2.83	2.04 / 2.78	2.00 / 2.71	1.98 / 2.68	1.95 / 2.62	1.93 / 2.59	1.92 / 2.57
19	4.38 / 8.18	3.52 / 5.93	3.13 / 5.01	2.90 / 4.50	2.74 / 4.17	2.63 / 3.94	2.55 / 3.77	2.48 / 3.63	2.43 / 3.52	2.38 / 3.43	2.34 / 3.36	2.31 / 3.30	2.26 / 3.19	2.21 / 3.12	2.15 / 3.00	2.11 / 2.92	2.07 / 2.84	2.02 / 2.76	2.00 / 2.70	1.96 / 2.63	1.94 / 2.60	1.91 / 2.54	1.90 / 2.51	1.88 / 2.49
20	4.35 / 8.10	3.49 / 5.85	3.10 / 4.94	2.87 / 4.43	2.71 / 4.10	2.60 / 3.87	2.52 / 3.71	2.45 / 3.56	2.40 / 3.45	2.35 / 3.37	2.31 / 3.30	2.28 / 3.23	2.23 / 3.13	2.18 / 3.05	2.12 / 2.94	2.08 / 2.86	2.04 / 2.77	1.99 / 2.69	1.96 / 2.63	1.92 / 2.56	1.90 / 2.53	1.87 / 2.47	1.85 / 2.44	1.84 / 2.42
21	4.32 / 8.02	3.47 / 5.78	3.07 / 4.87	2.84 / 4.37	2.68 / 4.04	2.57 / 3.81	2.49 / 3.65	2.42 / 3.51	2.37 / 3.40	2.32 / 3.31	2.28 / 3.24	2.25 / 3.17	2.20 / 3.07	2.15 / 2.99	2.09 / 2.88	2.05 / 2.80	2.00 / 2.72	1.96 / 2.63	1.93 / 2.58	1.89 / 2.51	1.87 / 2.47	1.84 / 2.42	1.82 / 2.38	1.81 / 2.36
22	4.30 / 7.94	3.44 / 5.72	3.05 / 4.82	2.82 / 4.31	2.66 / 3.99	2.55 / 3.76	2.47 / 3.59	2.40 / 3.45	2.35 / 3.35	2.30 / 3.26	2.26 / 3.18	2.23 / 3.12	2.18 / 3.02	2.13 / 2.94	2.07 / 2.83	2.03 / 2.75	1.98 / 2.67	1.93 / 2.58	1.91 / 2.53	1.87 / 2.46	1.84 / 2.42	1.81 / 2.37	1.80 / 2.33	1.78 / 2.31
23	4.28 / 7.88	3.42 / 5.66	3.03 / 4.76	2.80 / 4.26	2.64 / 3.94	2.53 / 3.71	2.45 / 3.54	2.38 / 3.41	2.32 / 3.30	2.28 / 3.21	2.24 / 3.14	2.20 / 3.07	2.14 / 2.97	2.10 / 2.89	2.04 / 2.78	2.00 / 2.70	1.96 / 2.62	1.91 / 2.53	1.88 / 2.48	1.84 / 2.41	1.82 / 2.37	1.79 / 2.32	1.77 / 2.28	1.76 / 2.26
24	4.26 / 7.82	3.40 / 5.61	3.01 / 4.72	2.78 / 4.22	2.62 / 3.90	2.51 / 3.67	2.43 / 3.50	2.36 / 3.36	2.30 / 3.25	2.26 / 3.17	2.22 / 3.09	2.18 / 3.03	2.13 / 2.93	2.09 / 2.85	2.02 / 2.74	1.98 / 2.66	1.94 / 2.58	1.89 / 2.49	1.86 / 2.44	1.82 / 2.36	1.80 / 2.33	1.76 / 2.27	1.74 / 2.23	1.73 / 2.21

* Reprinted, by permission, from G. W. Snedecor, *Statistical methods*, 5th ed., Ames, Iowa: Iowa State College Press, pp. 246–249, 1956.

An Example of Constructing a Theoretical Framework

In the past much research work was devoted to isolated studies. To advance the frontiers of knowledge, strong pleas have been made in recent years for the development of theoretical frameworks or models in various areas of knowledge that will stimulate, guide, and integrate research work. A study made of the characteristics of teachers serves as an example of one attempt to do this.

Over the years, information relative to teacher characteristics has been accumulated in an unsystematic manner with little attention given to building a theory of teacher behavior. Ryans[1] and his associates have taken steps in this direction. He states that his proposals "do not constitute a complete inventory of all assumptions required for a theory of teacher behavior. Nor is any particular claim made at this point for theoretical rigor. But if in the area of teacher behavior there are advantages in resolving and systematizing our thinking, a starting point is necessary regardless of how tentative it may be."

To develop a systematic theory, Ryans defined the term, "teacher behavior," stated the two major assumptions necessary for a theory of teacher behavior, and listed a number of implications or subassumptions (postulates) relating to each of them. From this theoretical framework he proceeded to make several propositions concerning teacher behavior in general terms that researchers could convert into exact and testable hypothesis form.

Definition

Teacher behavior may be defined simply as the behavior, or activities, of persons as they go about doing whatever is required of teachers, particularly those activities which are concerned with the guidance or direction of the learning of others.

[1] David G. Ryans, *Characteristics of Teachers*. Washington, D.C.: American Council on Education, 1960, pp. 13–26.

Basic Assumptions and Subassumptions

Assumption I: Teacher behavior is a function of situational factors and characteristics of the individual teacher. In setting out to formulate some theory of teacher behavior, the basic assumption might well be expected to bear resemblance to formulations made for similar purposes in connection with learning theory and personality theory. Indeed, in behavior theory, some expression of faith in the reliability, or consistency, of behavior is required. In the present case the basic assumption may be summarized in the proposition that teacher behavior is a resultant of (*a*) certain situational factors and (*b*) certain organismic conditions, and their interaction—or, simply, that teacher behavior is a function of certain environmental influences and the learned and unlearned characteristics of the individual teacher. . . .

Postulates

Postulate I-A: Teacher behavior is characterized by some degree of consistency. One implication of the basic assumption is that teacher behavior (and social behavior, with which education deals) is characterized by some degree of unformity; that, as Mill put it: " . . . there are such things in nature as parallel cases, that what happens once will, under sufficient degree of similarity of circumstances, happen again. . . ." We are stating simply that teacher behavior (a particular kind of behavior of a particular teacher) is not haphazard or fortuitous, but instead is consistent, or reliable, and therefore is capable of being predicted.

Postulate I-B: Teacher behavior is characterized by a limited number of responses. Another implication of the basic assumption (and perhaps it is so fundamental to scientific theory that it is unnecessary to state it explicitly with respect to teacher behavior) is expressed by Keynes' Postulate of Limited Independent Qualities, which states that: " . . . objects in a field over which our generalizations extend, do not have an infinite number of independent qualities; . . . their characteristics, however numerous, cohere together in groups of invariable connections, which are finite in number. . . ." Accordingly, the number of responses the individual teacher is capable of making, and the number of stimulus situations and organismic variables that may affect a teacher's behavior, are limited. This assumption is important if we hope to predict teacher behavior. It presents the researcher with a "tolerable" problem.

Postulate I-C: Teacher behavior is always probable rather than certain. All human behavior, characterized as it is by variability rather than by *complete* uniformity or consistency, must always be considered in the light of probability instead of from the standpoint of invariable cause-effect relationships. The error component resulting from such variability will inevitably be present in any assessment that is attempted of either (*a*) situational or stimulus conditions, (*b*) organismic conditions (genetic bases, past experience, motivation), or (*c*) teacher behavior (the dependent variable, or criterion). Behavior can be predicted only with varying degrees of probability.

Postulate I-D: Teacher behavior is a function of personal characteristics of the individual teacher. Teacher behavior is determined in part by the teacher's personal and social characteristics (e.g., in the intellectual, emotional, temperamental, attitudinal, and interest domains), which have their sources in both the genetic (unlearned) and experiential (learned) backgrounds of the individual. Knowledge of such characteristics contributes to prediction, within limits, of teacher behavior.

Postulate I-E: Teacher behavior is a function of general features of the situation in which it takes place. Teacher behavior is determined, in part, by general features of the situation in which it has its setting—features which may be observed to be common to situations of a general class and which, therefore, may be distinguished from the unique features of specific teaching situations. Information about such relevant features assists in the prediction, within limits, of teacher behavior.

Postulate I-F: Teacher behavior is a function of the specific situation in which it takes place. Finally, teacher behavior is determined, in part, by unique features of the particular situation in which it has its setting at a particular time. These features vary from situation to situation and contribute to the aspect of teacher behavior which is, to an extent, unique to the particular situation.

Assumption II: Teacher behavior is observable. When we attempt to study teacher behavior, we also make the assumption that teacher behavior may be identified objectively, either by direct observation or by indirect approaches that provide correlative indices of teacher behaviors. Examples of the indirect approaches are the assessment of pupil behavior, the use of tests of teacher abilities and knowledge, and the use of interviews or inventories to elicit expression of teacher preferences, interests, beliefs, and attitudes.

Several implications of this assumption may be noted here in the form of the following postulates.

Postulate II-A: Teacher behaviors are distinguishable. If teacher behaviors are observable, it follows that those with certain features must be capable of being identified and described so as to be distinguished from other teacher behaviors. Some behaviors have certain characteristics in common, which constitute generic or core components that may be abstracted to facilitate (a) communication of generalized descriptions of those behaviors, and (b) the identification of such behaviors in individual teachers. Teacher behaviors can be distinguished under observation.

Postulate II-B: Teacher behaviors are classifiable qualitatively and quantitatively. A second aspect of the assumption of the observability of teacher behavior is that teacher behaviors are classifiable, both qualitatively and quantitatively. A class, or category, of teacher behaviors is simply a grouping of specific behaviors which have many resemblances to one another and relatively few *important* differences. When we find such behavioral analogues, we take them as an indication that still other resemblances may exist, since resemblances in nature tend to go together in fairly large groups (Postulate of Limited Independent Qualities). When behaviors have been grouped together in the light of their resemblances, it becomes possible to abstract the general class description from the descriptions of specific manifestations and thereby provide the basis for a "concept" of teacher behavior of a certain kind and permit greater common understanding of the behavior.

Teacher behaviors that are similar, that have certain resemblances or common elements, may be classified in the same qualitative category. Within any given category, these behaviors may be further assigned to subclasses, which may be treated quantitatively. This is to say that teacher behaviors are subjectable to measurement—albeit approximate measurement. These quantitative subclasses may be of either of two types: (1) those permitting enumeration, or counting, only, or (2) those characterized by continuity and varying as a metric (exemplified at the lowest level of refinement by ordinal subclasses and at successively more refined levels by equal-interval and equal-ratio subclasses). . . .

Postulate II-C: Teacher behaviors are revealed through overt behavior and also by symptoms or correlates of behavior. Teacher behaviors may be revealed, or may be observed, either (1) by the representative *sampling* of specific teacher acts or behaviors, or (2) by specific signs, or indicators, or *correlates,* of the behavior under consideration.

In sampling behavior, we assume that the performance of the individual during the behavior sample is approximately (and at some level of probability) representative of the larger aspects, or universe, of his behavior. In judging behavior from signs or correlates, it is assumed that a behavior can be inferred or estimated approximately, in probability terms, from observed correlates of that behavior— from phenomena that are known to have been associated with that behavior in the past.

Some Propositions and Hypotheses

From the standpoint of the Teacher Characteristics Study, the foregoing definition and basic assumptions, together with their implications, provide a theoretical framework and starting point from which the researcher might reasonably proceed to propositions regarding teacher behavior—propositions that may be employed as hypotheses and tested against empirical data.

The number of descriptive classifications and specific propositions which might be generated with regard to teacher behavior is almost limitless, although we probably would not be interested in all such hypotheses even if it were possible to assemble them. Some classifications and some hypotheses seem more relevant than others. No doubt many of them could be incorporated in existing research designs and tested to determine their probable acceptability. . . .

Tests of a number of hypotheses about teacher classroom behaviors and other teacher characteristics were attempted by the Teacher Characteristics Study, and a major portion of this volume is given to reporting the data that were collected for these tests. It is not appropriate to list in this chapter—which deals with general theory of teacher behavior and problems related thereto—all the propositions of hypotheses which guided the research of the project. However, to illustrate the kind of propositions which may grow out of the basic assumptions and postulates stated earlier, a few of those to which the staff of the Teacher Characteristics Study gave attention are listed below.

Proposition: General classes of teacher classroom behaviors fall into relatively homogeneous clusters characterized by substantial intercorrelation of behaviors within a cluster. Teacher behavior *in toto* may be described in terms of a limited number of such major clusters of behaviors.

Proposition: The major clusters or families formed by teacher behaviors have the characteristics of *dimensions*. Individual teachers, in their manifestations of a particular behavior pattern, vary along a continuum between two behaviorally describable poles.

Proposition: Reliable estimates of teacher behavior constituting a major cluster (positions along a major dimension) may be obtained through assessments derived from the observations of trained observers.

Proposition: The classroom behavior of a teacher with respect to a major dimension, as represented by assessments made by trained observers, is characterized by substantial stability over considerable periods of time.

Proposition: The extent of intercorrelation among major dimensions of teacher behavior varies for different subpopulations of teachers, such as elementary teachers and secondary teachers.

Proposition: Correlates scales may be developed, using paper-and-pencil responses of teachers as indicators which will permit the indirect estimation of various kinds of teacher characteristics such as social attitudes, educational viewpoints, verbal ability, and emotionality.

Proposition: Teacher characteristics of the type described in the preceding proposition, as revealed by *correlates* in the form of paper-and-pencil responses of teachers to questions about their preferences, activities, and the like, are consistent and stable over substantial periods of time.

Proposition: Different subpopulations of teachers, classified according to grade level and subject matter taught, differ significantly in teacher characteristics.

Proposition: Certain teacher characteristics vary with the age of the teacher.

Proposition: Certain teacher characteristics are correlated with grades or marks earned by the teacher when in college.

Proposition: Certain teacher characteristics are related to the earlier youth activities of the teacher.

For some of these propositions there is considerable evidential support. For others considered by the Teacher Characteristics Study, lack of statistical corroboration or, equally often, absence of adequate controls, indicates that rejection, or at least suspended judgment, is in order. These findings are discussed in later chapters.

APPENDIX C

An Example of Hypothesis Construction

The problem of constructing hypotheses often perplexes students, and most examples in the literature are too complex for them to understand. Perhaps the following article[1], which informally explores a problem area in mental health and proposes several hypotheses, will provide a general understanding of the process. The article is written primarily for classroom teachers and does not present as rigorous an analysis of the problem and as precise statements of the hypotheses as the researcher employs. But it does reveal the types of explorations and explanations that investigators make in the early stages of problem evolvement.

Most classroom teachers are concerned about the mental health of their students for at least two reasons: they know that the level of interpersonal adjustment of the student has an effect on his level of academic learning, and they accept the *health* of the student as being important in its own right. This discussion of group mental health—the mental health of children in the classroom group—is intended especially for the classroom teacher. His job is essentially that of a group worker; and as such, he needs to have the understandings and skills essential to hygienic group management.

What follows, then, is an attempt to explore three questions which appear to be basic to an understanding of classroom mental health:

1. What differentiates a mentally healthy from a mentally unhealthy classroom —at least, as far as experience appears to indicate?

2. What kinds of things tend to influence the level of mental health in the classroom—at least, as far as human relations research appears to indicate?

3. What hypotheses, then, can be drawn regarding the management of mental health in the classroom—at least, as far as they sound psychologically reasonable?

Question 1 asks how we can assess the level of mental health in a classroom. Practically, the question asks for an identification of those dimensions along which one must observe in order to evaluate or judge the level of mental health within the classroom group. Four dimensions are suggested.

The amount of acceptance or rejection within the group. This refers to the extent of positive or negative affect in the classroom, or the degree of friendly versus unfriendly atmosphere. This is the kind of thing teachers find out by

[1] Allen Menlo, "Mental Health within the Classroom Group," *School of Education Bulletin, University of Michigan,* 31 (May, 1960) : 121.

397

doing a sociometric study on how much class members like each other, how much they think others like them, how much they like the teacher, how much they think the teacher likes them, and how much the teacher actually likes them. The assumption here is that the predominance of accepting attitudes and behaviors is healthier than the predominance of rejecting ones.

The amount of cooperative action or aggression within the group. This refers to the extent of active or passive movement with or against others, or the degree of helping versus force, threat, coercion, or harm. Teachers find this out when they ask students questions on how much they perceive themselves, other children, and the teacher as either being pushed around or pushing others around. The assumption here is that the predominance of cooperative actions is healthier than the predominance of aggressive actions.

The amount of involvement in or withdrawal from the class process. This refers to the extent of active or passive movement toward or away from others, or the degree of participation versus self-isolation and escape. Teachers assess this when they look for how much children appear to be, or feel they are, a part of the classroom experience. Here the assumption is that the presence of student involvement is healthier than the presence of withdrawal.

The amount of feeling of comfort or anxiety in the class. This refers to the extent of feelings of "at ease" or tension, or the degree of calm versus nervous feelings and behaviors. One way teachers evaluate this is by providing opportunities for students' expressions of happiness or unhappiness with respect to class procedures, other students, the teacher, and the general class situation. The assumption is that a predominance of feelings of comfort is healthier than one of anxiety.

Question 2 calls for a definition of the conditions which may influence a classroom group toward the manifestation of these symptoms. The findings of several studies strongly indicate a causative relationship between the exposure of human beings to certain conditions and their resultant demonstration of certain behaviors and attitudes consistent with the four sets of symptoms mentioned above. Specifically, these relationships are as follows:

When communication is cut off between people, they tend to develop misperceptions, misunderstanding, and even hostilities regarding and toward each other. When communication is open, people tend to develop realistic perceptions and positive feelings between each other.

When people have a perception of shared objectives, a feeling of cohesiveness, and see each other in a "good light" their contacts tend to produce accepting and mutually supportive attitudes and behaviors toward each other. People's contacts under conditions of uncommon objectives, lack of a spirit of "we-ness," and seeing each other's "poorer" side tend to produce unaccepting, nonsupportive attitudes and behaviors toward each other.

A highly restrictive style of leadership control tends to produce aggressive, scapegoating, and drop-out types of behaviors and attitudes among people. Less restrictive leadership control tends to produce cooperative, noncritical, and stay-in types of behaviors and attitudes.

People tend to get more involved in an experience when they participate in the planning of it, have opportunity to express their feelings about it, hear others' feelings about it, and have some active responsibility in carrying it out. People tend to resist those experiences in which they have no share in the planning, expression of feelings, or responsibility for implementation.

People tend to be attracted toward and feel more involved in activities which they see as having good chances of satisfying their own needs. People tend not to be attracted toward and not feel involved in activities which they see as having a poor chance of satisfying their own needs.

People tend to feel comfortable and secure in situations when they perceive themselves as having value and perceive others as representing friendly forces toward them. People tend to feel uncomfortable and insecure in situations when they perceive themselves as having minimal value and perceive others as representing unfriendly forces toward them.

The answers to the first two questions have described, thus far, the manifestations of healthy versus unhealthy socioemotional dynamics in a classroom group and have indicated the conditions which may be partially or wholly causative to these manifestations.

Question 3 is about the implications of all this for the teacher as a practitioner of hygienic group management. These implications follow in the form of hypotheses which are derived, more or less directly, from the foregoing material. These hypotheses are either partially or wholly untested and will probably remain unsubstantiated until teachers at various levels begin to research them within their own classes and schools. In the absence of experimental evidence, the teacher should find it interesting to test these hypotheses with his own classroom teaching-learning experiences.

Hypothesis A. Teachers who jointly plan classroom procedures and learning activities with their students contribute more to the mental health of students than do teachers who refrain from planning with their students.

Hypothesis B. Teachers who provide their students with opportunities for emotional ventilation and expression of feelings about what goes on in class, their peers, their teacher, and themselves contribute more to the mental health of students than teachers who do not make provisions for this.

Hypothesis C. Teachers who make maximum use of student services for leadership in the classroom contribute more to the mental health of students than teachers who give all or most of the services themselves.

Hypothesis D. Teachers who maintain flexible, uncrowded agenda of activity and subject matter in their classrooms contribute more to the mental health of students than teachers who keep crowded agenda.

Hypothesis E. Teachers who build motivation to learn by interpersonal cooperation in their classrooms contribute more to the mental health of students than teachers who build motivation by interpersonal competition.

Hypothesis F. Teachers who accept, and help their students accept, a wide range or variation in behavior and attitudes in their classrooms contribute more to the mental health of students than teachers who are, and help their students be, critically evaluative of individual differences in behavior and attitude.

The problem of maintaining good mental health in the classroom is one in which teachers are gaining more understanding and skill. Administrative and supervisory personnel are also becoming more intelligently familiar with the needs and the techniques, and their support, encouragement, and assistance do much to help the teacher accomplish his purposes.

An Example of Deducing the Consequences

Deducing the consequences of a hypothesis and discovering whether they are observable through appropriate tests is an important responsibility of the researcher. If factual affirmation can be found for one consequent, a hypothesis gains some support. If factual evidence can be found to support several entailed consequents, the cumulative evidence considerably strengthens the confirmation of the hypothesis. Since students often have difficulty in grasping the process of deducing consequences, the following discussion[1] of Newton's "theory" of the composition of white light may provide a helpful illustration.

Observing the colored spectrum which appears when sunlight is refracted in a crystal, Newton conceived the hypothesis that white light is a mixture of rays differing in refrangibility, and that the different colors of the spectrum correspond to the different degrees of refrangibility. This hypothesis entailed a number of consequents. We can represent the matter in this way:

If white light is a mixture of rays differing in refrangibility, and *if* the different colors of the spectrum correspond to the different degrees of refrangibility,

> *then* (1) rays of different colors cannot come to a focus at the same distance from the lens (and this explains the "blurred" images seen through earlier telescopes);
>
> *then* (2) for each color there must be a definite and specific amount of refraction and the refrangibility of every color must be constant;
>
> *then* (3) mixing in a due proportion all the primary colors should produce white light;
>
> *then* (4) the rainbow can be explained as the result of refraction;
>
> *then* (5) the "permanent colors of natural bodies" are the result of the reflection of light rays.

Here we have a hypothesis which entails at least five groups of consequents. If all of them are supported by the facts—and, through a series of ingenious experiments, Newton could show that this is the case—then the hypothesis may be said to be confirmed or verified beyond reasonable doubt.

[1] W. H. Werkmeister, *An Introduction to Critical Thinking.* Lincoln, Nebraska: Johnsen Publishing Company, 1957, p. 585.

APPENDIX E

An Example of Theory Construction

Theory building is a major concern of scientists. There are no existing cookbook directions for building a theory, but the following report illustrates one approach. To formulate their theory, the authors[1] borrowed the concept of symbolic transformation developed by Cassirer and Langer and applied it to phenomena in their field. They gave careful consideration to the definition of terms and concluded with suggestions for further research that needs to be done to test their theory.

Abstract

A tentative general theory of the meaning of human movement-kinesthesia as a somatic-sensory experience which can be conceptualized by the human mind was developed within the context of the basic assumptions of the philosophy of symbolic transformation as they relate to the nature of the process which enables human beings to find meaning in their sensory perceptions. The essential elements common to all forms of human movement were identified. A vocabulary was developed to refer to these elements in their most general form. Using this vocabulary, the relationships among these elements were analyzed in relation to the process of human thought. From this analysis, a tentative general theory of the meaning inherent in human movement-kinesthesia was formulated. The intent to attempt to validate this theory in subsequent papers is stated.

Movement is an essential element in all animal life. The feeling of moving in space accompanies and guides every reaction an animal makes to the stimuli that constitute its sensory perception of its internal and external environment. This is equally true for man, but there is a significant difference between animal and human movement, just as

There is an unmistakable difference between organic [animal] reactions and human responses. In the first case a direct and immediate answer is given to an outward [or inward] stimulus; in the second case the answer is delayed. It is interrupted and retarded by a slow and complicated process of thought. (1, *p. 43*)

Human movement differs from animal movement because man is able to *think* about his own movement. He can conceptualize his kinesthetic perception of his

[1] Lois Ellfeldt and Eleanor Metheny, "Movement and Meaning: Development of a General Theory," *Research Quarterly*, 29 (October, 1958): 264.

own movements. And he can try to "make sense" out of these conceptualizations by philosophizing about them within the context of his own structure of human meanings and values.

The somatic or structural aspects of movement have been studied by many investigators; but the significance of the human ability to conceptualize the sensory or perceptual aspects of movement has received little attention; and the questions relating to human meanings and values in this conceptualization of the structural-perceptual experience of movement-kinesthesia have scarcely been raised. The establishment of a coherent theory about the meanings inherent in the psycho-sensori-somatic experience of moving as a human being could do much to clarify the significance of physical education as the form of education which is primarily concerned with human movement experiences.

Statement of the Problem

The central problem of this study was the development of a tentative general theory about the meaning of human movement-kinesthesia as a somatic-sensory experience which can be conceptualized by the human mind. The logical solution of this problem was considered to be the first step in an attempt to develop a coherent philosophy of movement which identifies the meaning and value inherent in the basic human experience of moving and perceiving movement.

Procedure

The philosophical process of developing a tentative general theory which rested on identifiable basic assumptions and incorporated all observable aspects of the movement experience was implemented as follows: 1. A widely-accepted contemporary theory about the nature of the mental process which enables human beings to find meaning in their sensory perceptions was examined in terms of its relevance to the understanding of movement-kinesthesia; 2. Within the context of this theory, the elements which appear to be involved in all forms of human movement were identified; 3. To enable investigators to refer to these elements in their most general forms, a vocabulary was developed; 4. Using this vocabulary, the relationships among the general elements identified in human movement-kinesthesia were analyzed in relation to the process through which the human mind finds meaning in human experiences; and 5. Out of this analysis and synthesis, a tentative general theory of the meaning inherent in human movement-kinesthesia was formulated.

The Process of Human Thought

For many years, it was customary to describe the brain as a "transmitter system" similar to a telephone exchange in which sensory messages were received and motor messages sent out. This analogy provided a convenient explanation for reflex behavior. It was expanded when Pavlov and others demonstrated that reflexes could be conditioned, and a given response could be elicited by a substitute stimulus which became a "sign" for the original stimulus. The theory of conditioned reflexes accounted for many facets of animal behavior, but it provided no adequate explanation for man's ability to comprehend his own stimulus-response experiences and think about them in abstractions or ideas. Consideration of this unique ability "which appears to be the distinctive mark of human life" (1, *p. 42*) led to the conclusion that evolutionary development had produced a human *mind* which was significantly different from the animal *brain*.

> The functional circle of man is not only quantitatively enlarged; it has also undergone a qualitative change. Man has, as it were, discovered a new method of adapting himself to his environment. . . . As compared with other animals man lives not merely in a broader reality; he lives, so to speak, in a new *dimension* of reality. (1, *pp. 42–43*)

This concept of "a new dimension" in the human mind supplied the clue to a new analogy which incorporated man's unique ability to transform sensory perceptions into abstractions formulated as *ideas*. It is now recognized that while the animal brain acts essentially as a "transmitter," the human mind is better likened to a "transformer" in which sensory perceptions undergo a fundamental change of character during the process of stimulus transmission. The philosophy of symbolic transformation, developed initially by Ernest Cassirer (1) and later by Susanne K. Langer (4) and others, incorporates this concept of the transforming power of the human mind.

> Ideas are undoubtedly made out of impressions—out of sense messages from the special organs of perception, and vague visceral reports of feeling. . . . The material furnished by our senses is constantly wrought into *symbols,* which are our elementary ideas. . . . For the brain is not merely a great transmitter, a super-switchboard; it is better likened to a great transformer. The current of experience which passes through it undergoes a change of character, not through the agency of the sense by which the perception entered, but by virtue of a primary use which is made of it immediately: it is sucked into the stream of symbols which constitutes a human mind. . . . It is only when we penetrate into the varieties of symbolific activity . . . that we begin to see why human beings do not act as superintelligent cats, dogs, or apes would act. (4, *pp. 33–34*)

The human capacity for transforming sensory perceptions into symbols was emphasized by Ittelson and Cantril in their recent review of studies related to the nature of perception and sensation.

> In man the receiving of symbolic messages is undoubtedly one of the most important functions of perception. In lower animals it can be observed, if at all, only in a most primitive and stereotyped way. . . . In studying human perception, we have constantly to bear in mind that it is impossible to have any perception which is devoid of symbolic content. Furthermore, this symbolic content is not some excess baggage added to the perception, but is an integral and inseparable part of it. (2, *pp. 19–20*)

This capacity for dealing with abstractions which symbolize or represent his sensory perceptions is the basis of man's ability to find *meaning* in his life as a *human* being.

> . . . That symbolic thought and symbolic behavior are among the most characteristic features of human life, and that the whole progress of human culture is based on these conditions, is undeniable. . . . Hence, instead of defining man as an *animal rationale,* we should define him as an *animal symbolicum.* By so doing we can designate his specific difference, and we can understand the new way open to man—the way to civilization. (1, *pp. 44–45*)

Speech, a uniquely human development which is shared by no other branch of the animal kingdom, is prime evidence of man's capacity for symbolic transformation of sensory perception (1, *pp. 142–175;* 4, *pp. 83–115*). Sounds produced by vibrations of the vocal cords are transformed into *words,* which are symbols for concepts or meanings. Using these convenient abstractions of experience, the human mind is able to grasp, retain, and express *ideas* in a logical structure of discourse called language.

> The main lines of logical structure in all meaning-relations are . . . : the correlation of signs with their meanings by a selective mental process; the correlation of symbols with concepts and concepts with things, . . . ; and the assignment of elaborately patterned symbols to certain analogues in experience, the basis of all interpretation and thought. These are essentially the relationships we use in weaving the intricate web of meaning which is the real fabric of human life. (*4, p. 63*)

In recent years the implications of the philosophy of symbolic transformation for some of the "wordless" or non-discursive areas of human comprehension and expression have been tentatively examined, with specific reference to music, the graphic arts, and dance (3, 5). Essentially, it now appears evident that *animal symbolicum* transforms sensa into many different *kinds* of conceptual symbols, not all of which can be translated into words. A musical composition, for example, is a symbolic formulation of concepts in non-verbal sounds. A picture can never be completely described in words; it conveys its meaning in non-discursive visual symbols. Similarly, dance is recognized as a non-discursive art form which symbolifies concepts in movement.

> The recognition of presentation [non-discursive] symbolism as a normal and prevalent vehicle of meaning widens our conception of rationality far beyond the traditional boundaries, yet never breaks faith with logic in the strictest sense. Wherever a symbol operates, there is a meaning: . . . No symbol is exempt from the office of logical formulation, of conceptualizing what it conveys; however simple its import, or however great, this import is a *meaning,* and therefore an element for understanding. Such reflection invites one to tackle anew, and with entirely different expectations, the whole problem of the limits of reason, the much-disputed life of feeling, and the great controversial topics of fact and truth, knowledge and wisdom, science and art. (*4, pp. 78–9*)

The symbolic transformation of movement-kinesthesia has been explicitly recognized in dance as an art form, even as the symbolic nature of language is clearly identified in the language art form called poetry. But the symbolism of poetic language is only an extension of the first crude transformation of sounds into conceptual symbols which distinguish "the ape with the lalling instinct" from all other animals. So it would seem that recognition of the symbolic import of movement in the dancer's art would imply a fundamental human capacity to transform movement-kinesthesia into meaningful nondiscursive conceptual symbols. This line of reasoning suggests that the philosophy of symbolic transformation may provide the key to whatever meaning is inherent in movement-kinesthesia as man's most persistent sensory experience.

The Problem of Vocabulary

The current terminology of movement-kinesthesia is characterized by great diversity. In general, it has been developed by specialists concerned with specific aspects of movement. Anatomists, physiologists, neurologists, and orthopedists have studied structure and function; kinesiologists have identified principle of mechanics and dynamics; and those interested primarily in sports, dance, work, or therapeutics have all developed special terminologies. This concern with specifics has created a kinesiological Tower of Babel inhabited by specialists speaking in different tongues, unable to communicate adequately with each other about the general nature of the phenomena of movement and kinesthesia with which they are all dealing. Since "the whole purpose of general concepts is to make the distinction between special cases clear," (4, p. 43) any attempt to explore the general nature of movement-kinesthesia as a basic human experience with a vocabulary so contaminated by specific connotations can only add to the confusion.

A general vocabulary which identifies the elements common to all forms of movement is prerequisite to the development of a general theory of the meaning of movement-kinesthesia as a basic human experience. Such a vocabulary is presented below. It has been developed by logical analysis of the elements which are inherent in all forms of movement.

Considered in their most generalized form, the elements which appear to be common to all human movement may be classified as:

Structural— A dynamic somatic pattern is constructed by the changing positional relationships of the body masses.

Perceptual— The dynamic structure of this somatic pattern is perceived by the kinesthetic sensorium.

Conceptual—This dynamic somatic pattern has some significance as a response made by a human being to his sensory perception of external and/or internal environmental stimuli.

Words referring to these three general aspects of human movement have been developed by combining the root of the Greek word kinein (to move) with general word forms which identify the concepts of structure, sensory perception, and conceptualization. In the definitions which follow, the word "form" is used in its most general meaning as referring to a formulation of characteristics and the relationships among them which give an event its unique identity.

Kinestruct: n. A dynamic somatic form constructed by body masses in motion.
Kinestructure; v. To create a kinestruct.

Kinescept: n. A sensory form created by kinesthetic perception of a kinestruct.
Kinesceptualize; v. To perceive a kinescept.

Kinesymbol: n. A conceptual form which is an abstraction of the significance or import of a kinestruct and its kinescept within the socio-psycho-somatic context of a situation.
Kinesymbolize; v. To conceptualize the import of a kinestruct-kinescept.

These words are used in the discussion which follows.

The Nature of the Kinestruct

A kinestruct can never be described in detail because it is a dynamic form compounded out of continuous changes in tension in every muscle fiber of the body. (For example, "He raised his arm" describes only the gross nature of one aspect of a kinestruct. How did he raise his arm? What positions were assumed by the rest of his body? How were these positions altered by the raising of his arm? What changes occurred in the tension of the muscle fibers in his back? In his legs? In his neck? In what ways was the raising of his arm related to the total situation in which it occurred?) These uncountable changes in muscle tension which are synchronized into "a movement" are never random or spontaneous. They occur as a total response to the total situation in which the movement occurs.

The Nature of the Kinescept

Neither can the kinescept which corresponds to the kinestruct be described in detail. It is felt as a composite of the sensa transmitted by the entire kinesthetic sensorium as well as the "vague visceral reports of feeling" arising from continuous changes in homeostasis as the kinestructural response to the total situation is formulated.

The interaction among the muscular, neural, and biochemical aspects of movement is continuous, operating as a complex "feedback" system. The countless minute changes in the kinescept as the movement progresses are translated into motor-nerve stimuli which produce changes in muscle tension; these changes, in turn, provide new sensory information which modifies the kinescept and is utilized in turn to modify the motor-nerve stimuli, thus coordinating the kinestruct as it progresses in relation to the stimulus situation which initiated it. Through this interaction of situation-kinescept-kinestruct, the co-ordinated response of the *person* to his personal interpretation of the stimulus situation is kinestructuralized.

The kinescept provides a sensory record of the kinestructural response of the person to the situation even while it is controlling or guiding that response. This sensory record may or may not be consciously identified by the person, but it is always present. (The effect of obliterating one part of it can be illustrated by the difficulty of walking when the "foot has gone to sleep" and the local proprioceptors are deadened.) At times, the kinescept may be conceptualized at the cortical level of awareness, as it is when the person tries to "get the feel" of a movement pattern, or when he tries to recall "the feel of a movement" which he has previously performed. At other times, especially when the kinestruct is a familiar one, the kinesthetic feed-back may operate primarily at the cerebellar level, continuing to guide the kinestruct while the mover's conscious attention is focused on something else. In reflex movement, the feedback may operate primarily at the spinal level. But at whatever level neuromuscular interaction is effected, the kinescept of the kinestruct is always present, because without it co-ordinated movement is impossible (Cf. 6, *pp. 151–190*).

This sensory perception of the "feel of a movement" can never be satisfactorily described in words. Just as a sound must be heard, as a color must be seen, so a kinescept must be *felt* to be identified. It can be comprehended only in its own unique identity as a kinesthetically perceived and therefore non-discursive perceptual form.

The Nature of the Kinesymbol

A kinescept can be conceptualized as a unique perceptual "form" which conveys unique sensory information about one aspect of a person's relationship to the world. Since the human mind conceptualizes perceptions by transforming them into abstractions which serve as symbols of the meaning that the perceptions had to the person, it follows that kinescepts must also be subjected to this transforming process, becoming abstractions which are symbols of the meaning of the movement as perceived.

This conceptualization of kinesthetic perception cannot be expressed in the symbols of any other sensory conceptualizations; it is not verbal, visual, auditory, or anything else but what it is—a conceptualization of kinesthetic perception. It is a kinesymbol, an abstraction of a kinesthetic experience which contains its own human meaning in its own kinesthetically perceived form. This meaning may not be consciously recognized; it may be vague, fragmentary, or transient; it may be definite, organized, and long-lasting. It may be as functional as the meaning of locomotion or as non-utilitarian as "standing on your head to see if you can." But every kinestruct and its kinescept is a kinesymbolic formulation of personal experience which adds one more trace of *meaning* to a human life.

The characteristics which make kinescepts and kinestructs peculiarly well adapted to symbolic transformation are illuminated by Langer's discussion of the suitability of vocables for utilization as symbols.

> . . . The little vocal noises out of which we make our words are extremely easy to produce in all sorts of subtle variations, and easy to perceive and distinguish. . . . Not only does speech cost little effort, but above all it requires no instrument save the vocal apparatus and the auditory organs which, normally, we all carry about as part of our very selves; so words are *naturally available* symbols as well as very economical ones. . . . Vocables in themselves are so worthless that we cease to be aware of their physical presence at all, and become conscious only of their connotations, denotations, or other meanings. Our conceptual activity seems to flow through them, rather than merely to accompany them. . . . They fail to impress us as "experiences" in their own right unless we have difficulty in using them as words as we do with a foreign language or a technical jargon until we have mastered it. But the greatest virtue of verbal symbols is, probably, their tremendous readiness to enter into *combinations*. There is practically no limit to the selections and arrangements we can make of them. . . . Herein lies the power of language to embody concepts not only of things, but of things in combination, or situations. (4, *p. 61–62*)

This paragraph might be paraphrased into a description of kinestructs and kinescepts somewhat as follows:

> The little changes in muscle tension out of which we make our kinestructs are extremely easy to produce in all sorts of subtle variations, and easy to perceive and distinguish. They require no instrument save the physical apparatus which is a part of ourselves; so kinestructs and kinescepts are naturally available as symbols as

well as very economical ones.   These kinestructs and kinescepts are so much a part of our lives that we cease to be aware of their physical presence, and become conscious only of their connotations.   Our human activities seem to flow *through* them rather than to be identified with them.   They fail to impress us as "experiences" in their own right unless we have difficulty in comprehending or performing a new kinestruct, as we do with a new "skill" until we have mastered it.   But the greatest virtue of kinestructural-kinesceptual symbols is their tremendous readiness to enter into combinations.   There is practically no limit to the selections and arrangements we can make of them.   Herein lies the power of movement-kinesthesia to embody concepts not only of things, but of things in combinations, or situations.

As a person moves in many different situations, a given kinescept may acquire many encrustations of meaning derived from the intellectual-emotional responses *associated* with those situations, in time becoming a very complex symbol which can "stand for" the total meaning or import of the situations in which it was experienced.   For example, the "feel" of a golf swing is experienced within the context of the total meaning of the game situation in which the club is swung.   This context includes the mover's subconscious and non-conscious sensori-emotional reactions to the meaning the situation has for him as well as his conscious intellection about it.   Like other identifiable non-discursive perceptual forms, such as sight or sound, the kinescept is an integral part of the mover's total sensory record of the situation.   Accordingly, if it is abstracted from the situational context, it can represent or "stand for" that context in the same way that a picture or a song can "stand for" a total experience and "bring back" its complex sensori-emotional-intellectual connotations at some later date.   In short, a kinescept may serve not only as a discrete kinesymbol of the movement experience, as such, but also as a kinesymbol of the total import of a situation in which it has been experienced. Since all kinescepts are perceived within the context of a total situation, it seems probable that the meaning of all kinesymbols tends to become very complex.

The kinescepts of similar kinestructs may thus have very different emotional-intellectual import as kinesymbols for different people, depending upon the *meanings,* both obvious and subtle, in the situations in which they were experienced. (For example, the kinesymbolic import of the kinescept of "acute flexion of the thigh on the hip joint" may be quite different for a football player and a ballet dancer because the meanings and connotations in the situations in which their high kicks have been executed are not analogous.)   In time, a kinescept may accumulate many residual connotations, some of which may be mutually contradictory, and the performance of a given kinestruct may elicit conflicting emotions.

It may be noted that habitual postural kinestructs have long been recognized as kinesymbolic expressions of personality which reflect the influence of subconscious drives, motivations, and interpretations of self.   It seems probable that the kinesymbolic meaning of all habitual kinestructs involves similar emotional components derived from sub-conscious associations with other elements in the person's life experiences.

A Tentative General Theory

The distinguishing characteristic of human mentality has been identified as the ability to transform sensory perceptions into abstractions or symbols.   It has been shown that the sensory perception of movement, called kinesthesia, is susceptible to such symbolic transformation. Kinesthesia may thus be identified as a component of human mentality.

The experience of moving as a human being has been analyzed, and three distinct but interrelated forms have been identified: 1. A structural form called a kinestruct; 2. A perceptual form called a kinescept; 3. A conceptual form called a kinesymbol. The nature of these forms and their interrelationships provide the basis for a tentative general theory of the meaning of human movement-kinesthesia:

> *A kinestruct is the non-discursive kinesymbolic*
> *expression of the import of its kinescept.*

Discussion

The validity of this general theory must now be tested by determining to what extent it seems to account for observable manifestations of the phenomena to which it refers. Obviously, such an extended process is beyond the scope of this preliminary paper. A few illustrations, however, may suggest the approach.

How does a person comprehend or kinesceptualize a kinestruct created by another person? How does he create a similar kinestruct out of this first kinesception? What new dimension is added to the problem of "motor learning" by consideration of the kinesymbolism of the kinescept-kinestruct? Do the differences in kinesymbolism of "acute flexion of the thigh on the hip joint" provide an explanation for the mutual difficulty the athlete and the dancer may experience in attempting to perform each other's version of a similar kinestruct-kinescept? Exploration of the kinesymbolic import of habitual postural kinescepts may suggest ways to lessen the difficulties usually encountered in trying to "teach posture," i.e., establish a new postural kinestruct-kinescept.

Perhaps the perennially bothersome question of defining "quality of movement" may be tentatively answered by recognizing that the kinestruct and its kinescept are both kinesymbols, and that subtle differences in "quality" of similar kinestructs represent the subtle differences in their import as kinesymbols for the two performers.

These few examples suggest approaches to many problems related to the kinesymbolic kinescepts-kinestructs incorporated in the physical education program, but these must await further investigation. It is our belief, however, that the philosophy of movement which may be developed out of investigation of such problems can give new significance to "physical education" by illuminating the *meanings* and *values* inherent in movement-kinesthesia as one facet of man's ability to understand himself and the world in which he lives.

BIBLIOGRAPHY

NOTE: *Where two or more editions of the works utilized in this study have been published, reference is made to the edition most readily available to the general reader.*

1. Cassirer, Ernst, *An Essay on Man: An Introduction to a Philosophy of Human Culture.* New York: Doubleday and Co. (Doubleday Anchor Books A3),

1956. (Originally published by Louis Stern Memorial Fund, Yale University Press, 1944.)

The substance of Cassirer's work in the philosophy of symbolic transformation with reference to man's uniquely human attributes and their significance in the development of human culture.

2. Ittelson, William H. and Hadley Cantril, *Perception: A Transactional Approach*. New York: Doubleday and Co. (Doubleday Papers in Psychology DPP7), 1954.

A review of the nature of perception and the implications for the development of scientific psychology.

3. Langer, Susanne, K., *Feeling and Form*. New York: Charles Scribner's Sons. 1953. A theory of the meaning of art forms, including dance, developed from *Philosophy in a New Key*.

4. ———, *Philosophy in a New Key*. New York: The New American Library (A Mentor Book M25), 1948. (Originally published by Harvard University Press, 1942.)

The elements of the philosophy of symbolic transformation presented for the general reader. The logic of signs and symbols, the nature of meaning, and the nature of human mentality.

5. ———, *Problems of Art*. New York: Charles Scribner's Sons, 1957.

Ten philosophical lectures which provide an informal introduction to Langer's theory of non-discursive forms.

6. Sherrington, Charles S., *Man on His Nature*. New York: Doubleday and Co. (Doubleday Anchor Books A15), 1953. (Originally published by Cambridge University Press in 1940, with a revised edition in 1950.)

The physical basis of life, with emphasis on human consciousness and its origins in living substance. A classic in the contemporary literature of science.

APPENDIX F

An Example of Criticism of a Theory

A theory is likely to be unstable, particularly during the early stages of its formulation, but this is not a deterrent to progress. A proposed theory is not built for eternity; it is constructed so that a better one can be formulated in the future. After constructing a theory, a researcher and his colleagues critically analyze it and conduct studies to validate it. As a result of their work, they may reject the theory or suggest clarifications, revisions, or extensions that will lead to the formulation of a more generally acceptable theory. To illustrate, shortly after Ellfeldt and Metheny published their theory "Movement and Meaning" (Appendix E), Hubbard[1] carefully scrutinized it and offered the following criticism.

The new theory of "movement and meaning" though interesting, has several weaknesses. A basic fallacy occurs in the concept of kinesthetic feedback as presented in the statement that "the kinescept provides a sensory record . . . even while it is controlling or guiding the response" (p. 269). The kinesthetic input, or kinescept, is a *result* of the muscular action causing the movement and of the movement. Thus, kinesthesis is an inherent error-sensing mechanism. But the assumption that kinesthesis senses errors in the output in time to alter the action which produces it is highly questionable in the case of fast, skilled movements.

As a simple example, the skilled typist may sense that a wrong key was struck and stop to check visually. Very rarely does the typist block the stroke in time to prevent the error or in time to prevent additional letters appearing. Whether recognition of the wrong key being struck results from a discrepancy between the material being transcribed and the "kinesymbol" or a discrepancy between the "kinesymbol" leading to and the "kinescept" leading from the stroke is a moot question. The important point is that the error initiated tends strongly to occur and that feedback rarely occurs in time to prevent the error. Error prevention, when it does occur, is in terms of a temporary blockage of production. In sport, dance, or piano playing where the situation requires continued production, the error may be noted, but the general process proceeds.

[1] Alfred W. Hubbard, "Comments on the Article by Lois Ellfeldt and Eleanor Metheny, 'Movement and Meaning: Development of a General Theory,'" *Research Quarterly*, 30 (May, 1959): 244.

Kinesthesis may be error-sensing, but not error-correcting, in fast movements because of an inherent characteristic of the neuromuscular system. In fast, skilled movements, and especially those involving large segments of the body, the segment outruns the impressed force of the muscle, or muscles, initiating the movement. Thus, control is inherent in the combination of muscular forces initiating the stroke. Even though error is sensed as the movement is being executed, the error results unless the stroke is checked by an antagonist. Then it must be returned and restarted. Compensation for errors sensed through kinesthesis can sometimes be made in subsequent strokes of serial movement patterns. The result may be partially saved. And, of course, errors can be corrected in subsequent executions of the skill. In general, though, kinesthetic input is like a follow-through—it may indicate what went wrong but not in time to prevent it.

A second major weakness of the new theory is the suppression or disregard of the vital part other sensory inputs have in shaping skilled motor performance. The definitions (p. 268) establish a hierarchy from action to concepts based on kinesthesis, but kinesthesis without touch, pressure, and vision would be a relatively sterile sense. The quality, meaning, and effectiveness of motor performance depends on visible effects. Vision generally provides the basic feedback concerning the external effect of our actions. Vision also provides a basis for comprehending the action of others. Many "kinesymbols" originate in visual perception—seeing and trying are normal. Visual analysis of motor performance by skilled observers (coaches) often locates the source of motor errors and leads to better performance —and probably better "kinesymbols"—through discourse and demonstration.

Kinesthesis, touch, and pressure inputs accompany the production of action and precede the visible effect. A performer can predict the visible result from these inputs—once he learns to interpret them. He may "feel" the difference between two performances, but he cannot perceive good movement kinesthetically until he produces it. He cannot predict the outcome of performance from the "feel" during production until he determines what cues from kinesthesis, touch, and pressure correlate with good performance. Otherwise, old errors feel good. Obviously, vision is necessary to keep abreast of play in competition with opponents. But an individual executing a thoroughly practiced routine in gymnastics or figure skating, where he has only himself to control, might conceivably operate on the basis of cues from kinesthesis, touch, and pressure. He can, but partial or complete deprivation of vision produces considerable decrement in performance (1). This suggests that kinesthesis, even with touch and pressure, is not a sufficient basis for controlling previously well "kinesymbolized" skills.

A third weakness may be simply overstatement for emphasis. Statements that "a kinestruct can never be described in detail," that "the 'feel of a movement' can never be described in words," and that "conceptualizations of kinesthetic perception cannot be expressed in the symbols of any other sensory conceptualizations" are highly questionable. "He raised his arm" is concise and presumably sufficiently descriptive for the occasion. Describing any movement "in detail" is infinitely complicated and probably useless. Dynamic forms can be described, although precise description may confuse the uninitiated. Incidentally, human movement is compounded from discrete muscle impulses rather than "continuous changes in tension in every muscle fiber of the body." The "feel of movement" can be shared.

Prefacing statements with "it should feel as though" directs attention to kinesthetic, touch, and pressure sensations and, by directing a person to try for this feel, often bears fruit. The "kinesymbol," "kinescept," and "kinestruct" may be unexpressed operationally, but this does not mean that they are unexpressable or uncommunicable. Speaking is a motor response and thinking is done in terms of subovert movements. We translate words into action and action into words. We verbalize visual concepts, visualize verbal concepts, and express ideas with movements. And if a dancer can communicate concepts without discourse, discourse might communicate concepts without large, somatic movements—granting that both might miss the point in translation and both translations might result in jargon.

Finally, "recognizing that the kinestruct and its kinescept are both kinesymbols" and that these "cannot be expressed in the symbols of any other sensory conceptualization" makes all action and errors kinesymbolic and untouchable. Automatic feedback control of kinestructs by kinescepts makes action reflex and errors immutable since the movement is a motor image of the symbolic pattern. Thus, in trying to summarize the authors' position, but with no intention of distorting their meaning by injudicious quotation, we seem to find that movement has an untouchable origin and an immutable nature which presents physical education with an unsolvable problem and which makes any claims of teaching or training people in motor skills presumably fraudulent. The general theory (p. 272) might be rephrased to state that human movement is meaningful action based on the meaning of movement. This does not summarize the extensive findings concerning movement, perception, and their relations, but it at least leaves the door open for learning—*Alfred W. Hubbard, University of Illinois, Urbana, Illinois.*

BIBLIOGRAPHY

1. Graybiel, Ashton, *et al.*, "Russian Studies of Vision in Relation to Physical Activity and Sports." *Research Quarterly* **26:**480–85; Dec. 1955.

APPENDIX G

An Example of a Psychological Theory

Examples of the development of fairly complex hypotheses stated with some degree of precision are difficult to locate in educational literature. Admittedly, there are some relatively simple statements, but to find more sophisticated presentations one must turn to other fields. The following illustration from the field of psychology[1] presents a theory of error which includes four postulates. Note the care that has been given to the definitions of terms, the statement of the postulates, and the deductions derived from one of them.

Definitions

Error: A response other than that appropriate to the motor set present, where this response is appropriate to other parts of the stimulus complex.

Response: Observable striated muscular behavior by the individual.

Motor set: Bodily orientation for the performance of a given behavior, inferred jointly from the instructions given by the experimenter or subject to himself and the physical orientation of the person. We can to some extent get at it by asking the subject what he intends or intended to do, or by setting up an objective criterion for determining whether or not the physical orientation would allow the performance of the task.

Appropriate response: The response which the individual says he intends or intended to make and for which he is physically oriented is the appropriate response to the motor set. Appropriate responses to other parts of the stimulus complex are those which would be most frequently made if those parts of the stimulus complex were dominant.

Stimulus complex: Various components which make up the stimulus such as stimuli from motor set, specific drive stimuli, and external stimuli. Any of these can be changed relatively independently, changing the stimulus complex.

Dominance of a component of the stimulus complex: A drive stimulus is more dominant as the drive becomes stronger. When the subject is asked to describe

[1] R. B. Ammons, "Errors: Theory and Measurement," Kentucky Symposium: *Learning Theory, Personality Theory, and Clinical Research.* New York: John Wiley & Sons, Inc., 1954, p. 142.

414

a situation, a particular stimulus component is dominant to the extent that it is mentioned earlier in his description. Frequently, this dominance must be inferred from the past history of the individual. The report may not be accurate from the point of view of the experimenter, as in the case of the individual who has always hated a sibling and now reports that his emotion is one of love and affection, yet behaves as if he hated her. . . .

Drive stimuli: Those stimuli characteristically noted by the human organism in connection with hunger, thirst, sex frustration, fear, anxiety, etc. One could infer the presence of such stimuli in terms of strength of drive.

External stimuli: Environmental energies which affect the receptors of the organism. When the organism is oriented in such a way that the receptor can be affected by the energy and the energy is sufficient to stimulate the receptor, stimulation is normally assumed to take place.

Strength of the response tendency: Latency of the response, physical strength of the response, and probability of the response occurring in the presence of or closely following the presence of a given stimulus complex.

Stimulus similarity: Stimulus complexes are similar to the degree that they contain similar components and are relatively less separated along the various discriminable continua.

Strength of drive: Might be the self-rating of the individual or might be inferred from the past history of the individual with respect to the time since drinking, time since eating, number of times a pleasant or unpleasant consequence has followed a particular stimulus complex, etc. Thus drive stimuli can be associated with primary or secondary drives as conceived of by Hull. Emotions are considered to be drives.

Reward: The satisfaction of some need, goal-object consumption, or avoidance of noxious stimulation. . . .

Postulates

Postulate 1: To any stimulus component or complex, there are a number of possible responses. The strengths of the response tendencies differ. Thus there is present a "strength" hierarchy of responses to any given stimulus component or complex. . . .

Postulate 2: The more similar a stimulus component or complex is to another given stimulus component or complex which has regularly elicited a response in the past, the stronger the response of this kind now elicited by the new stimulus. . . .

Postulate 3: The stronger the drive, the stronger the response.

Postulate 4: The components of a given stimulus complex may in isolation elicit different responses. When the components are combined in the stimulus complex, the greater the dominance of a given component and the greater the strength of a given response tendency associated with it, the more likely the stimulus complex is to elicit this response.

Deductions

Deduction 4a: If a response has been regularly elicited under a low drive and is now elicited with a high drive of the same kind present, we will observe an increase in "errors," providing the strongest response tendencies to the motor set and the drive are different and that to the motor set is dominant.

Deduction 4b: If a response has been regularly elicited under one drive, and the drive is changed to another without altering the other stimulus components (especially motor set), there will be more errors, providing the appropriate dominant response to the drive-stimulus component from the original drive was the same as that to the motor set, but that to the new drive stimulus is different from that to the motor set, the motor set staying the same.

Deduction 4c: To the extent that a single stimulus component dominates the total stimulus complex, the successive responses given by an individual will be more similar to each other.

Strong emotion leads to stereotypy of responses, as does instruction induced "motor set," and the "same" physical stimulation. In free association, problem areas will be talked about more frequently than other areas. In the case of errors, we find that certain kinds are quite frequent, i.e., certain types of slips of the tongue and certain kinds of accidents in the accident-prone person. These errors should indicate the life areas in which the person has problems and thus be of diagnostic value to the clinician.

Deduction 4d: Other stimulus conditions being approximately equal, if one arouses a feeling about an error he should get real-life responses associated with a similar set, emotion, or drive more quickly than if no feeling is aroused. . . .

APPENDIX H

An Example of a Model

In recent literature of the behavioral sciences, the term "model" has become quite fashionable.[1] As more and more investigators use the term, it has taken on wider and more varied meanings. In general, it entails finding a structure that enables one to present concepts in such a way that researchers can gain useful insights into their phenomena. Some workers employ the term "model" as a synonym for theory, particularly for a theory that is highly speculative or quantified. Some workers employ the term to describe the structure employed in drawing an analogy. Scientists, for example, may use a theory in a field about which much is known as a model for constructing a theory in another field in which little is known. The biological theory, for example, has served as a model for a social theory.

Guilford and Merrifield have constructed a model to organize intellectual factors into a system. They define model as a "set of constructs specified in such a way that their formal connections are evident."[2] They depict the structure of intellect in the form of a three-dimensional rectangular solid as seen below, and carefully define their terms.[3]

The constructs in this model are the individual abilities, i.e., the cells in the three-dimensional matrix. The formal connections between the constructs are deducible from the categories with the three variables of classification: operation, content, and product. These three are considered as formally independent, so that no combination of operation, content, and product is logically excluded from the system.

The investigators do not consider the model to be perfect and the positions of the factors in it to be permanently fixed. They expect that additional empirical evidence may lead to some changes. They point out that[4]

[1] May Brodbeck, "The Philosophy of Science and Educational Research," *Review of Educational Research*, 27 (December, 1957) : 436

[2] J. P. Guilford and P. R. Merrifield, *The Structure of Intellect Model: Its Uses and Implications*. Reports from the Psychological Laboratory, University of Southern California, 24 (April, 1960), p. 13.

[3] *Ibid.*, p. 13.

[4] *Ibid.*, p. 13.

417

A model is used as a theory when connections between its constructs and the empirical world are hypothesized. The acceptance of a theory depends upon the verification of such hypotheses. For the structure-of-intellect model to be supported as theory requires two types of verification. First, previously found factors must be confirmed as distinct from each other, when interpreted in terms of their location in the model. Second, new factors must be hypothesized from the model, and their separate existences verified.

At present the investigators are testing "whether unknown unique abilities that are predicted by the model do, in fact exist as distinguishable entities."[5] The model has been used "as a basis for a rough consideration of problems of curriculum in education, in relation to teaching of reading, and as a basis for a systematic orientation with respect to psychological tests."[6]

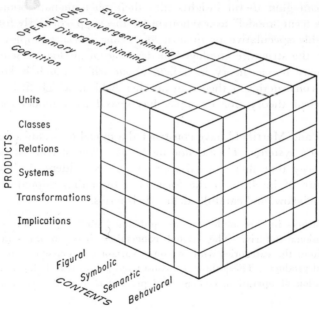

Figure A.

Definitions: The major concepts are labeled in Figure A. We shall begin with the kinds of operations and end with the kinds of products, also defining the parameters themselves.

Operations: Major kinds of intellectual activities or processes; things that the organism does with the raw materials of information.*

[5] *Ibid.*, p. 2.

[6] *Ibid.*, p. 3.

* "Information" in defined in a later section of this Report as "that which the organism discriminates."

Cognition: Discovery, awareness, rediscovery, or recognition of information in various forms; comprehension or understanding.

Memory: Retention of information in any form.

Divergent production: Generation of information from given information, where the emphasis is upon variety of output from the same source.

Convergent production: Generation of information from given information, where the emphasis is upon achieving unique or conventionally accepted or best outcomes.

Evaluation: Reaching decisions or making judgments concerning the goodness (correctness, suitability, adequacy, desirability) of information in terms of criteria of identity, consistency, and goal satisfaction.

Contents: General varieties of information.

Figural content: Information in concrete form, as perceived or as recalled in the form of images. The term "figural" implies some degree of organization or structuring.

Symbolic content: Information in the form of signs, having no significance in and of themselves, such as letters, numbers musical notations, etc.

Semantic content: Information in the form of meanings to which words commonly become attached, hence most notable in verbal thinking; involved in doing verbal tests, where the things signified by words must be known.

Behavioral content: Information, essentially non-verbal, involved in human interactions, where awareness of the attitudes, needs, desires, intentions, thoughts, etc. of other persons and of ourselves is important.

Products: Results from the organism's processing of information.

Units: Relatively segregated or circumscribed items of information having "thing" character.

Classes: Aggregates of items of information grouped because of their common properties.

Relations: Recognized connections between units of information based upon variables that apply to them.

Systems: Organized or structured aggregates of items of information; complexes of interrelated or interacting parts.

Transformations: Changes in existing or known information or in its use, as in production.

Implications: Extrapolations of information, in the form of expectancies, predictions, antecedents, and consequents.

Name Index

421

Subject Index